M

The Saltwater Wilderness

The Saltwater

GLENN VANSTRUM

Wilderness

OXFORD
UNIVERSITY PRESS

2003

OXFORD

UNIVERSITY PRESS

Oxford   New York

Auckland   Bangkok   Buenos Aires   Capetown   Chennai
Dar es Salaam   Delhi   Hong Kong   Istanbul   Karachi   Kolkata
Kuala Lumpur   Madrid   Melbourne   Mexico City   Mumbai   Nairobi
São Paulo   Shanghai   Taipei   Tokyo   Toronto

Copyright © 2003 by Glenn Vanstrum

Published by Oxford University Press, Inc.,
198 Madison Avenue, New York, New York 10016

www.oup.com

Oxford is a registered trademark of Oxford University Press

Library of Congress Cataloging-in-Publication Data
Vanstrum, Glenn S.
The saltwater wilderness / by Glenn Vanstrum.
p. cm.
Includes bibliographical references (p.).
ISBN 0-19-515937-3
1. Marine biology.   2. Marine biology—Pacific Ocean.   3. Deep diving.   I. Title.

QH91.V36 2003
508.3162—dc21   2002066348

All photographs by Glenn S. Vanstrum

9 8 7 6 5 4 3 2 1

Printed in the United States of America
on acid-free paper

For Diane, Erik, and Nicholas

May your course always take you downwind,
and may you be forever blessed by a following sea.

Preface

At the age of 14, I had the opportunity to join a group of fellow eighth-graders on a canoe trip into the arrowhead country of northeastern Minnesota. For the first time in our lives, nature unmarked by the hand of humanity surrounded us. Clear sparkling lakes, fresh air perfumed by pines, and countless splashing fish enveloped each canoeful of rowdy teenagers. Roadless tracts of forest stretched for miles in every direction, land known once to Anishinabe and voyageur, terrain that still harbored black bear, wolves, and mosquitoes by the billions. We were damp and cold for weeks, and many things that one might take for granted in the civilized world were absent, like toilets, electricity, stoves, and hot showers. But this first wilderness experience was, for most of us, heaven on Earth.

The trip left a deep mark and transformed me into a hopeless wilderness addict. Exactly what was so compelling about that northern world of water and nature was not clear; perhaps being in such a place stirred ancient Nordic memories of wild places, of travel by oar in ancient longboats.

Or maybe it was the adrenalin charge and stupidity of trying to shoot an unscouted rapids with my buddy, Chris Himmel. The counselors entrusted us, two adolescent stringbeans, with heavy food and tent packs, but we still tried to handle swollen spring white water that everyone else walked around. We paddled like banshees and made it down the first hundred yards or so. Then the river turned and dropped over a waterfall. Chris, in the bow, grabbed onto an overhanging birch tree to stop us, and the canoe pivoted around and over. Watching in horror as I disappeared over the falls, he was convinced of my early death. He was left struggling with the laden canoe caught half in raging water, half on the bank.

After bouncing me over endless haystacks of white water and rocks, the stream spat me out. I staggered back from the dead to join Chris in hauling on the canoe for a half hour or so. When we finally had her on the bank, we were exhausted, unable to move for an hour—all to save a mile-long portage.

Or maybe my wilderness addiction grew from the thrill of wildlife encounters, like the time we paddled our way through a shallow marsh past a bull moose feeding on the reeds. He carried an enormous rack and stood staring at us with water streaming from his muzzle; his nostrils, spewing clouds of condensed breath, flared wide at our presence. We were so close we could hear his snorting exhalations and the crunch of vegetation between his molars.

But whatever combination of character and experience rendered me vulnerable, the attraction to wild water grew, leading me far from Minnesota, eventually and inevitably to the sea.

Upon immersion in the ocean, all one's senses are overwhelmed. The touch of cool, liquid brine on skin, the taste of salt, the sound of lapping waves and snapping shrimp, the smell of seaweed, the visual delight of corals and flashing shoals of fish—all conspire to make one feel a surge of energy.

This is as it should be, for the ocean is the wellspring of life, the birthplace of primordial organisms, the source of our ancestors. Here was a teeming biota, a Darwinian struggle already running in high gear when the first land animals appeared hundreds of millions of years ago. Here is the elixir upon which all life, marine or terrestrial, depends.

Water: that near-universal solvent, that moderating influence that keeps planetary temperatures moderate, that sine qua non for photosynthesis. Astronomers study images of the surface of Mars, looking for telltale signs of erosion, glacial movement, or ancient river beds. They look for signs of moisture, because H_2O equals life.

Perhaps because Earth has so much water, then, it abounds with living things. The ocean covers almost three-quarters of the planet at an average depth of some 12,000 feet. As best as we can tell, nearly every cubic centimeter of this vast blanket of salt water contains biological material. Early

BREAKING WAVE, HORSESHOE REEF, LA JOLLA,

CALIFORNIA *"A wilderness, in contrast with those areas where man and his own*

works dominate the landscape. . . ."

seas probably held low concentrations of dissolved salt, but, after billions of years of runoff from land masses, seawater contains now, on average, 35 parts per thousand sodium chloride and other salts.[1] Although human blood has a tonicity, or salt concentration, about one-third of seawater,[2] it gives a hint of the close bond we have to the sea.

Yet, although in a sense we are made from it, and we may travel over it, on it, or within it, we air-breathing humans must maintain respect for the ocean. A beguiling but sometimes hostile three-dimensional world, the sea can be explored but never conquered.

Wilderness: "a region uncultivated and uninhabited; an open area of nature; a portion of a garden set apart for things to grow wild; a large confused mass or tangle of persons or things; a wild condition or quality." These are the options that *Webster's* dictionary[3] gives to define what others might call, simply, raw nature. The U.S. Wilderness Act of 1964 uses this:

> A wilderness, in contrast with those areas where man and his own works dominate the landscape, is hereby recognized as an area where the Earth and its community of life are untrammeled by man, where man himself is a visitor who does not remain.[4]

That the sea could fit all these definitions seems clear, hence the title of this book, an account of a personal marine journey that travels over time, over geography, and through changing philosophies. It is about seeking, experiencing, and conserving the ultimate wilderness: the ocean.

Surfing, diving, and exploring the sea have become a preoccupation through the last three decades, both in my adopted home state of California and elsewhere in the world. Compelled also to write, I've followed the first rule of literature ("write of what you know") and so produced this chronicle of marine discovery.

The tale that follows has an eclectic tone. Given a life spent as an underwater photographer, nature journalist, and physician, this should not be too surprising. Adventure (or, to be more accurate, misadventure), natural history, and science all appear along the way, along with profiles and interviews of some interesting maritime individuals.

Several of the chapters, or portions thereof, were first published in magazines or anthologies. "Beyond City Limits" (chapter 4) appeared in *Sierra* as "Just Beneath the Surface." "Of His Bones Are Coral Made" (chapter 6) was published in *Ocean Realm* as "Gorilla Diving in New Guinea." Portions of "Taking the Chance" (chapter 10) appeared in *California Wild* as "Where Wind and Currents Meet: Channel Islands Underwater." "Below Baja" (chapter 9) was published as "Oceans Mexico" in *American Nature Writing, 2001* (John Murray was the editor).

It should also be noted that in some of the chapters, names and appearances of certain people and boats were changed for legal reasons. The events and conversations, however, all took place as described.

Sentiments of attachment must be tempered with caution regarding the sea, for it can inspire darker emotions. Wrote Joseph Conrad in 1906, with the characteristic man-versus-nature sensibility of that time:

> As if it were too great, too mighty for common virtues, the ocean has no compassion, no faith, no law, no memory. Its fickleness is to be held true to men's purposes only by an undaunted resolution and by a sleepless, armed, jealous vigilance, in which, perhaps, there has always been more hate than love. *Odi et amo* may well be the confession of those who consciously or blindly have surrendered their existence to the fascination of the sea. . . .[5]

Studying this tempestuous liaison of human and ocean is important, even to persons dwelling in landlocked regions, for climate, weather, food, and transportation   nearly every aspect of our daily lives   has an intimate relationship to the oceans. Within the vastness of the saline wilderness lies a troubling paradox. Many today consider the living seas no longer to be the Conradian "too great and too mighty," but rather, to be in deep trouble. Under the combined assault of heavy human predation, runoff eutrophication (increased nutrients), and other synergistic pressures, many oceanic ecosystems are undergoing marked phase shifts. From 20%[6] to 50%[7] of the coral reefs of the world are undergoing stress from human activities. Certain scientists describe kelp forests in California, once teeming cities of life, as "ghost towns."[8] Worldwide fishing, according to a report from the National Academy of Sciences, occurs at unsustainable levels.[9]

All these things and more heighten our need to study the sea and, by extension, the evolutionary and ecological processes that affect it. As we embark on this nautical journey, I would like to keep a two-part question in mind: "Are there biological limits, over time, to the ocean? Or is marine life a non-zero-sum game?"

When we consider marine life, there are different perspectives. There is the concept of diversity: numbers of species, genetic variation within those species, and diversity of broad groups of basic body plans, for example, phyla, that contain species. That is one perspective.

Another way to look at life is by sheer size and number of creatures. Biologists have a word for this: "biomass." Ecologists, scientists who study how life forms live, evolve, and interact with each other and their environment, have a related term for how many individuals an environment can support: "carrying capacity." Their term for the amount of biomass found in a given volume or area at any given time: "standing crop."

Both perspectives, diversity and quantity, will play a role in helping us to answer the question, Are there biological limits, over time, to the ocean?

Considering this is important from a practical point of view. If the ocean is finite, we might consider it to function as an island of sorts. A very large island.

Now, within ecology lies the science of island biogeography. The two famous cocreators of the theory of natural selection as the crux of the origin of species—Charles Darwin and Alfred Russel Wallace—were island biogeographers. Both of these nineteenth-century pioneer theorists arrived independently upon their ideas from studying islands: for Darwin, the key was to be found in the Galapagos; for Wallace, it appeared in what is now Indonesia. To Darwin and Wallace, islands were natural laboratories, bigger and more real than a test-tube-filled room at Cambridge or Oxford, yet smaller and more manageable than a continent or an ocean.

A century later, in 1959, Robert MacArthur, a brilliant ecologist trained in mathematics (who suffered an early death), and Edward O. Wilson, an equally brilliant ant biologist, bumped into each other and decided to work in concert to try to pull patterns out of what was then the loose science of ecology. They, too, used islands as natural laboratories. In a seminal work, their book *The Theory of Island Biogeography*,[10] MacArthur and Wilson quantified and refined their field observations.

At the heart of their theory lay the concept of island equilibrium. They observed that plants and animals from continental land masses dispersed to far-flung islands. New species radiated from these initial colonists into unoccupied niches, or invaders ousted established species, which then became extinct. Over time came a sort of equilibrium, that is, a net effect of no gain or loss in species.

Today we suspect that such patterns may be idealized concepts and that punctuations occur in nature's equilibria. Ecologists have a term for upending events such as giant meteorites from outer space, rapid continental shifting, and sudden changes of ocean currents: "stochastic stresses." Wilson and MacArthur were aware that such abrupt episodes occurred, but they focused on finding broad generalizations and recurring themes for the stable periods between these stochastic events.

As natural laboratories, islands led terrestrial ecologists to discover truisms about animals and plants that live on land[11]: Larger islands support more species, and more abundant individuals, than do small islands. Rarity can predispose to extinction. Carnivores are more susceptible to extinction from stress and fragmentation of habitat than are herbivores, and large carnivores are more susceptible than small ones. Specialists are more vulnerable than are generalists. And so on.

As we humans swarm over the big land masses, we are causing a major stochastic stress. We are carving much remaining wild habitat into islandlike reserves and parks. In response, conservation biologists extrapolated principles of island biogeography to isolated sections on the continents. They developed theoretical constructs to explain how living creatures and physical processes on land interact in insular settings. These constructs included such concepts as minimum viable populations and population viability analysis, tools that ecologists used to help preserve rare species.

David Quammen, a nature writer, summarized much of this story of island biogeography in his book *The Song of the Dodo: Island Biogeography in an Age of Extinction*. Although not an ecologist by profession, Quammen is a keen naturalist and a seasoned world traveler. He coined the term "ecological naivety" for the unsuspecting innocence and unwariness many island fauna display toward human invaders. When a tree finch lands on your shoulder as you stroll about one of the Galapagos Islands, it is displaying ecological naivety—not stupidity or tameness. The finch and its ancestors adapted to a protected world where predation and competition from humans were nonexistant.[12] It never had a chance to learn that people might be dangerous.

To apply these ideas to the ocean, to take these theories and writings gleaned from the study of insular land habitats and make them fit the sea, is to turn things upside down. All the oceans of the world are connected. Conceivably, a hardy bacterial spore trapped in Arctic Ocean ice might be freed, cast into some mighty current, and end up in a tropical lagoon in the western Pacific. Or it might find itself caught in a 10-meter wave in the southern ocean. The sea knows no barriers—other than that presented by coastlines, the seafloor, and the atmosphere.

If the tools of island biogeographers do not work for the ocean, and some believe they may not,[13] then we retain a lot of uncertainty regarding limits in the sea. J.E.N. Veron, an Australian coral reef biologist, for example, writes: "Biogeographic concepts developed from terrestrial biota have very doubtful relevance to the ocean."[14]

Some parallels do exist, however. Many oceanic fauna display Quammen's ecological naivety, for example, and allow close approach by human marine explorers. Depending on currents, water and the larvae it carries may circulate only over small areas. An ocean may not seem all that big—to a whale. And so on.

The second part of our question is, in some ways, the first question recast into a different form: Is marine life (and that includes the entire squiggling, evolving mess, from viruses and bacteria to swordfish and sperm whales) a non-zero-sum game?

The mathematical field of game theory defines a zero-sum game as one where for every winner, there is a loser. Major league baseball, for example, is a zero-sum game. At the end of the season, when you add up all wins from all teams and subtract all losses, you get the number zero. Because of extra innings, there are no draws, no ties—only clear winners, and clear losers. When a marlin devours a sardine, the identities of victor and vanquished are just as transparent.

There is another way, though, to enjoy baseball. My wife, Diane, and I have learned from our two sons, Erik and Nicholas, that it is best to just play, have fun, and not worry too much about the score. And so, as we study life in the sea, as we follow the bluefin tuna, the opalescent squid, and the bottlenose dolphin, we might wonder, are there only winners and losers in the ocean? Is predation and digestion all there is? Or, given the right conditions, can marine biota play a non-zero-sum game?

It is my hope that in reading this book, you, too, may be inspired to ponder these questions of marine limits and zero sums. Perhaps you will reach different, more profound and original conclusions than my own.

It is also my hope that you might be inspired to examine your own relationship with the ocean. If you live inland and believe the distant sea to be unimportant, read on anyway, and you will find that the oceans and humanity are intertwined more than you may imagine.

So, wax up your board, check the pressure in your tank, and keep a sharp eye out for rogue whalers. It's time to slip overboard and get wet.

Acknowledgments

In the course of writing this book, I have been blessed with meeting and talking to some wonderful individuals. To get to know these people has been a thrill and a privilege. Ron Starkey, the late dive instructor, got me diving in California. Chuck Nicklin, the marine photographer, hauled me along on several wonderful trips to the South Seas. Paul Watson, the ocean eco-activist, spent long hours talking freely about a host of nautical issues. Gary Davis, the Channel Islands marine biologist, gave hours of his time as well. Jim Barry was kind enough to let me tag along as he took a submersible to 1,000 meters. Farooq Azam opened my eyes to the wonders of microbial oceanography. Pat Daily was very kind to take me on a number of expeditions on his dive boat. The nature writer John Murray got me writing in the first place and gave much time chatting with me about the art and science of distilling the wilderness onto paper. Joyce Berry, the acquisitions editor at Oxford, found something in the original, over-the-transom rough draft that somehow caught her eye and kept the book out of the slush pile.

Special thanks go to Kirk Jensen, the executive editor at Oxford University Press, who spent long hours editing multiple drafts of the manuscript. He elevated constructive criticism to a new height and, possessing unalloyed confidence in the project, made publication possible. Formally trained in the humanities, Kirk has, through his work at Oxford, an extraordinary grasp of things scientific, and his reviews, combining both worlds, were fundamental in shaping this work. He is also, I understand, one heck of a soccer coach.

A number of professional marine biologists and oceanographers reviewed the manuscript at various stages and offered expert criticism. Jeffrey Levinton, Professor of Ecology and Evolution at the State University of New York, provided a thorough and critical review that pushed the book to a higher level. Richard Grigg, Professor of Oceanography at the University of Hawaii, gave a no-holds-barred critique and followed up with a long and interesting e-mail conversation. David Au, a scientist at the National Marine Fisheries Bureau, reviewed several editions and gave much gentle insight and some head-scratching references, along with a number of long, involved conversations. Although these and other, anonymous, reviewers did their best to kept me in line and correct scientific problems, any lingering errors are, of course, my own fault.

Interviews, information, chapter reviews, and e-mails were gratefully supplied by many people. Many thanks to Craig Barilotti, Paul Dayton, Terry Rodgers, John Ugoretz, Pierre Kleiber, Pietro Parravano, Tom Raftican, Zeke Grader, James Bohnsack, Howard Hall, Marcy Remco, Pete Halmay, Forest Rohwer, Elaine Morgan, Alan Raabe, Flip Nicklin, Barbara Nombalais, Jerry Lieb, Carl Safina, Shana Beemer, Fred Van Dyke, Drew Kampion, Mary Lamberton, Alan Bowe, Alberta Thompson, Harold Mooney, Andrew Christie, Mizuki Hayashi, Stan Waterman, Michelle Morgante, Terry Rodgers, Doyle Hanan, Chris Banos, Fereidoun Rassoulzadegan, Brent Stewart, Tova and Navot Bornovski, Pat Colin, Kenneth Johnny, Lenny Oberg, Tom Johnson, Lisa Stallings, Richard Martin, Sylvia Earle, Patricia Watson, Ann Kitalong, Troy Ngiralkelau, Brian Caldwell, Phil Dustan, Paul Ponganis, Joe Gifford, and Ronn Patterson, among others.

I must acknowledge superb help from the Sharp Memorial Hospital medical library staff, who pulled, borrowed, and scrounged strange, exotic, and essential papers, at my request, on oceanography. Medicine and marine biology *are* related, as I hope the reader will agree.

A good deal of research went into this work, and I cannot thank enough those who put what I know to be an incredible amount of labor into each of the various books, peer-reviewed journal articles, websites, and newspaper and magazine pieces that provided so much valuable information for the manuscript. I have done my best to footnote all these sources; some of the most useful appear in the Short List of Related Readings section. My apologies to the authors of the many fine books and articles that belong in that section but couldn't be fit within it.

Greg Ochocki, another nature photographer, has been my comrade in arms on many journeys into the undersea realm, three being described in this compilation. Our enduring and long-suffering wives often wonder how a pair of intense personalities like ourselves can return from a trip without killing each other. Frankly, I'm still trying to figure that one out. Perhaps it is just that ocean magic working. But thanks, Greg.

Last, I am ever so grateful for the patience and understanding of Diane, my wife, and of my two sons, Erik and Nicholas, who put up with their dad typing like a maniac into the wee hours. To them, the loves of my life, I promise, no more books—at least until after the next baseball season.

Contents

The Saltwater Wilderness

CHAPTER ONE

If there is magic on this planet, it is contained in water. . . .

—LOREN EISELEY, *The Immense Journey*

First Contact

A Midwesterner Greets the Pacific and Meets Some Dolphins

Born in Minnesota, I was familiar with water in all forms but one. There was the swamp in front of our house, where pussytails grew tall, where blue-bell wildflowers on the bank sprang forth each spring, and where water filled with paramecia and amoebae made for long hours of microscopic schoolboy pleasure. A short walk to the north led to Minnehaha Creek, on whose frozen surface five of us skated the mile to Burwell Elementary late one November. A neighbor kid fell through thin ice on the way home, and even though we rescued him, stiff-legged, frosted blue jeans and all, his mother never let him play with us again.

There were the "Ten Thousand" northern lakes: Little Deer (one of 300 or so Deer Lakes in the state), Big Deer, Winnebegoshish, Ten-Mile, and Birch. We spent many days fishing in those lakes for northern pike, wall-eyed pike, and sunfish.

To the northeast loomed The Lake, Gitcheegoomee, Superior, its cobalt waters gleaming in the distance as we skied down glacier-carved hills to the lodge at Lutsen Resort. Here ships carrying taconite pellets of iron ore left Duluth for distant ports, and here great storms, Gordon Lightfoot's "gales of November come early," sank those ships.

Yes, Minnesota was a water state, although the water was crystallized more than half the year: snow, snow, and more snow. In the summer, violent thunderstorms, jet-black clouds, tornadoes, and, of course, more mosquitoes. Looking back, I know now that we were blessed, for we learned to swim like fish, to ski, to paddle canoes, to sail. One summer we had a diving hookah, a small, heavily polluting, two-stroke gasoline motor on a float that pumped air to a mask through a 30-foot hose. At the age of 11, I was diving in Big Deer Lake, staring eye to eye with a snapping turtle a foot in diameter, peering under logs for trophy muskellunge and northern pike, oblivious to the perils of air embolism, carbon monoxide poisoning, and the bends.

But there was one thing we didn't have in Minnesota: salt water. No ocean. No surfing. No coral reefs. We sang Beach Boys songs in our obligatory teenage rock band, but we were posers, wannabes, fakes. We could skateboard, but we could never surf, much less even see the ocean. We watched Lloyd Bridges play Mike Nelson on *Sea Hunt*, we thrilled to the adventures of Jacques Cousteau on the *Calypso*, but aqualungs were familiar to us only from television. The salt water we knew lay on the slushy winter streets of Minneapolis, where trucks poured tons of sodium chloride on stubborn ice. In short, we lived in an aquatic wonderland, but we felt cheated, landlocked, hopelessly provincial. We were ocean bereft, and we felt the less for it. But that didn't keep us from dreaming.

At the age of 17, my exposure to wilderness received a major boost. As a present for high school graduation, my parents sent me for a summer in Wyoming at the National Outdoor Leadership School. This was not an expensive school. We were given a sleeping bag, a backpack frame and woven nylon bags, a poncho, some food, and a tarp, and here we spent the summer above 9,000 feet in a roadless area of the Wind River Mountains, learning the art of no-trace camping and travel in the wilderness.

Our instructors taught us, on leaving a campsite, to hide all sign of our fires, to avoid leaving so much as a noodle at a cooking site (uncooked pasta takes months, even years to decompose). Cans and aluminum foil in the wilderness were *verboten*. Everything was carried in burnable bags. We learned how to climb mountains safely, how to rescue others, how to navigate with topographic maps. We learned to live off the land while traveling 50 miles over the Continental Divide during a five-day survival course. We learned that it was better to backtrack six miles to retrieve a lost bit of trash or clothing than to leave it and mar a pristine landscape.

The leader of the school, the mountaineer Paul Petzoldt, taught us a wilderness ethic. It was not based on personal gain. It was not based on fear of hell or punishment. It was based on the idea that wild land was sacred in its own right and deserving of celebration and that harming it in any way stood as a grave sin.

Upon graduating from Grinnell College in 1974, a liberal arts school nestled in the cornfields of Iowa, an even more landlocked state than Minnesota, I headed due west to the promised land of California. I had $300 in my pocket, an old VW Bug, and the address of parents of a college chum, gracious people who agreed to put me up for a few weeks. As my VW puttered across the Bay Bridge, San Francisco appeared out of the mist like a ship floating on the fog, bridges and skyscrapers looming, the superstructure of a monstrous, bizarre vessel. On my first pilgrimage to the Pacific, the water shocked me with the fury of bitter cold and the enormous waves of Ocean Beach. But the struggle for urban survival frustrated and delayed deeper acquaintance with the ocean until the next summer.

Peter Benchley's book *Jaws* had just come out that year. So close to the ocean and yet so far, and therefore ravenous for salty literature, I devoured every word. My imagination primed by Benchley, there came, finally, my moment of first immersion. On arriving one sunny weekend at Dog Beach in Santa Cruz with our household Airedale, Rusty, I failed to gather from the long lines of surf that it might not be the best day for a rookie bodysurfer. After warming up in the sand, I dove into the Pacific, my first experience swimming in the ocean.

Cold, the water was, 50°F, chilling to the bone with no wet suit, but there was no dwelling on numb limbs, for a solid six-foot swell was running. A decent swimmer overjoyed by the buoyant effect of salt water, I wasted no time in grasping the idea of sprinting to shore as a wave reared up, arching my body into a projectile, and sliding down the face of exploding water. After two or three of these wild bull rides, I swam back out to find the Airedale dog-paddling next to me. A fierce fighter who had lost one of his canine teeth in battle with another dog, Rusty feared nothing. The wave of the day reared up behind us, and I shouted,

"Go, Rusty, go!"

The wave launched both of us, and the thought came to me that Rusty had never been bodysurfing before, either. A giant, heaving wall of water threw us forward, twin projectiles, one human, one canine, a pair of aquatic, circus cannonballs.

A minute later at the surface, there was no sign of the dog.

Around me water boiled, and every ripple held the fin of a white shark. Panic seized me. Images from Benchley's book lurked everywhere. Rusty was first, I was next. That dark thing in the water—must be a shark. Ahhh!

It brushed my leg. I jerked back, imagination and reality merging. But the shark was only a piece of kelp.

Then, as the swell lifted me up, the sight of a furry form far away on the beach, drying off with a doggy shake, assuaged my fears. After a last adrenaline-charged dash, my own drenched body lay next to Rusty's, both of us near-frozen and collapsed on the sand. Every muscle was spent, every neuron overloaded with sensation: wonder, dread, delight, and terror all mixed together.

Bodysurfing, I learned, is a pure sport. There is no equipment other than a swimsuit. Unlike baseball, one does not keep score, except, perhaps, in some isolated competitions. The act is sport enough. The winning and losing is at a primordial level—perhaps this is the attraction: either you survive or you do not. It is the doing, not the winning, that makes riding a wave so wonderful.

A year passed, and events of good luck on land led me to acceptance in medical school at the University of California at San Diego. Perhaps a profession in marine biology might have suited me better, or perhaps a career as an underwater filmmaker. But at the age of 23, my life, terrestrially based until then, had a certain trajectory that led me to a eucalyptus-filled campus in La Jolla, a small peninsula jutting northward into the sea where Nobel laureates and surfers mingled and where, incidentally, Scripps Institution of Oceanography made its home.

Working for two years in Palo Alto, I'd saved enough to take the summer off before the big grind. Not able to afford a private place, I found myself a room with one Arthur Ley, a doctoral candidate in oceanography at Scripps. Art was a quiet sort with thick glasses and a mustache. His prize possession was a seven-foot surfboard with a decal of Jimi Hendrix on the deck. He was my kind of guy.

Art sized me up immediately as a surf geek, a goon from Minnesota who knew nothing of the sea and deserved little but quiet scorn. Oh, he was friendly enough, but I could tell it would take time to earn his respect. I wasted no time in buying a used surfboard at Mitch's Surfshop on Pearl Street, a real geek's board, bright green, but with nary a single ding and, at eight feet, big enough for a beginner to stand on.

That summer I paddled out three times a day at my selected learning spot, Twelfth Street in Del Mar, the race track suburb north of San Diego. There was the morning glass, when the still sea, unruffled by wind, gleamed, mirroring the morning sky, when small waves a foot or two high broke in perfect curls over the rocky reef. There was the afternoon session, when the

BOTTLENOSE DOLPHINS *"With each fin appearance, there was a loud exhalation—these were bottlenose dolphins."*

sun blazed and made up for the chop caused by the land breeze. And there was the evening, the squinting of near-sighted eyes into the setting sun, the hope of practicing skills on yet one more dark-shadowed breaker before dark.

Surfing is hard to learn. Everything is moving. Unlike skiing, where the mountain or hill stands still, you have to wait patiently for a wave to come. And when it does, and you fall off, there are long frustrating minutes of inactivity. There is no chair lift to carry you back out past the white water. You have only your arms to pull you along, and beginners like myself that summer tire out quickly.

But there are advantages. Apart from the high cost of living on the coast, there is no fee, no lift ticket as in skiing, no shepherds herding you into the lift line. There are today and were then, however, other surfers, some of whom were nice, and others who would run you over. After a time, muscles hardened, fat slipped away into the cold sea like wood into a bonfire, and I got in shape.

Most of all, from the first touch of salt water on bare feet, from the first breaking wave dunking my head on the paddle out, there was the thrill of the sea. Early that summer on a menacing, overcast day, as I rested outside the white water, gathering strength and nerve to try again, a dark fin knifed through the water. Again, memories of *Jaws* surfaced, and my heart skipped a beat. But the fin moved up and down. Then a second appeared, and a third. With each fin appearance, there was a loud exhalation—these were bottlenose dolphins. My panic receded.

From prior reading, I knew that the brains of these animals were as large or larger than human brains, in part because of huge regions related to echolocation and hearing.[1] There was the work of John Lilly that would suggest[2] (and be confirmed by others)[3] that dolphins enter deep, delta-wave sleep with only one hemisphere of their brain at a time.

Later, I found out that dolphins could recognize themselves and inspect marked body parts in mirrors. The self-awareness that this kind of mirror recognition implies was thought to exist in only great apes and humans, and suggests sentient intelligence.[4]

Then there were those enigmatic dolphin "signature" whistles. Dolphins produce these repetitive sounds, different from echolocation sounds, most probably to identify themselves to others in their species at a distance.[5] Dolphins announce themselves.

But for now, there was nothing better than this firsthand experience of seeing smooth, gray dolphin skin, hearing the soft blows, popping my head underwater to listen for a high-pitched sonar trill. All summer the same pod of dolphins entertained me as they darted in and around that surf break, fishing and riding waves.

San Diego was, and is, a populous city, one of the 10 biggest in the United States. Local beaches were home to substantial urban runoff. Trash of all sorts ended up below sea level: plastic bags, Styrofoam cups, flotsam and jetsam from boats and ships. Oil and organic residue from landfills washed into the water, as did sewage from broken mains and dog feces. Whenever a two-stroke outboard-powered speedboat chugged by in the distance, the smell of gasoline permeated the water as pungent organic molecules covered the surface for hundreds of yards. The Australian slang for a U.S. surfer is "seppo," short for "septic-tank Yank." Pollution or no, though, the ocean was still wilderness and, after those summers canoeing in Minnesota and mountaineering in Wyoming, this seppo had developed a keen taste for anything wild.

Despite slow progress, I kept at it, trying to learn the tricky act of paddling into the laminar rise of a breaking wave, leaping to my feet, and matching the forward fall of the wave with lateral motion. Riding the turbulent, chaotic white water proved to be near impossible. For every wave ridden without falling, a hundred knocked me down. But I kept at it. Eventually, persistence paid off.

As the years passed after that first summer, there would be surfaris to such places as southern Mexico, Indonesia, northern California, Baja California, and Costa Rica. I would never become a talented surfer, but that didn't bother me. There would be cold winter days at home blessed by monstrous swells; there would be tube rides, injuries, and wildlife encounters; there would be fresh memories overlapping those early learning days like fresh waves wrapping around a rock-studded point.

There was no forgetting, though, that first season of surfing. One sun-drenched afternoon in late August, the last day before the beginning of classes, stands out from the others and remains etched in my psyche.

The wave arose in La Jolla, at the beach break north of the Scripps Institution of Oceanography pier. A strong swell was running. A good-sized five-footer welled up behind me, lifting the tail of my green monster. Stroking hard, I sprang to my feet, turned hard off the bottom of the wave, and pulled up high on the shoulder. Through some kind of miracle, I didn't fall off.

Another surfer was paddling out. The green board, driven, perhaps, by divine intervention, turned down to pass harmlessly under the guy and shoot along, ever faster, just ahead of the breaking curl. On and on the mass of moving water went, carrying the two of us with it.

Finally, the wave lined up near the beach in what surfers call a "closeout."

Somehow the big, ugly board, under the illusion that its rider knew how to surf, turned up and over the lip, "kicking out" rather than "wiping out."

At that moment something came over me, a delicious sensation celebrating the junction of sea and wind and sun and land. I was, in surf jargon, stoked.

I'd become a winner in the game of surf. As a rule, only one surfer rides each wave. In that sense, surfing is a classic zero-sum game. A perfect wave rises up, the crowd of surfers scrambles, the deepest or most aggressive or biggest takes control and screams, "My wave," and everyone else backs off. One wave, one surfer. One wave, one winner.

Not all coasts support good waves for surfing. Great surf spots, places where the combination of bottom conditions, swell, and accessibility merge, are even more rare. As cities grow, and more people move to the shoreline, there is increased competition for each perfect, grinding tube.

But there is another way to think about it. After that one wave, there comes another. And another. And another. Waves will be coming long after every surfer has packed up and gone to bed, after they've all grown old and died, after the human race has disappeared. There is far-off surf in Mexico, Peru, and South Africa; there are waves all over this water planet.

Most of them remain unridden.

CHAPTER TWO

Gift of the Sun

Encounters with Wave Mountains in Oahu

EASTERN PACIFIC, LATE 1970s

Moving with geological slowness over a hot spot in the center of the tropical eastern Pacific lies a collection of large islands: Kauai, Oahu, Maui, Lanai, Molokai, and that youngster still perched over the volcanic vent, Hawaii. Jutting up from the abyss, these lava mountains receive a battering of waves across thousands of miles of fetch—landless, open water—in all directions. The power of the sun churns the Pacific Ocean, stirring up storms that blow across vast spaces. Solar heat is turned to wind, the wind stirs the waters, and waves settle out into organized swells. Reaching the coral reefs that surround the islands, these waves rear up, are held for long moments from breaking on north, west, and southern shores by northeast trade winds, and then pitch forward with incredible power and strength.

Hawaii is the most isolated archipelago on Earth. As a result, besides absorbing waves to make a surfer salivate, the islands harbor a multitude of rare, endemic species. On the rich soil of volcanic mountains and in verdant valleys, immigrant animals and plants found unoccupied niches—best thought of as ecological job descriptions—both above and below sea level. The islands are biologically well established (especially the more ancient, western ones), warm, and topographically steep. Deep ravines separate valleys, and marked climate variations occur on leeward and windward sides.

Because of this isolation and complex topography, speciation and adaptive radiation occur here that might, perhaps, have inspired Charles Darwin even more than the Galapagos, had he visited Hawaii. Here are, for example, honeycreepers, birds of every shape, color, and size. Here are 500 species of the fruit fly genus *Drosophila* alone.[1]

This extreme evolution of a few species radiating into unoccupied island roles is not limited to terrestrial creatures. Marine biologists estimate that one-fifth of the island's fishes, algae, mollusks, seastars, and brittlestars are endemic, unique to the chain.[2]

All this ran through my head as a plane carried me across a featureless Pacific, hurtling seven miles above the endless blue. A medical student in his final, fourth year, I'd engineered a swap with a similar student at the University of Hawaii and was sliding into Clayton Chong's car, apartment, and surfboard collection, just as Clayton was sliding into mine in southern California. For years, reading about surfing in Hawaii, about the legendary Banzai Pipeline, about riders of sea mountains, captivated me. The Polynesian settlement a thousand years before and the biological riches were no less fascinating. Now, at last, I was going to see for myself.

At Honolulu International, a buddy of Clayton's met me at the airport and asked if I was hungry. "Starving," I said. A few minutes later we were eating at an authentic Hawaiian restaurant. The thick, unappetizing paste that is poi, those tiny raw, whole crabs—it didn't take me long to decide that the culinary arts here were an acquired taste. But soon I was paddling out at Diamond Head reef, under the shadow of the ancient volcano, riding one of Clayton's boards, a clean, priceless classic hand-shaped by a surf legend, Gerry Lopez.

The sea tasted saltier to me than California water, the result of evaporation from a tropical sun. Even more apparent was the feeling of cleanliness, of trade winds blowing over thousands of miles of city-free ocean, of clear water reaching to vast depths, of freedom from California urban pollution and trash.

For an hour I enjoyed four-foot surf there on Oahu's south shore. Then a set wave arched up in front of me. Now, it is a statistical certainty that wave trains, blown by far-off storms, will combine at odd intervals. Any wave report gives only average swell heights, but one wave out of every thousand or so (perhaps every four hours) will be at least twice as big as the others.[3] This was one of those waves.

I turned and paddled hard, but the wave slammed into me with a violence that surprised me and upended me arse-over-teakettle. A wave starts to feel the bottom when it is about one-half the distance of its wavelength, wavelength being the distance between wave peaks over bottomless ocean. Because the wavelength of most Pacific or Atlantic storm waves is somewhere around 500 feet, this bottom effect appears at several hundred feet of depth, causing the wave to slow down and rear up. In places with continental shelves, then, waves lose speed long before they reach shore. Hawaii is not such a place.

Another mathematical oceanographic fact: when the bottom depth is about the same as the wave height (the distance from peak to trough), the wind energy in the wave starts to change form. Carried with little energy conversion through the seawater for miles, like the flutter you get when you shake a blanket, contact with the bottom changes wind energy to forward water motion, or as surfers say, the waves break. With shallow sloping bottoms, like at Waikiki Beach, this happens in water at a depth that is around 1.4 times the depth of the wave height. Where the bottom slopes up rapidly, as at Waimea Bay, on Oahu's North Shore, waves break in water that is about 0.8 times as deep as the wave is high.[4]

Before a wave breaks, water molecules pass on the wind energy from the sun, rotating in a circular fashion to assume a position near where they started when the wave first fluttered by. Over bottomless ocean, then, water moves in circles. But on breaking, that wind energy lifts up the water and casts it forward. If the wave is really big, it can travel at some 15–20 miles per hour.[5]

The reason for explaining all this is to point out why the waves in Hawaii strike so hard. There is no continental shelf to slow a wave impulse on these islands that have risen straight up from the abyss. Here, waves feel a sharply rising bottom, rear up, and break, all three events occurring in close proximity. To a surfer, this means, well, that the surf packs a wallop. And there, out at Diamond Head, I experienced for the first time this "Hawaiian Punch." Gasping for air at the surface, I realized Clayton's surfboard, attached to my leg with his old Velcro surf leash, was long gone, stripped from my ankle by water gone crazy.

I started swimming for shore but, in the failing afternoon light, saw no sign of the board. My near-sighted vision led me to one blurry patch of sea foam, then another. After 40 minutes of swimming and an hour of searching up and down the beach in the dark, it was clear that I owed Clayton a new board. Aloha to Hawaii, brah.

The next day dawned bright and cheerful. A mynah bird, a noisy black and white Asian immigrant, gave its melodious call and told me this was not Kansas. Clayton's radio gave the surf report: "Strong northeast trades, 15–20 knots. South shores two to four-foot surf, west shores running six to eight foot, windward shores are four foot and choppy. There is a high surf advisory on northwest shores, with swells reaching 10–12 feet."

My heart was hammering before a single sip of coffee. Ten to twelve foot waves. Yikes. Today, the North Shore held my destiny.

Still rueful over losing the board, I tucked my own—and soon to be Clayton's—eight-foot air-freighted California gun (from elephant gun, as in, a board to ride mammoth-sized waves) into his VW wagon and wound my way along Oahu's two freeways. Schofield Barracks appeared at the freeway's end, midisland, and then came sugarcane fields on a picturesque two-lane highway, where red volcanic dirt on the shoulder contrasted with yellow sunlight and green cane.

In the cool blue of the distant Pacific lay the fabled North Shore of Oahu. White lines appeared, visible from miles away, and my mouth turned dry. The North Shore is to a surfer what Mecca is to a Muslim, what a Nobel Prize is to a scientist, what . . . well, you get the idea. It is Nirvana. Valhalla. The Holy Grail. Best Actor, Best Actress, Best Picture, and all in one movie.

Giant waves strike this 20-mile-long coast every fall and winter, stirred up by violent storms in the North Pacific. The fast-moving, narrow Kuroshio Current carries solar radiation from the tropics as it moves north from the Philippines to Japan, where it turns eastward across the ocean and becomes the North Pacific Drift. The Kuroshio ferries enormous amounts of heat to the north, where it collides with cold winds blowing off the Asian landmass. All that heat is transferred to the atmosphere, which rises to create low-pressure cells and powerful surface winds. A similar scheme occurs in the North Atlantic, where the Gulf Stream meets cold winds blowing off Canada, but the scale is smaller. The result of this misnamed Pacific confluence of sun, heat, and wind is a spawning ground for the largest storms on Earth.[6]

Settled down by thousands of miles of fetch, waves from these immense winter storms catch trade winds blowing out of the northeast, from Kahuku Point at the northernmost tip of the island to Kaena Point at the northwest corner and down the west side to the south shore. Unimpeded by continental shelves, the faces are blasted smooth by these offshore trades, with great plumes of spray cast behind each wave. At last, as the waves break over coral reefs, lips pitch forward into Greyhound bus–sized tubes.

To be sure, there may at times be waves as big at select surf spots near the North American mainland, at Maverick's in Half Moon Bay, California, or at Cortes Bank, a hundred miles offshore from San Diego, or at Todos Santos in

Ensenada, Mexico. Surely there are giant waves at the Antarctic convergence, where never-ending westerlies blow in an endless circle of fetch down in the cold southern ocean.

But no place else on the planet has warm water so kind, trade winds so perfect, coral reefs making waves so ridable, and the number of legendary surf spots so large as on the North Shore. Laniakea, Haleiwa, Pipeline, Rocky Point, Sunset, Waimea, Off-the-Wall—the list goes on and on. All were familiar to me from surf magazines. All thrilled me, all scared me to death.

Passing through Haleiwa, a small town at the end of the highway from the south, I saw a peculiar, battered sign on Kamehameha Highway, the main route along the North Shore: "Civil Defense Warning: Large Dangerous Surf." My own imagination added, of course, the obligatory "Abandon all hope ye who enter here."

The first spot visible from the road was Laniakea, a point reef break that was packed with 50 surfers. One surfer after another scored a hall-of-fame tube ride. This was it. Throwing caution to the trades, I paddled out.

A rip whisked me into the lineup. A giant wave reared up as spray peppered my face and made vision impossible. Just as I was ready to launch, another surfer appeared, already riding, lining up for a tube beneath me. The size of the waves amazed me, and the speed, and the power. Hawaiians, in a sort of perverse machismo, measure waves from the back, unlike oceanographers, who measure them from peak to trough. For the locals, a 10-foot wave is what we would call, in California, a 20-foot wave. Again and again I tried to catch one of these beasts, but to no avail.

At last, I found a wave to myself, rode it in my own inimitable style— butt sticking out, arms flailing, semi out of control—and then wiped out. The velocity and strength of the swell were hard to believe. Even though the wave held me in its grip for what seemed only a moment, it carried me a hundred yards before burying me under an avalanche of white water. Ecstatic, I paddled to shore, exhausted and exhilarated.

Jumping back into Clayton's car, I pushed north. The day was not yet done. At Waimea Bay, where 20- to 30-foot waves could be ridden, only a few surfers were out, the swell not big enough to make the place happen. I stopped anyway to gaze and recall a classic surf story from 1943.

During that war year, two young, pioneering surfers, Woody Brown and Dickie Cross, paddled out at Oahu's Sunset Beach into large, 15-foot surf. They soon realized that they had made a mistake, as the wave size increased dramatically over the next hours. By the time they reached the safety of deep, offshore ocean, giant mountains of water now broke in long, unridable, closed-out lines between them and the beach.

Knowing there was no hope of making it to land at Sunset, the two men, in faltering light, decided to paddle the three miles or so west to Waimea Bay, where they stood a better chance. As they reached their goal, the sun kissed the horizon. They watched in horror as waves too big to surf, 50-footers, now thundered across the entire mouth of the bay.

Woody called over to his mate and told him he planned to ditch his board and swim. Dickie replied that he thought the best chance was to go for it and surf in. Said Wally Froiseth, another surfer from the era:

"They were sitting there when this huge set came. Dickie started to paddle for it, to take off on it. And Woody told him, 'No, no, don't take it, it's all the way across the bay. There's no chance of you going any place.' But the last thing he saw was Dickie dropping into it; we never saw him again."[7]

That night a bone-chilled Woody Brown was found unconscious on the beach. Dickie Cross's body was never recovered. Woody went on to invent the catamaran and spend much of his life sailing. To this day, now in his 80s, he is still surfing.

Starting up and cruising down the next stretch of Kam Highway, I saw a place called Pupukea Beach Park. Something made me pull the VW in here, for it was my guess that this was the access to the Banzai Pipeline surf break. Pipeline, during the early years of surfing, was regarded as a place where certain death lay, where the most tubular, dangerous waves in the world broke on a nasty reef impossibly close to shore.

By the time I first got there, in the late 1970s, it had been conquered, and the most prestigious contests in surfing were held there on a yearly basis. But a reputation as a dangerous place still tainted the spot.

Upon my arrival, a paramedic van flashed its lights on the edge of a crowded parking lot. A fourth-year med student and full of hubris, I ran up only to stop short at what will forever be my impression of Pipeline.

A local Hawaiian lay on the sand, his face purple, his trunks sandy and wet. Paramedics had inserted an endotracheal breathing tube through his mouth and were ventilating soggy lungs with an Ambubag. Two more paramedics were pumping on the unfortunate man's chest. In the distance, huge breaking barrels scorched in from the horizon, breaking like mortar shells only 20 yards or so from shore. Before there was time to react or try to help, the paramedics lifted the man up on a wooden backboard, never once stopping their resuscitative maneuvers, and loaded him onto their van.

Welcome to Pipeline. I sat back in shock with the rest of a stunned crowd to watch riderless waves crashing toward shore. That day did not see me paddle out at the Pipe, nor any day since. Although not a superstitious type, I know an omen when it appears.

DANE KEALOHA—PIPELINE, OAHU, HAWAII *"But a reputation as a dangerous place still tainted the spot."*

There were many more days in the sun surfing after that first one. Most, thankfully, were not quite as dramatic. There was a Thanksgiving trip to Maui, where we surfed 10-foot Honolua Bay, one of the longest, most finely wrought point-break tubes in the world. There was the time I paddled out at eight-foot Rocky Point, a break that is prime in the four- to six-foot range, and discovered why only a few guys were out—the place is too dangerous at eight feet and up. There were a number of other times when the size of the waves fooled and outclassed me. This happened at Sunset and Haleiwa on the North Shore, and Makaha on the west side. In each case, the surf was over 15 feet, my demise seemed imminent, and there were futile vows never to repeat such a mistake.

One of those episodes occurred during that first trip to Oahu as a medical student, late during my three-month stint there. A December swell struck the island from the northwest, with massive waves whipped up by the usual low-pressure area in the North Pacific basin, somewhere southeast of Russia's Kuril Islands. By that time I'd bought a used seven and a half–foot gun shaped by the well-known surfer Ben Aipa, but that board seemed small for the 20-footers breaking on the North Shore.

Thinking the waves there might be less formidable, I decided to drive to Oahu's sunny, leeward west side, where trade winds blasted straight offshore after having all moisture wrung from their soul by the Waianae Range. On this desertlike, parched side of the island lay Makaha Point, a famous break that could handle big surf.

The west side of the island is local Hawaiian turf, where many a haole has been punched out for any offense, real or imagined. "Haole" (literally, "of another breath") is popularly thought to mean "without soul" and is the Hawaiian perjorative for a white or Caucasian. And so I was careful to be on my best behavior, whether in the water or out. At the parking lot, two Hawaiians, a middle-aged man and a boy of 14 or so, were also preparing to go surfing. The three of us sat with our boards and cars for a long while and waited for a set. The sea was calm for the moment, but a heavy mist hung over the coconut palm–studded beach.

A dark line appeared on the horizon, then several lines, a kind of oceanic corduroy. My stomach wrenched as the first wave broke far outside, for it was bigger than anything I'd ever ridden. It took a good three seconds for the water to fall from top to bottom. It had perfect shape, though, and in my mind I surfed it, outracing the section known as the "Bowl," where Makaha can close out into unridability and nail you.

I was about ready to jump in the car and go home when the Hawaiian guy, a stocky gent who appeared to be in his 40s but looked fit and muscular, walked up and started examining my board. After a time he looked at me and smiled. "I remember when I made this board," he said, smiling even more.

"Are you," I gulped, "Ben Aipa?"

"That's me, brah," he said, and I shook his offered hand. Ben invited me to join him for a surf. I had no choice but to accept. After waxing up the deck of the board to keep my feet from slipping, I followed the two Hawaiians out. At Makaha, each wave bounces off the shore and ricochets back into the next wave, creating a spectacular and sometimes dangerous backwash. I was shaking, sprinting through this section, but made it out and paddled for a long time in the rip between Makaha and Klausmeyer's, the break to the south. Finally, Aipa and friend appeared, bobbing in the swell, waiting for me far from shore. We were way past the point, so far out that the buildings onshore were invisible.

None of us was truly ready for those waves. Every time a set would come, we'd yell for the others to go. But looking down each face through blinding spray, I could sense a 30-foot or so vertical drop, then feel a moving mountain of deep blue water sweep up and cascade down past me, Niagara-like. The roar each time a wave broke was deafening, the blazing noon sun on the white water, blinding. Time and again I would paddle with all my strength into one of the monsters, but the offshore wind would hold me back until the wave was vertical, and the thought of getting caught in the bowl would hold me back even more.

"Even if you don't ride it, watch the wave as it breaks inside," Aipa counseled the boy and me. "Learn from each wave."

To tell the truth, I can't remember Aipa or the boy catching a wave, either, although they probably did; a memory that remains clear, in addition to my own timidity, was the three of us meeting on shore some two hours later, exhausted, thrilled just to be out among the big waves.

"How big would you call it, Ben?" I asked. Although Aipa was past his prime, he had a lifetime of Hawaiian surfing under his belt, not to mention a pair of brass balls.

"Oh," I remember him replying, nonchalant, "maybe 15 foot or so."

Work as an emergency doctor on the North Shore, at a little place called Kahuku Hospital, kept me busy for several years after a surgical internship. Here, surfers of all stripes came to be sutured: local Hawaiians, Brazilians, Peruvians, Frenchmen, Australians, and Californians. I saw and heard things that often failed to make the surf magazines or the newspaper. There was the last surf of a guy who paddled the mile offshore into huge Avalanche, a mysto reef break that became ridable only in giant swells. He wiped out, slit the popliteal artery behind his knee, and bled to death trying to get back to shore. There was the surfboard tip that spiked the rectum of a famous surfer at Pipeline, earning him a colostomy bag for a couple of months. There was the drug deal shootout, the Samoan hit on the head by a Tongan hammer, the Tongan beat to a pulp by a Samoan, and innumerable head-on car wrecks on Kam Highway. There was even a hurricane, the events of which will appear later in these pages.

One day during this period I nearly drowned while surfing in big surf at Sunset. An oversized wave pitched me onto my ear, rupturing my left tympanic membrane and breaking my surfboard leash. But there was no time to dwell on the strange whistling that emanated from my head as I tried to hold my breath. The wave had carried me into what surfers call the "impact zone," where the lips of the waves curl over and land. Needless to say, this was not a good place in which to tarry. To compound matters, a long set of similar, beefy waves continued to pour in.

Again and again I held my breath and dived deep, actively breaststroking down, trying to ignore the pain in my ear, sensing the ocean thundering some 20–30 feet above. A dark cloud appeared each time in my visual field just before surfacing. After five or six of these desperate dives, the thought dawned in my thick head that this might be a serious, possibly even a life-threatening situation.

Shallow-water blackout—more deadly to the free diver than any shark. Feared by spearfishermen, underwater whale photographers, and surfers alike, it kills you only inches from the life-giving air. Here's how it works, as told to me by marine mammal and avian diving physiologist—and human anesthesiologist—Paul Ponganis. (Paul works with me 10 months of every year in the hospital and then goes to Antarctica for two months to study Weddell seals and emperor penguins.)

Buildup in the blood of carbon dioxide stimulates air hunger when you hold your breath. When a diver, before submerging, hyperventilates with two or three deep breaths, the level of this gas is lowered, and down time can be prolonged. Between each wave, I did just that.

But there is another gas to consider—oxygen. At too high a level, as when diving with compressed air to, say, 300 feet of water, or 10 atmospheres, elevated oxygen in the blood can cause fatal seizures. This, obviously, was not a problem for me that day. But too little oxygen can also cause brain dysfunction—blackout, fainting, or syncope. And too little oxygen was my problem, according to Paul.

Partial pressure, the key to understanding shallow-water blackout, is the given portion of a mixed gas exuding pressure. In this case the mixed gas is air. To know the partial pressure of oxygen where there is one atmosphere of pressure, that is, at sea level, you multiply 0.21 (because air is 21% oxygen) times 760 mm of mercury (the weight of all the air stacked above to outer space as measured by a column of that heavy, liquid metal, mercury or Hg). Thus, 0.21×760 equals 160 mm Hg, the partial pressure of oxygen.

At a depth of 33 feet, pressure doubles; it becomes twice the pressure generated by Earth's atmosphere. Each time I swam down under one of the mammoth breakers, oxygen pressure in my lungs and blood also nearly doubled. At 33 feet deep, the partial pressure of oxygen becomes 0.21 of 1,520 mm Hg, or 21% of two atmospheres—320 mm Hg.

At this depth, for me at Sunset, all was well and good (except for the water entering my middle ear). And because I'd hyperventilated, the doubling of CO_2 didn't seem to bother me much. But my exercising body used up oxygen quickly, lowering the partial pressure of that gas in my lungs to, say, 75 mm Hg. This is still a number high enough to supply vital organs adequately. But, when I rose to just beneath the surface, as Paul Ponganis pointed out, the already lowered oxygen pressure now halved—to around 37 mm Hg. This is a dangerously low level, about the amount of oxygen found in an acclimatized climber's blood on the summit of Mt. Everest. Brain cells need oxygen to function; when the group of cells in the brainstem that keeps you awake, the reticular activating system, shuts down, you lose consciousness.

Low oxygen pressure in the blood is a stealthy murderer. There is no frantic urge to breathe, as there is with increased CO_2. There is only a sneaky, subtle loss of awareness. Sometimes there is a visual deficit just before unconsciousness, something I was noticing.

Somehow my foggy brain realized that Sunset was gaining the upper hand. Throwing caution to the wind, I stopped fighting, relaxed at the surface, and let the next wave explode on top of me. There was an instant mighty impact, something like a bomb going off, a thrashing, a pulverizing, and then a quick drag across coral reef. Seconds later the wave spat my body to safety on the coarse Sunset Beach sand.

The contrast between the medical and the surfer's life proved, in the end, to be too much for me. One afternoon dreamlike eight-foot Sunset captivated me until five minutes before my shift at the emergency department. Racing in, I changed in the car and roared the short distance to the hospital, to find everyone trying their best to revive a two-year-old drowning victim. With salt water still pouring from my maxillary sinuses (an occupational problem many surfers have), I helped the pediatrician in that futile exercise, then had a long, heart-rending talk with the hysterical parents. This sort of juxtaposition of perfect joy and sudden death didn't work for me, and I moved back to California, a place that has been my home to this day.

But let me make one thing clear. Hawaii is a wonderful place, and the Hawaiian ocean a special corner of the Pacific. Surf rules here. There is something alive and special about the sea surrounding these islands. Maybe it is the crystal clarity of the water, unmarred by human pollution. Maybe it is the soft, pristine air, swept clean by the ever-present trade winds blasting across endless tracts of blue ocean.

It is here, perhaps, more than any place else, that the ocean, with all its thundering violence and deep mysteries, gives one the impression of infinity. Infinite power, infinite cleanliness, infinite numbers of perfect waves—the concept of limits in the sea is not an easy one to accept out here, a thousand miles from any other land.

Topside, though, at least, it is clear that infinity applies less well to biodiversity and longevity of Hawaiian species survival. Many of the native honeycreepers, many native plants, and many insects have gone extinct in Hawaii, victims of human destruction of habitat and human-borne mainland immigrants (including avian malaria and the *Culex* mosquito).[8] Endemic fish, barnacles, and mollusks, for all we know, are doing better. The monk seal, though, is teetering, protected, safe for now, but still dancing with oblivion. The warning signs that all is not perfect in paradise are hard to ignore.

Terrestrial, modern Hawaii makes a good case for a zero-sum evolutionary game. As life first colonized the raw volcanic islands, it encountered few limits. A non-zero-sum game was in effect, and what ecologists call "r-selected" organisms—those with high fecundity, short life spans, and rapid growth—thrived. Birds and insects hitchhiked in on the wind and on floating debris. Current-borne fish and larvae found their way across an immense fetch. They found wide-open, uncolonized territory.

These founding immigrants radiated and filled open, available ecological niches. Whether they achieved some kind of biotic steady state between new speciation or immigration and extinction before people arrived is open to debate. But humans did indeed arrive. And with them, avian malaria came, rats, pigs, and goats came, sugar cane and pineapple fields came, and exotic honeycreepers left. The Hawaii *mamo*, the black *mamo*, the *ula-ai-hawane*, the Oahu *nukupuu*, the *amaui*, the *kioea*, and the Oahu *oo* all left.[9] Gone for good.

"*Pau*," as Hawaiians say. "Finished."

The status of life in the unruly Hawaiian seas, though, remains an open question. Perhaps no one knows those seas better than Richard Grigg. Rick, whom I met at a wedding on the North Shore, is a compact, muscular man with piercing blue eyes, a ready smile, and a quick wit. He has a big reputation in both the surfing world, where he is famous for his style in riding giant Waimea waves (waves that would keep me on the beach), and in the oceanographic world, for his work on the coral reef biological community.

Grigg the oceanographer is not as fanatical about the plight of coral reefs as some. He admits that reefs are under siege, particularly near urban centers in Indonesia, the Philippines, and parts of the Caribbean. But he told me, "There are plenty of healthy reefs out there as well. In Hawaii, over 90% of our reefs are as healthy as ever."

In 1994 Grigg published a study that looked at the abundance of reef fishes in Hawaii.[10] Using sophisticated techniques, he measured biomass and species variety of fish in a number of habitats. He found that pollution from deep outflow pipes actually increased fish abundance and that the biomass and number of species of fish in any one of Hawaii's 11 no-fishing areas (Marine Life Conservation Districts) were markedly higher than in fished areas. Such places as Hanauma Bay and Honolua Bay, where fishing is banned, were, predictably, chock full of reef fish.

Even more interesting, Grigg noticed that high relief reefs, places with complex topography due to lava formations and coral growth, had much more biomass. Hawaiian fishermen have known this for years; there is even a word for such an area, koa, meaning "fish house" in the Hawaiian language.

This is the kind of evidence that makes me wonder about limits. Now, perhaps these fish simply moved in from elsewhere, and there was no net loss or gain of biomass at the reef fish trophic level overall. Maybe, though, these tropical fish represent increased survival of juveniles. Only 10 out of a million fish larvae may survive to become adults, and the critical bottleneck in fish populations is the larval period.[11] Food is probably not the limiting factor for many kinds of fish; this is suggested by events during World War II, when intense fishing (what ecologists call predation or "top-down" pressure) in the North Sea was suspended. Total fish biomass doubled during the war years, and there was little evidence of this growth slowing in most species before fishing resumed.[12] These events suggested that "bottom-up" pressure, from lack of nutrients and prey, was not a problem for North Sea fish.

Grigg's study hints that, perhaps, life in the ocean might not always be playing a zero-sum game—not, at least, over time. As volcanoes spew and corals build, habitat may become more complex, more "high-relief," and more larvae might survive to adulthood. Quantity and diversity of life might then accelerate.

As waves break, though, events may take a different turn.

For another paper, Rick Grigg wore both of his hats—oceanographer and surfer. In 1993 the Sierra Club sued the City and County of Honolulu for alleged violations of the U.S. Clean Water Act. Although court proceedings failed to produce solid evidence that sewage was harming the marine environment, the judge did stipulate that the city spend a million dollars on further study.

This funding allowed Grigg to study the impact of sewage discharges, runoff from land, and "natural sources" upon corals in Mamala Bay (a 36-km tract that includes most of Honolulu and runs from Barbers Point to Diamond Head).[13] "Natural sources," it must be understood, is a code word for "surf." The study, in which Grigg examined quadrats, or physical squares, at 29 stations and used historical data ranging over 25 years (corals have annual growth bands similar to tree rings), did not find what the Sierra Club hoped.

Until 1977, raw sewage did have a serious, localized effect on the reef corals. In that year, the City of Honolulu upgraded sewage treatment and extended outfalls to deep water (greater than 200 feet of depth, or 65 meters). The researchers could not detect an impact on corals from sewage after that time.

But, in 1982 and 1992, two magnitude 5 hurricanes, Iwa and Iniki, with winds greater than 150 mph (240 kph), generated waves in excess of 20 feet (7.5 meters). Such waves, although a yearly event on the North Shore, are unheard of on the southern coast of Oahu. Grigg demonstrated that, as a result of these waves, coral cover of well-developed offshore reefs plummeted from 60–75% to 5–15%. Wow.

I relayed the gist of this study to a surfing acquaintance, who rephrased and summarized the results for me using surfer's vernacular.

A Jeff Spicoli–like character (Spicoli was the archetypical, zoned out, hedonistic surfer played by Sean Penn in the 1982 movie *Fast Times at Ridgemont High*), this to-remain-nameless surfer gave a scatological reply. I did, however, have to give him points for succinctness and alliteration.

"I get it, dude," he said, "Hawaiian surf . . . is stronger than shit."

And I take off on the last wave—it's the outside reef at Steamer's—and I make the take-off,

and it's dark, and I don't know where the hell I'm going. I'm afraid I'm gonna hit a piece of

kelp, but I make it to the bottom and turn up the face . . . then, right in front of me, a sea

lion pops out of the wave and starts surfing, throwing water off its chest, and I hear it going

shhhhh-shhhhhhh-shhhhhhhhhh . . . —FRED VAN DYKE

Home, Sweet Horseshoe

Surfing Adventures and Natural History of La Jolla

It was in California that surfing became a stepping stone for this middle-aged surfer, a portal into a new world. Settling down, I started to pay more attention to what had been before only superfluous parts of the activity—wildlife, subtleties of geology, my own impact upon nature, and nature's impact upon me. Oh, don't get me wrong, surfing was still the manifest celebration of marine joy. But the act led me to dwell on other mysteries.

LA JOLLA, LATE 1980s

It was a brilliant, Santa Ana day out on Horseshoe Reef. The dry January winds, sizzling off the Mojave desert, carried strange vapors of creosote bush and mesquite, odors that overpowered the usual sea smell of kelp and crab. I waxed up my eight-and-a-half-foot surfboard, a size suitable for an old man (the only things that get bigger as you age are your waistline and your surfboard), and the familiar, candlelike fragrance of the stuff—the brand name is Sex Wax—mingled with the inland scents to bring back memories of a thousand other surf sorties like this one.

Paddling through the beach break took more concentration than usual. I'd been working earlier that day, and my mind was elsewhere. As you well know, surviving in any walk of human life is far from easy, and my life as a doc was no exception. I was ambivalent about medicine. When you are in private practice, like myself, you are basically doing variations on the same thing every day, trying to bat 1.000, working to stay up on the latest advances and technology, and hoping to stay out of court. My anesthesiology practice was more brutal than most, with a lot of night and weekend work, and many emergency trauma, cardiac, and neurosurgery cases. (Anesthesiologists keep people alive while surgeons operate on them; they also try to make the process pain-free.) My partners and I took pride in our care of the sickest of the sick; we gave anesthesia for heart and kidney transplants, brain tumors, and garroted throats alike. We did it well, but no matter how good we were, sometimes the Grim Reaper won.

The public has a full belly of "doctors-as-gods"; the media plays on public fears, always looking to publicize the latest doctor screw-up. Then there is the whole managed-care phenomenon, the pressure to do more cases, in a shorter time, for less money, with less sleep.

Despite these complaints, many physicians become trapped by their income in what might be called the "golden handcuffs of medicine." Many doctors would love to get off the treadmill and do something less stressful and more creative (as perhaps evidenced by the large number of docs becoming "disabled"—physician's disability insurance premiums have soared in response), but it is hard to give up the high income and start a new life.

Don't get me wrong, though. To help people out, to ease their pain, to do something right and get a sincere thanks, is rewarding. Take the card that appeared in my mail not long ago with the neat, handwritten inscription, "Thank you for helping to save my son's life." It cheered me for weeks. But as in any job, the more experienced you become, the more mundane your work seems. After many years, there were times when burnout became a real problem. Hence, to get rejuvenated, to heal myself, I went to the ocean whenever possible.

As always, the clutter of city thoughts and urban tension vanished under the pressure of survival at sea. The first shore pounder nailed me, threatened to slam me into the sand. Cold salt water entered my wet suit, chilling my head like a great gulp of ice cream. Vigorous paddling brought me over a second and third wave, and soon I was in the relative safety of the rip zone, where surf from 10 different directions wrapped over the curved reef, churning the water into a swirling chaos, a corral filled with milling, nervous mustang waves.

Horseshoe was, and is, a special place for me. It is the closest reef to my house, close enough to walk, a serious spot where beginning surfers might want to reconsider testing their luck, a place where I have come close to dying on several occasions. It is home. There is an old, rusted iron horseshoe nailed to the weather-beaten railing on the beach access stairway above the break.

There is a double meaning to the reef's name. It curves in a great U turned sideways, such that the mighty norths of winter break toward the right as you face shore, and the cleaner souths of summer break left across the inside in what surfers call a freight train barrel.

Geologists would call the reef a "wave-cut terrace," a flat tabletop carved from a rock cliff that appears at low tide.[1] The terrace rock is tough enough to withstand the relentless kicking of the waves, but the surf has, over thousands of storms, carried missing soft strata into the depths and gouged deep, sand-bottom channels that return wave-tossed water to the sea in violent rip currents. The result of all this excavation activity, the sea floor "U," is one derivation of Horseshoe's name.

The other, of course, is what the place can deliver—a fatal kick to the cranium.

Summer chubasco hurricanes in Mexico swing westward past Cabo San Lucas and send their energy bundles north in long, pristine lines of power. When summer waves break hard at the Shoe, the water can warm to 70°F, and surfers climb out of the woodwork from up and down the coast to ride them. At low tide, when the surf is most hollow and the tubes most deep, the inner reef is exposed, and you can see aggregating anemones, knobby sea stars, surf grass, purple braided hair algae, and, of course, iron-hard rock.

This is what oceanographers call the "littoral," the place where sea and land meet.[2] Here lies a complex and competitive world, where creatures must dwell at times underwater and at times in the air, where surf can batter the largest boulder into rubble, and where nutrients and opportunity abound. In and around the littoral dwell sulfur sponges, sandcastle worms, mossy chitons, keyhole limpets, Kellet's whelks, and, of course, knob-kneed surfers.

At the intense, crowded take-off point, tempers can flare, and a wipeout can mean disaster.

One August, I committed myself to a big left, jumped up, and then saw from the corner of my eye, too late, some guy with a long ponytail pulling in front of me as my board launched into the barrel. He'd committed a cardinal sin, known as snaking, cutting off, dropping in, and a host of other pejorative names. Surfing is a sport of quick reactions and microseconds. To avoid spearing the guy, I banked hard right, down into the flats in front of the wave—and paid the price.

The thick lip of a 10-foot wave blasted me off my board. The impact drilled me head first into the reef.

Something snapped in my neck, but I came up for air still moving arms and legs. A vivid history from the hospital came to me at once, a surfer who did the same thing, injuring himself in the same way at the same spot: he twisted his neck to see if he was OK and pithed himself. Although his mates rescued him, dragging him to shore, he earned a fate some would consider worse than death, instant quadriplegia. So, without moving my neck an inch, I paddled in, paying no attention to the guy with the pony tail and his "Sorry, dude," and made my slow way home.

Of course, a reasonable person would have called the paramedics on the spot and been strapped to a backboard with a cervical collar. Instead, I had my wife, Diane, wrap my neck in a towel and drive me to the hospital emergency department. The X-rays, as it turned out, showed no fracture, but for some years after that, my relationship with Horseshoe remained uneasy.

Another time at the Shoe in summer, during a bad wipeout, a board fin sliced a two-inch gash on the sole of my foot. The doctor sewing it up had to sit on my leg farrier-style to inject the local anesthetic—sensory nerves congregate on the sole, and reflex withdrawal made that limb twitch around the operating table like the hindleg of a nervous colt.

Oh, yes, I know Horseshoe well. But I love the break still.

When summer conditions are right, you can slip into a long barrel and come out, your hair dry, your soul on fire. And in the winter, you can drop in on steep, huge faces and crank turn after turn on a moving wall of multidimensional water. When it's on, Horseshoe is insane.

There are other joys to the place. When the surf is small and the water clear, bright orange garibaldi, that most territorial of damselfishes, stand out like exclamation points as they guard their sections of the Shoe. Black-and-white western grebes paddle through the shallows, darting below to peck for crustaceans. Harbor seals pause here to hunt, looking for an unwary kelp bass or a sheephead. California spiny lobsters and two-spotted octopi skulk in tiny caves and crevices. Brandt's cormorants fly by in columns, their necks extended, their eyes peeled for sardines. When the ocean calms, the reef is an aquarium, bursting with wildlife, a place to swim and snorkel and savor the sun.

Horseshoe has its downside, to be sure. There are days when unridable waves break over the shallow reef, closed out and unforgiving. There are days when every other break in La Jolla is firing and Horseshoe is strangely quiet, nearly flat.

Then there is the large storm drain on shore that, after a heavy rain, turns the water murky with runoff. The City of San Diego performs coliform counts after storms, and lifeguards close the beach at times with little yellow signs warning of risks of hepatitis and influenza.

On this day, though, none of that bothered me. Surf was the only thing on my mind. Big surf. The Santa Ana winds blew straight into each wave as it broke, holding up the face in the manner of the Hawaiian trades, casting behind it a heavy horsetail of spray as it finally collided with the coast. There was a solid 8- to 10-foot swell from some mid-Pacific gale thousands of miles to the west. But that was not all. A second, bigger swell from a storm in the Gulf of Alaska was spewing waves down from the north. The two systems were churning, first a set from one, then a lull, then a set from the other. Each series had its own personality—the steep peaks of the west, the long, angry cleanup sets from the north. Sometimes they merged into a saddle, a couloir of water, and these were the biggest and the baddest. They reminded me of giant waves converging at Sunset Beach.

Stroking through the rip, I could see only one other surfer. In winter, the water was cold—you had to wear a wet suit—and the waves hit huge. You could last only so long, and then, no matter how conditioned your arms, no matter how strong the latissimus dorsi and trapezius muscles in your back, you had to rest and warm up. And then someone else could have a turn.

Now my adrenalin started to pick up. Caught inside by a big, set wave, I tumbled in the turbulence of the white water, then regained my balance and paddled hard. Caught again, and my weary arms screamed for mercy. At last the forces of nature smiled. I broke free of the surf zone and found deep, calm water. The rip had carried me far to the south, and it was a long haul north to where the other surfer bobbed in the drink, a black, wet-suited horseman sitting on his board, a knight waiting for the joust.

For January, the weather was unbelievable—sunny, warm, glowing. A line of brown pelicans in mating plumage glided by, first a gold-crested, red-pouched adult, then two gray adolescents, then two more gilded grownups, then two more kids. Just as they neared the surfer, a wave poured in, and the big birds rode along the face, only darting off the updraft as the offshore wind blew white spray high into the air.

Pelicans feed by plunge-diving; they hover some 30 feet in the air over a school of baitfish, then, wrapping their wings into an aerodynamic bullet shape, they strike the water with barely a splash. Underwater, the pouch under their beak expands to grotesque size, filled with struggling fish and water. The big birds, their wing spans reaching more than four feet, then surface, eject the water, and swallow their prey.

When I first began surfing in the 1970s, it was rare to see a line of pelicans gliding over the spray. Indeed, the species, a survivor for some 30 million years,[3] became endangered during the early part of that decade. DDT, (dichlorophenyltrichloroethane), the post–World War II pesticide of choice, concentrated in their tissue as toxins do in apex predators. Heavy organic pollutants are not metabolized in organisms; as a carnivore at the next higher trophic level consumes them as prey, the chemical increases in concentration. This process is called biological magnification.[4]

DDT, although relatively nontoxic to people, lasts for years, as do its breakdown products. Especially effective against mosquitoes, it showed up in marine organisms as remote as Antarctica and was biomagnified in some commercial fish, such as mackerel, to exceed the U.S. Food and Drug Association's permissible level of 5 ppm.

Brown pelicans were, however, a special case. DDT adversely affects the deposition of calcium in avian eggshells.[5] *Pelecanus occidentalis* developed especially high levels, because the water near an Anacapa Island nesting site carried high DDT concentrations that were eventually traced to a Los Angeles factory that produced a majority of the world's supply.[6] The pelican eggs became so thin that they were crushed by nesting parental weight, and successful breeding essentially disappeared in the Channel Islands off southern California.

It took a seminal piece of literature by Rachel Carson, *Silent Spring*, the resulting Earth Day, and a lot of political activism before the pesticide was banned. Today the big birds are back in numbers.

Surfers feel a special kinship with brown pelicans, for they, too, seem to love big waves. Although I've often seen them plunge-diving, even tried to photograph the practice underwater (without success), I've never seen pelicans windsurfing big waves stop to feed. Never.

Now, utilitarian animal behaviorists would no doubt postulate that the birds are using the surf as a kind of trolley, a bird freeway for transportation from one feeding site to another. And I couldn't argue with that possibility.

But it is an odd coincidence that, when the waves are huge and glassy, like they were on this day, the big birds come out in large numbers to ride up and down the coast. It is not easy to ascertain a bird's emotion, after all, and there is agreement now among scientists that they probably evolved from dinosaurs. They have a reptilian air about them. But an aura of joy surrounds every pelican I've seen when it's riding the smooth, laminar wave updrafts, as it barely moves its wings, as it soars over the nexus of sea, land, and air. My guess is that they windsurf for fun, pure and simple.

A perfect rainbow appeared, then vanished. A second wave broke, this

BROWN PELICANS RIDING WAVE UPDRAFT, HORSESHOE REEF, LA JOLLA, CALIFORNIA *"But it is an odd coincidence that, when the waves are huge and glassy, like they were on this day, the big birds come out in large numbers to ride up and down the coast."*

one with the surfer sliding right on a long face, another rainbow forming behind, the tiny drops of offshore spray working as prisms to cast an arc of blue, yellow, and red.

Distracted, I realized too late the wave was about to break on me. It was a big wave, a moving, apartment building–sized wave. Frantic, I paddled due west and just made it though, the wind casting spray and colored light around me in a crazy sunstorm.

The surfer paddled back outside the surf zone, a grin plastered on his face.

"Hey, bud," he said, California-style but, improbably, with a thick Scottish brogue. It was a friend of mine, Brian Caldwell, a guy who arrived in the States from Edinburgh 10 years ago, his accent so thick that we Yanks could barely understand him, his surfing skills far from honed. Now Brian ripped big waves and had metamorphosed his dialect into Valley-speak.

"Killer wave," I said, grinning back, and he was stoked. Surfers tend toward the taciturn, and to get praise in the lineup means something. It was hard not to admire Brian's tenacity, his love of the sea and surfing, his loyalty to this particular reef. Most adults paddle out once or twice, get beat up, realize how tough a thing it is to master, and then quit. Although surfing is a motion sport akin to skiing or skateboarding, waves, unlike mountains or sidewalks, are moving, evanescent, transient entities. When you fall off, they don't wait around for you to practice your moves and get it right. My choice for learning was a gentle wave to the north, a forgiving wave. Brian chose the Shoe.

It was hard to concentrate on surfing out there, waiting for a set, what with all the activity. Friends, rainbows, pelicans. Then a black hump broke the surface 50 yards beyond us, and a huge plume of water vapor rocketed skyward.

"Thar she blows!" A California gray whale, *Eschrichtius robustus,* migrating south to Magdalena Bay, on its way to find sex and society. There was a hint of rainbow in the spout, too.

"Where?" Brian shouted.

"One o'clock!" I yelled.

We saw two, three blows, then a long curve of broad, barnacled back, then the great flukes. The whale had sounded, perhaps to rake its mouth over the bottom, sifting sand and sea grass for invertebrates and small fish. As it surfaced, it spat out water and detritus through its baleen, sieving gallons of protein, amphipods, mollusks, and worms, the reward for its diving effort. By plowing the benthic (sea-bottom) marine community, cetaceans such as this leave whale-sized, irregular depressions and so become important ecological disturbance forces.[7]

Although it eats only small stuff, the whale is a carnivore nevertheless. "Devilfish," the nineteenth-century whalers off the California coast called them; these seemingly placid creatures did not go to harpooned graves without taking along their fair share of boats and men. They may have been aided in their mayhem by a small symbiont, the barnacle *Cryptolepas rachianectes*, that is found only on the gray whale.[8] How this relationship evolved is a mystery, but the rows of razor-sharp barnacles can transform the powerful head, flippers, and fluke tips of a whale from battering rams to slicing maces.[9] In this sense, the barnacle provides a service to the whale, but more often than not, it is a parasite, adding through the weight of great numbers an immense drag to the whale's hydrodynamics. For this reason, perhaps, cetaceans turn over their skin cells up to 290 times faster than humans—just to keep ahead of barnacles.[10]

In centuries past, gray whales were common in the Atlantic and the western Pacific as well as here, off the California coast. But the last of the Atlantic population was killed around 1700, the Icelandic and European grays having been decimated before that. A small population may or may not survive off the coast of Japan and Korea, but it is only on the west coast of North America, where we were surfing, that the now-protected animal thrives. Worldwide, the population is slowly coming back, at somewhere around 20,000 individuals.[11]

One of the greatest migrators in the world, the eastern Pacific gray whales make an annual pilgrimage of over 10,000 miles. From May to early October, these 40-foot-long cetaceans feed in shallow waters off Alaska and Siberia; then, they swim south to pass San Diego in late December and January (as this one was doing now) and continue down to the great bays of Baja California, their warm calving and mating grounds. In southern waters they eat little if at all, and so they turn around and swim back in spring for the bounties of the north.[12]

How do they find their way? Most probably, gray whales, along with tuna, marine turtles, and other marine mammals, use Earth's magnetic fields to navigate. Scientists have found chains of magnetite (Fe_3O_4) both in magnetotactic bacteria and in tuna, where the magnetite was entwined with nervous tissue;[13] this may explain the anatomic mechanism. They have also correlated mass strandings of marine mammals on the East Coast of the United States and in England with geomagnetic contour lines—lines that whales may follow like roadways—that cross from sea to land.[14]

Brian and I searched for the spout; the whale rewarded us by blasting again in the distance. For a moment I was seized with the urge to paddle after it, to get closer, but I knew the chase would be fruitless. The big mammals had been hunted heavily during the past in their brush with extinction; now, there was something to be said for leaving them alone.

A wave set came. I forced myself to paddle for shore, looking back to see if the whale was still there. Waves, like whales, come and go; neither can be ignored. The first one in the set was perfect, a west peak. The wind hit me first, and then a blue semicircle of liquid joy lifted me up. Paddling in a furious sprint, I clawed downward into the offshore gusts, through the rainbow, and leaped to my feet. Board and body rocketed down a laminar face, held together by a precarious combination of torque and gravity.

The wave soared in 20 different planes and twisted in four dimensions. As it broke, a thundering wall of turbulent foam and white water chased me, only a split second behind. I kicked out, flopped onto my board, and paddled west with anxious hands. Not for me getting creamed on the reef inside, where brilliant green surf grass showed above the lowering tide.

Back in the lineup, Brian laughed.

"Bitchin' wave, mate!"

Wipeouts are my specialty, and riding a wave without falling remains an amazing personal triumph. But before I could indulge in any prolonged, prideful glory, another dark spot in the water distracted us. No, two, three spots. Dorsal fins. Spouts. Glistening bodies, wrapped in blubber. Small whales —bottlenose dolphins. Like the pelicans, the dolphins came when the waves were biggest—they wanted to ride with us, to share the liquid stage.

Tursiops truncatus is the familiar dolphin one sees presented like a circus animal in oceanaria across the world. Compared with many wild animals, it is easily trained to perform acrobatics, locate hidden objects, and play with human toys such as balls and hoops. The military has worked with the animal for years, especially here off San Diego, where captive bottlenose squeal at surfers who boat around Point Loma to anchor off a Navy facility and surf a prime spot named Dolphin Tanks.

Immortalized in the television show *Flipper*, the supposedly friendly beasts, many of whom weigh a thousand pounds, have recently been implicated in injuring or even killing humans. There circulates a story, perhaps apocryphal, perhaps not, of a boy swimming in shallow water with a wild bottlenose off Brazil who thought it might be funny to stuff a snow cone into the animal's dorsal breathing orifice. The infuriated animal promptly butted and killed a nearby innocent swimmer.

Make no mistake, dolphins are wild animals and must be treated with respect. People who work with them daily know they are individuals, different from us humans, each with a unique personality and a different life experience with our kind. Something that day out there with Brian told me we had nothing to fear from these bottlenose. Something told me we were not playing the usual surfer's zero-sum game.

Paddling into a big right, one of those Alaskan waves from the north, I was startled by a gray-black shape darting under my board. I turned hard at the bottom of the wave, the peak feathering above my head, and a dolphin, eight feet long, popped out of the wave in front of me. A perpetual smile grinned beneath a melon-shaped forehead; a high-pitched squeal cut through the roar of the spray. The animal, its brain bigger than any human's, its temporal auditory centers spilling into its parietal lobes,[15] the entire cerebrum huge from processing three-dimensional echolocation, knew my position exactly, cut right when my board cut left, cut up where I cut down, and chattered the whole time in dolphin-speak. When the wave petered out in the rip channel, the sea mammal was gone, leaving me speechless.

After riding one more wave, a long, winding, walled right that ended in an ignominious fall, my arms felt like overcooked linguine. My own cerebrum was overloaded with images of wildlife and waves and reflected prismatic light. It was best not to get too greedy. I turned to shore and paddled hard as a pair of set waves from two directions combined into a big saddle wave. By my calculation, it would break well behind me, and then I'd ride the white water in. There was not much left in my paddle. I was pretty well spent.

I heard the wave crashing behind me and braced myself without looking at the wall of turbulence. My hands gripped my board with every last vestige of strength. The roar was deafening now, any moment . . . KABAAAAAAM

The Shoe hit me hard, slamming my jaw into the board with irresistible and sudden violence. Kicked in the chin by a wild, aquatic equine, my body was blown off the surfboard, jerked into the maelstrom. Up, down, there was no way to know. Cornered in the corral of reef, I was at the mercy of a cold, white stallion, kicking, organic, furious, alive.

The wave had its way with me. My hands and arms covered my head and neck. I prayed for safe passage over the rocks. Then it was gone.

One learns not to struggle and waste precious oxygen. I rose to the surface, felt the thick foam, flung it aside, and took in some air. A second wave loomed, this one just as big, just as brawny. One more breath, one more dive deep to escape.

Back on the surface, I swept the foam clear and took another gasp of atmosphere. Another wave, another dive, another embrace against the reef. I knew the routine. I also knew it couldn't go on forever. Eventually one of us, myself or the Shoe, would have to quit. Usually there were only three or four big waves to a set; close to exhaustion, I was banking on it.

When it comes to waves, there are no limits. Only lulls. But how about the gray whales and the bottlenose dolphins, the brown pelicans, and the double-crested cormorants? They were the real harbingers of joy there on the reef—were they safe in an infinitely vast sea, or were they bumping into lethal boundaries?

As the years crawl by, it is perhaps inevitable that one day surfing might become my own lethal limit. But not yet, and not on that most perfect of days. There were powerful smells in the surf that January, in that magical place where land and sea collide: Sex Wax, seaweed, and chaparral filled the air.

The scent of death, though, was not among them.

CHAPTER FOUR

"If we didn't die, we would not appreciate life as we do."

—JACQUES-YVES COUSTEAU

Beyond City Limits

Exploring Underwater Mysteries of Kelp and Squid

After years of surfing and staring down into the ocean's depths, something finally convinced me to find out just what lay beneath the surface. It is a different sort of celebration, diving, compared with the wild physical nature of surfing. Sometimes it is better when surfing to turn off thought and let your primitive coordination centers, your cerebellum, run things. While diving, you need to keep rational at all times, to remember that you are but a stranger in a strange land. There is little margin for error at depth, your equipment must work perfectly, and such simple acts as breathing and clearing ears are ignored at peril. The world below also fits a more cerebral mindset, for dive training teaches early on to touch as little as possible and to delight in watching, in learning about life under the sea. No matter how fascinating things get, though, one must always remember such basic items as, "How much air is left in my tank?" and "How deep am I?"

Recently, the oceanographer Mia Tegner, a veteran of thousands of dives, died at Wreck Alley among kelp forests here off San Diego. Her husband, photographer Eric Hanauer, wrote this about the tragedy:

"Mia was working . . . doing a survey of fish on the wrecks for a new project on artificial reef communities. Her slate was filled with notes. . . ."[1]

Tegner was studying the new artificial reef created by the sinking of the Canadian destroyer Yukon. . . . Perhaps she was wrapped up in wondering if, by adding *complexity, by making the underwater world "high relief," as Rick Grigg describes it, humans can multiply possibilities for life in the sea. Perhaps she was wondering if the increased fish found at wreck sites had simply been recruited from elsewhere, or if they represented larvae that, having found good habitat, survived when they might have died. Perhaps she was thinking about ways to avoid limits in the sea, about non-zero-sum games . . . perhaps she was thinking about infinity.*

Hanauer went on to say:

"Although we may never know what really happened, I think she was so engrossed in her work that she didn't check her air and ran out, having to make a rapid ascent.

"Sometimes we get so comfortable underwater that we forget that we are riding a tiger."[2]

LA JOLLA, 1990s

One by one, two by two, we gathered in near silence on the La Jolla sandstone bluff that bright, February afternoon to pay our last respects to a guy named Ron. Old friends murmured greetings, nothing more. A small knot of wetsuit-clad divers attended to a wreath of flowers down on the beach, only feet from the harbor seal haulout. A few of the pinnipeds watched them with one eye, but most just stretched out luxuriously on the sun-warmed sand. The ocean breeze carried up to us the salty tang of kelp and the dank, gym-socks odor of seals.

Just 10 feet from where I stand, a bagpipe player split the clear day with the sharp, sudden force of an ax blade, blowing an Amazing Grace so startling, so piercing, that every one of the seals stared up at us and started barking in dismay. Slowly now, as if careful not to harm a single blossom, the divers slipped the wreath into the chill eastern Pacific and started swimming for the open sea.

In one step, they left the civilized megalopolis behind and entered the territory of the kelp forest and the opal squid. The megalopolis, the greater San Diego–Tijuana border complex of some four million human souls, is my home. A Minnesota boy with a strong addiction to wilderness, there is only one reason I've been able to stay here—the "big wild" that borders the city, 64 million square miles of wild, one-third of Earth's surface. The Pacific.

For many years after moving to California, I was content to explore the surface of the ecotone, the zone where ocean meets land: the surf. Wrapped around a board waiting for a set, dangling my feet in the drink, I often wondered what was down there. At times a garibaldi would swirl in an orange flash or a dolphin would crease the surface with a knife-edged dorsal fin, but it seemed to me there was only one way to get to know the real Pacific: put on a tank and drop in.

Snorkeling and free diving, I gleaned brief glimpses of the blue-green undersea world: startled schools of barracuda, a scuttling crab, the gentle sway of kelp. Air hunger, the constant need to clear my ears with each dive, and the difficulty in making photographs made these excursions less than satisfying.

Unfortunately, an experience in medical school delayed my scuba (the acronym for self-contained underwater breathing apparatus) career for some years. We admitted a young, formerly fearless Navy SEAL (sea, air, land) to our internal medicine ward for hyperbaric treatment. He'd been diving mornings with his unit and then moonlighting in the late afternoons working underwater salvage. All this bottom time got the poor guy bent, and he ended up with rotary nystagmus—unable to control his ocular muscles, his eyeballs spun around and around in his head, putting him on perpetual bed rest. He couldn't walk and could barely talk. He just lay there, gripping the mattress, trying to get things to stop spinning. My rotation on that ward was 12 weeks long; when I left, he was still there, white-knuckled, hanging on to his bed for dear life.

Then came a trip to Hawaii in 1989 when my surfing buddy Joe Gifford talked me into going down with a scuba tank. Joe has a receding hair line and a mischievous smile. He looks and acts a lot like the actor Jack Nicholson.

"Just remember," he said, "clear your ears when ya go down, and come up real slow. Don't hold your breath comin' up, 'cause the air will expand in your lungs and kill ya."

"What about the bends?" I asked, whimpering.

"Don't worry," said Joe, "we ain't goin' deep enough."

That first dive was near a cemetery, at a site called "Five Graves." We slipped into clear water and swam, weightless, past some whitetip sharks into a cave. I followed Joe through a long tunnel into a small lava cavern. There was an air pocket there where we took off our masks and felt the atmospheric pressure rise and fall with the swell. On the way back, amidst abstract sculptures of rainbow-hued hard corals, we saw a trumpetfish, a moray eel, and a vast school of blue and yellow surgeonfish that darkened the water. Astronauts in inner space, free from gravity and civilization, we were visitors in an alien world.

After getting certified, I started diving back on the mainland, although with some reluctance. California diving was a different animal from Hawaii diving. The water was bitter cold. The visibility was often poor. The wildlife, though, was just as fantastic. Sea lions, leopard sharks, moray eels—they were all there. The city planners, showing foresight and wisdom, established a biological preserve in 1970 along the La Jolla coast and prohibited the taking or harming of sea life there in any form, ensuring that my local coastal waters would remain pristine, if frigid.[3]

The reserve is located where the Rose Canyon fault enters the sea. This giant slash through a hundred-foot cliff, a place where water mysteriously appears and oozes out to create a small cliffside oasis, is where the tectonic plate of our fair city rides north from the rest of San Diego, creating La Jolla Cove and La Jolla proper, a sort of miniature peninsular version of San Francisco. The fault continues down into the sea, and in the underwater park one can find four distinct habitats: kelp forest, sandy plateaus, rock reefs, and subterranean marine canyon.

One day, checking out the visibility at a spot within the reserve called Second Reef, trying to screw up courage, I saw a kelp-draped figure crawl out of the sea, a man who looked like Neptune himself. Squinting up at me through weathered, sparkling eyes, handlebar mustache dripping salt water, strands of surf grass stuck to his wet suit, he broke into a Pacific-sized smile.

"How was it?" I asked.

"Un-be-lievable," he answered in a voice rough as beach sand. "I'm down there at about 60 feet, 60 feet, you understand, and I feel this pecking at my shoulder. I turn, and do you know what it is?"

"A kelp bass?" I ventured.

"A cormorant! Un-der-water!" he said. "Can you believe it? A bird! And he's pecking away at my mask, peck, peck, peck, like he's trying to figure out what I'm doing down there. Can you be-lieve it!"

This was Ron Starkey, soon to be a good friend, a dive instructor still full of amazement at the discoveries to be made under the sea. If it wasn't a cormorant at 60 feet, it was a pair of tame moray eels wrapped around his neck or an inflamed garibaldi defending its nest. It was Ron who spurred me to forget the cold and poor visibility of the eastern Pacific and just go diving.

For starters, Ron hauled me out on my first night dive. After all the hype and talk about sharks, I wasn't too sure about restricting my view to a small light. On a moonless night we waded out into the wilderness from the warm glow of a seaside restaurant. The incongruity of it struck me—inside the restaurant, elegantly coiffured ladies and well-heeled gentlemen were sitting down to a five-course meal, while a few feet away, we were slipping into the cool black ink of the unknown.

Ron had a powerful flash, and my fears washed off with the incoming tide. In quick order, he showed me a cusk eel burrowing into the sand, a he-man-sized lobster dancing over the bottom with ballet legs, and a round stingray. He scooped the ray up and held the stinger and tail, letting me touch the sandpaper-like skin, then gently released it. We turned off our lights, and an iridescent violet and yellow jellyfish wafted by, all but invisible, shimmering ghostlike amid trails of glowing plankton.

There is something both peaceful and exhilarating about swimming along 30 feet deep in the quiet Pacific at night. The warm glow of the torches limits one's visual field and focuses attention. Daytime fish such as garibaldi and bass disappear, and a new shift of characters, octopi, crabs, and eels, comes out to explore and feed.

As I got to know Ron, it became clear he was obsessed with getting wet. Recovering from a bitter divorce, he seemed blind to topside life, ignoring non-diving-related culture and events, smoking too many cigarettes as if uncomfortable inhaling noncompressed air. An old injury from the construction trade left him with pinched nerves in his neck, a painful condition relieved only while weightless underwater. The classic surfer adage fit him well: "At sea, one leaves the problems of land far behind." He made maybe five or six dives a day, taught hundreds of students, and lived, talked, ate, and breathed scuba. Maybe he was a bit of a maniac, but his love of the ocean was real, almost palpable.

Another dive with Ron did not go so well. It was my first trip below in serious kelp forest. The ocean off San Diego, like much of the West Coast, is blessed with the world's fastest growing "plant," the brown algae *Macrocystis pyrifera*—commonly known as kelp. Widely quoted to be able to grow up to two feet per day under perfect conditions,[4] kelp produces dense forests in water from 15 to 90 feet of depth, where rootlike holdfasts grip the bottom. In and around these "trees" live, or used to live, marine mammals, fish of every description, and invertebrates from holothurians to cephalopods.[3]

Some taxonomists place kelp, as a multicellular alga, in the kingdom of the Plantae, although they would place one-celled algae and the protozoa (amoebae, paramecia, diatoms, dinoflagellates, and the like) in the kingdom of Protista. Others, because algae neither develop from embryos nor have vascular structures as do plants,[5] place all algae in Protista. However one classifies it, *M. pyrifera* uses photosynthesis via sunlight-grabbing leaflike structures called blades. It supports itself with stemlike structures named stipes and with oval bulbs named bladders, miniature buoys filled with gases, including the poisonous carbon monoxide, that keep the plant upright. Kelp secretes polysaccharides, and the resulting "slime" acts like oil on seawater, making it glassy smooth.

When you break through the glass and enter the sea surrounding this most beautiful of forests, the brilliance of the colors hits you first, that and the shock of the cold water. Green blades shimmer in the current, blue water surges in gentle motion from side to side, and golden rays shimmer down, cathedrallike, from the surface. Crawling up the kelp are Norris top snails, with their orange-red feet. Schools of silver-blue blacksmith bustle through waving stipes, blades, and bladders. On the bottom lie bioluminescent anemones and red gorgonian corals.

Kelp may only be an alga, but the forest it creates is sublime.

Ecologists know kelp forests, along with coral reefs, to be regions of high productivity, with productivity defined as the creation of complex carbon compounds—sugars, proteins, and nucleic acids. Remember the photosynthesis equation from biology? In the presence of sunlight and nutrients,[6]

$$6CO_2 + 6H_2O \rightarrow C_6H_{12}O_6 + 6O_2.$$

In plain English, green plants use chlorophyll to take carbon dioxide and water and produce the sugar glucose and oxygen. This primary production, or carbon fixation, lies at the base of both marine and terrestrial food pyramids. Productivity in the ocean is measured in grams of carbon fixed per square meter per year—gC/m^2/year. By convention, each square meter of surface ocean also represents the water column under it that reaches all the way from the surface to the sea-bottom. Open ocean, far from land and upwellings, is a sort of desert, with $18-50$ gC/m^2/yr.[7] Kelp forest, on the other hand, produces from 800 to 2,000 gC/m^2/yr.[5]

Researchers at the University of California, Paul Dayton and the late Mia Tegner in particular, found that the southern California kelp forests, despite—or because of—that production, are often starved for nitrogen, an element needed for building amino and nucleic acids. This starvation for fertilizer can worsen during El Niño warming events.[8] When the City of San Diego's outfall pipe (a tunnel that is now nearly 300 feet deep and extends over four miles from shore) ruptured near shore during just such an event in 1992, primary-treated sewage poured into the middle of the kelp bed. To the surprise of Dayton and Tegner, the kelp plants responded positively to the spill, probably because of the increased nitrogen. Stress from lack of nitrates persisted in the La Jolla kelp beds, a *de facto* control for this serendipitous experiment.[9]

When normal conditions prevail and there is no break in the pipeline, the sewage remains in deep water and gets nowhere near the kelp—a sun-loving, photosynthetic organism that grows in the Point Loma bed at about 70 feet of seawater or less.

Craig Barilotti, who, like Dayton and Tegner, received a doctorate in marine biology, is now retired after spending a lifetime working on—and in—the kelp. Some call Barilotti "Mr. Kelp" because of his expertise and passion for the habitat, although he himself would grant that title to Wheeler North, a scientist who initiated the kelp "movement" in the 1950s and has been a mentor to many kelp bed biologists (North was ill at the time of this writing but has managed, until recently, to continue diving). Barilotti, who talked to me at length on the sewage/kelp relationship, maintains a skeptical view of any foolish notions that sewage might be beneficial for the kelp ecosystem as a whole. Paul Dayton, I should add, would be the first to agree.

"Coliform bacteria levels along the offshore edge of the Point Loma bed dropped after the outfall was extended to its current position in 1993," Barilotti told me, "indicating that the wastewater plume no longer impacts the kelp bed as it did prior to the extension. Therefore, the kelp plants are receiving negligible nutrients, if any, from discharged wastes."

Barilotti went on to point out that since the 1993 extension, the alga now grows in deeper water and in places where it hasn't been seen in decades. Such evidence hints that, except perhaps during El Niño events, sewage wastes may have harmed the kelp in the years before the deepening and lengthening of the pipe.

One hundred miles north, the 12-mile-long Palos Verde kelp bed died off in the 1950s from a combination of ocean warming, sewage, and DDT, PCBs (polychlorinated biphenyls), and other chemicals. The demise of the alga occurred when a Los Angeles outfall opened at about 90 feet of depth, just under the thermocline (the boundary layer between warm water at the surface and cold water beneath). The Palos Verdes underwater forests started to rebound in the early 1970s, after the City of Los Angeles reduced discharge of solids and industrial chemicals and improved treatment and "source control"—that is, banning the release of DDT and PCBs. The Palos Verdes bed also got some help from direct planting.

"The Department of Fish and Game and Caltech brought in 2,000 transplants [of seaweed spores] and got it going again," said Wheeler North,[10] who as a Caltech research biologist and professor has studied kelp since 1956.

Sorting out these issues is far from simple. Human wastes, ocean warming events, industrial pollution, fishing, and marine biology all affect kelp science, making it a complex and contentious issue in California.[11] Exactly how kelp maintains its high photosynthetic production—for it can do so in places without major cities and outfall sewage pipes—remains to be elucidated.

Here off San Diego's Point Loma, kelp ships run in reverse as huge circular mowing devices on their sterns cut and haul aboard the seaweed, harvesting only the surface fronds. The resulting product, algin, is used in making such foods as ice cream, pie, puddings, and beer.

Although the kelp off San Diego is still doing well, the animal life that makes the beds unique has been decimated. Overfishing and use of bottom-set gill nets, now outlawed, have depleted local populations of sheephead, rockfish, and bass. San Diego divers in the 1940s and 1950s commonly found monster-sized black sea bass in the forest, some weighing up to 500 pounds. Although these fish can still be encountered off San Clemente Island, 50 miles offshore, the coastal waters tell a different story.

"Early divers in the Point Loma region talk about seeing several on a dive," said Mia Tegner in 1997[12] about the now-protected, grouperlike creatures. "Our group [at Scripps] has made about 20,000 dives at Point Loma [in the kelp bed] in the last 27 years and never seen one."

The kelp ecosystem evolved as a complex interaction between algae, sea urchins (that eat the algae), and sea otters (that eat the sea urchins). The now extinct Steller's sea cow also played a key role, grazing the tops of the beds; this manatee-like creature was eliminated from most Pacific kelp beds by aboriginal hunting and then was finished off by Europeans in 1768.[13] The fur trade eliminated sea otters from southern California by the early 1800s, but the forests themselves did not begin to disappear until intense exploitation led to ecological extinction of other sea urchin predators and competitors, such as sheephead, spiny lobsters, and abalone. This started in the 1950s. Fishing for sea urchins in the 1970s and 1980s has resulted in healthy, well-developed kelp forests—with few herbivores and fewer still carnivores.[14]

San Diego is replete with old-timers who dived in the 1950s. They spin wistful tales of how abalone used to carpet the bottom, grazing on the algae; today the tasty mollusks are so depleted that four of the five species are in danger of local extirpation. The white abalone, *Haliotis sorenseni*, in fact, is in danger of total extinction. These animals were heavily hunted in the early 1970s, and recent field surveys by research submarine vessels have led scientists to estimate that only about 1,500 animals survive.[15]

This single-shelled mollusk, six inches or so in diameter, brings us back to island biogeography and the balance between immigration (or speciation) and extinction. Although it is a long way from theory to wildlife management, biologists needed a way to estimate "minimum viable populations," the absolute limit below which an animal might become extinct. In 1980, Ian Franklin, a fruit-fly geneticist, and Michael Soulé, a California ecologist, came up with what evolved into a rough rule of 50/500 to fit this concept to reality.[16] They suggested, as a general starting point, that 50 animals is the absolute short-term limit below which genetic problems result, and that 500 breeding animals is the minimum for a long-term population to survive.

This 50/500 rule has a checkered past and is disputed by some. For evaluating species and extinction in the sea, two Australian marine biologists, G.P. Jones and U.L. Kaly, state flat out that most conservation biological theories (like the 50/500 rule) are deficient.[17]

In the ocean, the vast majority of species are rare, in that they have rare local abundance. But bony fishes (also called teleosts) and 70% of marine invertebrates (such as the white abalone) reproduce by free-floating eggs and sperm, with larval stages carried by currents—the larvae are part of the plankton, that group of drifting organisms of the sea that have their lateral and vertical movements determined by water motion.

Even though they may be locally rare, larvae can disperse over wide areas of ocean. As Jones and Kaly point out, "Just as rare species are not necessarily at risk, species at risk are not necessarily rare."[18] For this reason, marine extinctions have been thought by biologists to be uncommon. One of the first to write of this was Jean-Baptiste Lamarck in his *Philosophie Zoologique* of 1809:

> Animals living in the waters, especially the sea waters, are protected from the destruction of their species by Man. Their multiplication is so rapid and their means of evading pursuit or traps are so great that there is no likelihood of his being able to destroy the entire species of any of these animals.[19]

Although the fossil record is replete with extinct marine animals, there has been only one recorded post-Pleistocene extinction of a marine invertebrate, that of the limpet *Lottia alveus*, last found in the eelgrass beds of eastern North America in the 1920s.[20] Marine mammals and birds are another story, with the loss of the Steller's sea cow and the great auk being well known. Today blue, fin, humpback, sei, and southern right whales are considered endangered, as are manatees, dugongs, most sea turtles, and other large vertebrates. But we don't really know about animals with planktonic larvae.

Jones and Kaly, the Australian marine biologists, believe that many of the tools used to quantify land animals, especially on islands, will not work in the marine world. They believe, for example, that the genetic factors that led to the 50/500 rule are not problems for "small 'open' populations of marine organisms with high levels of gene flow among subpopulations."[21]

Michael Soulé (who fashioned the 50/500 rule with Franklin) and Michael Gilpin, another California ecologist, published in 1986 a more complex and refined tool than the 50/500 rule, what they called "population viability analysis."[22] Recognizing the problems with the simplistic 50/500 rule, they believed that conservationists should integrate data about any given species from four broad areas: demographics, inbreeding, habitat fragmentation, and adaptation. Rather than use a magic number, there would be a systematic process to yield a particular diagnosis.[23]

But even this sophisticated tool, argue Jones and Kaly, is less applicable to the high levels of dispersal found for marine species. As seagrass beds and coral reefs decline, there will be increasing fragmentation of marine habitat, acknowledge the two Queensland-based scientists.[24] But because there are such huge gaps in our knowledge about subpopulations, reproduction, larval dispersal, and other complex ecologic data, they argue that we can't use Gilpin and Soulé's model as a good handle on how to quantitate which marine animals are endangered and which are not.

Given the interconnectiveness of the sea, the preoccupation of land-based conservation biologists with corridors connecting fragmented habitat also probably doesn't hold for the marine world. But, as 1,500 remaining white abalone illustrate, there is potential for extinction in the ocean.

Art Ley, my old roommate, cooked some fresh abalone for me in 1976. The muscular foot is the preferred cut, and it is so tough that Art pounded each sliver of meat with a special toothed hammer to make it palatable. But oh, my—after a light sautee in olive oil, what a taste! Too bad. There is a reason abalone commands a premium price in restaurants, and that price and poaching go hand in hand.

The oily meat of the dodo, *Raphus cucullatus*, that ungainly, naive, and flightless bird, led hungry and poorly provisioned Dutch explorers to contribute to its extinction on the Indian Ocean island of Mauritius (sharing the blame with the introduced, egg-eating macaque monkey).[25] So the flavor and texture of abalone meat may lead us Californians to a similar tragedy. Relatively immobile creatures, the invertebrate mollusks need to be close together in large enough numbers at spawning time to fertilize each other. When numbers drop below a certain level, none of the gametes can pair up, and the population plummets.[26] For the white abalone, then, there is no question regarding limits. The ocean in general and the kelp forest in particular form a finite world.

Two British marine biologists, Callum Roberts and Julie Hawkins, disagree with Jones and Kaly's assessment of the poor fit of island biogeographical principles to the marine world. They write: "Many species . . . do not have planktonic larvae or high mobility as adults . . . large numbers of invertebrate species have 'crawl away' larvae that disperse only meters from their parents. Others are planktonic only briefly up to a few kilometres."[27]

Roberts and Hawkins list a number of fish and invertebrates that, if not extinct, are teetering on the brink. These include Boschmai's fire coral, *Millepora boschmai*; the Galapagos damselfish, *Azurina eupalama;* the spotted handfish, *Brachionichthys hirsutus;* the barndoor skate, *Raja laevis;* the Banggai cardinalfish, *Pterapogon kauderni;* the coelacanth *Latimeria chalumnae;* the Texas pipefish, *Syngnathus affinis;* the emerald seaslug, *Phyllaplysia smaragda;* the horn snail, *Cerithidea fuscata;* the rocky shore limpet, *Colisella edmitchelli;* and the totoaba, *Totoaba macdonaldi*.[28]

It is their contention, and that of other marine biologists,[29] that the confidence of those who believe marine extinctions to be rare may be falsely bolstered by the great difficulty of detecting them. It is almost impossible to know when the last individual of a fish or mollusk has been caught—unlike the public death in 1914 in the Cincinnati zoo of Martha, the last remaining passenger pigeon. It is hard to prove a negative. Unsampled habitat maintains the possibility of persistence, and studying marine habitats can be difficult—especially for a novice diver like myself.

On this clear Friday the 13th in October, hoping to view at least some wildlife, Ron Starkey and I hopped onto a boat, got a dive briefing from the skipper, and dropped in. Assuming that my years of surfing taught me everything there was to know about kelp, I plummeted with the glittering sunbeams into a murky, blue-green world 95 feet deep, at four atmospheres of pressure. Despite the sun, the visibility was only five feet, and the kelp was as dense as Amazon rain forest. Ron was my dive buddy, so I tried to follow him as he darted ahead, but I soon fell behind, hung up in shiny green stems and stipes. An improvised 360 degree roll not only failed to free me but got me stuck even worse.

I whipped out a dive knife and started whacking kelp fronds, using up a lot of air, trying not to panic, trying not to cut my regulator hose. Free from the kelp, I started rising, overbuoyant. Aluminum tanks become lighter as they empty, and a nervous diver can suck air like a snorting race horse.

I tried to dump air from my buoyancy vest. The thing had . . . overexpanded. Couldn't find . . . air release valves. Rocketing for the surface . . . rush of bubbles . . . open mouth scream . . . terror . . .AAAAAAAHHHH!

A champagne cork released at 16 fathoms, I bobbed up to my waist in the bright sunlight in a wad of bubbles and fear. The skipper looked over from the boat in surprise, saw that air embolism and the bends had spared me, and shook his head at my idiocy.

Ron came up 15 minutes later, angry, sputtering, going off. "Where did you go? I mean, you disappeared! Some buddy! All I could think was, Friday the 13th, Friday the 13th, and man, you are gone."

After a lot of discussion and debate, we reviewed the lessons learned from this dangerous uncontrolled ascent, an inexperienced-diver mishap that could easily have been fatal: Never roll in the kelp. Never let yourself get grossly overbuoyant while worrying about some task. And never approach any dive without realizing that dropping into the ocean is no different than mountaineering—one slip, or series of slips, and you are history.

The key to safe sport diving, I learned, is to stay reasonably close to the surface and to avoid prolonged bottom times that require decompression on ascent. This allows a diver to make just such a rapid emergency retreat to the atmosphere as I did so unwillingly in the kelp. If a diver follows this rule, no matter what kind of equipment failure, no matter what kind of animal encounter, he or she can always rip off a weight belt and shoot up to the fresh air.

Most of the problems and dangers of diving involve pressure and depth. As noted in chapter 2, pressure increases one atmosphere's worth of air for each 33 feet or 10 meters of water. Partial pressure of gases increases in the lungs proportionately. The deeper one goes, the higher one's oxygen and nitrogen blood levels become.

Nitrogen, the inert gas that makes up some 78% of the air we breathe, is normally insoluble in the body. But at high pressure, it wiggles its way into blood and body tissues. In the brain, it causes a druglike high (or low, depending on the circumstances). There's an old adage that you should not go diving with someone that you've never gone drinking with, the idea being that a wild and unpredictable drunk might act the same way under the influence of nitrogen.

Getting nitrogen out of the body can cause decompression illness, or DCI. Slow, methodical ascents help in letting nitrogen diffuse harmlessly into the lungs and out of the body. Rapid ascents, like my unplanned rise from the kelp, especially if made after long dives, can cause big bubbles to form in brain, spinal cord, or coronary tissue, with catastrophic results. Treatment consists of hyperbaric oxygen or, failing a nearby chamber, breathing pure oxygen topside. Failing that, one can recompress at shallow depth with a second bottle of air. Modern dive computers help sport divers avoid these kinds of problems.

Another enemy of the ascending diver is air embolism. Had I kept my mouth shut during my emergency ascent, the compressed air in my lungs, at around four atmospheres, or 30 meters, would have expanded to almost four times my lung volume at the surface. In so doing, air would have invaded my blood stream, that is, embolized, and probably would have killed me. But my mouth remained open, the air rushed out, and only my pride was injured.

After the misadventure in the kelp, I started, paradoxically enough, to doubt the wisdom of buddy diving. Chasing after Ron, trying to keep my buddy in sight no matter what, led to my getting entangled. A buddy, I realized, could drag you into trouble that you might have avoided. A buddy might want to go deeper, or be braver in exploring wrecks, or be less patient when photographing. A buddy could give you false assurance when you needed to rely on your own skills and equipment, and anyway, things could go sour too fast for a buddy to help. And so, upon learning of the great squid run, I ventured out solo.

Each January, there is a spectacle that occurs in the ocean wilderness off La Jolla Canyon, a spectacle with everything Hollywood could want and more — sex, violence, death, and rebirth. Millions, maybe billions, of opal or market squid, *Loligo opalescens*, swim inshore to gather and spawn. These cephalopods form one of the bulwarks of the ocean food web, taking up a position somewhere in the chain above the zooplankton and below the tertiary predators. Just about every big fish, marine mammal, or sea bird loves to eat them; by the same token, these voracious animals gobble up anything they can wrap their beaks around — crustaceans, bait fish, smaller squid. For years fishermen neglected them. Now, as markets in the Far East develop, and as Americans get used to the idea of calamari as a food (it's rarely called squid on the menu), human predatory pressure is increasing.

Marcy Remco, a squid specialist from the California Department of Fish and Game, told me that until recently, there was no regulation of the industry. California boats hauled in a record 79,000 tons of squid worth $30 million in 1996; the harvest in 1997 dropped to 71,000 tons. Because of El Niño–induced ocean warming, the catch for the next year was only 1,600 tons. With the return of cool water, the squid take rebounded to nearly 100,000 tons for each of the next two years. Although the fishery, the largest in the state, is now permit limited, there are no limits on catch size, and except for weekend closures, year-round fishing is allowed. According to Remco, the brief, year-long life span of the animal is the key factor in this volatility. Opal squid, like flies or frogs, are what ecologists call "r-selected" organisms; because of their small size, short lives, and fecundity, their numbers can grow quickly to take advantage of a bloom of resources. "K-selected" organisms, on the other hand, such as elephants or whales, have large size, long lives, and slow reproduction.

Exactly how to measure rising and falling squid populations, though, has yet to be determined. Gary Davis, a National Park Service marine biologist for the Channel Islands, told me that our state of knowledge of this and other fisheries amounts to a mismanaged checkbook.

"We know the value of the checks that are being cashed," he said, "but often we don't know the size of the balance."

Squid are fascinating creatures; they use water jet propulsion to move, they release ink clouds to protect themselves, and they have remarkable nervous systems. Chromatophores in their skin change color with kaleidoscopic speed. Although not as brainy as their cousins the octopi, squid have neurons similar enough to our own that they have been used for decades in medical research.[30]

It was not only a general fascination with cephalopods, though, that led me out one evening to photograph the great January spawning run. Opal squid have this odd method of reproduction. They don't just have sex and smoke a cigarette. There is more involved; the stakes are higher. Once a male deposits his spermatophore packet with a special tentacle in the female, and once she safely plants the fertilized egg packet into the sandy bottom, both die. Like salmon, they perform one final, heroic act, and it's over.

There are nuances to this coital behavior, I learned, that illustrate how odd and crafty these creatures are. Offshore, where there is room to maneuver, pick, and choose, females find the male of their choice, mate head to head, and retain the sperm packet in their mouths, where they hold it for months.

"That way," said Roger Hanlon, a marine biologist at Woods Hole, Massachusetts, "if a female meets 'that one special guy' early on, she can hang onto his sperm."[31]

Inshore, where eggs are deposited, sexual mayhem and orgy are the norm. Squid cloud the seas. They jet forward, reverse, and sideways via their directable siphons and tail fins. Large bully males fight for mates, grab the female they desire, and deposit sperm under the female's mantle near her egg chamber. Their bodies pulsate with flashes of purple, green, and brown. With all the pushing and shoving, there is no time for offshore-style squid fellatio.

Near the sandy bottom, a female withdraws her 4–10-inch-long egg packet, holding 200 or so gelatinous eggs, and releases from her mouth the stored sperm of her choice, early mate. But with her tentacles occupied, she can no longer fight off the ever-present and pesky small males, who dart in and deposit sperm directly on the eggs.

MATING OPAL SQUID, LA JOLLA, CALIFORNIA "Inshore, where

eggs are deposited, sexual mayhem and orgy are the norm. Squid cloud the seas."

While this is going on, predators knife through the water to devour distracted, love-struck squid. Birds, fish, and marine mammals all take advantage of the mass of bioprotein. On the bottom, squid-hunting crabs and lobsters find their way past satiated horn and angel sharks that lie motionless on the sand, chunks of half-eaten squid hanging from their overstuffed jaws.[32] Bony fishes—cabezon, sculpin, and sea bass—join in the feast as well. Blue sharks, California sea lions, and harbor seals attack active, mating squid farther up in the water column. When the orgy is over, exhausted male and female cephalopods die, their bodies, if missed by predators, littering the ocean floor among the egg sacks and in places piling up to over a foot deep.[33]

In hopes of seeing this display of sex and violence, then, came one novice solo diver, yours truly, loaded with a new, heavy photo strobe, a camera, and the sparest of information: "Just swim out to where the sea birds are the thickest and drop in there . . ." was the thin advice somebody gave me in a dive shop. I'd dived the canyon before, during the daytime with Ron, and was confident that the terrain would hold no surprises. The setup: a gentle sand dropoff, punctuated by vertical cliffs. The walls were pockmarked with holes favored as home by the ubiquitous red and blue goby, a beautiful fish the size of a toothpick.

As the sun settled on the horizon, I punched through small surf and kicked due west out to sea, toward a raucous gathering of hundreds of gulls, cormorants, and pelicans. The long swim took me much farther out than my recollection of where the dive spot should be. At last, there were as many birds inshore as to the west; diving, resting, and conversing avians surrounded me. An unseen bird bomber splashed the back of my head, a little too close for comfort, and got my teeth chattering—a gift, no doubt, from the late Alfred Hitchcock.

The sun by now was long gone, and the reds and oranges on the horizon were fading fast into a deep indigo-violet. Resting on the surface after the long swim to slow my heart rate and calm down, I checked my gear once again—plenty of air, no weird leaks, camera OK.

Weighed down by the new strobe, I left the surface without effort. At 90 feet, my flash showed a brief vision of twirling miniature submarines, jetting every which way in pairs. My descent was so rapid, though, that the scene appeared but for a moment, and then down, down, down I dropped.

Not wanting to overcompensate and rocket to the surface again, I cautiously added air to my vest. My ears kept requiring clearing, telling me I was still sinking, and the water turned blacker than the night sky of Neptune. After taking his bathysphere to a record depth, William Beebe wrote of this place, the abyss, a world so dark, "It seemed as if all future nights in the upper world must be considered . . . twilight."[34]

I was flying totally on instruments; there was no bottom, no point of orientation. And no bathysphere. My heart pounded at hummingbird tempo. La Jolla Canyon dropped here to a depth of 900 feet. Once again panic seized me. I added air to my vest, "pssst, pssst," then shined a light at my depth gauge. Uh-oh—144 feet. Recreational divers were not supposed to go over 130 feet.

At last my ginger efforts at neutralizing buoyancy paid off. I rose back to 90 feet, saw the squid once again, but rose past them. My heart whirring, my ears popping, all drive to be a squid voyeur withered and vanished. Finally neutral at 30 feet, I checked my body. Everything seemed normal, all limbs wiggled; my brain, though pulsing with adrenalin, functioned. It was time to turn east for shore. The squid would have to wait another day.

Once again I suffered from a bad case of beginner buoyancy-itis, in this case the combination of a lack of external reference to my depth—diving at night in blue water—and fear of overinflating from my previous mishap in the kelp led me astray. Looking back, it is clear that I lacked the experience for such a dive; a dozen daylight dives in clear water would have helped prevent this second, unplanned near-disaster.

Experience can be defined as "having made that mistake once before." Trouble is, in the alien element of the underwater world, errors can kill you before you can learn from them. Hundreds of dives later, these two events remain scorched in my memory as the lucky escapes of a foolish beginner, and (knock on wood) I've yet to repeat anything like them.

Twenty-four hours later I returned with a new strategy—dive in 30 feet of water, follow the sand bottom down, and never mind the birds. The scheme worked perfectly. At 60 feet, squid surrounded me by the thousands upon thousands. Opal-eyed, mantles flashing red with passion, oblivious to the big, clumsy mammal that spouted bubbles and was so easy to avoid, they rocketed about in a furious, intricate mating dance.

Each creature was six to eight inches long and festooned with 10 tentacles. Some were clearly engaged in that final, heroic act of reproduction, the males wrapped around the females, their tentacles probing, their quivering a universal sign of coitus. There were times, though, when a third squid joined the party. Later, at a Scripps Institution of Oceanography lecture, I learned this was just what it appeared to be: a *ménage à trois*. "The females clearly have certain males they prefer," said the researcher in sterile science-speak. "If you are a male that is eschewed, you still have a chance at reproduction. These males manage to insert a sperm packet into a female that is otherwise preoccupied by a desirable male."

There were other strange going-ons, as well. The females planted egg cases in the sand by the millions, giving a snowy appearance to the bottom. Hovering to photograph them, I concentrated on timing images to give the best combination of natural history and design. An eery feeling came over me while working, disrupting my concentration—something was watching me. Looking up, my flash revealed a huge bat ray, holding motionless above, wings barely quivering, a living, inner spaceship studying an odd, bubbling intruder.

I wondered how this silent, cartilaginous fish could make me aware of its presence. It made no sound hovering motionless in the black water, but perhaps it made me sense some kind of electric life charge. Sharks and rays have lateral lines that pick up pressure changes, ampullae of Lorenzini that detect bioelectric signals—perhaps submersion in the ocean activates ancient, vestigial sensory organs in the human body. More likely, compressed air expanded my cerebrum through nitrogen narcosis, the rapture of the deep.

This concentration of life—birds, fish, cephalopods—made it clear that the squid formed a vital link in the ocean food web. Bright lights offshore told of commercial fishermen shining the spawning creatures, luring them into their nets. But many fisheries concentrate on taking carnivores that exist at the fourth trophic level, such as shark or tuna [phytoplankton (level 1) are eaten by herbivore zooplankton (level 2), which are eaten by squid (level 3), which are eaten by the fourth-level carnivores]. In years past, blue sharks gathered in great numbers off San Diego to feed on the squid.

Doc Anes, a diver who has made a living chumming blues with his secret, nauseating, dead fish sauce, dons a chain mail suit and leads divers into a shark cage at Thirty-Mile Bank off San Diego. In the good old days, dozens of blues would answer his dinner bell within minutes. Now you might wait for hours to see one. Perhaps the sleek hunters are nearly gone, fished out for their fins, caught as by-catch on longlines or in gill nets, or perhaps they have just relocated. But it bothered me to consider what might happen to our local ocean if animals supporting the base of their food chain, such as the opals, were also overharvested.

Like the crucial stone holding an arch together, a keystone species exerts a marked influence over an entire ecosystem. The concept, originally devised by biologist Robert T. Paine, refers to apex predators whose removal causes major changes in ecosystems.[35] Ecologists also use it to refer to single species that have a marked effect on their immediate environment. Beavers, for example, alter northern temperate forests by clearing trees and building dams and ponds.[36]

What would happen to this web of life if *Loligo opalescens* were to disappear? Was it a keystone species? Perhaps overfishing of squid could make the whole coastal oceanic world undergo dramatic change. Or perhaps some other marine creature would rise to the occasion and take the squid's "near-shore pelagic" niche.

Pondering these and other things, I found myself driven to dive with the oversexed multitudes many times. Although no further diving misadventures befell me, more questions came with each exploration. Why must the mating couples die? Do their bodies provide nutrients for the voracious young? Does their death remove competition for food? If squid nervous systems are like ours, does sex feel good? Does dying hurt?

On some nights, dozens of divers were in the water, photographers diving solo, mostly, each carrying a torch that punctuated the 90-foot black depth with an eery halo of light. Ron was among them, but he always brought a buddy. With each exposed image, strobe lights flashed like silent artillery, adding a surreal element to an already bizarre spectacle.

Ron appeared at the dive shop one February afternoon; we shared stories and photographs and dreamed of the South Seas.

"Why don't you travel to Fiji or New Guinea on a dive trip someday, Ron?" I asked.

"Hell," he answered, in his sharkskin voice, "I've already made plans. I'm heading to the South Pacific, and soon." He shifted to a conspiratorial tone, a wild light shining in his eyes. "But I'm using a one-way ticket, man. Once I get there, I'm not coming back."

He asked me to join him for a squid dive that afternoon, and I thought about it long and hard. "Come on," he said. "It's just about time for the egg sacks to hatch. Let's go watch life begin!" Exhausted from working the night before, I passed, regretful about missing something great.

I did miss something, but it wasn't great. That night, on the evening news, viewers watched rescuers pull a diver through the surf at La Jolla Canyon. Paramedics pumped on his chest as lifeguards loaded him into an ambulance. I stared at the diver's face, pale, squid-white, endotracheal tube protruding. It was Ron.

Why my friend died never became clear.[37] His novice buddy said the dive was uneventful, a 95-footer, and that, after surfacing, Ron started waving his arms around, reaching for her wildly. Then he went limp and sank. In 15 feet of water, the dive student was unable to inflate his vest or release his weight belt; by the time lifeguards brought him up, it was too late. Most probably he suffered a heart attack or cardiac dysrhythmia and just happened to be diving. Perhaps an errant nitrogen bubble fizzed into a crucial artery in his heart or brain. Only Ron could tell us for sure, and Ron wasn't talking.

One thing was certain: He died doing the thing he loved.

So here we were on the bluff, a crowd of people touched by a diver, a keystone species sort of dive instructor, someone who managed to interest hundreds of people in the magical, dangerous wilderness so close, and yet so far, from the city limits. Would our fascination for the sea collapse now that Ron was dead? No. In death there was rebirth. We'd learned that much, at least, from the squid.

The seals became used to the bagpipes. They returned to their sunbathing, although they did not seem as relaxed as before. The swim was starting to get tough, now; the divers rounded the breakwater with the floating wreath and hit the surf. Kicking hard with their fins, they broke through the waves and stroked out into calmer, deep water.

A Forster's tern, its elegant black cap molted to winter white, plunge-dived for baitfish near the group of wet-suit skinned humans. As we watched the swimmers' progress, a fleet of 10 brown pelicans cruised southward in single file, surfing the updraft wind on an obsidian-edged wave. Gliding motionless as long as they could, the pterodactyl-like pelicans flapped their wings at the last instant to pull up as the wave hammered into the breakwater. The adults were dressed in their best winter mating plumage, their gullets a bright crimson, their crests a golden wheat color.

At last the divers were far enough out and, with a small prayer, set free the wreath. It drifted in the current toward the kelp beds, dwindling to a tiny speck. Only when it was out of sight did the bagpipe player cease, releasing the day to the wind and sea.

Note: On May 29, 2001, *the federal government officially listed the white abalone as an endangered species.*[38]

CHAPTER FIVE

The clearness of the water afforded me one of the most astonishing and beautiful sights I have

ever beheld. The bottom was absolutely hidden by a continuous series of corals, sponges,

actiniae, and other marine productions, of magnificent dimension, varied forms, and brilliant

colours. It was a sight to gaze at for hours, and no description can do justice to its surpassing

beauty and interest.—ALFRED RUSSEL WALLACE, *The Malay Archipelago*

Soft Coral Paradise

Beneath the Surface in Fiji

As with surfing, the lure of exploring far-off oceans soon gripped me. Without a doubt, diving in warmer seas than the San Diego ocean, an ocean cooled by the south-flowing California Current, held many attractions. Diving in warm water is easier. Intrinsically buoyant wet suits are thinner, if worn at all. One uses, for that reason, less weight to stay submerged. Cold water, fertilized with upwelling nutrients, favors the growth of diatoms and other plankton, and these decrease visibility. Warm tropical water, on the other hand, is much more sterile, because, with few exceptions, tropical oceans are stratified and a sharp thermocline separates warm water and rich, cool water. As a result, the nutrients are locked in the depths and visibility increases.

In tropical seas, one can see underwater 30 feet or more, even 100 feet. All this makes diving easier and safer, for it is harder to get lost and easier to make it back to a dive boat. Mentally, too, diving feels more joyous and less dangerous in warm, clear water—but it can also lure you deeper.

There are different biota to observe in tropical oceans as well. Coral reefs only thrive in water warmer than 64°F, or 18°C. Tuna and their fast-swimming cousins also favor warmer climes. It took little persuasion, then, to get me on a plane to what would surely be a tropical paradise.

Paradise was not the first word that came to mind as the 110-foot sloop *Nai'a* pounded through the late-autumn Fijian gale. Great gray walls of water loomed up out of the driven rain to starboard. *Nai'a* reared her bow and slammed down, her solid iron keel damping what would send a lesser boat into a capsizing roll. She was a good boat, a solid boat, and to her this storm was a trifle. To me and my stomach, on the other hand, it was a major problem.

I collapsed topside on a bench amidships, bored with lying around in my bunk in a Dramamine daze. Peni, a big bear of a Fijian, sat smiling across from me, calmly smoking a cigarette. I managed a weak grin in return, but Peni's smoke didn't agree with me, and yet another wave smacked the boat and exploded over the bow. As I crawled, defeated, back to my bunk, pausing to upchuck in the stateroom sink, my stomach twisted in misery. My mind, though, was exultant. Like all storms, this one would pass, and when it did, there would be diving in one of the most amazing biological regions of the world. Nirvana would be mine.

The broad expanse of equatorial ocean that extends from Africa eastward to Hawaii contains, in its shallow, sunlit waters, coral reefs that form what is the world's most biodiverse marine province. Many fish and invertebrates living in these Indo-Pacific waters have free-floating egg and larval stages, a method of reproduction that, as described in chapter 4, can allow dispersal over a wide area.

Because of powerful trade winds that blow from the northeast in the northern hemisphere, and from the southeast in the southern, the prevailing surface currents in the tropics flow to the west. Behind this simple statement lie some key oceanographic principles.

As the sun warms the atmosphere and evaporates moisture from equatorial oceans, this warm, moist air rises. In the northern hemisphere, cool, sinking air some 30 degrees north then pulls this air away from the equator. Meanwhile, the cool, sinking air is pulled south by the rising air from the equator. This circular, cylindrical flow of air, called a meteorologic cell, would run north–south if not for Earth's rotation.

But because a spot such as Bogata, Colombia, on the fat part of a spinning planet near the equator, travels faster than a place directly north, like Montreal, Canada, a place situated on a thinner section, there is a tendency for moving objects in the northern hemisphere to curve clockwise. The opposite is true in the southern hemisphere. This principle is called the Coriolis effect, in honor of Gaspard Gustave de Coriolis, the French scientist who deciphered the mathematics in 1835.[1]

Take a globe and spin it for a while. Watch how quickly the equatorial regions move, and how slowly the polar regions move. This is the key to the Coriolis effect. Tom Garrison, a professor at the University of Southern California and author of what many consider the classic oceanography textbook, explains the phenomenon as follows (using different cities): "Buffalo doesn't have as far to go in a day as does Quito. It must move eastward more slowly to maintain its position due north of Quito."[2]

If we were to fire a cannonball from Buffalo, Garrison continues, aimed due south at Quito (which lies at the same longitude), the ball would curve to the right, because it is moving more slowly than its target. Or if, conversely, Peruvians were to aim a large cannonball at Buffalo, it, too, would curve to the right, because it is traveling faster than its target. The opposite is true in the southern hemisphere—moving objects swerve to the left.

Trade winds created by the uneven warming of Earth do not run north–south, then, but veer to the west. Although there are several equatorial countercurrents that flow to the east, because of the trades the general flow of tropical surface water, and the planktonic larvae the currents carry, is westward.

How much the bewildering complexity of reefs in the western Pacific is the result of larval transport is unclear. Some of the reason for the relative sparseness of coral and other reef species in, say, the eastern Pacific may be due to geological reasons, to the deep dropoffs and canyons of California and Peru, as well as to the cold California and Humboldt currents sweeping toward the equator.[3]

Another explanation for the relative paucity of marine species in such eastern Pacific locales as Hawaii is isolation. Marine life, like terrestrial life, disperses via island stepping stones; a continuous necklace of islands stretches across the South Pacific from Sumatra to Tahiti, for example, and may explain the increased species found in French Polynesia as opposed to the otherwise geographically analogous Hawaiian Islands, which are separated by a thousand-mile barrier of open ocean from the Phoenix, Line, and Marshall islands.[4]

But no one can deny that the Indo-Australian Archipelago, the heart of the region, including Malaysia, Indonesia, the Philippines, New Guinea, and northern Australia, harbors the greatest wealth of oceanic species in the world.[5] Different sources estimate that there are anywhere from 450 to 700 species of coral for divers to explore in the western Pacific, for example, compared with the Caribbean, which has only from 67 to 80.[6] On tropical

Indo-Pacific reefs live about 5,000 species of mollusks and 2,000 species of reef fish; on Atlantic reefs occur 1,200 mollusk species and 600 reef fish species.[7]

Fiji, a group of 844 islands about 1,500 nautical miles east of New Guinea, lies just outside the Fertile Triangle formed by Malaysia, the Philippines, and northern Australia. What diversity the country lacks in overall faunal richness it makes up for in unique, endemic animals. Fiji also happens to have, on its verdant shores, a warm-hearted, generous race of humans. No place is immune to trouble, of course, and violence has erupted between the indigenous people and the Indian immigrant population.[8] In the outer islands, though, little of this tension was evident.

As the storm abated, Ravai, our Fijian captain, steered *Nai'a* through an atoll pass, the break in the coralline chain surrounding an island where rainwater, snared from the trade winds by igneous mountains, escapes to the sea. Suddenly, as if a set were changed in a play, the sun came out, the surf calmed to glass, and orchid blossoms released their fragrance from a coconut palm–studded shore. We had arrived at Wakaya Island. Paradise was about to unfold.

Like many islands in the Pacific, Wakaya is volcanic in origin. First magma arose from Earth's mantle to shoot through an ocean floor "hotspot" or fracture zone and create an underwater mountain and, eventually, a cone-shaped island. With shallow, clear seawater and plentiful sunlight, coral polyps thrived, laying down their limestone skeletons by the billions and forming a fringing reef.

In a process first hypothesized by Charles Darwin during his voyage as naturalist on the *Beagle*, the weight of solid igneous rock caused the crust under the island's center to sink a few millimeters each year, and the fringing reef, ever growing to make up for the sinking bedrock, became a coral atoll, a ring complete with protected lagoon.[9] On many islands, no trace of volcano remains, all the igneous rock having long disappeared. To test Darwin's theory, scientists have drilled at such places as Enewetak, a mature atoll in the central Pacific that barely rises above sea level. Here they found the volcanic base at 1,219 meters of depth.[10]

As *Nai'a* slipped into a calm lagoon, I stared at a verdant, jagged mountain, a peak that proclaimed Wakaya to be geologically young. Distant surf thundered on the calcareous reef, but only tiny ripples washed through to us on the inside.

It was time to go diving. We gathered our gear and hopped into an outboard-powered inflatable. On went buoyancy compensator vests and tanks, masks, and fins. At the site, we kicked over backward into the warm water.

DENDRONEPHTHYA SOFT CORALS, NIGALI PASS, FIJI

"Each colony looked liked a gaudy fluff of cotton candy; taking a bite, however,

would not be advised."

As I drifted down, clearing my ears with gentle blowing while pinching my nose, a kaleidoscope of life reeled below. But we did not tarry in the shallows—we saved that for the end of the dive.

Down we plunged into the blue. A wall lay before us, covered with sea fans, soft corals, and darting schools of reef fish. At 100 feet, Rusi, the divemaster, motioned to a spot on the vertical cliff. I moved closer, squirting a bit of air into my vest to keep neutral buoyancy—similar to how a fish uses a swim bladder. There, in a hole within the reef, a brilliant blue creature stared at me with canary yellow eyes, her mouth agape. It was a blue ribbon eel resting in her cave, waiting for the nighttime hunt. Males are black and much less gaudy, but the females are dressed to kill.

We ascended slowly. A cavern unfolded filled with black coral, intricate fan-shaped colonies of animals that weave lacelike patterns shining, under the light of a torch, in reds and silvery yellows. Schools of crimson, nocturnal cardinalfish stared at us from deep within the grotto through dark, owl-like eyes.

As we reached 60 feet of depth, the current hit us and we were forced to swim hard to stay in one place. Here lay vertical fields of underwater wildflowers. Arguably the most beautiful creatures in the sea, soft corals of the genus *Dendronephthya* are animals possessing colors that stagger the imagination. Vivid reds, iridescent yellows, dazzling purples, startling oranges— they come in every hue imaginable. Fiji, with its lagoons and currents, is one of the best places in the world to see *Dendronephthya*. Each colony looked like a gaudy fluff of cotton candy; taking a bite, however, would not be advised.

Like all corals, soft corals are members of the phylum Cnidaria (formerly called Coelenterates),[11] a broad collection of radially symmetric invertebrates that also includes jellyfish, anemones, hard corals, and hydrozoans. Most corals form colonies of animals that gather planktonic or free-swimming food; soft corals lack the limestone skeleton of the hard corals; instead, they form a stem supported by calcium-containing spicules. Each tiny animal at the periphery of the soft coral colony extends eight tentacles (making it an octocoral) from its polyp body to collect food; these tentacles possess microscopic stinging cells called nematocysts. If a careless diver should run a bare hand over these tentacles, a most unpleasant sting will result. Rusi kept a vinegar solution topside to pour on one's skin after a clumsy encounter with the nematocysts.

Soft corals are one reason many divers come to this island paradise. Not just another pretty face in the ocean, their biology hides a great mystery. Their relatives, sea fans and hard corals (called by some hexacorals, for having six tentacles), often become covered with hitchhiking hangers-on: feather stars or crinoids, algae, sponges, and ascidians. But soft corals rarely put up with such characters. They possess chemical secretions that repel these marine boarders and, as such, are a focus of much research.[12] Japanese scientists, for example, have isolated a group of steroids in *Dendronephthya* that are lethal to barnacle larvae at low concentrations.[13]

William Fenical, an organic chemist at Scripps Institution of Oceanography, has helped isolate a group of compounds called pseudopterosins from sea whips, soft corals found in the Caribbean.[14] These chemicals possess anti-inflammatory properties; they have been licensed by several cosmetic companies for use in skin care.[15] Bryostatins, compounds found in bryozoans (platelike organisms that cling to docks and bottoms of boats), inhibit leukemias and form an additional example of this sort of bioprospecting. Eleutherobins, also from soft corals, are yet a third group of organic alkaloids; these prevent cell division much like the anticancer drug taxol.

Donald Gerhart, a professor of marine biology at North Carolina State University, studied a Caribbean octocoral named *Plexaura homomala* that devotes 5% of its body weight to producing hormonal prostaglandin. Although studies to use the chemical as a birth control method failed, it works fine for the coral, which resists predation by making its attackers vomit. Gerhart also found a sea squirt, *Phallusia nigra*, that possesses sufficient vanadium to kill a sea lion and secretes sulfuric acid from acid vacuoles.[16]

Because they are soft-bodied, Fenical explains, soft corals and other shell-less creatures use chemicals rather than armor for defense in the competitive world of the coral reef.[17] In this diverse, eat-or-be-eaten world, water-diluted, biologically active compounds, such as those used by soft corals, have evolved to become concentrated, varied, and potent. As such, they hold promise for new medicines. They also make clear that life is far from easy in the deceptive beauty of the coral—predation is fierce, competition is keen, and predators abound.

In studying corals, it became clear to me that the taxonomy, or naming, was more than a little complicated. In a process begun in pre-Darwin times by the Swede Linnaeus, biologists have delighted in classifying life in ever-narrowing groups, from domain, kingdom, phylum, class, order, family, and genus to, finally, species. Because they have evolved over many millions of years, tropical ecosystems possess phyla diversity—as opposed to species diversity—far beyond that found on land. (A phylum is a basic, major grouping found in animal taxonomy, just below kingdom, that is based on body plan.) Robert Jay Wilder, author of *Listening to the Sea*, writes of this complexity: "Life in its greatest variety is biased toward marine environments."[18]

E.O. Wilson, coauthor of the classic *Theory of Island Biogeography* (1967), has become a renowned champion for biodiversity. He notes that all 36 described phyla occur in the sea, as opposed to only 10 on land. These include two phyla discovered only within the last 30 years, the Loricifera, "miniature bullet-shaped organisms with a girdlelike band around their middle," and the Cycliophora, "plump symbiotic forms that attach themselves to the mouths of lobsters and filter out food particles left over from their hosts' meals."[19]

In thinking about these phyla, most of which are invertebrates, we humans are often guilty of considering them primitive and inferior.

"This," write marine biologists Patrick Colin and Charles Arneson, who specialize in their study, "is a popular misconception. These species have continually evolved and adapted to changes . . . for periods far longer than any vertebrates. . . . Today it is understood," they continue, that "even a simple sponge may have highly evolved chemistry which enables it to compete effectively for living space with 'higher' animals on the reef."[20] A better word for "primitive" or "inferior," then, by this line of thinking, would be "ancestral."[21]

The taxonomy and classification by morphology of corals can be complex (brace yourself): Corals, in the phylum of Cnidaria, fall into the class of Anthozoa, except for fire corals, which are in the class Hydrozoa. Soft corals are often thought to include their relatives the sea fans, sea plumes, and sea whips. These animals fall into the subclass Alcyonaria; all have eight bipinnate tentacles on each polyp. Hard corals can be found in the order Scleractinia, a part of the subclass Zoantharia, which includes sea anemones, corallimorphs, and zoanthids. Although many of these creatures have six tentacles, some Scleractinia can have hundreds, sea anemones, for example.

Is this confusing? You bet. But just wait. At the level of the species, marine life, especially coralline marine life, can become almost hopelessly blurred, at least according to Australian field biologist J.E.N. Veron. In his book *Corals in Space and Time*,[22] Veron presents a novel theory that, according to Hawaiian oceanographer Richard Grigg,[23] "challenges Darwin head on"—for corals, at least. It is not so much competition that drives natural selection and evolution, according to this line of thinking, but stochastic forces such as changing oceanic conditions. Veron notes that corals, carried near and far by ocean currents, develop races and subspecies in response to local conditions, often producing widely differing colors and shapes depending on local nutrients, predators, and wave action. He postulates that, although the concept of species as a biological unit that interbreeds and should be given protection is important, "nature, especially marine life, does not come in discrete units which have clear boundaries."[24]

Three recent discoveries have sustained Veron's arguments, according, again, to Grigg.[25] First, there is the fact that 75% of all corals are known to spawn, relying on external fertilization in the water column for the union of gametes. Next, scientists have discovered massive spawning events off the Great Barrier Reef of Australia, where dozens of species of corals release gametes in annual synchrony to make a rich, reproductive soup—a sexual stew ideal for mismatched fertilization and hybridization. Finally, it is now known that many of the hybrids formed from these mass spawning events are viable.

Taking these three discoveries, and adding a lifetime of field study, Veron has concluded that there can be, for corals, a sort of species complex of races and subspecies that he calls a "syngameon." And he postulates that it is ocean currents that drive this genetic mix.[26]

As planetary temperatures wax and wane, the relative strength of ocean currents varies. In times of strong currents, coral larvae are scattered far and wide, and there is rapid genetic mixing and hybridization. Although some of the hybrids formed may be sterile, others may be fertile. When currents are strong, species dwindle and are well defined. In other words, as currents increase, seas act like continents.

During times of weak current, there is less distribution and more speciation. The definition between species becomes blurred as subspecies and races appear, molding themselves to narrow, variable local conditions of surge and wave impact, food sources, and coral-eating predation. Gametes are synthesized. Now, we have a syngameon. With less movement of water, parts of the sea become isolated places that are hotbeds of speciation and evolution. In short, seas now act like islands. Writes Veron:

> For any given "species," the currents of any one geological interval create patterns of hybrids, subspecies, and races. These patterns will last only as long as these currents last, then they will change. What changes is not just distribution, but the composition of the "species": all distinctions between "species," "subspecies," "races," and all other such taxonomic units become blurred. It is as if the genetic composition of each of these units becomes re-packaged into different units. When currents change again, the re-packaging starts all over again, and so on and on in an unending process.[27]

Syngameons formed from hybridization have been described in terrestrial plant genera, including *Quercus* (oaks), *Eucalyptus*, and *Iris*.[28] Veron's hypothesis, what has come to be known as "reticulate evolution," may apply to other marine animals that spawn, including crustaceans, mollusks, polychaetes, and echinoderms.

No doubt some scientists would argue with this thought and insist that more field research might elucidate the taxonomy of corals and that the definition of a species, an interbreeding group of animals, is still a valid idea. Grigg[29] believes that only molecular genetics may prove or disprove Veron's postulate.

But that is the joy and curse of science: Theories are built up and knocked down, and firm understandings are replaced with new, confounding data. Science is an uncertain business; probabilities outnumber axiomatic facts. Only one thing is certain: one can look at a coral reef from many perspectives, as a beautiful mosaic, as a maze of genetic conundrums, and as a tangled web of intricate behaviors, predator–prey relationships, and adaptations.

Working hard in the current, I used up much of my compressed air and rose to the shallow 30-foot depth. Here the current relaxed, and knobs of hard coral ("bommies" in Australian slang) provided home to a complex world of small fish and invertebrates. Hard corals, also called stony or hermatypic corals, build the foundation of any coral reef, along with coralline algae. Each individual coral polyp is nothing more than a fleshy sack with a mouth surrounded by six tentacles. But the fleshy sack secretes a limestone (calcium carbonate) skeletal case where the polyp can hide from predators in daytime. At night, the polyp spreads its nematocyst-bearing tentacles wide. As the corals die and new generations appear, the skeletal remains build the reef. The living skin of the hard coral reef, though, remains about one tenth of a millimeter thick—paper thin.[30]

As stony corals build reefs, they are helped by coralline algae, red algae that precipitate calcium carbonate, $CaCO_3$, like corals but spread out in thin sheets over the reef, cementing the colonies together.[31] Coralline algae are especially important in wave impact zones.

Virtually all hard and some soft corals live in a symbiotic relationship with zooxanthellae, a type of dinoflagellate algae.[32] The algae, living in the gastric tubes of their hosts, can make up 80% of the soft portions of corals.[33] Through photosynthesis, they take carbon dioxide that the polyps release through respiration, add sunlight and water from shallow seas, and produce carbohydrates and oxygen that benefit the corals. The predatory corals, with their carnivorous if microscopic diet, excrete raw material for the algae. Both species use phosphates and nitrogen to build nucleic acids for DNA and amino acids for proteins. In the nutrient-poor (upwelling-poor might be a more accurate term) seas of the tropics, it is through cooperation that both organisms can survive.[34]

Like kelp forests, coral reefs have high primary productivity, estimated by various sources[35] to be from 1,500 to 5,000 grams of carbon/m²/year, compared, once again, with the open sea, where 18–50 grams of carbon/m²/year is the norm. Why are the reefs such oases in vast areas of desertlike, nutrient-poor ocean?

Although there is some disagreement as to the reason for the high productivity of coral reefs, the fact itself is not in dispute, not even for remote atolls far from any land. Most blue-water plankton, larvae, and bacteria are absorbed by the many biofiltering reef fauna, that is, by sponges, mollusks, worms, and the corals themselves. But it may well be symbiosis that lies at the heart of this abundance. Close coupling of zooxanthellae within coral polyps means that algae will not be swept away by currents and surge and that scarce nutrients will be fully utilized by both cnidarians and algae.[36]

J.E.N. Veron, ever the contrarian, has a different take on coral symbiosis. He acknowledges that there are many advantages, such as "the removal of metabolic wastes, the enhancement of calcification, direct nutrient contribution, and concentration and recycling of limited nutrients."[37] But he also points out that the evolutionary price of mutualism is high. Zooxanthellae depend on photosynthesis; hence, corals are limited to the photic zone, the surface area of the ocean that receives light. During the Cretaceous-Tertiary mass extinction from the Yucatan meteorite, when light levels were low, one-third of all families and over 70% of genera of corals were wiped out. Writes Veron: "Apparent disadvantages of light dependence arise because of the addictive nature of symbiosis."[38]

In this competitive, dangerous place, the coral reef, a place where poisons and treachery abound, the entire ecosystem depends on cooperation, at least at the coral/zooxanthella level. Reefs can grow so large that they are visible from space, like the Great Barrier Reef's 600,000 km² expanse. One might think that, apart from the next giant meteorite, there are no limits to the continued increase of coral communities, other than the need for shallow water and low latitude. One might not harbor doubts about their survival—yet, such doubts exist.

Corals, soft and hard, are fastidious animals. They thrive to build their epic reefs only in waters that have average temperatures between 64°F and 86°F (18–30°C), although some species do survive in high latitudes, such as *Astrangia danae*, an Atlantic stony coral found off the northeastern United States. They must have clear water, plentiful sunlight, and salinity near 35 parts per thousand. In other words, they prefer the very conditions that make sport divers drool. Too much heat, too much cold, too much ultraviolet radiation, too much sediment runoff, and the colonies, or their symbiotic algae partners, die.

Corals need and benefit from shifting ocean currents; strong Fijian currents bring planktonic prey to extended nematocyst-armed tentacles. But once a year these ancestral cnidarians time their sexual behavior to slack seas. As on the Great Barrier Reef, where 87 of 105 species spawn within three to five nights after the November full moon,[39] in Fiji every spring corals synchronize the casting of millions of eggs and sperm into warming waters. This mating launches fertilized eggs in huge numbers to the vagaries of the open ocean, usually when neap tides occur and currents are subdued. Scientists speculate that the relatively calm water allows better chances for union of egg and sperm. Witnessing this underwater storm of gametes forms the dream of many an underwater adventurer; unfortunately, the coralline orgy would not happen for us on this autumnal trip.

Somehow, through the crucible of time and evolution, the immobile corals have evolved to mix genes in this way, timing the event for the tides and moon, sending some of their progeny far from the harsh, competitive life that is the coral reef, keeping most, perhaps, close to home. Predators may eat their fill during the spawn, but the astronomic numbers of eggs ensure that many larvae survive.

Writes Gregory Wray, a Duke biologist specializing in marine larvae, "Setting great numbers of offspring adrift in the ocean increases the chance that at least some will survive and be delivered to suitable locations, a strategy contemporary ecologists call bet hedging."[40]

Some scientists have toyed with the idea that, rather than bet hedging, the larvae are cast into the water column to use a different food source from the adults. But others, including Richard Grigg, the University of Hawaii oceanographer, who for five years was editor-in-chief of the journal *Coral Reef*, disagree.

"Corals are more often space limited than food limited," he told me. "However, an isolated reef may be recruitment limited."[41]

The coral reef can be an inhospitable place for tiny larvae that drift over billions of extended nematocysts, whereas in blue water, nutrients are sparse and death by starvation becomes a possibility, as does predation by pelagics. Natural selection has favored ciliated and motile coral larvae, or planulae, seeded with symbiotic algae from their parents, that swim about for a few days or even several weeks before settling onto a reef somewhere. Once planted, they undergo a rapid metamorphosis and begin their fixed, sessile, second stage of life.

Wray remarks that beyond bet hedging, the ability to drift long distances can provide a mechanism for genetic mixing: "Many adult marine inverte-brates have only a limited ability to move," he writes, "and some, such as corals and barnacles, do not move at all. Inbreeding is a real danger for crea-tures that are stuck in one place. Widespread dispersal helps ensure that when larvae do settle down, their neighbors—and potential mates—will be unrelated."[42]

Others, such as Jeffrey Levinton, professor of ecology and evolution at the State University of New York at Stony Brook, disagree with this idea, ar-guing that "there is no evolutionary model that can make this an evolved strategy, and that local mixing might be enough to avoid inbreeding."[43]

A sailing friend of mine from early surfing days in La Jolla, Phillip Dus-tan, is a coral reef specialist and professor of biology at the College of Charles-ton in South Carolina. Phillip sailed on *Calypso* with Jacques Cousteau in the Caribbean and the Amazon in the 1970s. I asked him about the distribution of coral larvae.

"We really don't know," he told me. "The larvae can be planktonic, drift-ing for long periods of time, for days, for weeks, before finding the red cal-careous algae that attracts them to settle down. But we really don't know how far they drift or how widely they scatter."

For many years, biologists thought the spread of invertebrate reef life to be random. Scientists have found evidence that some inhabitants of the coral reef, at least, find their way back to their place of birth. Headed by Harvard professor Stephen Palumbi, a group of researchers found, through DNA studies, that mantis shrimp exhibit "genetic segregation into multiple dis-tinct populations in spite of free floating planktonic life stages."[44] In plain English, like gestating salmon, these babies make it back home. If this phe-nomenon were to prove true for corals in the planular stage, as studies by Sammarco and colleagues on the Great Barrier Reef have implied,[45] the im-plications are tremendous, for multiple conservation areas might be needed to assure protection of coral reef species and communities, not just a few large preserves.

Despite their fastidious nature, it is hard to imagine a disaster killing off all corals, even though the colonies have many enemies. Eventually, one would hope, the currents would bring fresh larvae to start growth anew. Yet powerful tropical storms, like the one that hit us on the *Nai'a*, kill a lot of corals. Cyclones (also called hurricanes) kill many more (see chapter 2).

Freshwater runoff kills coral, too. Too much nitrogen-bearing human waste and fertilizer in that runoff (eutrophication) can cause exuberant over-growth of algae sediment—which kills coral. This effect occurs most com-monly in embayments and other current-protected areas. Even though corals depend on zooxanthellae, there are species of filamentous, fleshy algae that smother corals and thrive when excess nitrogen and phosphorus appear in the water column.

Then there are the herbivores. Angelfish, those brilliant hallmarks of the reef, hunt in male–female pairs searching for tasty bites of algae and coral mucus, material entwined with the coral. Parrotfish, whose excreta make up much of the sand on tropical beaches, scrape on hard corals all day long as they feed on algae and leave dime-sized scars with fused teeth that form powerful beaks.[46] Most of these fish, however, evolved with the corals over millions of years. Preferring filamentous algae over zooxanthellic algae, they benefit the reef overall, despite some localized damage.

A good example of the fragility of the complex, dynamic, coral reef ecology may be found in Jamaica. The waters surrounding this large island in the Caribbean hold some 60 species of corals. Human population growth in Jamaica, typical of many poor countries, has an exponential growth trajectory. Early fishery reports suggest that people removed most large herbivorous fishes before the twentieth century;[47] by 1973, continued harvesting of both algae-eating herbivores (parrotfish and surgeonfish) and carnivores (sharks, jacks, and groupers) removed fish at a rate that was twice — or even three times — the sustainable take.[48] As fish disappeared, populations of an algae-eating competitor, the sea urchin *Diadema antillarum*, exploded. During the 1970s, the reefs appeared to be surviving well, as *Diadema* took over the niche of herbivorous fish, keeping the fleshy, filamentous algae under control.

But then, in 1980, Hurricane Allen smashed shallow-water corals, and before recovery could occur, in 1982 a water-borne pathogen attacked the urchins, resulting in mass mortality of *Diadema* throughout the Caribbean. The result? An explosive algal bloom swallowed Jamaica's reefs, increasing coverage from 4% to 92%, with coral cover declining from 52% to 3%.[49]

Controversy surrounds another natural predator of corals, the crown-of-thorns sea star (*Acanthaster planci*). This slow, poisonous creature lumbers over a hapless coral and everts its mouth to suck the life out of colony after colony. Large stretches of the Great Barrier Reef in Australia have been laid waste by these predators; debate rages as to whether this is a natural boom-and-bust phenomenon or the result of activities of man.[50] There is little doubt that humans have decreased some *Acanthaster* predators, such as the Triton's trumpet (a large, rare, colorful mollusk valued for its shell) and the humpheaded wrasse (a tasty, overhunted reef fish), who hunt juvenile crown-of-thorns.[51]

Other scientists point out that studies of *Acanthaster* spines from Holo-

cene sediments on the Great Barrier Reef of Australia show population os-
cillations of the sea star to have been cycling over thousands to millions of
years.[52] As the crown-of-thorns become abundant, they may only kill off the
living reef in discrete areas, and then starve and die off.

More overt, manmade disasters await corals in the Indo-Pacific. For years
fishermen have used dynamite to catch fish. Bombed out craters are common throughout the region from this practice; on our dives, though, we neither saw nor heard signs of blast fishing.

Native fishermen throughout the Fertile Triangle and beyond, lured by
merchants who pay exorbitant cash sums for live fish, have taken to cyanide
reef fishing. Although deadly to wide swaths of reef, some fish, especially the
prized Napoleon wrasse, are only stunned by dilute cyanide and can be captured and transported alive to Asian cities for sale in the restaurant trade. I
have seen rows of tanks holding these fish in the Aberdeen section of Hong
Kong, awaiting delivery. After they arrive in restaurants in the Central District, the fish, still nominally alive, are put on display. Customers pay around
$300, pick out their victim for the chef, and then dine on a plate of ultra-
fresh, tasty wrasse lips.

Cyanide, a nasty compound of carbon and nitrogen that disrupts respiratory metabolism, kills fish weeks or months after exposure. Tropical
aquarium fishes bought here in the United States often die after several
months. The reason? They were captured with reef-killing squirts of the poison in the Indo-Pacific.[53] More than half of the reef fish caught in this way
for the aquarium trade once came from Indonesia. Some now estimate[54] that
only 6.7% of the country's coral reefs remain in a healthy state, 30% have
been ruined, and the remaining reefs are in critical condition. Coral is the
keystone of the habitat, and killing it takes a host of other creatures with it,
something like clear-cutting a forest. Although some corals reach full size in
a couple of years, the annual bands on others show them to be hundreds of
years old. Recovery of today's destroyed reefs—if humans could find a way
to leave them alone—might take from 25 to 100 years or more.

A school of purple and orange fish called anthias zipped by me through the
antlers of a staghorn coral colony, while a scarlet anemone, also a cnidarian,
harbored neon-orange clownfish within its deadly tentacles. In places the
corals were brown, green, and yellow. This was the sign of healthy zooxanthellic algae living within the cnidarians. In other places, the corals were
pure white, or bleached—these hard corals had lost their symbiotic algae.
The condition, although not immediately fatal, will eventually kill the colony
if the algae do not recover. Many corals, though, do bounce back.

It is bleaching that some scientists studying coral reefs consider one of the worst dangers facing the ecosystem worldwide. As global warming continues, whatever its cause, vast acres of reef may, these scientists say, turn pale and die. Whether or not the combined force of all the above assaults has made Indonesia's problem typical of tropical coastlines is a matter of debate.

There is evidence from other marine areas, though. For example, an unusual joint study by Israeli and Jordanian scientists showed that a fifth of the coral in the Red Sea's Gulf of Aqaba Marine Peace Park has died off in the past two years.[55]

Peter Glynn, a respected coral reef biologist based in Miami, believes that recurring El Niño events, those periodic intense warmings of eastern tropical Pacific (ETP) waters, may prevent the formation of the large, diverse reefs found in the western Pacific.[56] He developed this hypothesis while documenting in Panama the probable extinction of a species of reef-building fire or hydrocoral, *Millepora* sp. nov., an extinction most probably due to the 1982–83 El Niño.[57] There are corals in the ETP, off Mexico and Central America, but the reefs they build are small and their species few in number. If hot water does keep ETP coral at bay, and global warming might increase numbers of El Niños, the implications for reefs worldwide are sobering.[58]

Richard Grigg is a champion for the robustness of corals and their reefs.[59] He believes that corals evolved with surf and storms and other stressors and that they are able to bounce back after severe abuse, whether caused by humans or not. In his view, first presented by Grassle in 1973.[60] "Reef communities form a temporal mosaic in space—that is, a patchwork . . . in different stages of recovery from various disturbances."[61] This school of thought considers coral ecosystems to be unstable, dynamic, and unpredictable.

To Grigg, some marine biologists exaggerate reef problems in such places as Indonesia or the Red Sea to advance their own agendas or to get grants funded.[62] He called the worst offenders "false Cassandras" in an article on the crown-of-thorns sea star invasion.[63] Others share his sentiments.[64]

Phillip Dustan, the coral biology professor at the College of Charleston, holds opinions on the other side of the aisle. He is a researcher for the Cousteau Society; he was also the principal investigator for a U.S. Environmental Protection Agency (EPA) assessment project on Floridian corals. A soft-spoken, wiry waterman with an iron-hard will and a strong sense of ecological morality, he told me that the sum of all the hazards worldwide is creating a crisis of enormous magnitude for the world's corals and the reef communities they support.

"In our EPA project that started measuring in 1996," said Dustan, "the average loss of living coral coverage throughout the Florida Keys was 38%

from 1996 to 1999—that's three calendar years. The reef that I worked on, Carysfort Reef, lost 68% of its coral in that time alone. Diseases are up about 400% from 1995. And recruitment is virtually zero. We find some new baby corals, but it's nothing like it should be."

"What's doing it, then?" I asked.

"Well," he replied, "it's a series of nested stresses. There's local, there's regional, and there's global stress. The local stress is 'take and break' and sewage pollution. The regional is all the pollution from the Mississippi and the other rivers, all the different watersheds of the United States and Central America. As for global, we've got things like toxic dust from Africa, the decrease in the ozone layer, and global warming.

"So as the corals become stressed, they become more susceptible. They are very sensitive to temperature and thermal pollution. But as the water quality degrades, the corals become more susceptible to disease, more than anything. Diseases have really hammered the corals in the Florida Keys. There's one, for example, we discovered; we call it the 'white plague.' It wipes out coral.

"Pogo had it right. We have met the enemy, and the enemy is us."

Thomas Goreau, an American marine biologist, considers modern coral reefs to be less than 5,000 years old, for the most part, and agrees with Grigg that they undergo change, succession, and "urban renewal."[65] Nevertheless, he has become a strong scientific and political advocate for coral reef protection, research, and restoration. He is now president of the nonprofit Global Coral Reef Alliance.[66]

Why? Goreau has witnessed, while diving around the world, a marked mortality in coral reefs since 1998, and he's documented these massive die-offs from warm temperatures, pollution, and coral diseases. "At this point, at least one-half of the reefs in the world have been seriously impacted by global warming and pollution," said Goreau.[67] "We're right up to the limit of what the corals can stand."[68]

The 1998 mortality, fueled by the 1997–98 El Niño, was, he said, "horrifying. There's hardly anything alive." Nine-tenths of the coral reefs in Indonesia, according to Goreau, "are already dead, and the Caribbean islands are just beginning to experience the same phenomenon."[69]

For Goreau, who—with his father and grandfather—has studied and photographed corals for decades, the loss of today's reefs, even though they may be "only" thousands of years old, is an unmitigated catastrophe.

So are the coral reefs of the world in a state of emergency? When it comes to professional thought on their status, there is a range of opinion, from cautious, guarded optimism to strident alarmism. I wondered if Grigg's impressions might be fueled by his pristine, home Hawaiian ecosystem, and Dustan's by his more populous and battered Caribbean. Goreau, though, with his worldwide perspective, tilts the balance toward the alarmists.

All scientists, however, agree that, especially near urban centers in the Philippines, the Caribbean, and Indonesia, coral is under stress and that overfishing is a big problem; reef fish keep filamentous algae in check, and we can only surmise the multiplicity of other ways that healthy populations of reef fish interact with invertebrates on the reef. Removing them wholesale, as is often done, is disastrous for coral reef communities.

A global perspective is needed, supported by global data. A satellite dedicated to studying coral reefs worldwide,[70] as scientists now study rain forests, may prove one way to get a handle on just how endangered the habitat really is.

But there are reasons why some marine scientists and nongovernmental organizations (NGOs) may be tempted to exaggerate pending environmental catastrophes, although how much they do is a matter for debate. One reason is that many are up against formidable opponents—large fishing groups such as At Sea Processing, the Recreational Fishing Alliance, American Pelagic Fishing, and Taiyo Fishing Corporation, as well as an assortment of industrialists and developers, lumber companies, and many others.

And there is no comparison regarding comparative funding. For every marine biologist who gets, maybe, $30,000 a year working for an environmental NGO, there are perhaps a dozen lobbyists in Washington and elsewhere making much more pushing for increased fishing, opening up minke and sperm whaling, or cutting down the last bits of old-growth salmon forest.

The Center for Responsive Politics is a nonpartisan NGO that publishes amounts of contributions in the United States to politicians and their parties from a wide variety of contributors. Data from this group are widely quoted in the media by both right and left. Numbers from their website provide some interesting perspectives on the relative funding and power of corporate versus environmental funding.[71] For example, total contributions since 1990 from all energy and natural resource industries total $226,107,690. Total donations from the construction industry over the same period are $171,332,144. The chemical industry? $38,168,937. Sea transportation? $16,408,784.

Compare these numbers, individually or in aggregate, with $8,240,682, the combined political contributions since 1990 given on behalf of all environmental organizations and their lobby groups. One can understand why some greens feel outgunned and slip into exaggeration to benefit their arguments.

It's also important to realize that protecting the environment today is a legal game—if you want to set aside, say, 20% of a certain coral reef as a no-take fishing zone, you can't ask for 20%, because you'll get, maybe, if you're lucky, 8%. So, you claim a 50% zone is needed and settle for 20%. Unfortunately, the objective truth gets lost in this kind of negotiation. There is scientific truth, and there is the perverse truth of the legal/business/negotiating world.

Environmentalists also look ahead farther than do businessmen. Consider, on a more terrestrial note, Yellowstone National Park. When the U.S. Congress established that corner of Wyoming in 1872 as the first national park in the world, there was wilderness aplenty in the country. The park was conceived mostly to protect thermal features, Yellowstone Canyon, and other unique geology. Now, as development steadily encroaches on wild lands, Yellowstone has become important as a refuge for grizzlies and other wildlife. So even though setting aside large areas of coral reef or temperate coastal waters today may seem unnecessary, when one extrapolates ahead 100 years, the precedent of those reserves will become essential—all because of the reality of so many human beings.

The coral in Fiji appeared to us to be in good shape, as is the reef situation in much of Oceania,[72] although the World Resources Institute classifies two-thirds of Fijian reefs as "at risk."[73]

Why this relative reef health? Fiji is remote. The entire island chain contains only some 700,000 people. That helps, compared with the burgeoning millions inhabiting Indonesia and the Philippines. Fiji is relatively far south from the equator and so escapes the brunt of warm climate change and El Niños. Also, there is the tradition of reef stewardship by local groups that may help to preserve coral reefs.

Families control the customary fishing rights beyond each parcel of land from the reef to the shore; local fishing grounds, called qoliqoli, are not part of a commons. They belong to the locals. The fisherman's mantra, "Catch all the fish now, before someone else does," might not apply in Fiji, at least for demersal reef fish—some would say that here Garrett Hardin's[74] "tragedy of the commons" has been averted. Others would point to Japanese boats that visit to buy local crustaceans and sea cucumbers and wonder whether this is really true.

Coral reef horrors such as cyanide fishing and dynamiting are, for the most part, unknown in Fiji. Each tribal group owns its own fishing grounds, and the tribal chiefs control use of the reef, including diving. In fact, we were only able to dive in this qoliqoli because the owners of Nai'a met with the local Wakaya chief, paid a tribute of "goodwill money," and assured him of our honorable intentions (no fishing, only photography).

Similar schemes have helped coral reefs elsewhere. Off the Great Barrier Reef, for example, limited licenses for fishing and collecting crustacea have reduced the "get the fish quick before someone else does" mentality that leads to barren seas in other parts of the world. (However, J.E.N. Veron, an Australian coral biologist, states that because of fishing, "the central and southern Great Barrier Reef is nowhere near as 'pristine' as is sometimes claimed."[75]) In Bonaire, in the Caribbean, a strict "don't anchor, don't collect" ethic has led to an ecologically sensitive diving community and thriving reefs.[76]

On the skiff ride back to the boat, we spied a pair of manta rays feeding on plankton in the Wakaya channel. For exhilarating minutes we snorkeled with them, watching as they performed graceful circles under shimmering solar rays. Cousins of the sharks, these mammoth creatures are dramatic to behold, and sighting them convinced us all the more of the biological health of the island's waters.

During the night, Nai'a raised anchor and sailed onward to the large island of Gau (pronounced Now). Here, the local Fijians have overfished beche-de-mer and lobster almost to extirpation. Richard Grigg has visited Fiji and gave me his impression: "In general, Fijian reefs undergo enormous change; bleaching is common, but so is recovery. Overall, based on personal observations, I would say their worst problem is overfishing."[77]

But here also awaited one of the most spectacular and "fishy" dives in the world. The skipper, Ravai, took us through a coral pass with great care the next morning. At the dive preview, the divemaster, Rusi, explained our plan.

As ebb tide occurs in the lagoon, silt- and sediment-laden waters exit, but through another pass. An anomalous ebb current from the open sea is then forced in via Nigali Pass, the break in the atoll chain where we are now anchored. The dive, on chalkboard, anyway, appeared simple: Jump in, get down to 100 or 120 feet, ride the current in and up. And be nice to the sharks.

Moments later, the familiar warm water of the South Seas caressed me. Deep into a natural canyon I plunged with the others, waiting to feel the current. A warm, liquid breeze grabbed me and took me on a whirlwind ride.

Like monsters popping up in a funhouse tunnel, the sharks appeared and flashed by, some close enough to touch. But these were not fake apparitions—these were the real thing. Facing into the current, scanning the inflow for a free meal from the open sea, swam one, two, four, eight gray reef sharks, several blacktips, and more whitetip reefs than I could number. It was, however, the gray reef, a 6–10-foot-long animal, that demanded the most respect. A territorial shark, this creature will let you know when it disagrees with your presence by arching its back and pointing downward with pectoral fins. Although fatal attacks are rare, gray reefs have been known to administer a single, nasty warning bite. But these females seemed relaxed, oblivious to the bubbling creatures that joined them.

Carried like coral eggs by the current, we shot by dozens of sharks. I noticed one on the sea floor, motionless, sleeping. I swooped in for a closer look, but it awakened and moved on.

On the canyon walls, meanwhile, were soft corals. Red, purple, orange, pink—the usual colors, but bathed in the clear rush of water, they seemed magnified, intensified, saturated with hue and pigment. Between the exhilaration of the current, the sharks, and the rainbowlike soft corals, it was hard for me to imagine anything more from this dive, but the finale, too, held a surprise.

The push of lucid, deep-ocean water from beyond the reef petered out at 30 feet in a warm, sun-drenched shallows. On the bottom was an enormous, golden-brown cauliflower coral colony, some 50 feet in width, much of it covered with yellow fire coral. Corals reproduce sexually in the great timed spawns that defeat reef predators with abundance; once they have settled into the sessile state in their permanent limestone dwellings, they use fission-style asexual reproduction or budding. Each animal in the cauliflower possessed identical genes, and so the colony represented millions of copies of a single creature and hundreds of years of growth. Darting over it were angelfish, parrotfish, anthias, and a host of wrasse, damselfish, and other creatures that captured the eye but defied identification. Their home was the grandmother of all corals.

Nigali Pass: One of the most beautiful, thrilling, underwater locales on the planet.

That night, we went ashore for a visit to a village on Gau, where we renewed acquaintances with the chief who controlled the *qoliqoli*. It was high tide when we took a skiff to the island, and we walked across a tidal plain of deep mud perforated with clam siphon holes. In the village it was raining, but it was a warm, pleasant rain, and we were greeted by smiling faces. The local people, influenced heavily by missionaries, were dressed conservatively: the women wore ankle-length skirts, the men, shirts and long pants. We sat cross-legged on reed mats in a thatched long house, where we began the kava ceremony. In a giant basin in the center of the room, water was poured over kava roots and steeped into a thin tea.

After a long, opaque introduction in Fijian, the chief clapped his hands and offered a bowl of kava to Rusi, our leader. Clapping his hands in turn, Rusi took and drained the bowl, delivering a long, sonorous response, praising the island and its rich and varied waters.

A smiling young man held the bowl out to me. I, too, clapped, then received and raised the heavy hardwood to my lips. The tea tasted something like thin dishwater, numbing the tongue slightly and leaving a strange, not unpleasant, aftertaste. I finished my drink manfully and blessed the islanders for letting us share the magic of their ocean. For some 20 minutes the bowl made rounds, each person speaking, ignoring language barriers. Then, without warning, everyone jumped to their feet and a cassette player released a slow, Fijian song, something like Hawaiian music but even more gentle, if that can be imagined.

Now young ladies in ones and twos were asking men to dance. Two approached me, and knowing full well that world peace depended on it, I accepted. For an hour this went on, partners changing, everyone smiling and dancing arm in arm, girls in their long skirts and men in their long pants, dive explorers from America and local Fijians, no one left out, everybody delighting in the mix of cultures and people.

Dance over, we departed into darkness and soft tropical rain. The tide had dropped, and we skittered in pain over the reef, one agonizing step at a time, stepping on the living coral we have come to know so well, some of us in bare feet. It was not a pretty sight. One hundred yards out, we finally reached the anchored skiff. Back on *Nai'a*, we poured hydrogen peroxide on our foot wounds, reflecting on the night, on the razor blade feel of invertebrates on skin, and on the warmth of the Fijians.

Late that evening Peni, the sailor, took a few of us for a night dive. The rain was gone, and as the skiff slid into the dark lagoon, the stars burned with unusual intensity. The air, freshened by southeast trades from oceans south of Tahiti, carried exotic land smells of breadfruit and frangipani; it flowed clean and clear, unblemished by the smog and bustle of mankind. The Milky Way draped across the sky, a sparkling diamond necklace strung over the heavens. I looked for familiar constellations, Orion, perhaps, but recognized only a group of five bright stars: the Southern Cross.

After checking gear, three of us slipped into the water. Night dives require special courage—during the wee hours the gray reef shark transforms from Dr. Jekyll into Mr. Hyde. We felt the need, however, to see the corals during their most active time.

At 10 meters, the reef looked familiar, but different. Gone were the schools of gaudy fish, the anthias, the angelfish. A lone parrotfish had spun a gauzy cocoon and was sleeping in a coralline nook. Squirrelfish were out

LIONFISH, FIJI *"In the dark of night, it was invisible to its prey."*

and about, the reason for their large, light-catching eyes now apparent. An octopus danced along the reef with dancing limbs, colors changing with each step of its ballet to blend into the mosaic.

The soft corals reached out into the dark water with seductive, extended tentacles. The hard corals, too, sprouted uncountable millions of small white flowers. It was feeding time for the cnidarians.

I found an interesting feather star, also called a crinoid, a delicate echinoderm with 20 or 30 arms, each possessing numerous, fine side branches called pinnules. Each pinnule is coated with a sticky substance that helps the crinoid catch plankton and bits of organic matter, food that is then conveyed by cilial hairs to a central mouth.[78] Crinoids are gaudily dressed in brilliant pigments—this one was covered in horizontal white and green stripes with long red lines running down each arm. They possess skin toxins and, like many toxic creatures in the animal kingdom, have evolved their bold patterns to serve as a warning to foolish predators. The unusual thing about this one: it was wrapped around a red and green *Dendronephthya*. Odd, I thought. Perhaps the coralline chemical this bougainvillea-of-the-sea used to keep away intruders has failed. Or, perhaps, the crinoid somehow developed an antidote.

A red lionfish caught my eye. Under the light of my flash its red, orange, and white stripes seemed improbably garish, but in the dark of night, it was invisible to its prey. Long red-and-white striped spines loaded with poison warned predators to keep a safe distance. Watching the animal as it moved slowly over the coral, I followed it with just the edge of the light beam. A small cardinalfish wandered too near, and in a blindingly fast motion, the lionfish darted forward and inhaled its unlucky victim.

After a long hour at 30 feet, I surfaced. One hundred yards distant, Peni and the small light on the skiff bobbed in and out of sight through the waves. For a moment I put out my waterproof torch. The sea around me shimmered with glowing phytoplankton, the sky above afire with distant, ancient galaxies undimmed by incandescent illumination.

Something nudged my wet-suit-covered leg. After a minute, my heartbeat slowed, my eyes accommodated, and the cause became visible. Small squid surrounded me, darting, feeding, glowing like their prey, voracious. Perhaps these were vampire squid of the genus *Vampyroteuthis*, members of an ancestral yet newly discovered species endemic to Fiji that come up from the depths at night to feed. Perhaps they were related to *Euprymna scolopes*, a squid endemic to Hawaii that possesses luminous bacteria symbionts.[79] I should have been terrified, lying there on the surface in the dark, strange creatures bumping into me.

But for reasons hard to explain, perhaps the high of diving, perhaps the thrill of floating in this warm, primordial soup of life, my state of mind could only be described as ecstatic.

Five years after my visit to Fiji, marine filmmaker and photographer Howard Hall spent hundreds of hours diving in Fijian waters with the Nai'a. Although he saw and experienced many wonderful things, Hall noted the following changes at one of the dive sites that had been, for us, pristine and magnificent:

> "The coral reef surrounding the lagoon is essentially dead," he said. "Something terrible happened here. . . . There are almost no living hard corals on the reef. Rob and Cat (co-owners of Nai'a) say that this reef was alive and vibrant only two years ago."[80]

CHAPTER SIX

Full fathom five thy father lies;

Of his bones are coral made;

Those are pearls that were his eyes;

Nothing of him that doth fade,

But doth suffer a sea change

Into something rich and strange . . .

—WILLIAM SHAKESPEARE, *The Tempest*

Of His Bones Are Coral Made

Marine Biodiversity and Diving in the Bismarck Sea

After cutting my teeth on Fijian coral, I was ready to hit the nexus of marine biodiversity, New Guinea. Before leaving, I read the stories, Peter Matthiessen's first-hand observations of ritualized warfare, books by Jared Diamond on tribal use of upland rain forest flora and fauna, and the story of the revenge killing of the young Rockefeller heir—he had the misfortune to be the first foreigner to appear in a remote valley just after another stranger murdered a tribesman there. By the time my trip began my excitement was at a fever pitch. I was not to be disappointed. But my adventures were more in the realm of biology than anthropology.

PAPUA NEW GUINEA, 1990s

We were zipping in a skiff to the dive boat *Febrina* from the dock at Kavieng, New Ireland, on the final leg of a marathon voyage. Alan Raabe, our sun-baked, slightly mad Aussie skipper, squinted through the midday equatorial sun at underwater film maestro Chuck Nicklin.

"The diving, mate. The diving has been incredible—that is, when the current is right. When the current is wrong, it's no bloody good, and I won't deny it. But we've got it wired, mate. Gorilla diving, that's what we've been doing, gorilla diving. An early morning deepey at 6:30, breakfast, and two more dives before lunch. An afternoon nap while we move, another dive, a bit of tucker, a night dive, and dinner. After that, digger, we can take a nap and do it again."

Nicklin laughed, his blue eyes sparkling. He looked to be in his 50s, but he'd been *diving* for 50 years. This was his sixth trip with Alan Raabe, and he knew Alan could pull off whatever he promised. Chuck had spent two months filming beneath six feet of ice in Antarctica; he had been one of the first to dive the 240-foot-deep wreck of the *Andrea Doria* in murky, cold water with howling currents. Gorilla diving—Chuck and Alan's private slang for gnarly, dangerous, difficult diving—was nothing new to him.

The rest of us listened in jet-lagged stupor. But after a couple of tune-up dives, a banquet dinner, some good Adelaide cabernet, and a good night's sleep, we were ready to rock at a quarter to six when the *Febrina's* motors revved the morning wakeup.

The morning Alan was different from the midday Alan. Bleary eyed, he stared dully at a passenger firing questions about the dive spot. "Ah, just go down the mooring line, mate, over the wall, and turn right at the sea fan," he muttered, working his way fore to the cockpit. The first mate and divemaster, Francis, an eloquent New Guinean with a crisp Aussie accent, filled us in on the dive site details, drew a map, answered dumb questions, the works.

We hit the warm water and worked hard into the current. Hand over hand we struggled, down to the reef, over the edge of the invertebrate-carpeted wall. Like wind tearing at apes brachiating through a rain forest, the incoming tide from the Solomon Sea gusted and blustered and threatened to wash us away. Down, down, down, we pushed. At last the current relaxed its grip. The visibility was limitless. The mother of all sea fans sat at about 90 feet, festooned with a dozen crinoids, each a different color. Swarms of reef fish darted in and out of the wall mosaic. A big, blue-finned travally cruised past. Turning right, we watched a dense shoal of jacks school by, unperturbed at our presence.

Looking for rubble at the wall's base, a place to melt in and wait for other, open-water pelagic fish, I set my knee set down with care in what appeared to be dead coralline debris. Something wiggled out from underneath. Stonefish. My heart skipped a beat, but there was no screaming agony, no sting at all. One of the most toxic denizens of the deep, stonefish are legendary for killing an unwary diver—like myself—quickly and painfully. *Synancia hor-*

rida, over a foot long, bears the perfect reef camouflage, even down to the bits of algae hanging from the poison-bearing spines. After my initial glimpse of the living rock, I froze, tried to find its new location, could not, and was only able to thank Poseidon for sparing me.

A squadron of chevron barracuda, maybe two, three dozen, distracted me from my stonefish encounter as they cruised by almost within reach. Unlike the lonely giant barracuda, chevrons favor schools, the bigger the better. They kept tight formation as they whirled around me, pectoral fins almost touching, wingtip to wingtip, Blue Angels of the sea.

To my surprise, Alan appeared; it is a rare dive he will miss. He pointed into the blue, and we saw a silvertip shark, no, a pair of silvertips. They, too, gave us a fly-by. Like most requiem sharks, a group that includes such maneaters as tigers, bulls, and oceanic whitetips, silvertips are serious sharks with thick, powerful bodies and substantial jaws.[1] Chuck filmed them a sea fan or two away. Somebody left the wall for a closer look, and the sharks disappeared.

Back on *Febrina*, Alan told me that he's injected stonefish wounds in the past with the local anesthetic lidocaine.

"It's the agony that kills most people," he said. "You can lose your ruddy mind from the pain. It's hard to surface safely from 30 meters when your bloody leg feels like it's bein' fried in bacon fat."[2]

We ate and dived, dived and ate. Rarely did we stop more than once at a site: Planet Channel, Big Fish Reef, Barrons Strait, Albatross Channel, Leslie's Knob. Decompressing, looking up from the anchor line, we saw silhouettes of outrigger canoes tied to *Febrina*, locals peddling fresh fruit and vegetables. We logged five, then six dives a day. We got into the rhythm. Things started to blur.

One morning I was all set to go for an early morning deepey, ready to hit the water. Film in the camera, mask, fins, weight belt, all systems were "go." I put my hand over my mask, preparing to jump, when Francis and the crew burst into hysterical laughter.

"Your tank, mate, your tank. You forgot your tank!"

Another day, trying to eke out my last few pounds of air in the shallows, I drifted past *Febrina* and needed to swim, against strong current, a hundred yards or so back to the boat.

"Be careful, I promised your wife I'd bring you home," chided Nicklin. Two dives later, he did the same thing.

"Be careful, I promised your wife I'd bring you home," I rejoined.

Current diving is no joke. There was, for example, the Louisiana couple left behind on the Great Barrier Reef by an Aussie dive-cattle-boat. They'd

REEF SEASCAPE, PAPUA NEW GUINEA *"The mother of all sea fans sat at about 90 feet, festooned with a dozen crinoids. . . ."*

drifted off some distance in the current and, at a cursory role call, the crew failed to note their absence from the large party of divers. A search begun four days later never found their bodies, although it did produce a single fin, dive hood, buoyancy compensator, and tank. Also found: a dive slate with a help plea written on it.[3] It's a big ocean, the Pacific.

Wimps that we were, four or five days of this proved tiring.

"No more gorilla diving, Alan," said Chuck. "We're ready for someplace easy and pretty." And so we motored across the Bismarck Sea, leaving the wilds of New Ireland to head south to Walindi Plantation, Kimbe Island, and the calmer wilds of New Britain. The water was like glass. Flying fish scattered from the bow. And, although we all used dive computers to avoid the bends, there was no doubt that nitrogen bubbled through our veins.

Somewhere in the middle of the Bismarck, just off the smoking volcano at Rabuul, the water stood two miles deep. A pod of spinner dolphins, Alan's private troupe, appeared as if on command.

Stenella longirostris, those most gregarious of blue-water mammals, are the dolphins that, along with their cousins the spotted dolphins, have died in the thousands in the eastern Pacific in tuna seine nets. Boisterous, athletic animals, they delight in riding bow waves and in shooting high into the air, twirling in 360-degree spins.

"Everybody in!" Alan called, as he proceeded to drive the boat in an ever-narrowing circle around us, a pod of finned snorkelers. Sunlight shimmered down to the abyss. We could feel, deep in our bodies, high-pitched, whistling sound waves as the dolphins sent echoes our way. Perhaps they were looking to see if our stomachs were full, or if any of us were pregnant. Marine mammal scientists have shown that bottlenose dolphins, at least, can probably elucidate such things with their sonar.[4] The spinners enjoyed the bow wave for a quarter of an hour, keeping a wary distance from us humans; then they were gone.

"I'm worried about Chuckleberry," said Alan. I agreed. Nicklin did look a bit peaked. We checked his temp—103.5 Fahrenheit. Too much. We'd not seen a mosquito the whole trip, well, maybe a couple on a village shore visit. Too early for malaria—or was it? Too much fever. Raabe started Nicklin on oral high-dose quinine, then held forth on his dislike of prophylactic mefloquine.

"Ten years of nonstop diving, and only five blokes I've sent for decompression to Australia. It's some aircraft ride to Darwin, too, 50 feet off the water for $50,000. Not a bloody one of the five had the bends—the problem is that mefloquine. It gives 'em the same symptoms: headache, girdle pain, focal findings. We get stuck and have to air-vac 'em. Read the package insert, 'do not use while operating heavy machinery.' Well, now, isn't that cute? Don't operate machinery—how about diving down to five atmospheres? And, the worst thing about mefloquine—you can get malaria on the damned stuff."

Raabe convinced us to take doxycyline and chloroquine. He nursed Nicklin, but progress was slow. Then I saw the infected cut on the cinematographer's shin. Inflamed, red skin surrounded the laceration and tracked up to the knee. This was not malaria, but cellulitis.

"No problem, mate, I've got just the stuff!" Ignoring my ribbing about practicing medicine without a license, the skipper replaced the quinine with horse-size penicillin shots and oral cephalosporin antibiotics. Soon Chuck was back in the water, only missing 24 hours of diving from his brush with blood poisoning.

The next day we found a sandy plain between bommies (coral heads), a bland tennis-court-sized area covered with rubble. Alan took me down and motioned to a tiny pair of creatures. A goby, resplendent with bulging black and white eyes and orange body spots, a fish the size of my fingernail, lay at the opening of a small hole in the sand. Next to it, an industrious shrimp, pink, with pale yellow extremities and white body stripes, worked valiantly at pushing great boulders (for its size, anyway) up and out of the cave. I glanced around the plain and noticed similar pairings every foot or so. I ventured too close, and the goby wheeled and dived into the hole, followed by the shrimp. Only later did they reappear, first the goby, then the crustacean bulldozer.

This was mutualism at its finest. The sharp-sighted goby served as a lookout, the blind shrimp as the contractor. Each pair of symbionts occupied a duplex cave equidistant from the others. There was cooperation here, but also competition; territoriality played a role in this community as well as mutualism.

Symbiosis is the general association of members of two distinct species. It is an umbrella term that includes three kinds of relationships: mutualism, where both species benefit from the interaction, commensalism, where one species benefits and the other is unaffected, and parasitism, where one gains and the other loses. Mutualism occurs, for example, among corals and zooxanthellae, as well as in these gobies and shrimps. An example of commensalism would be the association of pilot fish with oceanic whitetip sharks[5]— the little fish don't give anything to their host, but their eating of scraps from the big animal's messy meals doesn't really harm the shark. Parasitism would include the ever-present barnacles and remoras that plague whales, mantas, and other large creatures, as well as the frequent internal worms found in many marine vertebrates.

Just above the goby/shrimp plain, perched on a bommie, an anemone, a crimson and green cnidarian, waved tentacles loaded with poisonous nematocysts in the current. A bold anemone fish, one of many species of the genus *Amphiprion* found in New Guinea, this one orange with white stripes, swam in and out of the forest of waving arms, oblivious to the stingers. Biologists have found that these fish slowly acclimatize themselves to the nematocysts, coating themselves with anemone mucus.[6] Once their slime coat is complete, the anemone perceives them as self, and the nematocycts fail to discharge toxin. By both their bold markings and their behavior, the orange clownfish attract potential predators and turn them into anemone prey, some morsels of which they will share.

A meter distant from the anemone lay the blue-green mantle of an open giant clam, one of six species of the genus *Tridacna*. Most bivalve mollusks orient their hinge toward the water, their mantles hidden, and their muscular foot embedded within the substrate of the reef. Not the giant clam. The exuberant colors seen on the soft tissue layer are pigments that absorb excess light, protecting the clam but allowing enough light to enter. Photosynthetic zooxanthellae live within the clam, leading to both the unusual posture of the animal and the pigments.[7] Clams with zooxanthellae have flourished, and natural selection on the crowded, competitive reef yields yet another example of the "addiction" of mutualistic symbiosis.

On the next dive, Alan took me to about 60 feet, where a crimson cuttlefish hovered, colors changing to green, then flashing back to red, then back to green. A cephalopod, brainy cousin of the squid and octopus, this creature had chromatophores in its skin that allowed it this chameleonlike display. Unlike chameleons, though, who change colors more slowly via the autonomic nervous system, the cuttlefish can change appearance in the blink of an eye, in this case an eye that is W-shaped, perhaps to enable it to see backward and forward at the same time.[8]

The key to cuttlefish colors lies in specialized muscles and cells. Chromatophores, cells filled with red, yellow, black, and orange pigments, are pulled to the skin's surface by specialized papilla muscles in response to messages from the complex cuttlefish brain. Another type of cell, the iridophore, made of layers of chitin that bend light, gives rise to shimmering blues, greens, and silvers. And leucophores, flat, branched cells, reflect all types of light.[9]

Sharp-eyed hunters, cuttlefish can detect polarized light that enables them to find concealed or even transparent prey. Using their chromatophores, they camouflage themselves to avoid large marine carnivores by matching coloration with the seafloor.[10] Color changes also happen when the cephalopod is disturbed or feels threatened. This hovering cuttlefish was, perhaps, signaling to us its indecision, its inability to fathom whether the two bubbling creatures watching it were friend or foe.

Later we made a night dive. I found a crab at 20 feet that bore no resemblance to any crab I've ever seen. The animal stared at me from a crevice in the coral, crimson body glowing in the light of my torch, multiple eyes sizing me up. Topside, poring over the *Febrina*'s library, I discovered a photo of the creature in Colin and Arneson's *Tropical Pacific Invertebrates*.[11] The caption: Unidentified Crab.

The next day, a large pufferfish guarded the mooring line, modeling for us, daring us to touch his poisonous essence, to test a finger in his formidable incisors. Although clearly of the genus *Arothon*, after another futile search in the library, I couldn't identify the species.

As for sessile invertebrates, we discovered the same problem, only worse. Soft corals of every hue and description, sea squirts, fans, anemones—for every one that was named, for every species pinned down, there seemed to be another with an "unidentified" caption. Just as in a rain forest, rare species were common, and common species were few.

Through the shifting climes of the geological ages, millennia of glacial ice, then heat, then winter, the water in New Guinea has remained tropical, the fight for survival has had stable conditions, and the pressure to change, to speciate, to develop and find new niches has been, and is, tremendous.[12] Lying before our eyes was the result, arguably, the greatest biodiversity of any aquatic realm.

That, anyhow, is one theory. Another theory, and the two are by no means mutually exclusive, is that as planetary ice ages came, the rich tropical underwater life in the Indo-Pacific region contracted into small, isolated seas of warmth and comfort as waters dropped. These pockets of ocean were analogous to oceanic islands like Hawaii and the Galapagos, with their endemic species, or to refugia forming during cool periods in terrestrial tropical regions such as the Amazon basin. They allowed the marooned members of a species, such as my unidentifiable crab, to drift, as in genetic drift, and thus become a distinct population.

"The passing ice ages," said Richard Grigg, the Hawaiian oceanographer, "lowered sea levels, isolating small individual seas that went their own evolutionary ways and produced great diversification."[13]

As conditions became warmer and these islands merged into a tropical, oceanic continent, so goes the theory, our crab and his island mates could rejoin their long-lost relatives but no longer reproduce with them. And voilà! By definition they became a new species.

Ivan Valiela, an ecologist at Woods Hole in Massachusetts, lists a total of six theories explaining species diversity, some of which are variations on the two mentioned above.[14] There is the time hypothesis, that older communities are more diverse. There is the spatial heterogeneity hypothesis, that the more complex or higher the relief of an environment, the more diversity. There is the competition hypothesis, that more and more species fill narrower and narrower niches. There is the environmental stability hypothesis, that there will be fewer extinctions with steady nutrients, salinity, oxygen, and so on. There is the productivity hypothesis, that the greater the fixation of carbon, the greater the resources and the more species. Finally, there is the predation hypothesis, that "top-down" pressure lowers competition between prey species and increases diversity.

Valiela notes that most of these theories, taken alone, falter. He does point out that often a specific predator or disturbance may keep any one organism from taking over an ecosystem (recall that Jamaican sea urchin described in chapter 5). This type of stochastic challenge promotes diversity best if it is intermediate in effect. Thus, boulders in California intertidal zones that are intermediate in size and moved about some, but not constantly, by surf, have more complex communities than do giant, stationary boulders or small rocks.[15]

Pollution, though, almost invariably decreases numbers of species. Studies with plankton, such as diatoms, and benthic fauna, including worms, are clear on that point.[16] Human disturbances, evidently, are often more than intermediate in effect.

Whatever the cause, from Malaysia to northern Australia and up to the South Philippines, there is no greater biodiversity of aquatic creatures on the planet.[17] New Guinea lies near the center of this Fertile Triangle. Here the wide range of phyla, those broad groupings of basic body plans, is greater than that found in the tropical rain forests, even given their botanical, microbial, vertebrate, and, especially, arthropod diversity. All of the 36 known phyla taxonomists use are represented in this marine storehouse of species: Cnidaria (soft and hard corals, anemones), Chordata (fish, mammals, reptiles), Arthropoda (crabs, lobsters), Mollusca (mollusks, octopi, squid, seashell-bearing gastropods), Porifera (sponges), Platyhelmintha (flatworms), Annelida (Christmas tree worms), Echinoderms (sea stars, brittle stars, feather stars)—the list goes on and on. Upon a single canyon wall a sharp-eyed biologist or naturalist might spy dozens of these phyla.

After species diversity and diversity by phylum, there is a third type of diversity, diversity at the genetic level within a given species. This is the type of diversity that makes rescue of endangered mammals so difficult, for example, when numbers fall to the genetic bottleneck of 50 or fewer individuals (the 50/500 rule discussed in chapter 4). Studying individual variation in a place like underwater New Guinea or, for that matter, in a tropical rain forest is difficult, for, once again, in tropical hotspots of diversity the rare is common and the common few. Finding 50 of anything in these New Guinea seas was difficult, unless one considered the swarms of fusiliers that came from nowhere to cloud our underwater seascape and then leave, their blue bodies and gold tails flashing in the current, or the similar shoals of barracuda, jacks, and butterflyfishes.

British marine biologists Callum Roberts and Julie Hawkins have studied size ranges of coral reef fishes in detail.[18] Their findings shed light both on why wide diversity is found on coral reefs and why members of an individual species may be few.

From a sample of 1,677 species, 9.2% were restricted to an area of less than 50,000 km^2, a size often used to classify terrestrial species as restricted. Twenty-four percent of fish species had limited ranges less than 800,000 km^2 (roughly the size of the Great Barrier Reef, or two-thirds the length of the Red Sea). They also found 41% of 169 black corals, 28% of cone shell species, and 11% of stony corals to have restricted ranges by this second criterion.

Roberts and Hawkins have also found that reef fish with their median restricted range of 150,000 km^2 had suitable habitat, on average, of only 500 km^2. This size is about the same as a circular coral reef with a diameter of 25 km.

In a sense, then, even without an ongoing ice age, a significant percentage of the biota in coral reef communities, although connected by deep water and currents, remains insular. Many species maintain small ranges and hence have more opportunity for genetic drift and speciation. By the same token, because ranges are small, overall numbers may also be limited. By extension, and by the principles of island biogeography, these creatures may then be vulnerable. The kicker in all this, of course, is the work of coral biologist J.E.N. Veron (see chapter 5), who makes clear that current strength is a powerful factor in how big "insular" areas of ocean really are.

Now, there are those who insist that only biodiversity will save life on Earth, should a massive meteorite strike the planet like the mile-in-diameter object that struck the Yucatan 65 million years ago and ended the reign of the dinosaurs. They say this because complex ecosystems have been thought by Robert MacArthur[19] and other pioneering ecologists to be more robust and better able to withstand violent perturbations than are simple ones. The idea seemed intuitive to MacArthur, but scientists have since cast doubts on his theory.[20] A spate of theoretical publications[21] in the 1970s showed that stability was reduced in diverse systems. This sort of thinking ran as follows: as a system gets more and more complex, with more and more complicated parts, destroying any one portion will be more likely to break the whole thing.

But an answering salvo of publications appeared, showing that changing the models made complexity increase stability.[22] Much of the debate revolved around the difficulty of defining stability or its opposite, perturbation. Woods Hole marine ecologist Ivan Valiela pointed out that it is difficult to formulate testable hypotheses because of "the ambiguity of the concept and the often tautological nature of discussions of stability."[23] As a consequence, for many years there was little experimental work done, and, as one scientific comic wrote, "The marked instability of attitudes regarding diversity-stability relationships in ecosystems arises from a low diversity of empirical tests of the hypothesis."[24]

Nevertheless, there are some field studies. Removal of sea otters from kelp forest ecosystems such as California's did not result in immediate overgrowth of sea urchins and loss of kelp, because of redundant species that either eat or compete with sea urchins, such as sheephead, lobsters, and abalone.[25] In Alaska's more simplified Aleutian kelp ecosystem, a similar loss of sea otters from killer whale predation resulted in rapid devastation of the kelp.[26] Likewise, a 15-year terrestrial field project at Cedar Creek by scientists at the University of Minnesota implied that plant ecosystems diverse in species are more stable and productive.[27]

In recent years, more literature has appeared,[28] and the debate over biodiversity and stability has intensified.[29] Led by ecologists David Tilman of the University of Minnesota and John Lawton of Imperial College, Britain, those in favor of the hypothesis distributed a pamphlet through the Ecological Society of America (ESA) to members of Congress touting the importance of biodiversity. The pamphlet recommended the "prudent strategy of preserving biodiversity in order to safe-guard ecosystem processes vital to society."[30]

Believing the experimental evidence to be premature at this stage, critics such as Michael Huston of the Oak Ridge National Laboratory[31] and Phil Grime of the University of Sheffield in Britain fumed, firing a commentary back to the ESA calling the research "biased," "politically motivated," a "propaganda document" that promotes "unjustifiable actions based on a house of cards."[32]

Although these comments may seem tame compared with, say, what one might encounter in sports or politics, for the staid world of academic ecology they were incendiary. As with climate studies, experiments involving the complexities of the biodiversity/stability hypothesis are difficult to construct and easy to find fault with. Subtle ecological concepts are central to the arguments. For example, there is the "sampling effect"—the higher production seen in multispecies environments may be from a few highly productive species. To overcome this effect, "overyielding" must be demonstrated—productivity of the diverse system must be shown to be greater than that of the sole most productive species grown in isolation.

As with disputes over the greenhouse effect and global warming, the debate on whether the data on biodiversity are robust enough to inform public policy may continue for some time. Because changing humanity's present course, regarding either carbon emissions or intrusions on nature, has huge economic implications, the stakes are high—and the rhetoric increasingly heated.

In addition to advocates of the complexity/stability hypothesis, there are those who value biological complexity because they feel it is vital for mankind to have the ability to manufacture drugs and chemicals from a wide variety of rain forest plants and tropical reef creatures. Still others will say that biodiversity is vital because we humans depend on the existence of other species for our own survival.

I would lay claim to the idea, though, that maintaining a diverse world genome, whether by species, or by phylum, or through individual variety, is a valuable thing of and by itself. You can have boring, monochrome simplicity, or you can have stunning, kaleidoscopic complexity. For me, the choice is simple. *Vive la différence!*

Thirty-eight dives and nine days later, we docked at Walindi. Alan strode around, his arms up in the air. Verdant vegetation enveloped him, casting a green glow to his hide.

"God, I love this place," he cried, to no one in particular.

Glad as he was to be on terra firma once again, Alan still seemed more aquatic than terrestrial, lying at the edge of some human genetic bell-shaped curve, part of a DNA drift from the terrestrial center to the marine extreme. Perhaps if any of us lived long enough on a dive boat in the Bismarck Sea, we, too, might evolve into a similar sort of semiaquatic mammal.

In fact, a theory that an amphibious lifestyle did play a role in the evolution of *Homo sapiens* has been knocking around the fringes of cloistered academia for decades. Scientists joke about it, whispering about it at the edges of lecture halls, unwilling, for the most part, to stake a career on pursuing it, but, until the fossil record reveals more information, the idea refuses to die. German biologist Max Westenhofer in 1942[33] and British marine biologist Sir Alistair Hardy in 1960[34] suggested, to explain some curious quirks of human anatomy and physiology, that early humans led a semiaquatic existence. Welsh writer-researcher Elaine Morgan then developed the theory in several books, including the 1999 *Aquatic Ape Hypothesis*.[35]

Unlike any other primate, we are essentially hairless, except for our heads and genital regions. Unlike any other primate, we possess a well-developed layer of subcutaneous fat. Unlike any other primate, we are bipedal and walk upright. These may have helped our ancestors to adapt to the then marshy swampland regions of Ethiopia, where, some five million years ago, advancing seas encroached upon what is now the Afar Triangle. In this region, the northeast Horn of Africa, three rift systems converge, seven active volcanoes exist, and the Miocene geological record shows periodic dry salt layers, from dessication, and shale layers, from flooding. Morgan makes the case that, even as the Mediterranean broke through the Bosporus into the Black Sea 8,000 years ago, seawater may have flooded into Afar from the Strait of Bab el Mandeb.[35]

This kind of sudden event, a punctuation in the Miocene equilibrium, may have been the circumstance that led us to become hairless, upright, and full of subcutaneous fat, or so goes the theory. In shallow, warm seas, mollusks and other easy-to-find marine nutrients may have been gathered by bipedal, wading and swimming *Homo*s, and some of Africa's fierce predators could be avoided, especially lions and hyenas.

Hairlessness has been thought to increase swimming speed—hence the swim racer body shave—and blubber helps preserve heat. Both are common in aquatic or semiaquatic animals, not just in dolphins and whales, but in elephants and hippos, too. Perhaps these things evolved in humans, according to Morgan, Hardy, and Westenhofer, to handle an existence half in water, half on land.

Another quirk the hypothesis explains is our possession of a descended larynx, something other apes do not have (their larynx rides high). We own the same sort of larynx that sea lions and walruses have; it has the downside of allowing food or liquid to go into our windpipe and lungs but the upside of enabling us to take quick, deep breaths, a useful tool for vigorous swimming. Natural selection might favor such a trait in an aquatic environment. That it also enables complex vocalizations was, say theorists, a lucky byproduct. (Others suggest that language and improved communication were the sole driving forces for the selection of descent of the larynx.)[36]

Coupled with the human ability to breath-hold at will, a trait essential for swimming—something that chimps and gorillas cannot be trained to do—

the descended larynx may, or so goes the theory, have paved the way for our development of language. With language and the tool-holding upright posture permitting the same sort of rapid positive feedback loop that led dolphins to grow large auditory lobes, our brain capacity increased.

Morgan presents additional clues supporting the theory. The diving reflex, a marked slowing of the heart rate caused by immersion in cold water, is more pronounced in *Homo sapiens* than in the great apes. Our teeth differ, too, and seem to aquatic ape theorists to be better adapted to soft marine foods than for tearing flesh and chomping on hard vegetation. Sometime near our evolving away from chimpanzees and gorillas, *Homo* lost the large canines that these animals possess.

Of course, the hypothesis fails to tell us why sea otters, who are also semiaquatic and have similar tooth structure to humans, rely on fur for warmth and not blubber. Polar bears, although they have blubber, also have hair and swim very well indeed. It fails to state why sea lions, seals, and other pinnipeds with fatty layers also have fur. Hairlessness is no longer considered important for swimming speed; in fact, scientists studying hydrodynamics know that subtle imperfections on a surface increase laminar flow.[37] Shark skin, for example, has denticles. Racing yachts no longer have perfectly smooth hulls. The theory also fails to tell us how those curly, wading humanoids avoided the crocodiles and hippopotami that lived then and kill so many Africans today.

But if a period of semiaquatic existence did lead to our split from the other apes, it would not be the first time in evolutionary history that mammals have reentered the sea. Cetaceans, pinnipeds, dugongs, and manatees all evolved from land-based ancestors to become completely aquatic. Semiaquatic mammals include polar bears, beavers, and otters. Marine biologist Richard Ellis, research associate at New York's American Museum of Natural History, points all this out in a discussion of the aquatic ape theory in his book *Aquagenesis*.[38] He feels the concept, although not accepted by conservative anthropologists, explains the existing fossil record better than the old savannah hypothesis, the idea that, roughly stated, ancient humans assumed the upright posture, lost body hair, and started talking upon descending from the trees and moving onto Africa's grasslands.

Phillip Tobias, a South African anthropologist, agrees, writing, "Elaine Morgan, in her remarkable book, *The Scars of Evolution*, came to the same conclusion that we had reached from quite different lines of evidence: the old Savannah Hypothesis was not tenable."[39]

Hairlessness, bipedal posture, the descended larynx, and the presence of subcutaneous fat form the cornerstones of the aquatic ape hypothesis. Unfortunately, the fossil record is notoriously weak during the crucial time, around five million years ago. Fossils show only bones and, rarely, feathers. They make detection of hair, cartilage, and fat, to say the least, difficult.

I e-mailed Elaine Morgan in Wales and asked if she thought we could know, roughly, when *Homo* became hairless. She replied, "Nobody can do anything but guess. The [obese] Paleolithic carved figures look hairless but it must have begun much earlier, in my opinion."

Morgan is the first to admit that the aquatic ape theory is a minority view. Only new discoveries in the fossil record will prove or disprove it. Yohannes Haile-Selassie, an anthropologist at the University of California at Berkeley, recently found hominoid (common to both ape and human ancestors) specimens from Ethiopia that dated between 5.2 and 5.8 million years ago.[40] A toe joint suggested upright walking, and surrounding sediment implied a wet, forested environment. If these bones prove to be hominid (belonging to human ancestors), the finding differs from the image of humans leaving the trees to walk upright on a dry savannah.

However, DNA evidence leads most scientists to think that the split between humans and the other apes occurred about one-half million years later[41]; thus these bones may well prove to be pongid (belonging to ape ancestors). Fossil findings similar to these—and clues to environmental conditions in surrounding sediments—from that crucial five-million-years-ago period will ultimately decide whether or not the hypothesis holds water.

What the fossil record does tell us beyond doubt (although still argued by some religious zealots) is that we did evolve from ancestral apes, who did evolve from other terrestrial vertebrates. These pioneering creatures of the land, in turn, evolved from ancient, ancestral amphibians, who evolved from marine vertebrates.

Diane, my wife, has her own theories about human origins. She is willing to accept that I evolved from an ape.

"That's obvious," she says, "but my own ancestors were all people."

Ignoring such objections, it remains safe to say that even if the aquatic ape theory ends up in the permanent dustbin of rejected scientific hypotheses (and it may or may not), there is little doubt that we humans did ultimately evolve from the sea. And whenever I think of people like Alan Raabe or Chuck Nicklin, people who seem more at home underwater than above, those origins come to mind.

For that matter, after spending so much time in the ocean, my own body seems to have changed. There are bony growths narrowing my external ear canals, so that, despite one round of corrective surgery, my ears resemble the closed, internal auditory apparatus of a dolphin. (Sound travels well enough underwater that, for a fully aquatic animal, an open external canal becomes unnecessary.)

Then there is this increasing subcutaneous body fat. My waistline, for example, has increased several inches lately; I've broken down and been buying the next-size-larger blue jeans and swim trunks. There has also been more and more loss of hair, especially above my forehead.

Diane thinks, of course, that I'm just growing old. But I prefer to believe these changes represent a kind of dolphinization process, proof that my roots lie deep in the ocean.

Cosmic sounds, electronic sounds, the music of the spheres shimmer through the soft gurgle

of the sea with the resonance of an echo chamber, and with them soft bell notes and sweet

bat squeaks, froggish bass notes, barks, grunts, whistles, oinks, and elephantine rumbling,

as if the ocean floor had fallen in. No word conveys the eeriness of whale song, tuned by

the ages to a purity beyond refining, a sound that man should hear each morning to remind

him of the morning of the world.

—PETER MATTHIESSEN, *Blue Meridian*

Sea of Giants

Among Humpbacks in Tonga

Fulfilling *for the senses as coral reef communities can be, they still pale before contact with a fellow mammal. Something about meeting large creatures that are like us, yet different, stimulates new and strange emotions and empowers the soul. "Charismatic megafauna," people call them, at times in a negative sort of way, as though we should be ashamed for loving big mammals more than radially symmetric invertebrates. Clearly, at least to my thinking, all the parts of the biotic community are essential and fascinating. But there is no denying that emotions do well up for those same creatures that have become environmental icons—tigers, polar bears, grizzlies, and . . . whales.*

VAVA'U, TONGA, 1990s

We drifted weightless, waiting in blue water. Sunbeams danced into the unfathomable depths; deep basso notes rocketed into soprano sirens and wails, then dived back down to spine-vibrating profundos. The humpbacks were here.

We waited. There was no rush. The water was gin clear. We could have been in outer space. Time slowed, then stopped. Our senses became hyper-acute; sight, hearing, smell, touch, taste—all focused on the moment. Wondering what secrets the abyss held, we hung suspended, and we waited.

Some Aussie sport fishermen had pulled a big marlin to their boat the day before, planning to tag and release, when a six-foot oceanic whitetip shark took two bites, killed the marlin, and made off with a good twenty pounds of fish flesh. We spent long minutes at the wharf inspecting what was left of the billfish. Here, in addition to the whales, there were other denizens of the bottomless blue, citizens of the sea that did not believe in mutualism and cooperation; citizens that were not above eating the flesh of humans.

A lone jellyfish and a school of tiny red fry distracted my attention to the surface. Behind them, as if in slow motion, a large indistinct form glided closer. A female humpback. Her newborn, pale and squid-white, drafted in the current of her pectoral fin. They passed by at right angles, still in slow motion, and, with one slow flick of momma's giant flukes, disappeared. It was the first time I'd seen a whale up close underwater; for days I would relive this watery vision.

We had flown over from Fiji to visit the 170 islands carved of lava, limestone, and coral, 126 of them uninhabited. Tonga lies east of Fiji at 20 degrees latitude south—about one century due yesteryear of Honolulu. Jet planes and scuba diving have not much altered the relaxed Polynesian lifestyle of the Friendly Islands. Although tourism in recent years has been growing, the country today still sees many fewer visitors than does Fiji.

The lack of commercialism makes the islands a special treat to western travelers, mostly yacht sailors and fishermen visiting the northern group of 34 islands at Vava'u (pronounced va-vow). Some sailors fly here to rent and navigate the protected waters between the islands. Others, crossing the Pacific the hard way, make Tonga their first landfall after traveling west from Tahiti. The islands are also becoming known to divers and naturalists. Our party fell into this last category: Greg Ochocki, a tall, intense, bespectacled abstract painter turned nature photographer; Chuck Nicklin, a lean, calm, blue-eyed cinematographer with a host of movie credits; and myself.

Marlin and other pelagic, deep-water fish patrol the outer reaches of the reefs. Taking advantage of this bounty, local fishermen have moored fish aggregation devices, shadow-producing buoys, some miles off Vava'u, a practice done all over the Pacific. Schools of dorado, tuna, and shark gather under them in abundance. Blue-water diving off one of these buoys is a real treat, but oceanic whitetips and the odd tiger shark restrict the activity to the experienced and the brave. There was a buoy only five miles out that we planned to explore, but a big storm blew it away, and we were stuck with reef diving. That, however, was far from a disappointment.

The protected inland waters of Vava'u are pristine, with hard corals, volcanic caves, sea fans, and soft corals untouched by the fins of the masses. Tropical reef fish abound; there are two live aquarium fish exporters on the southern island of Tongatapu,[1] but there are none in Vava'u. Visibility is often 200 feet or more, because of the small land masses and the lack of runoff. The Tonga Trench sits just east of the islands, so one can find coral-studded walls with depths of 180 feet only 30 feet from land, and 1,800 and 18,000-foot depths not too much farther offshore.

There is huge diversity in the enchanting underwater worlds below Vava'u, and we made a point to visit as many as we could. Hunga Magic, a hard coral head, had current-plying jacks and barracuda at 80–100 feet and a red-orange soft coral and fairy-basslet (a small, orange fish) paradise in the shallows. Afternoon sun washed Swallows' Cave with godbeams; numerous swimthroughs and side-branching caverns offered visions of big-eyed soldierfish, black corals, and lobsters. Schools of teira batfish stood guard in the harbor bay over the wreck of an old copra steamer. The invertebrate-encrusted hull, the length of a football field, lay in the eery silence typical of shipwrecks at 90 feet. And, in the wicked current of a site bearing the whimsical name King Neptune's Sea Fan Grotto, an underwater valley was home to hundreds of ancient, scarlet gorgonian sea fans, some measuring 10 feet across.

Wintering humpbacks, though, are what make Tonga special to the discerning traveler, and they are the real reason we came here. Although the southern humpback population is severely depleted from an estimated original population of 120,000, some 10,000 are left.[2] Many of these beautiful, white-bellied humpbacks migrate from their Antarctic feeding grounds north every austral winter to the calm, warm waters of Tonga. Here male singers dive to 10 or 20 fathoms, hold themselves nose down and flukes up, and sing long, complex songs that carry for miles and change in subtle ways from year to year. Here females give birth to calves they nurse with milk that is more than half fat. And here rival males, full of lust and testosterone, square off in epic sea battles.

Little mixing occurs between these whales and their dark-bellied cousins on the other side of the equator. Tongan and Maui humpbacks are separated not only by thousands of miles of Pacific Ocean but also by time. The north–south migrations of the two groups are exactly six months out of synch, precluding, at least most of the time, any chance liaisons at the equator.[3]

Humpbacks share a number of attributes unique to their species. They are among the most acrobatic of large cetaceans, often making somersaults by leaping belly up into a breach, diving back down headfirst, and circling underwater to their original position. They have the largest pectoral fins of any whale (*Megaptera novaeangeliae*, their Latin name, means "large-winged New Englander"). And, although we will not see the behavior here in Tonga, they emit bubbles while spiraling beneath herring and other baitfish in high latitudes; the bubbles entrap the fish, and the whales then rush into the school to capture tons of prey within their baleen.

But krill, a large shrimplike creature about two and one-half inches long, *Euphausia superba*, makes up the bulk of the southern humpback diet, as it does for other baleen whales, such as the blue, the sei, the fin, and the minke. Primarily a herbivore, krill (Norwegian for "whale food") feeds on diatoms and other phytoplankton that bloom in nutrient-rich Antarctic waters during the long days of the austral summer. Scientific knowledge of the animal is limited, and estimates of its total biomass vary from 75 million tons (close to the annual total of worldwide human fishing) to 1.35 billion tons.[4] As *r*-selected organisms, krill numbers can expand rapidly should their favorite prey, ice algae, be favored by expanding ice sheets, or should their chief competitor, a jellyfishlike salp, *Salpa thompsoni*, decline.[5] Humpbacks, though, as *K*-selected creatures, are saturation selected and use a "few-large" reproductive strategy.[6] Dependent on krill numbers, they cannot rapidly respond to changes in prey availability.

It is the haunting music, though, of the male humpback singers that is the humpback's most peculiar and fascinating quality; it enchanted us as we dived over the untouched Tongan hard corals and fans. The alien yet accessible melodies carry long distances underwater and never cease to thrill. Complex moans and cries, yups and snores, whos and ees and oos, they range all over the human hearing frequencies and beyond, from the very deepest bass notes that a diver cannot hear but only feel in the gut, to high-pitched squeaks that recall a balloon being tortured by a four-year-old. But most of the humpback songs are soothing, beautiful tonal mixtures that delight the human ear.

Roger Payne, one of the world's foremost whale researchers, found that songs overlap during successive years but become more different as time elapses, with nearly all portions changing after five years.[7] The new versions, though, spread rapidly throughout the singing cohort. The dialects of song are the same among Mexican and Hawaiian populations, for example, but different from Caribbean populations, whose songs in turn differ from the Tongan whales.

After spending years listening to humpbacks with hydrophones, Payne has found that cetacean music is similar to human music in many ways. The whales employ similar rhythms, for example, and use phrases of a similar length to our music—a few seconds—to build themes. Like human composers, they keep reiterating these musical ideas, sometimes even stating a theme, developing it, and then restating it in *sonata allegro* form. The length of the whale songs averages 15 minutes—a length similar to that of many human classical music compositions.[8] The humpback singers use intervals in their melodies not too different from our own scales, with rare percussive effects, like tympani in an orchestra, punctuating the more frequent tonal sounds to keep a rhythm as steady and rolling as the ocean waves.

Scientists like Payne are not sure why the singers sing; they suspect the practice may serve a territorial purpose to ward off rival males, or may serve to attract females impressed by musical novelty and beauty, or both. Whatever their exact purpose, humpback songs, one of the most intriguing mysteries of the animal kingdom, form strangely beautiful symphonies in the reverberant halls of the ocean.

Only two decades ago, His Majesty King Taufa'ahau Tupou IV banned humpback whaling by decree in Tonga; before that, a group of fishermen living on Hunga Island near Vava'u "took" around 10 humpbacks a year. As recently as 1995 a Tongan living in Japan, Tasi Afeaki, pressured the king to allow the resumption of whaling, proposing a kill of 50 humpbacks, 200 sperm whales, and 100 minkes (Tokyo fish markets pay as much as $70.00 per pound for whale meat.) The government rejected his proposal in two days.[9]

Allan Bowe, a heavily bearded New Zealand expatriate and owner of one of Tonga's premier whale-watching businesses, made a point at the time to personally visit the king. Bowe, who took the three of us out in his fine humpback search boat, told me about the meeting:

> I was chartered by Tom Curren and Kelly Slater, then the two best surfers in the world, along with a *Surfer* magazine photographer and an ESPN crew. Our plan was to search out and ride the best unridden waves on Tonga. I'd seen a photo, from the thirties, of the King riding a wave, so I called the palace up and asked his agent if he'd like to meet the boys. Next thing I know, we're scrounging up sport coats and trousers from the yachtees to visit the King.
>
> I made a pitch to him at the time about the whales, and he assured me that he'd never allow whaling to resume. So, no worries . . .

Whether the King's heirs will carry on the whaling moratorium remains to be seen. In his late 70s at the time of this writing, although he has lost a third of his former weight, the monarch still tips the scales at around 300 pounds. This is a lot for good health, even for a Tongan—like the Samoans, the local people include some of the largest-boned individuals in the world. While downing suds in a local bar, we heard from some yachtees, marooned here by choice for 10 years, that the king's son, HRH Crown Prince Tupouto'a, is a bit of a playboy but also switched on to the modern world. He established the official Tonga website, for example, and understands the global importance of the Internet. As heir to the throne, his commitment to the environment remains to be established, but preliminary signs are good.

As far as we could tell, whale watching was thriving on Tonga, and with luck, the economic pressure it generated would help maintain the ban. Harassing the whales is illegal, but swimming and photography near them is allowed. An afternoon's cruise might yield, with luck, a pleasant encounter with a female and calf and a checkout by a lone male passing through. Near Submarine Island, the whales congregate in the afternoons, and there one has a good chance to witness a breech.

Chuck Nicklin and Rick Rosenthal, two hardworking nature filmmakers, had been in Vava'u filming humpbacks for BBC/NPR the previous August. "Lucky" Nicklin told me about his most memorable Tongan humpback encounter:

> We spent the whole day without getting in the water with a whale . . .
> until 4 P.M. We were four or five miles out to sea when we saw a whale
> tail-slapping. Rick had dressed and said he could get some [photos]
> topside. I just figured I would put my gear on. We stopped where the
> whale went down, waited, and then he was under the boat. I scrambled
> in the water and he stayed with me, at times coming up from deep
> water right to my face. . . . the visibility was 200 plus. When he left
> Rick put his gear on, and we went to where the whale was slapping his
> tail. He came to both of us two more times . . . the best experience I
> have ever had with whales.

Whale watching can be like that, and it certainly was for us—hours of waiting, moments of ecstasy. Such is the tempo of the South Seas. Life on Vava'u, both in the water and topside, pulses to ancient rhythms. People take time to chat, time to smile—only crazy visitors from the mainland are ever in a hurry.

The human inhabitants of the Kingdom of Tonga, though, as in all rural societies in Earth's far-flung, pristine regions, must navigate the turbulent waters of the global cash economy. The lure of quick money is forever present, from the capture and sale of tropical reef creatures for the aquarium trade, to the slaying of turtles to provide shells for unthinking tourists, to the vending of rights to a zealous international commercial fishing industry. And always lurking is the temptation to resume the hunting of humpback whales.

Walking through town one day, I encountered a battered truck overflowing with whale bones. A local Tongan woman, walking next to me in a flamboyant red and white dress, told me these bones were from the old days when whaling was legal. The men, she said, will spend months carving them and then sell the resulting scrimshaw to tourists. It occurred to me that there is a ready market for more than just whale meat, should whaling resume here.

To a humpback, one might conjecture, the ocean, for all its vastness, has definite limits. It is probable that these animals communicate with deep-pitched elephantlike sounds over vast distances. They can travel from one side of an ocean basin to the other in a matter of weeks. They have evolved body size, motility, and communication skills to deal with the problems of scale the ocean holds. Unlike whale sharks and other large fishy inhabitants, the big mammals are also constrained to make periodic trips to the atmosphere. Those fateful spouts, so harmless for so many years, almost led to the end of the whales, for the blasts of moist air gave their position away to human hunters. But humans halted industrial slaughter of these animals a hair's breadth before the ultimate biological limit, extinction, was reached.

Industrial whaling, intensified in the southern oceans since the late 1920s, took humpback numbers down to about 5% of their estimated initial stock.[10] Whalers acted as marine predators typically do, harvesting the largest prey first, the blues, and then switching to fins and humpbacks. In the 1960s, the bigger animals became scarce, and what whalers remained targeted sei and minke whales. Over 46 million tons of whale biomass were reduced, in a few decades, to 8 million tons.[11]

Annual krill consumption by whales then went from 190 million tons to 40 million tons,[12] and pinniped populations thrived, as did the few remaining whales. This hints that whale populations tend to be food limited, in contrast to fish populations, which seem to be larval-survival limited.[13]

Large animals, especially carnivores, often occur in small numbers. Why? Consider the oceanic food web. Herbivores such as copepod and krill zooplankton, also called primary consumers, graze upon photosynthetic algae, the primary producers that transform carbon dioxide, hydrogen from water, and sunlight into oxygen and organic matter (sugars and proteins). Carnivores, such as anchovies and herring, also called secondary consumers, then eat the herbivores. Tertiary consumers, such as humpbacks and tuna, then eat those carnivores. Of course, this is a simplification, for animals cross levels and skip layers. Energy flows through complicated food webs, not the neat food chains of classical biology. Krill, for example, feed on zooplankton at times, making them carnivore/herbivores. Baleen whales, when they feed on krill rather than herring, become secondary or tertiary consumers, depending on the krill's diet.

Accepting the simplification, then, as energy is transferred, there is roughly about a 90% loss at each consumer trophic level.[14] By the time a humpback feasts on high-latitude herring, there is much less energy available (10% of 10% of 10%) than there is for a creature at the lowest level. Because of this energy depletion, tertiary consumers are, almost by definition, rare.

It is now important to take this "rare" quality a step further. To state once again what may be, in the marine world, a deceptively obvious idea, we know from island biogeography that an uncommon animal can all too easily become an endangered animal.[15]

Unlike many inhabitants of the saltwater wilderness, whales reproduce slowly, gestating their offspring in utero and then feeding them milk after birth. This adds to their relatively low numbers—remember, there are six billion humans and only 10,000 southern humpbacks.

Perhaps, then, another reason why conservationists have latched onto megafaunal carnivore icons like grizzly bears, tigers, and whales is that, besides exuding charisma, they can, with ease, be forced into oblivion. The reason they are so vulnerable is because they are so rare.

As we cruised on a small boat out of Vava'u harbor, I wondered if the Tongans would be able to choose a course that might preserve the biological riches of their homeland. Sustainable tourist industries—diving, sailing, surfing, and whale watching—might be better able to withstand the long run. There are dangers in tourism, of course: any native Hawaiian can tell you about cultural imperialism. There are worse dangers in biological exploitation, though, and cyanide fishing in Indonesia, dynamite fishing in the Philippines, and just plain overfishing in the United States and Mexico all provide ample testimony for that.

My sympathy lies less, I should confess, with humans, Caucasian or Tongan, than with the whales themselves. Large, gentle creatures, animals that could crush you with a single fluke tap but do not, animals that talk to each other in exotic love songs half an hour long, animals that cannot fail to thrill on sight—it is impossible for me to think in a rational manner about the pros and cons of whaling, for I am attached to the big, strange, marine mammals. In some circles "saving the whales" and "loving whales" have become slogans of ridicule, icons of foolish, utopian, idealistic liberalism. I suspect that those who make light of animals so near to extinction are persons who never got close to a wild whale in the ocean. There are few who can have such an encounter and remain unmoved.

Sly, our Vava'un skipper, navigated the boat along a channel between two limestone islands. Days of heavy rain were behind us, and the sun reflected off mangrove trees ashore, their leaves a deep green, their black roots probing deep into the salt water. A scent of jasmine blossoms hung in the air, and the sea was a vivid, deep blue.

Today Chuck Nicklin was staying topside. Greg Ochocki and I decided to trade off swimming with the humpbacks, and it was Greg's turn. But after waiting for hours in wet suit and fins, he slipped into more comfortable threads. When the chance came, only yours truly was ready to seize the moment.

"There he is! You see him? He's coming right at us." Like many Tongans, Sly's English had a down-under accent. "It's a male, and he's on a mission. Into the water, mate . . . now!"

I slipped over the gunwale into the crystal-clear sea. Moving as gently as possible, trying to keep my fins from stirring the water, I floated to a point that would intersect the whale's path. There was a faint, dark shape looming ahead. It came closer. My heart rate picked up. The thing was big, really big. With each steady swing of its flukes, the humpback swam nearer, ignoring me as if I were nothing more consequential than, well, a human. I gazed at the ivory abdomen, at the calm eye the size of a saucer.

His white belly glistened. He exhaled, then took a breath, and the dank, seasalt spray of the spout was caught, sparkling, in the trades. A wash of whale current hit me as his 70,000-pound bulk passed, swirling me around like a piece of driftwood. His flukes, steady and resolute, carried his massive body forward 20, 30 feet with every stroke. His heart, a muscle the size of an automobile engine, pumped five gallons of blood with every bradycardic contraction. As marine biologist Graham Worthy points out, if we were to measure physiological time by heartbeat, then one day for a shrew would equal twelve days for a porpoise, would equal three months for a whale.[16] To understand whales, we must understand how they read time. For them, a month-long journey across a vast expanse of ocean might seem as a trip of a few days would seem to us.

The humpback kept cadence to this primordial tempo as he swung his body in the slow rhythm that was the cetacean dance. Flukes and song, heart and soul, the giant throbbed in synch with Tonga.

SOUTHERN HUMPBACK WHALE, VAVA'U, TONGA

"His white belly glistened "

CHAPTER EIGHT

There is a pleasure in the pathless woods;

there is a rapture by the lonely shore;

there is society, where none intrudes;

by the deep sea, and music in its roar.

I love not man the less,

But nature more.

—LORD GEORGE GORDON BYRON, *"Don Juan"*

Caribbean Symbiosis

Adventures with Barracuda and Dolphins off Roatan, Honduras

By this time in my dive career, I was getting a little burned out from travel. At six foot four inches, I do not fit well in airplane seats. Keeping all that camera and diving gear straight seemed more like work and less a labor of love. Then there was the idea of leading a low-impact life. Traveling less meant less jet fuel, fewer camera batteries, less film, less disruption of exotic ecosystems. Most of all, there was the pull of a lovely wife and two small children. Fatherhood has done more to temper my adventurous instincts than anything.

On the flip side of the environmental argument, responsible ecotourism that infused revenues into native economies could encourage local people to protect their wildlife and ecosystems. On the flip side of the pain-in-traveling argument, there was always the option of taking some Dramamine and sleeping my way through discomfort. On the flip side of the family argument—well, there wasn't much, other than, when the kids are big enough, they're coming along.

Every now and then, the chance for a trip came up. Most of the time I passed. But not always.

A horde of no-see-ums and mosquitoes gnawed at bare feet and ankles on my walk across the hot sand. Rotting papayas, guavas, and coconuts littered a fertile, Honduran shore. Pungent wood smoke, somebody's cooking fire, hung in the air. The current in the lagoon ran parallel to the beach, and I headed opposite the flow of water, as far as the insects would allow, carrying nothing but a mask, fins, and snorkel, wearing nothing but a pair of old surf trunks.

Events had forced me to cut my journey here short. Unable to go diving with the others, I was killing time waiting for a plane. The land above the sea, sprinkled at first with shacks and the odd, small beach resort, widened into dense, pristine rain forest. Shriek and screech of unseen macaw and cicada pierced the thick, humid atmosphere. There was not a breath of wind to cool my sunburnt skin.

At last the heat and bugs and waiting drove me into the warm Caribbean. Viscous muck welled up between my toes and soothed the itching of insect bites. The water was too tepid to be refreshing. A good hundred yards from shore, I slipped on gear and left gravity behind.

In an instant, the sea washed away sweat and blurred thoughts of land. The mud flats, scattered with conch shells, revealed millions of small holes, some spouting mysterious clouds: filter-feeding shellfish spewing wastewater.

Mud gave way to sand and coral heads. Purple sea fans waved against the current, seizing nutrients and plankton. A cloud of baitfish darted by, silversides, enveloping me for a moment, then vanishing.

All thoughts of time were gone. There was no sound but noisy breathing into the snorkel. I relaxed and inspired slowly, trying to become silent as a staghorn coral. A crackling noise chattered in the background. Snapping shrimp, invisible, but not unnoticed.

A sudden chill warned of change. A chasm opened beneath me: Spooky Channel. I peered down into the depths, hoping to see a grouper or a hammerhead. Circling over the edge of the canyon, I saw a yellow-green brain coral, maybe eight feet in diameter, at the mouth of the channel. It glistened in the shallows.

A great barracuda, nearly motionless, hovered over the mammoth coral, flaring its fins and gills, opening its mouth in a great yawn. It was a host fish, advertising to cleaning fish by ritual movements that it needed servicing. A pair of wrasse, cleaners with yellow, blue, and black stripes, read the barracuda's intentions and were reciprocating. They nibbled away near powerful jaws, fearless, cleaning rows of needle-sharp teeth.

The lone barracuda must have been seven feet long, his body six inches in diameter. Each scale shimmered in the sun, gray ones with a greenish cast above, white underneath. There were large doglike teeth, shearing teeth on the sides.

Attacks on people from such fish are rare but have been recorded, mostly on people attempting to spear the beasts, people swimming with other speared prey, or waders or swimmers in murky water.[1] It's not a good fish to kill and eat, should one be so inclined, for many large adult barracuda like this one carried the ciguatera toxin, a poison bioaccumulated from their prey that causes bizarre neurological symptoms, including reversal of hot and cold sensation.[2]

I became motionless myself, near the aura of the large, content beast, trancelike in its enjoyment of the dental hygiene. A school of 20 blue tang swooped in a circle at a distance; if they wished to be cleaned, they needed to wait.

One wrasse, pecking at unseen parasites, disappeared into the open mouth of the giant. Another worked its way along gills held wide in submissive reef pose. The barracuda, wild and free, submitted to the flossing like a boxer in a dentist's chair; in return, he spared the sparks that formed wrasse lives.

Cleaning hints that there may be more to the interaction of marine species than the brutal big-fish-eat-little-fish Darwinism that dominates the popular conception of life under the sea. Cleaning behavior is not rare; when a diver looks for the activity, it becomes all too common. Off Maui, green sea turtles lie in bliss within coral heads while cleaner damselfish peck on their shells and bodies. Nearby, in Molokini Crater, unicornfish line up to get cleaned by yellow and blue cleaner wrasse nearly identical to those that tended the barracuda. In the Sea of Cortez, manta rays glide along as Clarion angelfish nibble at parasites on their broad wings. In Fiji and in Hawaii, cleaner shrimp will leave a moray eel to clean a human diver's mouth, assuming, of course, that the diver exudes peaceful vibes, removes her regulator, and leaves her mouth wide open.

There have been interesting experiments done with cleaner fish. Writes marine biologist Paul Billeter: "After all cleaners were removed from a small reef, most other species [of fish] left the reef. The territorial species that remained exhibited an increase in ectoparasites, invasion by microorganisms, and frayed and ragged fins. . . ."[3]

Another study from the Great Barrier Reef showed that fish on reefs de-

SWEET LIPS AND CLEANER WRASSE, PALAU, MICRONESIA

"Cleaning hints that there may be more to the interaction of marine species. . . ."

nuded of cleaner wrasse had, on average, almost four times as many gnathiids (a parasitic isopod).[4] And an elegant, noninvasive study from the Red Sea[5] showed that reef stations with cleaner fish had, on average, 26 species of fish, whereas those without had only three. This supports the idea that species diversity is related to coevolution and symbiosis.

Because field studies like these are difficult to do, scientists have used game theory to get a theoretical handle on the problem of cooperation and non-zero-sum games in life—such as cleaner fish and their "customers." Through computer models, researchers set up evolutionary scenarios and make predictions about ecosystems and live nature.

In the 1980s, a political scientist at the University of Michigan, Robert Axelrod, working with W.D. Hamilton, an evolutionary biologist, studied the same kind of mutual altruism seen in cleaning behavior through a deceptively simple game known as the Prisoner's Dilemma.[6] The game evolves from an imaginary example of two prisoners in jail, both charged with a serious crime. Each prisoner has two choices, from the point of view of the other prisoner—not the cops: rat on his confederate ("defect") and gain the advantage of clemency for cooperating with the authorities, or keep his mouth shut ("cooperate"). Now, given that each prisoner does not know what the other is up to, there are four possible outcomes.

In the first and second outcomes, one prisoner defects and the other cooperates, or vice versa. In either case, one gets a heavy jail sentence and the other gets off scot-free. In the third outcome, both defect and both get a stiff but somewhat reduced sentence, because both played along with the authorities. In the fourth outcome, both cooperate and both get a small sentence for a lesser offense.

Given only one game, both prisoners invariably turn each other in. There is no way of ensuring trust; both prisoners go to jail, and both miss out on the benefits of cooperation. But, should a large number of games be played out, patterns emerge and trust can develop.

This is the sort of game Axelrod and Hamilton proposed, Iterated Prisoner's Dilemma, where "iterated" refers to multiple rounds of the game (in this case, 200 moves). They invited 14 game theorists from the fields of economics, sociology, political science, and mathematics to submit a computer program with strategies for the game. And then they played everyone against each other in a round robin tournament, to see what strategy would prevail. "The payoff to a player," they write, "is in terms of the effect on [the player's] fitness,"[7]—that is, survival and fecundity. Game theory, then, uses arbitrary numerical values that act as best guesses for weighing natural phenomenon.

To their surprise, "nice" strategies, or strategies that involved cooperation over time, won over "nasty" strategies. Axelrod and Hamilton defined a nice strategy as one in which a player never initiates defection. But nice does not mean total pushover. Anatol Rapoport of Vienna submitted the most successful strategy. He called it Tit for Tat. This program was simple: it cooperated on the first move and then on all following moves did whatever the other player had done on the preceding move.

In a second tournament with 62 competing entries from six countries, this time including professors of evolutionary biology and physics, everyone knew in advance that Tit for Tat had won the first tournament.[8] Yet Rapoport's strategy won the second round robin as well.

Tit for Tat has three features that combine to make it so robust: "It was never the first to defect," write Axelrod and Hamilton, "it was provocable into retaliation by a defection of the other, and it was forgiving after just one act of retaliation."[9]

With a little imagination, we can see game theory strategies in action with our fish. The barracuda could devour the little cleaner and benefit from an easy meal. Or the wrasse, having the barracuda in its expectant trance, could dart in and take a solid bite of tender flesh and beat a hasty retreat. (Indeed, certain small fish have evolved to mimic cleaners in appearance and make a specialty of nibbling cleaners.) But at the brain coral I was watching, over time each has learned the benefit of cooperation.

Axelrod and Hamilton note that cleaning fish behavior is only found in territorial reef animals, which perform repeated, "iterated" rounds of the Prisoner's Dilemma: "Aquatic cleaner mutualisms . . . seem to be unknown in the free-mixing circumstances of the open sea."[10]

The geneticist and science writer Richard Dawkins, in the chapter "Nice Guys Finish First" from his book *The Selfish Gene*,[11] discusses the Prisoner's Dilemma and non-zero-sum games. He points out that besides cleaner fish, a large number of mutualistic/cooperative relationships exist in nature. There is the sharing of blood among vampire bats—"unlucky" bats who have failed to slurp up a tasty sanguinous meal can, on any given night, get enough regurgitated blood from "lucky" bats (who are related or otherwise familiar) to avoid starvation. There is the sharing of sexes among a certain hermaphroditic sea bass—even though being female, laying eggs, and raising young require more energy and work, *Hypoplectrus nigricans* take turns at playing both sexes equally. And there is the pollination of fig trees by egg-laying fig wasps—wasps pollinate many more figs than they fill with destructive eggs, although the latter course might benefit them more in the short term. All these interactions can be viewed as real-life variations of the Prisoner's Dilemma.

As long as the participants view the game of life as a non-zero-sum game (a game without clear winners and losers or possibly, even, one with many winners and no losers), Dawkins points out that everyone benefits and "nice" strategies like Tit for Tat dominate. But some players display what Axelrod termed "envious" play, that is, the striving to get more points, or more money, or less jail time, than the other guy. The goal of these players is not so much to do well, but to do better than the other player—to win.

Dawkins presents divorce court[12] as an example of how splitting couples, who could both walk away with much more of their assets without the burden of legal fees, become "envious." The lawyers play a non-zero-sum game, both attorneys reaping their fees (and laughing together on their way to the bank) by getting man and woman to fight a zero-sum, win–lose, *Kramer vs. Kramer* battle. Here the legal teams cooperate, through unwritten rules of noncooperation and noncommunication, to benefit themselves by leading their clients into a win–lose game. The divorcing, "envious" pair, though, loses out.

Psychologists have set up the Iterated Prisoner's Dilemma between real people. They find, as do divorce court survivors, that players who succumb to envy do poorly.

Asks Dawkins, "Which aspects of human life do we *perceive* as zero or non-zero-sum? Do we assume, in real life as well as in psychological experiments, that we are playing a zero-sum game when we are not?"[13]

Besides this game of the Prisoner's Dilemma, as played by barracuda and cleaner wrasse, there was the integrated symbiosis found in the coral, the perfect, gargantuan, large-grooved brain coral. This colony of millions of tiny animals, voracious and efficient carnivores themselves, catches planktonic prey by extending tentacles laced with poisonous nematocysts. But, as described in chapter 5, the animals also live in harmony with plantlike, photosynthesizing, zooxanthellic algae. The coral builds calcium carbonate walls and provides nitrogen and phosphorus; the algae contribute nutrients synthesized from carbon dioxide, water, and sunlight. The algae also give a wide palette of color to their coral hosts. Should the algae perish from pollution or temperature change, the brain coral would turn a bleached white, and if new algae fail to recolonize, die.[14] In these nutrient-poor tropical waters, it is by the grace of mutualism that the brain coral survives.

Game theory models "how organisms make decisions when outcomes are contingent on what others do."[15] By changing the arbitrary rewards for cooperating or defecting, evolutionary biologists can mimic subtle variations between cooperative behaviors found in nature. These include reciprocity (where an animal gives something today for an anticipated return favor tomorrow), by-product mutualism (where there is no value in defection and cooperation is favored), and synergistic mutualism (where cooperation produces more than the sum of two independent behaviors).[16] An example of reciprocity would be the sharing of sea lion prey by killer whales with other pod members in Punta Norte, Argentina.[17] An example of by-product mutualism would be intraspecific cleaning behavior in a number of fishes.[18] And, an example of synergistic mutualism might be coral and algae, or communal harpoon hunting of sperm whales by the Lamalera tribe of Nusa Tenggara Timor.[19]

Lee Alan Dugatkin, a biologist at the University of Louisville, has noted that the harsher and more adverse an environment becomes, the more cooperation is favored (the "common enemy" hypothesis).[20] With its sparse nutrients, harsh sunlight, and deadly hurricanes, the reef might well be thought to epitomize a harsh and adverse marine environment.

There is no question that, on coral reefs as elsewhere in the sea, there are a multitude of species scrambling for preeminence. There is no grocery store on the reef; if, as an animal, you are hungry, you must go out and capture food. If you are a parrotfish, you must find and eat algae. If you are a white-tip shark, you must catch fish; if you are a moray, you must find your preferred snack of octopus.

Similarly, there is no lack of parasites. Every shark has its remora latched on, adding drag, scarfing up missed nibbles. Mantas and many whales are stuck with these hitchhikers as well. Microbial predators and parasites also abound. There is a whole universe of pathogenic viruses, bacteria, and protozoa that infest all manner of marine animals.

In chapters 2 and 7 we looked at carrying capacity, K, and growth rates, r, and although these values vary in their mathematical fit to reality based on various equations, they all point to one thing: in the wild, there must be competition for resources.[21]

But cooperation may play as important a role as competition and predation, only in a different, more intimate way. In 1909, Konstantin S. Merezhovsky first argued that the green specks in plant cells that made sugar from sunlight—chloroplasts—evolved from foreign symbionts. A few decades later, Ivan Wallin promoted the notion that symbiosis was essential to evolution. Adding experimental substance to these ideas, Andrei Famintsyn grew chloroplasts isolated from plants in his Russian lab. Their work and views were ignored and forgotten until more recently.[22]

Lynn Margulis is the modern champion of the concept of microbial symbiosis; she has built a formidable career theorizing that many eukaryotic organisms (complex creatures such as plants and animals that have nuclei in their cells) coevolved with ingested microbes. Instead of becoming digested, these bacteria and archaea, ancestral life forms with simplified structures, established détente with their predators and became organelles. Through this stalemate, or what might even be called cooperation, creatures that could have been microbial prey survived to enable the complex cellular structures that define today's blue whales and redwoods.

Margulis's work and that of others now suggest that some of the cell's most vital organelles—chloroplasts in plants and energy-producing mitochondria in both plants and animals—are integrated former bacteria.[23] Humans are no exception to this rule. Not only do we possess two distinct genomes, our own nuclear genome and the genome of our maternally transmitted mitochondria, but we also harbor multitudes of bacteria in our gut that help us digest food. Ten percent of a human being's dry weight, and a substantial majority of the total number of cells in our bodies, for example, are bacteria.[24]

My wife, Diane, it should be noted, has her own ideas about this aspect of symbiosis. She refuses to take personal responsibility in accepting these facts.

"All those bugs may live in your body, perhaps," she says, "but they certainly do not live in mine."

A peculiar protein arrangement in the ciliae that line our respiratory tracts and our sperm cells, a bizarre structure of nine pairs of protein molecules arrayed in a circle around a single pair in the center, is common to both eukaryotes like us and bacteria. Because of this shared structure, Margulis suggests that distant relatives of today's 8,000 or so species of spirochetes (a diverse group of bacteria that include the syphilis-causing pathogen *Treponema pallidum*) also became symbiotic with our nucleated cells. By this line of thinking, it is quite possible that spirochetes gave us, as eukaryote donor–recipients, motion and motility, and perhaps even the microtubules that support our nervous systems.

"Hungry squirming symbionts," she writes, with her son, Dorion Sagan, "attaching to cells for their own purposes, could have become the cell whip system. . . . They could do so by obeying the same old story lines of vicious attack, compromise, and ultimate partnership of victor and vanquished."[25]

Reef-building corals, with their complex association of cnidarians and zooxanthellae, take this kind of symbiosis to an even higher level. One might consider that they possess five different genomes of once independent organisms.[26] The coral polyps have their own genome plus their mitochondrial genes; the zooxanthellae possess their distinct genome, plus alga-specific mitochondria, plus the photosynthesizing chloroplast genes from remotely ingested (but not digested!) blue-green algae.

Richard Dawkins thinks Margulis is on the right track in emphasizing symbiosis but believes the argument could be carried even further, to the level of the individual gene itself. He sees replicating genetic material competing in a selfish way and settling into profitable mutualism with other genes, both within any given clownfish or coral, and without, as symbiosis between different animals. In his view, genes "clubbed together to build large 'vehicles'—bodies—for their joint housing and survival."[27] Dawkins takes issue with Margulis's invocation of "the poetry of cooperation and amity";[28] he stresses that selfish competition at all levels drives coadaptation and co-evolution.

Writes Dawkins in his book *Unweaving the Rainbow*:

> Margulis and Sagan are in a superficial sense not too far from being right here. But they are misled by bad poetic science into expressing it wrongly . . . the opposition "combat versus cooperation" is the wrong dichotomy to stress. There is fundamental conflict at the level of the genes. But since the environments of genes are dominated by each other, cooperation and "networking" arise automatically as a favoured manifestation of that conflict.[29]

Just how big a role cooperative behaviors such as cleaning or cooperative hunting play in the ethology of more complex marine animals is still unknown. It remains a relatively unexplored area of study. A dive guide in Maui told me once, though, that she often sees *uluas*, or jacks, following a prowling moray—when the eel finds prey, they join in for the feast. In the eastern tropical Pacific, tuna and spinner and spotted dolphins are commonly found together; this fact has led tuna fishermen to practice "fishing on dolphin" and has resulted in the deaths of many dolphins caught in the seine nets. There are different theories as to who is following whom, but some kind of mutualistic (benefits both) or commensal (benefits one, is neutral to the other) behavior is most probably at play. Recall other examples from these pages: the anemone fish and the anemones, the giant clams and their zooxanthellae, the species-specific barnacles living on the gray whales that both weigh down the mammals as parasites and arm them as mutualists.

Marine photographers spend many hours observing life on coral reefs. Even during night dives, watching one animal devouring another is not a frequent occurrence. More commonly, one sees the multitude of species bustling about, each with a specific agenda, but with overt confrontation rare. Most predation occurs during the transition hours of dawn and dusk[30] and is hard to witness. It is easy to see how, for example, filmmakers Michele and Howard Hall, who make thousands of dives and nearly live at times under the sea, might make this observation:

> A coral reef is the combination of thousands of species forming a single living entity. The reef is like a city. Every individual is concerned with its own survival. But at the same time, the reef couldn't exist without a confederation between species, an alliance of cooperation between citizens.[31]

Yet much predation occurs at night. Other feeding, such as that of the crown-of-thorns sea star on corals, is slow and subtle to the casual observer. There would be no need for reef creatures to evolve their incredible array of camouflage, poison, and other defenses if the coral world were not a cut-throat, dangerous place where predation and fleeing predation are not primary concerns. The reef is a city, all right, full of potential muggers, murderers, and mayhem.

Beyond predation, there is constant competition for resources, for light, for space, for nutrients. But Margulis believes that there is more to it than digestion and competition, and the fact that the reefs exist at all, oases of high productivity in vast tropical ocean deserts, proves her point: "Life is really far more a non-zero-sum game than many realize."[32]

Here off Honduras, just east of the Yucatan Peninsula, were waters rich in evolutionary history, for not far from here lay the impact crater of the great iridium meteorite that ended the Cretaceous Age—and the reign of the dinosaurs—65 million years ago. The Caribbean, it occurred to me, must have been ground zero for marine evolution. Most living organisms probably died. Perhaps the Caribbean lay sterile for millennia, to be repopulated by immigrants. Whatever the particulars, it seems plausible that the meteorite and the resulting disappearance of huge, reptilian, marine predators opened niches for large fish, including gilled, teleost fishes like the barracuda.

Teleosts, representing at 20,000 species more than 90% of existing species of the class Osteichthyes, or bony fish,[33] have reached their fullest extent in the last 50 million years.[34] Their most distinctive feature is the homocercal tail, that is, a tail symmetric from the midline, a tail in which the upper portion forms a mirror opposite of the lower. This structure allows rapid and powerful swimming with efficient body motion and, in an example of convergent evolution, is also found in white and mako sharks.

Beyond cleaner fish relationships, carnivores like this teleost barracuda play a key role on the reef. They stabilize the marine environment by top-down control of lower trophic levels—although it is difficult to study because of historical human fishing,[35] too many herbivores, surgeonfish, and parrotfish, if uncontrolled by top-level predators, may well have deleterious effects on reef ecology.

My dreamlike state shattered. The setting, the fish, the coral, the cleaner wrasse: It was all too perfect. The photographer in me came alive. Backing off quietly, I retreated and then, in high gear, raced the half mile to shore for my camera, kicking and stroking as fast as possible, hoping against hope the enormous, wild fish would still be there on my return.

My brother Grant and I hadn't seen each other in years, and we thought a dive trip together in Central America would be a good idea. One of the resorts here on Roatan Island, 50 miles or so from mainland Honduras, is famous for allowing divers to swim with bottlenose dolphins, and we thought we'd make some photographs of them during our reunion.

Grant is a slim, muscular redhead now gone gray, with an easy manner and tons of diving experience. As soon as our ancient, Casablanca-style DC-3 landed on the island, we grabbed our gear and rolled off the dock to explore Spooky Channel.

Grant insisted that my photography gear stay onshore. I can count on one hand the dives I've made without a camera—someday, I always told myself, I will become a Zen diver like my brother and just be. This first plunge off Roatan was my chance.

With freedom from the need to worry about f-stops, light, and backscatter, it was a pleasure to follow Grant and his pal, Peter Vickers, through the complex coral-lined chasm I would snorkel over later. Peter is a great, square man with a tan down to his bones. His accent lies somewhere between English and Australian, exactly where he's spent most of his life, in London, Sydney, and the South Pacific. He knows the tropics like a hermit crab knows its stolen shell. We let him lead us through the mazelike twists and turns of the channel.

Invertebrates of all colors and descriptions lined the walls. Most noticeable were the giant red barrel sponges, apartment houses of the reef, transparent shrimp and tiny fry hiding in their every nook and cranny. A big Nassau grouper sat patiently, lurking in ambush with jaws wide open. Wide-eyed black-barred soldierfish hid from the daylight in the dark crevices, waiting for the cloak of night.

The chasm became a winding cave, dark and mysterious, with moray eels lurking in the far recesses. Then it opened up to a sunlit shelf at 40 feet; now there were studded, crenelated fire corals, brain corals, lettuce corals, and anemones. Sea rods and staghorns made spikelike silhouettes, schools of gold and black sergeant majors swam in formation, tiny blue chromis fish blazed in glowing iridescence, black wire corals coiled, and striped grunts fed on plankton. Just when my brain neared overload and could absorb no more, the shelf disappeared, dropping off in a sheer wall to the depths of forever.

Now, I am able to put away a few beers from time to time and hold them pretty well. Nitrogen narcosis, rapture of the deep, has never affected me much. But when we flew over that wall, weightless, and the primordial abyss appeared without warning, an orchestra went off in my brain. French horns started blaring, string players sawed away like mad, and on top there shrilled a piercing piccolo.

Imagine flying over a kaleidoscopic landscape, complex beyond belief, a city of rainbow life forms, intricate, busy, bustling, and then . . . it all falls away into blue nothing. A rich blue, a royal blue, a cobalt blue so clear and deep that you could dream in blue forever and never grow tired of it—that was the color of the water. Something about it made me hear the roaring thunder of Beethoven.

We drifted down to a 100 feet and looked out from a wall draped with black corals. A hammerhead twice my size cruised by, an unblinking, lateral eye looking me over for a tense moment; then, the silent fish moved on out of sight with a swing of its tail. The overture over, only noisy scuba bubbles now disturbed the quiet.

The next day Grant and Peter slipped out at 6:00 A.M. for an early morning "deepey." This involved using a single tank of air, dropping down at the wall motionless to 300 feet, and then slowly coming up.

Such a dive was a dangerous enterprise, by any measure. At 300 feet (90 meters), or 10 atmospheres of pressure, each breath of compressed air equals 10 breaths at the surface; running out of air at depth can happen easily. At 300 feet, the partial pressure of nitrogen reaches nearly eight atmospheres, because 0.78 (78%), the concentration of nitrogen in air, times 10 atmospheres of air, equals 7.8. So the risk of getting the bends on rising to the surface is also magnified. But the most dangerous aspect of diving to 300 feet involves oxygen toxicity.

At 10 atmospheres, oxygen pressure reaches about two atmospheres of pressure, or 0.21 (21%), the concentration of oxygen in air, times 10. At oxygen partial pressures above 1.6 atmospheres, the risk of sudden, unheralded grand mal seizure increases dramatically. The longer the underwater exposure to high levels of oxygen, the higher the risk of toxicity. And surviving such a seizure underwater is close to impossible.

The U.S. Navy, during World War II, experimented with rebreather underwater systems. Because of the limited technology at the time, these devices used 100% oxygen. Rebreathers circulate gases, scrubbing out exhaled carbon dioxide with soda lime, and release very few bubbles—a real advantage for underwater demolition teams.

But diver after diver died in mysterious seizures related to oxygen toxicity, and the Navy learned that such rebreathers were only safe to a depth of one and one-half atmospheres, or 15 feet. With 100% oxygen, diving to 33 feet, barely deep enough to escape wave surge, caused partial pressures of oxygen to reach 2.0 atmospheres—the same levels Peter Vickers would hit on his early morning plunge.

Peter's been doing these deepies for years, though, and maintains that it's safe "if you come up without muckin' about down there." He also swore, later at breakfast, that he saw a bright red barrel sponge under ambient light at 50 fathoms. It's well known that there are few red light rays underwater after 15 feet of depth, the yellows fade by 40 feet, the greens by 100 feet. There is precious little color at 300 feet, even in the Caribbean—only blue. It's *dark* down there. My thought was that he was getting himself one hell of a nitrogen high. Later, I learned that some corals, through bioluminescence from symbiotic algae, produce their own light and that Peter might not be as crazy as he seemed.

Phillip Dustan, the coral reef expert who is science adviser for the Cousteau Society and biology professor at the College of Charleston in South Carolina, said this about the phenomenon:

"As you go deeper, once the red light is gone, at 15, 20 meters, you sometimes see red corals. The red is from natural fluorescence in their algae, a byproduct of photosynthesis."

"How about sponges?" I asked.

"Not unless they have zooxanthellae. For algae, this glowing is a kind of photochemical sweat. Sponges do have other kinds of pigments and organisms on them, cyanophytes, for example, and they could have zooxanthellae on them, glowing red, sure. . . ."

Maybe it was just another case of nitrogen narcosis that made Peter's sponge appear reddish. Maybe it was bioluminescent light. There was no way I was going to drop that deep to see for myself.

After a day of reef scuba, my brother and I visited the bottlenose dolphins. With some reservation, we forked over a pile of local currency for the pleasure of diving with *Tursiops truncatus*.

A cheerful Rastafarian in dreadlocks, who spoke only English, and a stoic Honduran in a faded Yankee baseball cap, who spoke only Spanish, piloted us up the lagoon channel in an ancient skiff. How the crew communicated with each other was impossible to determine. The dolphin pens came into view through the early morning mist. Each was about 100 feet square, with submerged netting hanging from a low wooden frame. It seemed a comfortable situation for a dolphin, plenty of room and nothing preventing a leap to freedom.

Then I recalled that dolphins, for unexplained reasons, seem unable to deal with nets and, despite their intelligence and echolocation, cannot jump over them. This, of course, is why the eastern Pacific practice of setting on tuna with dolphins can be so deadly for the mammals. Today, though, after a good deal of pressure, most boats "back down" their nets and the dolphins jump out easily.

David Au is a marine biologist at the National Marine Fisheries Service in La Jolla who has studied dolphins and tuna for many years. A soft-spoken, thoughtful scientist who is deeply interested in ecology, he is a friend, one of the few people I know who enjoys discussions about such arcane topics as stability and diversity of species, or exactly why dolphins, if they're so smart, can't escape nets.

"My hypothesis as to why dolphins don't jump over nets," he told me, "is that their jumping behavior has evolved for only two purposes: communication/sexual display and high speed swimming, both of which are inappropriate for the circumstance."

In other words, dolphins may be displaying ecological naivety (David Quammen's term) to objects that are not part of their culture or evolution. They are killed by tuna nets for the same reasons that a Galapagos finch will land fearlessly on a human shoulder.

We soon found ourselves out on the reef, waiting at 60 feet of depth for the arrival of the marine mammals. Conch, shellfish living in spiral homes a foot or more in diameter, littered a sandy plateau surrounded by healthy corals. The crew on the second boat, luring them with mullet handouts, brought out two dolphins, a big, friendly male and a shy female. Ten-foot torpedoes each weighing a thousand pounds wasted no time in dive-bombing us.

The big male, Ajax, after checking us out, started twirling nose down in the sand, spinning like a boat propeller. Sand whirled, Ajax whirled, and then up he popped, a razorfish in his mouth. Grant and I wasted no time mimicking this behavior, and Ajax shot around us, curious, nodding his head up and down, blowing bubbles. Shrill dolphin sonar flooded the water with sound waves and penetrated deep into our tissue.

Ten minutes went by before I remembered there was photography to be done. Ajax did not seem to mind my bright strobe. His female friend, though, was camera shy. This did not bother us, for at a similar resort a female dolphin bonded a little too well with some tourist guy. After she pressed herself against him in amorous fashion for an hour, he tried to leave the water. Heart broken, sad to see him go (or so it seemed), the female *Tursiops* gave him a parting love tap on the jaw, enough to break it in two places and give him a concussion.

Our air gone too soon, we surfaced, boarded our boat, and headed back to the pens. The dolphins, led along with fish handouts, followed. At any time they could have bolted and taken off for the open ocean. But, like golden retrievers, they'd given up their chance to be free.

Investing a few hours at the dolphin institute, I met Jeri, one of the trainers. A dark-eyed, deeply tanned, cable-thin expatriate from California, Jeri was dressed in ancient cutoffs and a faded T-shirt. She lived, breathed, and thought dolphins. She told me how one year ago, the hotel received a pod of seven captive dolphins from a bankrupt Florida oceanarium. Various authorities forbade the institute from letting the dolphins out of their pens. This restriction was placed because of fears that these animals, born in captivity, would fail to survive if returned to the open ocean.

The Honduran hotel abided by this, at least temporarily. Researchers at the institute were in the process of getting permission to teach the dolphins to make forays out into the channel, when a hurricane struck.

Heavy rain and winds turned the normally placid lagoon into a roaring cauldron. Waves poured over the barrier reefs. The dolphin pens were destroyed by an Amazonian outflow of storm surf and rainwater. Concerted rescue attempts were foiled by persistent heavy surf, wind, and near-Biblical rain.

As she got to this part of the narrative, I noticed Jeri's brow furrow. A distant look appeared in her eyes.

"At last the storm passed," she told me. "Our boats scoured the reefs for dolphins. Flotsam and jetsam everywhere. A total bitch."

For long hours Jeri and her fellow trainers navigated through heavy swells looking for dolphins amid partially submerged coconut palms, deck chairs, and broken pier beams. The Honduran animals, though, needed no help. They swam in, of their own accord, through the familiar channel they knew so well. The Floridian dolphins were another story.

After days of searching, institute staff found the unlucky seven several miles offshore in a tight pod. They tried to lure them back through the channel. Jeri told me her first sighting made her fearful, for the dolphins failed to keep watch on the depths. The Honduran dolphins, when they are over deep water, are much more cautious; they constantly turn, send out sonar, and look down. The Florida pod paid no attention to the possibility of deep-swimming, ambush-prone sharks. They crowded around the boat like excited children, jumping for fish handouts. The trainer doubted they knew how to hunt. Several had raw wounds on their bellies, probably from coral damage.

Each time Jeri brought them to the reef pass, the dolphins would scatter. She would lead them back with mullet, but before they could find the channel, they would retreat, led back out to sea by their female leader. Perhaps they'd tried crossing the reef before and were injured, storm surf thrashing their skin on the fire coral. Jeri tried for two days. Finally, on the third morning, they failed to appear and were never seen again.

As we motored back to our sandy digs, the bilingual crew running the boat, I asked Grant what he thought of our dive.

"I thought the whole thing was goofy," he said. This surprised me.

"Why?" I asked.

"Those dolphins just didn't seem right. They may be smart, but they seemed bored. They lacked pizzazz. I think those people, feeding them so much fish, ordering their lives, have taken the spark of living out of 'em."

It was impossible to say if he was right. The mammals seemed pretty lively to me, but, then again, I don't speak Dolphin. Neither, I may add, does my brother. Perhaps he was thinking in anthropomorphic terms. Perhaps he objected to the idea of any form of captivity and read this into the dolphin's behavior.

"No way those dolphins were the same as wild dolphins," said my brother. "They've been spoiled, and spoiled rotten."

Perhaps humans, using insidious fish treats to trick them, addicted the bottlenose to their current soft and spineless existence. Or perhaps they willingly gave up the chance to be free for the safety, food, and boredom that went along with human–dolphin symbiosis. Who were we to judge? What if we had to catch our meals every day? What if we were on the menu for swift, ravenous ambush predators?

There was no way to know. Jeri never told me where the local dolphins came from. Perhaps they were born in captivity and never really knew the sweet taste—or terror—that can come with pure freedom. But did we ourselves know the flavor of that rare cuisine?

That night I phoned home. There was bad news. Erik, my son, was sick.

"I didn't know what to do . . ." said my wife, Diane, during the hour-long conversation. Her voice shook. "He just couldn't stop coughing . . . he started turning blue. . . . I took him to Children's Hospital emergency, and they treated him for asthma and he's better . . . for now . . ."

BARRACUDA AND BRAIN CORAL, ROATAN, HONDURAS

"The image of the barracuda and the brain coral was ingrained in my mind, an etching

of Nature, wild and primeval."

Diane is a calm and together person, one of the many reasons I love her, but just then she came close to breaking down.

"Don't worry," I said. "Forget the dive trip. Forget the brothers' reunion. I'm coming home."

So there I was, snorkeling in paradise, while my son was sick thousands of miles away. The reason I was still there: there was no flight from Roatan Island to the Honduran mainland until the next day. Even if there had been a chance to leave right away, I'd made four dives the day before, including a night dive, and was a candidate for aviation bends. At altitude, especially in an unpressurized DC-3, residual nitrogen has a nasty habit of bubbling up to block arteries that feed important places like the brain.

I swam at full speed, venting frustration and guilt. A pier extended 100 yards toward Spooky Channel. I climbed up a ladder slippery and green with algae, hid snorkel gear under a coil of ancient rope, and sprinted for shore. The image of the barracuda and the brain coral was ingrained in my mind, an etching of Nature, wild and primeval.

I greased O-rings and loaded film, then raced across the sand, the littered coconut husks scraping my feet. Gear retrieved, fins, mask, snorkel on, and the warm Caribbean surrounded me once again. My vision was different now, my mind-set altered. Hurry, hurry, hurry, the left side of my brain told me. To capture the barracuda photo, something needed to be sacrificed.

Nearing the mouth of the channel, I forced myself to relax. The Zen-like trance from before had long faded.

Would the big fish still be there? Wary, I stopped swimming and floated unmoving, then inched toward the brain coral. Behold the primitive hunter. Eons of ingrained memory aided the stalk.

The barracuda had not moved an inch. The cleaners disappeared, though, and the fish no longer fanned its gills. The hunter in me released the bowstring, hurled his photographic spear. Gotcha! Hoping for an even better shot, I ventured closer.

For a moment, a pair of steady eyes took my measure. With a flick of its homocercal tail, the fish wheeled and turned. It disdained my photographic hunt. It knew too well the danger of humans. In sadness, I watched it disappear.

The big guy had not given up much, though, only a spot at the cleaning station. It remained lord of these rich, coralline waters. The barracuda did not follow mullet handouts. It answered to no one—except cleaner wrasse.

I, too, answered to symbiosis, the symbiosis of family. Without loved ones, my fins turned frayed and ragged, my gills became clogged, and predators attacked me from the depths.

Slow, deep strokes took me back from the brain coral to the no-see-ums and mosquitoes on shore. The acrid odor of evening wood fires carried out to sea. Sunset reds and oranges blazed across a foreign sky. Should the barracuda below have peered upward, it would have seen, perhaps with relief, my wake scoring the still surface of the sea.

We were curious. Our curiosity was not limited, but was as wide and horizonless as that of

Darwin or Agassiz or Linnaeus or Pliny. We wanted to see everything our eyes would

accommodate. . . .—JOHN STEINBECK, The Log from the Sea of Cortez

Below Baja

Exploring the Waters of Mexico

After diving in the South Seas and the Caribbean, it was hard, later, to refuse the *offer of a voyage on a private dive boat out of Cabo San Lucas. The eastern tropical Pacific is known as "the Land of the Big." Here the attraction to a diver is not so much reef complexity, but large underwater fauna. The prevailing current system moves west, and replacement upwelling of rich water from deep, polar currents combines with divergences along shearing current boundaries created by the east-moving Equatorial Countercurrent. All this moving water brings nutrients to the eastern tropical Pacific and buffs up the food pyramid. Whale sharks, tiger sharks, mantas, marlin, and tuna all live here and grow to prodigious size.*

The kids were healthy, and my gracious wife urged me to get outdoors for a while and destress from doctoring. I wanted to go in the spirit of E.F. Ricketts and John Steinbeck; I wanted to travel with clear and objective vision. As it turned out, the trip opened my eyes to problems in the human relationship to the creatures of the sea.

CABO SAN LUCAS, 1990s

For three days we patrolled Gorda Bank, a sea mount that rises from a thousand fathoms to 120 feet beneath the surface. We were five nautical miles southeast of Cabo San Lucas, somewhere in the transition between the eastern tropical Pacific and the Sea of Cortez. As was often the case, I was seasick. Every roll of the boat, every pitch, every twisting yaw sent perverse signals from my inner ear to my stomach.

A storm spiraling clockwise under the Southern Cross flung a choppy swell at *Tiberon Tigre*, our 75-foot, twin-diesel dive boat. If we could've seen the animal we were searching for, I could have slipped underwater and been cured of my *mal de mer*. But there were no whale sharks.

Rhincodon typus grows up to 40 feet in length and can weigh as many tons. Gentle to humans, a terror to plankton and baitfish, the beast soars above such places as Gorda Bank, filter-feeding for protein. I'd seen photographs and films of whale sharks but had never seen one for real. I knew they had white spots covering their dorsal surface and that their young are ovoviviparous, that is, born live from eggs hatched within the uterus. In Taiwan, fishermen harpooned a pregnant whale shark and found 300 embryos in her uterus, with pups free from the yolk sac measuring up to 25 inches long.[1]

I knew that their mouths were miniature ecosystems, cavernous pits where remoras and other fish live. I knew of a report showing that a whale shark, equipped with a satellite tag, traveled 14,000 miles in 40 months.[2] But I did not know what it is like to swim with one.

Mexico—somehow, a journey here never turned out the way you expected. A hot, sometimes swollen, often parched land, generous in its deceptive fruits and fish, our southern neighbor could do worse than make the unwary *gringo* seasick.

Of course, the United States could be just as bountiful, just as hazardous. There remained a major difference: aquatic wildlife in the south remained in better shape. The forces of destruction were not as far along as they were up north. Life in the ocean world down here was still abundant.

Or was it?

Fed up with searching for nonexistent whale sharks, Dick, the skipper, revved our engines and sent us north into the Sea of Cortez. A legend among Cabo captains, Dick knew these waters better than any *yanqui*, better than most Mexicans. He'd fished and dived here for three decades. A towering, muscular blond, his skin was burnt to parchment from the sun. Now a family man with a daughter in San Diego, the seagoing life he led was less appealing than it once was. Six months away each year was too much. But whatever the changes in his personal life, Dick remained, at heart, a fisherman. He loved catching fish, he loved taking people to fish, he loved cooking and eating fish, he loved the whole fishing program.

Tiberon Tigre was, after all, a fishing boat most of the year, and Dick ran it as such. Even on dive trips like this one, whenever the skipper took her out of port, he always threw a pair of lures attached to heavy tackle over the stern to troll for wahoo or dorado. Should the call "Hook-up!" shatter the air, he eased back on the throttle and expected any idle passengers to haul in whatever was on the line—whether you wanted to or not. This was no nature cruise, no whale-watching boat where fish and meat to feed passengers were bought in the grocery store and someone else did the dirty work. *Tiberon Tigre* caught her own, and if you voyaged on her, you were sure to get blood on your hands.

Past the Greek Wreck, almost up to La Paz, Dick threw anchor near a black rock some 400 yards from shore. "Roca Mosca," they called it, "rock of the fly." We slipped on our dive gear and powered through the current to what, underwater, was a pinnacle. There was a break in the unrelenting sun. I peered upward. Rain clouds? No. Jacks. Thousands of jacks. Wall-eyed torpedoes, each one 20 pounds of dynamo fish, each able to take their pound of flesh in one bite, they surrounded me and blotted the light. Some were so close I could touch them.

For a moment my nerves got the best of me. Then I remembered to be a photographer and circumnavigate the pinnacle, looking for the right angle. (A confession: much as I love photography, I use it in this way at times to calm paranoid fears of diving dangers.) The reef was covered with rust-colored sea fans. Cortez angelfish, resplendent in turquoise, yellow, and black, darted amid the jacks. A small school of trumpetfish scooted by, their narrow bodies reflecting silver and blue—when the jack thundercloud let a sunbeam through.

The jacks continued to block the light. An opening appeared, the rays glistened, I made a photo. Then there was darkness again. The darkness of fish cloud.

A fishy place, we all agreed. And we dived there again and again. Terry, the owner of *Tiberon Tigre*, told me that the sea life of Baja California, astounding as it seemed, was but a remnant of the past, the glory days before drift netters and trawlers swept the waters clean. Terry, like Dick, was a unique individual: heart surgeon, jet pilot, owner of multiple businesses, he brought us here at his expense. A calm man with a down-home Tennessee accent, he'd been coming to Mexico for 30 years. Terry had seen changes here and had himself gone from spear fisherman to underwater photographer. He was unimpressed by the huge school of jacks.

"I remember my first visit here, in 1968," he recalled. "We'd anchor off some island and watch the sun set over the water. There would be fish jumping in all directions, splashing all the way to shore, all the way to the horizon. I thought it could never be fished out. I was wrong.

"There's an island up north," he continued, "a snow white island that once was home to thousands upon thousands of pelicans, gulls, and boobies. Each species nested at a different level on the island and bleached it in layers of guano. Today, the bleach remains—but the birds are gone. No bait fish for them to feed on; they've all been netted, sold as food or fertilizer.

"Some people have stopped calling it the Sea of Cortez—Dead Sea is more like it."

We hoisted *Tiberon Tigre's* anchor and started the long haul around the cape to Magdalena Bay. Dick knew a place where the sardines still schooled and the marlin fed. Perhaps we would see something. As usual, he dragged a pair of lures in our wake. Tired from diving, I drifted off under the rack of rods and reels in the forecastle.

Baja California—the great, thousand-mile-long peninsula. A tectonic phenomenon, lateral movement between the Pacific and the North American plates, is ripping the peninsula apart from mainland Mexico, its coastal cousin. The Sea of Cortez, born from this tearing asunder at the infamous San Andreas fault, is part of what geologists call the East Pacific Spreading Center.

"Hook-up!" someone yelled, shattering my reverie. Curious at what had been caught, I wandered up to the stern, where Dick thrusted a heavy, saltwater rod and reel into my hands.

"Pull that fish in, will ya?" he said. "It's dinner."

I hauled and reeled, hauled and reeled. I could feel the power of the fish, but the heavy monofilament and leverage of the resin pole were too much.

"Come on," Dick shouted. "He's gonna get away."

Redoubling my efforts, it occurred to me that it had been years since I caught a fish. Growing up in Minnesota, catching crappie, northern pike, and muskellunge in northern lakes, I'd thought nothing of clobbering a fine fish on the head, slicing the belly open to strip out the guts, filleting flesh from bone. And why not? They were only fish. They were meant for us to eat.

In Wyoming one summer, on a survival course as a famished teenager in mountaineering school, I once ate a trout whole—head, eyeballs, the whole works. My wife and I loved the taste of fish, sauteed in garlic and olive oil: swordfish, ahi, halibut, more recently, the heavenly Chilean sea bass, bursting with fat and flavor.

But by this time things were starting to seem different. I'd read *Sea Change* by Sylvia Earle,[3] the famed oceanographer and explorer. I now found it hard to swim with an animal, photograph it, and then kill it. The last wild game on Earth to be hunted as a commercial enterprise is fish. Eating blue-fin tuna or swordfish, writes Earle, is like eating panther or eagle. When you consume such a meal, you are eating a top predator, an animal known now by scientists to be at least somewhat warm-blooded, a creature created by millions of years of evolution. And a creature whose numbers are fast dwindling.

Chilean sea bass turns out to be Patagonian toothfish, fish that take a century to mature. In only a few years the "sea bass" fishery has all but forced this strange creature to extinction.

Many eastern seaboard chefs recently began a boycott of Atlantic sword-fish as swordfishermen gave up inefficient but selective harpooning of large adults for lucrative, indiscriminant long-lining. Such fishermen, immortalized —without a trace of irony—in the bestseller *The Perfect Storm*,[4] have de-pleted both juveniles and adults, and in response, average catch size has plummeted.[5] Oceanographer Carl Safina, commenting on the 60-mile long-lines, each with hundreds of hooks baited with squid and Cylume light-sticks, told the *New York Times*:

"Longlining shouldn't be allowed, period. Fishing for swordfish should be confined to rod and reel and harpooning. There are a couple hundred longline boats. We should buy them out or pay them not to fish."[6]

Giant bluefin, the biggest, fastest, sleekest tuna in the sea, fish whose bodies are maintained at a constant 28–33°C no matter what the water tem-perature,[7] each fetch thousands in the Tokyo markets. It is no wonder that, from 1971 to 1991, their numbers dropped.[8] During this time, the indus-try was regulated by the International Commission for the Conservation of Atlantic Tuna (ICCAT, also called by some wags the "International Commis-sion to Catch All the Tuna"[9]). Despite ICCAT, the Mediterranean bluefin tuna population dropped 50% and western Atlantic bluefin numbers dropped a staggering 90%.[10] As described in chapter 4, California's abalone population, especially the white abalone, is barely surviving. Yet more and more Americans are switching from red meat to heart-healthy fish. Six bil-lion humans worldwide, six billion 70-kilogram omnivores, and many of us armed to the teeth with technology, tools, and hubris.

I reeled in with half my heart in it. Perhaps the fish might get away. But no. "Hey, look, he's tail-wrapped!"

I looked down at a 40-pound wahoo, the lure caught in its mouth, eyes flashing, the monofilament wrapped around a regal, homocercal tail. Dick reached down and gaffed the animal, grunted, and, with a two-handed pump, plopped him on deck. The wahoo's back was silver blue, the belly white. Sleek muscle strained in vain. The tail beat a paradiddle against the fiberglass hull. Blood poured from the mouth. Gills gasped in the strange medium that is air.

Wahoo—*Acanthocybium solandri*. Proud member of the family Scombridae, the tunas and mackerels, a fish esteemed by anglers for its fighting qualities and flavor. Like the dorado, it is not considered part of a population at risk. Unlike the bluefin tuna,[11] the swordfish,[12] or the lamnid sharks (mako, white, porbeagle, salmon),[13] it is not thought to be warm-blooded, yet it is one of the fastest fish in the ocean. Not until the 1970s did scientists figure out that some fish maintain temperatures higher than the ambient water, especially in the swimming muscles, brains, and eyes. They conserve heat in vital hunting organs via a countercurrent network of capillaries, the *rete mirabile*, or "wonderful network" described by George Cuvier, a French anatomist of the 1830s who detailed the structure but failed to understand how it worked.[14] Arteries and veins hold warm blood in one place by means of this heat-exchanging capillary network; similar countercurrents appear in human kidneys to concentrate salts and in diving mammals to concentrate oxygen.

Heat in billfish, tunas, and lamnid sharks is not only conserved but created by extra energy-generating organelles, or mitochondria, in their muscle cells. It is heat that makes these fish so special, heat that gives them the incredible energy to course through the water at speeds up to 40, 50, 60 miles an hour, heat that gives them the edge over cold squid and other prey in the chill depths, heat that makes them the fighting choice of fishermen.

The wahoo, on the other hand, possesses rete networks—but the networks are not thought to create heat. How, then, does it maintain the high metabolism that keeps it in league with tuna and billfish as a fisherman's prize?

The answer is a mystery. It may lie in ram jet ventilation. As the wahoo zooms through the sea, oxygen-bearing water pours through its mouth and through its gill filaments, much as air pours into a ram jet aircraft engine. In the gills, where complex folds and filaments increase surface area and tissue/saltwater contact, countercurrent-fed, oxygen-poor hemoglobin grabs electron-bearing oxygen to stoke the furnace of the animal's fiery metabolism. Perhaps the wahoo somehow milks this phenomenon more than the sharks, tuna, and mackerel[15] that share this adaptation. Or perhaps the explanation for the wahoo's legendary speed and strength still awaits science.

In any case, there was no way for this wahoo to speed through the ocean like an underwater jet; there was only the spending of every last bit of precious, stored energy. The animal stared at me with a wild-eyed look, its large, alien orbs losing their luster and turning glassy and opaque.

Do not go gently into that good night,
Rage, rage against the dying of the light.

The words of Dylan Thomas to his dying father rang apt, perhaps, for fish as well as men. I found the driftwood club the crew used to kill fish and struck once, twice on the skull above the eyes, each time making a dull, wet smack. At last the fish was still. Dick and Terry reeled in two more wahoo moments later.

"Well, Dick, that should be enough fish for a week, at least, don't you think?" I ventured.

He looked at me with the peculiar, screwed-up smile he reserved for tree-hugging Sierra Clubbers.

"I want to catch all the fish," he started, each word measured and powerful. He was kidding, I thought.

"All the fish. I want to catch all the fish." His chants crescendoed, each repetition louder and more forceful until Ahab himself was shouting, "I WANT TO CATCH ALL THE FISH!"

I stumbled back to my bunk and dozed.

The dinner bell awakened me. Subtle odors of garlic, fresh seafood, and spice permeated *Tiberon Tigre*. My stomach ground, seasickness replaced with hunger as, zombielike, I stared at Dick's wahoo melts, mouth-watering chunks of fresh wahoo, onions, jack cheese, and butter, broiled over English muffins. I hesitated, torn. A day spent at sea makes one ravenous, and the smell of Dick's creations was intoxicating. I reached over and sampled a melt, the explosion of delicious flavor helping me to rationalize about my right to be on the food chain, my omnivore heritage, and so on. Maybe someday I'd become a vegetarian. Today, though, the spirit was willing but the flesh all too weak.

We motored past Cabo San Lucas into hard swells coming from the northwest. After a long night, we found ourselves off the great bay, Magdalena, where gray whales come to give birth and mate every winter, fasting on their epic journey from the Bering Sea.

The sun beat, the boat rocked. Off to the horizon, like a breaching humpback, a black marlin jumped, spun, and landed with a splash. Perhaps it was trying to rid itself of barnacles and remoras. Perhaps it was showing off to a female. Perhaps it was just celebrating life. Who could fathom the mind of a marlin?

Dick was looking for sign of a baitball, a horde of packed, frenzied sardines, herring, or anchovy. He called them "meatballs." The only way to see them from a distance was to look for the birds. Marlin, dolphins, tuna, or sharks trapped schooled fish against the surface, while frigate birds and brown boobies attacked from the air, tipping off a keen observer from miles away.

We scanned and scanned, motored and motored. Dick got bad news on the radio from San Carlos, the little fishing town within the bay. Nobody was catching marlin, nobody had seen any baitballs. But we didn't give up.

Last year *Tiberon Tigre* brought a pair of British natural history filmmakers here to film marlin and baitfish using the wide-format IMAX camera. Dick told us that it was no easy thing to winch the delicate, 265-pound machine into the sea; maneuvering the refrigerator-sized camera and housing underwater to film wildlife was even harder.

The strange thing the filmmakers learned was that baitfish could figure out, in short order, that divers were not a threat. The biggest problem during the shoot was avoiding the clouds of fish that gathered around the photographers, pressing on all sides. The prey, of course, were harmless. The darting, hunting predators were another story. On the far side of a meatball from the cameraman, the film's producer took a marlin bill through the hair. After the dive, everyone wondered why he was quiet for so long; it took a while for his psyche to recover to the point where he could relay what happened.

"Meatball ahead!" Diesels slowed. A dozen black frigatebirds, their forked tails quivering, skimmed the water scooping fish. Here and there the water erupted in frantic boiling.

"No marlin, those are blacktail skipjack below!" cried Dick.

Terry and I slipped into the warm sea, Terry with scuba, myself snorkeling. I swam all out, chasing the 20-foot cloud of sardines, *Sardinops sagax*. Below, like shadows, a dozen or more tuna lurked, diving through the bait every so often, leaving a trail of scales to drift in the sunlit water.

I looked for Terry. Bait surrounded him. A Michelin Man of fish, only his flippers, hands, and head were visible. Then they enveloped me, too. I felt frantic protein-energy bundles against my body, gentle, frenzied taps of terror. These were not just fish. These were fellow living creatures, and they knew fear. Of that I swear. There was electricity in the water. That, and the smell of piscine genocide.

Something punched me in the mouth, knocking the snorkel free. An errant skipjack. Enveloped and invisible within a cloud of silvery sardines, I swam for freedom; a trail of small victims, hoping the large, strange, bubbling creature would provide shelter, followed. *Tiberon Tigre* trolled by. The school left me to hide beneath her hull.

With astounding rapidity, the fish disappeared. Had every last one been devoured? Or did they dive and escape? Terry told me he'd seen satiated marlin herding bait for hours. When they dived to evade the death trap against the surface, a single billfish would follow, bringing them back in a lazy, workmanlike pace. Skimmer-feeding frigatebirds and plunge-diving boobies further decimated the trapped prey. With deliberate moves, the marlin readied themselves, then took turns diving at warp speed through the center of the school, their slashing bills leaving a trail of blood and death. In this manner they finished off every last one of the silvery plankton eaters.

Schooling, the sardines' reflex to danger, led to their doom. Yet, over evolutionary time, natural selection has made schooling the predator avoidance behavior of choice for these fish. Tight formations, apparently, work better at avoiding predator detection than isolated fish scattered over a wide range of ocean, or schooling helps the sardines find their own prey better, or, perhaps, so many fish so close together favors reproduction.

In all marine environments, organisms and nutrients are "patchy"—their distribution is irregular. The prey of sardines, r-selected zooplankton copepods, appear in dense aggregations as they multiply to take advantage of similar dense patches of dinoflagellates, the predominant tropical phytoplankton. As a result, sardines, too, congregate in schools, as do their predators, the tuna and billfish.

The patches of abundance that appear here and there in the nutrient-poor oceanic gyres act like moving islands. This is especially obvious when great rings of warm water, some 100 miles across and 3,000 feet deep, break off from the Gulf Stream and persist for two or three years in the central Atlantic.[16]

Like new volcanic islands rising from the deep, upwellings of nutrients, cleared areas from human trawling, and oceanic rings are all subject to colonization by new species. Just as a forest goes through succession, so may these types of habitat. An element of uncertainty lies over this, for how things proceed depends on how fast creatures can breed (r selection), how efficient they are at using resources (K selection), and many other factors.

The marlin and the blacktail skipjack tuna, the top predators in this uncertain game, made it their business to range over enormous areas of empty seas, searching for islands of abundance. Their behavior when they found them made it clear that they must not have read about Axelrod's Iterated Prisoner's Dilemma or Tit for Tat. They did not use a "nice" strategy. It was not their style. They played a strictly zero-sum game.

Dick anchored off another sea mount, this one called Thetis Bank. Like Gorda, it started at 120 feet. We rolled into the water, savoring the weightlessness, the familiar unfamiliarity of the alien element. Down the anchor

DIVER IN BAITBALL WITH SKIPJACK TUNA BELOW

"I looked for Terry. Bait surrounded him. A Michelin Man of fish. . . ."

line we plunged, leveling out at depth. There was something strange here. A large white rock, some seaweed. My brain, thick with nitrogen, was slow to register.

That white outcrop was no rock. That algae, no seaweed. An abandoned trawling net was draped across the pinnacle, and pulling up on it, a pale float of putrid gas and decaying meat, was a dead loggerhead turtle. Swimming next to it was a live turtle, its flippers barely moving, its motion a graceful, solo tango. It was hard to believe it was a reptile, an ancient reptile at that. And an endangered species.

With streamlined shell and long flippers, marine turtles move without effort through the water; on land, they are clumsy and defenseless. All are classified as endangered because of human predation.[17] Large sea turtles, once numbering in the millions a few centuries ago in the Caribbean, for example, now number in the tens of thousands. As herbivores, their cropping of seagrass beds kept things healthy; with the functional removal of the reptiles, vast amounts of plant detritus fueled microbes, increased oxygen demands, and promoted hypoxic water or "dead zones." In Florida Bay, local extinction of the green sea turtle has led to the demise of turtlegrass beds.[18]

Unlike freshwater turtles, marine turtles cannot retract their heads and limbs within their shell and are vulnerable to shark attack. To excrete excess salt, they use special eye glands that secrete copious, gluey tears visible only on land.

Loggerhead hatchlings have both light sense and magnetic sense for orientation. Newly hatched turtles, born from land-laid eggs, find their way to the ocean by light from the moon or stars reflected off the surface of the sea. Once they are in the surf, they use wave motion to get them to deep water; if the sea is calm, they use the magnetic sense,[19] a sense that is somehow set by light. They continue to use these senses over the 10 years or so a loggerhead takes to reach breeding maturation. Then, describing ocean-sized migratory cycles, they return to natal egg-laying sites every two or three years.[20]

Whether this living descendant from the Triassic Age, making slow circles around the net, was grieving the death of its mate, or just looking to grab a meal, no one could know. I dipped under the dead turtle, trying to get a shot into the sunburst, 140 feet above. I looked at my gauges. Uh-oh. Air went quickly at six atmospheres—each breath used six sea-level breaths from my tank.

Up the line, a short dive, yet full of pathos. After a careful, slow ascent, I returned to the swim step to breathe the foulest odor my nose has ever encountered. Eau de dead turtle. Linda, Terry's high-energy, mile-swimming girlfriend, had cut the corpse loose.

DEAD SEA TURTLE IN ABANDONED FISHING NET, THETIS

BANK, MEXICO *"That white outcrop was no rock; that algae, no seaweed.*

An abandoned trawling net. . . ."

A fearless, attractive blonde who is invariably the first one in the water, Linda felt compelled to sever the net and send the bloated body rocketing to the surface:

"The other one was mourning. If we didn't free it, it would have drowned down there, too."

Much as I doubted that Linda was right, it was impossible to know what the animal thought, or even if it thought at all.

It is my experience that wild creatures feel something, though, even the lowly fish and reptiles. One has to feel the terror of the fish in the baitball or see the look in the eye of the turtle at the grave of its mate to forgive these odd lapses into anthropomorphism. Showing that animals have emotions and thought has been done with higher life forms such as chimps and dolphins. No one has proven that any creature other than a human is sentient and has self-aware consciousness.

Consider, though, the mirror recognition studies done in dolphins.[21] Consider also the work of Donald Griffin, the Harvard biologist who discovered echolocation in bats. A champion of animal thought, he emphasizes that the inability to prove fails to disprove.[22] Intelligence, like everything else in life, has evolved over time in fits and starts along a punctuated continuum. Although we are much different from reptiles like the loggerhead, we are also much the same. The difference is that we are carnivores who often exploit animals in a zero-sum, win–lose game. With the exceptions of the few humans killed each year by grizzlies, crocodiles, and great whites, we are invariably the winners. As such, it is to our cultural advantage to minimize and downplay nonhuman thoughts and emotions.

We picked up another diver in Cabo and headed south 225 nautical miles to the four Revillagigedos Islands: Benedicto, Socorro, Clarion, and Roca Partida. I dosed myself once again with antihistamines for the cruise. I was near comatose in the bow. This was a good thing, for we rocked and plunged so hard that several pitches bounced me three, four inches off the bunk.

The islands are a Mexican wildlife preserve; it takes a special permit to visit. No commercial fishing is allowed within a 12-mile zone, but some report the law to be poorly enforced. More hurricanes strike these isolated rocks than perhaps anywhere else in the world. Other than a handful of Mexican military, who live here with their families in steel-reinforced concrete block houses on Socorro, the volcanic islands are ruled by boobies and frigatebirds topside, Galapagos and tiger sharks beneath the seas.

We reached Benedicto first. Gale force winds swept across the island's barren, smoke-gray pumice. We could not breathe on deck for the volcano-born dust. Dick kept motoring, on to Socorro. I drifted off again in the bow.

We declared ourselves by radio at the tiny harbor that is Socorro customs. Everyone anteed up passports, visas, permits, and the fishing licenses that Mexican law required us to have. We waited long, tepid hours. It was maddening in the heat. At last some bored sailors paddled over from the pier. They made their unhurried way to our boat in a tiny skiff with two inches of freeboard. How many more hurricanes would each endure before returning to the mainland? We offered them sodas from the cooler. Dick gave a bottle of brandy to the *jefe*. All in all, our visit was cordial.

At last we got to a dive site and slipped into the gin-clear, 80°F water. The bottom was carpeted with orange sponges and stony corals, *Porcillopora*, for the most part. Swarms of gaudy tropicals went about their business, unafraid of us. Most noticeable were the Clarion angelfish: the orange and blue-striped juveniles played coy; the adults were in our faces, defending territory or, perhaps, offering cleaning services. Skulking through the coral and sea fans were parrotfish, cleaner wrasse, butterflyfish, scorpionfish, puffers, trumpetfish, and surgeonfish. Lobsters the size of cocker spaniels lurked in daytime caverns. Snapping shrimp, unseen, clattered percussion in the background, a constant drumming behind our noisy bubbles.

After almost every dive, a manta appeared near the boat on the ascent. I learned to carry a spare camera in my buoyancy vest with a wide-angle lens for such encounters. The vision of these other-worldly creatures became routine, as routine as the sighting of a thousand-pound animal with a 15-foot wingspan can be. Plankton feeders (like whale sharks), mantas beat their wings with a steady, sinusoidal grace; to my surprise, they often slowed down near us divers, as if to get a better look at what must be to them clumsy intruders.

On one dive I watched three Galapagos sharks, six to eight feet in length, follow Terry's and Linda's flippers up to the swim step. Perhaps they were curious, perhaps just biding their time. These "brownies" made night diving here all but impossible—as the sun went down, their aggression levels went up. I swam to the step, trying to convince myself that they weren't watching me.

Tales of tiger sharks abounded here in the islands, but our ambivalent desire to see the great carnivore, the namesake of *Tiberon Tigre*, remained unsatisfied. Besides the Galapagos sharks, we sighted silvertip and reef whitetip sharks. Dropping down to 120 feet, Kevin, the diver we picked up in Cabo, and I spotted a pair of hammerheads. They saw us and our bubbles, wheeled, and disappeared.

Kevin was a world-class climber. His mission: "exploring the spaceship." In the late 1960s and 1970s, Kevin hung out with other climbing rats at Camp 4 in Yosemite, scaling Half Dome and El Capitan. Like Terry, he was a heart surgeon; he also dived, rode motorcycles, and flew hang gliders and small planes.

"You'll never catch me dying of cancer or heart disease in a hospital," he would say. "I plan on having a traumatic death."

A wiry man with a graying beard, Kevin has a lithe, spidery build. As we trolled along Socorro, he talked Dick into anchoring at an overhang, a beyond-vertical, igneous cliff. He scrambled unaided up some 40 feet. We watched, our jaws dropping. Sure, if he fell, he'd land in the surf, but still. . . .

Then Kevin reached a group of nesting boobies at the peak of the overhang. There was something wrong with one of the birds. A long trail of monofilament nylon trailed from its neck. After struggling 50 feet up, Kevin grabbed the line and pulled in the terrified boobie. Two slashes with his knife and it was soaring over the sea, free from the fisherman's burden.

Trolling for tuna on our way back to Benedicto, Dick hooked up—but reeled in nothing but a wahoo head. Oceanic whitetip? Tiger shark? Only Poseidon knew who owned the buzz-saw teeth that severed wahoo vertebrae and muscle.

We hooked up again. The fish leaped, and we saw the most beautiful fish in the sea: mahi-mahi, dolphinfish, dorado, whatever name you care to use. Indigo, green, then yellow, these rainbow-hued delights fade fast to a dull gray when they die. As Dick gaffed this particular 30-pounder, a second fish hovered in the blue water. Slipping in, I swam over, camera in hand. The dorado, clearly nervous, feared my presence, yet seemed unable to leave the vicinity. Once again, there was the sensation of piscine emotion—sadness, maybe, even anguish. Nonsense, I thought, rank anthropomorphism.

Back on deck, Dick declared, "Oh yeah, if you catch one there's always a second nearby. Male and a female. They mate for life, you know. . . ."

We ignored Clarion and Roca Partida, two other distant volcanoes, to try again at the Boiler, a sea-mount dive site off Benedicto. The winds had died, and the spot was on. Dense schools of amberjack circled while 50-pound bluefin travally, sky blue and streaked with yellow, lumbered by in small schools. The pinnacle peak was covered with corals, sponges, morays, and the usual tropical reef fish. A pod of dolphins zoomed by to check us out. Spinners, I thought, but they were in and out so fast that it was hard to tell. Omnipresent mantas circled over deep water nearby. On one ray I spotted a pair of Clarion angelfish, adults, cleaning white parasites off the manta's back. Two fat, lazy remoras rode alongside, loafing, oblivious. Here ran the whole gamut of oceanic relationships. Mutualism: the angelfish feeding on ectoparasites, the manta getting cleaned and hydrodynamic. Parasitism: the manta providing the remoras with a free ride, at the expense of increased muscle effort. Predation: the manta scooping up zooplankton and phytoplankton, the angelfish eating the barnacles.

This was paradise. Dive, eat, sleep. Loaded on a near-overdose fix of wilderness, I was in a state of ecstasy and contentment. The Boiler was perfection: big, wild animals everywhere, doing their wild thing on a wild reef in the middle of nowhere. Dive, eat, and sleep.

Dick, however, was bored. He decided to chum up tuna. Ladles and ladles of putrid fish guts went overboard. We were not surprised when no tuna, only aggressive Galapagos sharks, answered the dinner bell. A dozen swirling predators churned the water. Madman that he was, Dick dived in and snorkeled around, then popped back onto the swim step. It was the quickest swim he had ever taken; the sharks were nipping on his fins as he scrambled out of the water.

"Bastards," he said, spitting the word out in anger. "I've seen them ruin a ten thousand dollar fishing charter so fast. . . ."

Dick grabbed a bang stick, a long pole with a shotgun shell mounted on the end.

"I'm going to kill one of the bastards. You'll see, the rest will leave."

I protested but he ignored me. He popped a six-foot brownie in the head and stared as it sunk into the depths.

Dick was hopeless. He just didn't get it. Never mind that these sleek predators represented millions of years of evolution, that they were matchless relics of the age of dinosaurs. He just had the need to kill.

Angry at my impotence, I returned to my bunk. Dick had many admirable qualities—a kind and loving father, he took great care of his family. While hardly an environmentalist, he had been known to slice an illegal fifty-mile-long line (although he made sure to salvage a hooked thresher shark for the pantry from the line before it sank) and then fend off a furious fishing crew with bland, innocent denials. Hooking up a dolphin by mistake, he endured savage palm lacerations trying to cut the line as close to the animal's mouth as possible. But in spite of these things, he angered me to the point of speechlessness by his wanton Galapagos shark killing. For a long time I lay there in the bow, fuming, staring at the rods and reels hanging over my head.

After long days at the islands, we headed north. Dick had been yakking with his buddies on the single side-band radio. Following the gut-pounding return run of 20-plus hours, we came full circle to Gorda Bank. Dick said there was a rumor, something about big fish. Linda, the first diver in the water (as usual), came rushing back topside, screaming for her wide-angle lens—a definite clue.

Slipping into planktonic seas, Kevin a stroke behind, I swam down the anchor line, fighting a brisk current. A fish the size of a Greyhound bus cruised toward us at 70 feet. Whale shark. Kicking mightily, I circumnavigated the animal as it dived deeper, pausing at the cavernous mouth, where five remoras stared at me from their peculiar domicile.

Yes, divers who have been coming to these waters for decades bemoan the exponential drop in sea life found here. Last year, 10 years, 20 years ago—it was always better then. "You could walk across the Sea of Cortez on the backs of marlin." "Mantas with wingspans of 20 feet carried you on endless journeys." "Baitballs were everywhere, and big, 100 feet across." Now . . . there is less. There remains a lot, only less.

There are few if any studies from two decades ago delivering census data on overall sea life in this part of the ocean. The Sea of Cortez conservation organization Sea Watch reports that many commercial fish species in waters surrounding Baja California have decreased between 70% and 95% over the last 17 years. Nine of the 17 species they have followed are commercially extinct.[23] Anecdotal reports from such experienced divers as *Tiberon Tigre*'s owner, Terry, confirm these numbers.

Howard Hall, the underwater photographer and filmmaker, writes of his 20 years of diving off Baja:

> Ten years seems to be a good period for measuring change in an undersea wilderness. It doesn't matter when you make your first dive in an area, ten years later the site will almost always seem "dived out." You enter a wilderness environment on a time-line that represents diversity and abundance as a declining curve. Whether you make your first dive in 1945 or 1992, you enter the curve high and leave it low. . . .[24]

In 1995 marine biologist David Pauly wrote a paper echoing this sentiment, coining the phrase "shifting baseline syndrome,"[25] a scientific term for the phenomenon that Hall describes. Tim Smith, a National Oceanic and Atmospheric Association (NOAA) fishery scientist, is leading an international taskforce to recover the history of commercial fishing and whaling.

"By not including . . . historical information," said Smith, "[fishery] stock assessments frequently suffer from the shifting baseline syndrome, in which, as ecologist Jeremy Jackson noted, 'everyone, scientists included, believed that the way things were when they first saw them is natural.' "[26]

There is a paradox contained within these Mexican waters. Despite sentiments like those of Howard and Terry, a neophyte like myself, seeing a huge school of jacks, or a whale shark, or a giant manta, or a meatball, comes away with the impression of uncommon abundance. Never mind that one must run south 200 miles through hurricane alley to find it. Life—and death—still thrive off Mexico, where everything still seems more than up north. More wild, more primeval, more savage.

Could species of fish like the whale shark become extinct? Could it join the cousin of the California grays we met before, the Atlantic gray whale, *Eschrichtius robustus*? Could it disappear, like the Steller's sea cow, *Hydrodamalis gigas*, like the 10 seabirds that have become extinct, including the great auk, *Pinguinus impennis*? Could it vanish like the eelgrass limpet, *Lottia alveus*, or the San Diego mudsnail, *Cerithidea fuscata*?

Census data on marine species tend to be thin and irregular.[27] For example, fewer than 10 specimens of the megamouth shark, *Megachasma pelagios*, only first described in 1983, have been found to date. A coelacanth, that rare, ancestral, deep-abyssal fish discovered some 50 years ago off Madagascar, was found in Indonesia in 1998, 10,000 km from its previously known habitat.[28]

The IUCN World Conservation Union, the nongovernmental organization that keeps track of rare species, listed (as of 1996) 117 marine fishes as threatened, compared with 734 freshwater species.[29] With 60% of the described fish in the world living in salt water, this difference in listings might be due to the more widespread dispersal of fish larvae in the sea, or might be because marine species monitoring is very spotty.[30] The take-home summary from all these facts: we don't have enough information to make accurate analyses of threatened marine species.

For fish that are harvested commercially, there are better data. Since 1994, the 400-year-old fishery of Atlantic cod, *Gadus morhua*, has been suspended on Canada's eastern coast, yet the species is still classified as vulnerable, and the fishery has not yet rebounded. *Thunnus thynnus*, the Atlantic bluefin tuna, has extremely low populations, as does the southern bluefin tuna of the Pacific. The barndoor skate, *Raja laevis*, formerly a common "trash" fish taken by accident in shallow-water trawl fisheries in the northwest Atlantic, is now considered on the brink of extinction.[31] And invertebrates such as the queen conch and the giant clam are depleted across their range in tropical waters.[32]

Along with a relative lack of knowledge and increased difficulty of study, compared with our better grasp of endangered land creatures, is the worldwide disturbance of marine ecosystems, especially the loss of coral reefs and mangroves. Coral reefs, as noted in chapters 5 and 6, are hotbeds of biodiversity. Comprising only a tenth of a percent of the area of the world's oceans, they hold some 25% of all marine species[33] and 4–5% of all species.[34] Although some scientists such as Richard Grigg are sanguine about the status of corals, others claim that 27% of the world's reefs are at high risk.[35] What this means regarding extinctions, we can only guess; analogies comparing coral reef and rain forest as biodiverse treasure houses of species, however, hold true. If the syngameon theory of J.E.N. Veron (the idea that ocean currents and hybridization dominate coral speciation) is correct, rapid loss and gain of species may just be a normal aspect of coralline history. But how the fish and invertebrates that live within this ecosystem respond to changes in coral biodiversity is unknown.

Mangroves, trees that are salt-water tolerant and line many tropical coasts, have complex, mazelike root systems that provide nursing areas for fish and invertebrates. Yet, about 50% of the world's mangrove coastlines have been lost, victims of the human desire to live and work at land's end.[36]

For the past two centuries, trawlers have been scraping the bottom of larger and larger expanses of ocean. They scrape, pulverize, and dredge the seabed, transforming diverse assemblages of species, what were complex, organized systems, into sand and mud. Carl Safina, an oceanographer who works for the Audubon Society and authored *Song for the Blue Ocean* (1997), estimated that an area equivalent to the entire planet's continental shelf is trawled over every two years.[37] What species have been lost from trawling— other than the near extinction of the barndoor skate—is anybody's guess.[38]

I have mentioned how some biologists believe that, because of numerous subpopulations and the millions of larvae and wide dispersal found at sea, rules of conservation biology (especially, "rareness predisposes to extinction") fail to hold in the ocean.[39] Thus, marine extinctions ought to be few and far between. But others are not so sure. Writes Safina, "A general misperception is that small invertebrate marine bottom dwellers are highly fecund and reproduce by means of drifting larvae that can recolonize large areas quickly. In truth, key creatures of the bottom community can disperse over only short distances."[40]

And I have also mentioned how some marine ecologists believe that human activities are challenging biodiversity at sea.[41] They believe that the scarcity of oceanic extinctions may reveal nothing more than the difficulty of proving them. Hundreds of mollusks, for example, are "missing in action," but it will be difficult to prove that they are extinct.[42]

How about whale sharks? They bear their young live, and they are big and rare. All these things, we have learned, predispose to extinction. Scientists such as Callum Roberts of York, who investigates Caribbean popula-

WHALE SHARK, GORDA BANK, MEXICO *"Eye to fist-sized eye*

with the largest of all fish. . . ."

tions, and Brent Stewart in San Diego, who studies eastern Pacific animals such as the one here at Gorda Bank, are following this elusive, plankton-eating creature, but gaps remain in our knowledge of the animal's behavior and ecology.

Eye to fist-sized eye with the largest of all fish, slipping past 120 feet, I shivered with delight. The animal's hide was painted with circular spots, a pattern from the op-art 1960s. Dermal denticles—hardened scales—gave it texture. These toothlike structures were packed together with their tips facing backward to give the shark skin a rough, abrasive feel when rubbed against the direction of water flow. The denticles shed microvortices, decreasing drag and increasing hydrodynamics, and made the skin tough and durable. For many hundreds of years, shark hide was used by weapon makers to produce nonslip handles on knives and swords, handles medieval fighters could grip during the bloodiest of battles.

I longed to touch the skin for a moment but resisted. Living sandpaper, it looked tough, but there are anecdotal reports that human contact has been linked to fungal infections in the whale shark's cousin, the manta. I felt the sensation of calm, patient, overwhelming strength, the same thing one feels in the presence of other large beings such as elephants and whales. They are an ancient species, whale sharks, hence, by definition, a successful one. How do they know when and where to go to find the planktonic upwellings and the hordes of red crabs? How do mates find each other in the vastness of a blue-water planet?

A new, legal whale shark industry in the Philippines and Thailand is decimating Asian populations, and once plentiful animals there are now rare. Because scientists know these animals migrate over immense distances, perhaps even the entire range of the Pacific, they could form a single, interbreeding population—a population with fishing-imposed limits, a population that might be a big loser in the zero-sum game we humans have decided to play with nature. The future, then, could be grim for our beast as well.

A wave of sudden shivering over a 40-foot expanse of dotted shark skin warned that the creature was, perhaps, aware of me. No, came the more rational thought, the creature did this shimmer every few minutes to resist barnacles and other sea parasites. Even so, I felt my presence was no longer appreciated. I backed off, careful not to get struck by the tail as it powered back and forth like a great barn door.

Rising above the mightiest fish in the ocean, I noticed bubbles spouting from the broad, rough-skinned back. Kevin was hitching a ride on the five-foot dorsal fin.

Now, to some environmentally correct souls, to approach a wild animal is heresy; to get as close as Kevin was, blasphemy of the basest sort. Both animals and dive sites can be "loved to death." Balance is a good thing, though, and perhaps these folks have gone overboard. Roger Payne, a biologist who has spent his life studying whales, believes that swimming with large sea creatures has more positives than negatives. He writes in his book *Among Whales*:

> I feel there is a danger that in our zeal to protect [whales] from harassment we may overprotect them, and thereby disallow even careful approaches by experienced people. If this occurs we will be stifling the kinds of friendships that might otherwise form between humans and whales. . . .[43]

Adds Howard Hall:

> Make no mistake, for every manta touched by a sport diver . . . thousands die in gill nets. For every hammerhead disturbed by a photographer, thousands die on longlines. And, especially in the Sea of Cortez, for every fragile coral damaged by the fin of a diver, miles of sea floor are ripped up and desolated by shrimp trawls. . . .[44]

The mountaineer sailed out of sight into the current-swept deep, one more remora drafting on the body of a giant. Swimming with the whale shark had taken us both far from *Tiberon Tigre*. There would be long minutes ascending in blue water, with no means of orientation but depth gauge and compass. Kevin and I drifted, weightless, at the mercy of upwelling and tidal flow, suspended in the azure void.

Some years after our voyage to Mexico, Howard Hall, that indomitable and tireless underwater filmmaker, visited the Revillagigedos Islands for two weeks as a scout trip for a film extolling the marine riches of the region. Here is an excerpt from his letter to Mike McGettigan, director of the conservation NGO "Sea Watch":

"I found our March trip to Los Revillagigedos Islands disturbing. During our two weeks diving at the islands, I saw only one shark at Socorro, six sharks at Partida, and no sharks at Benedicto. . . . Sharks were not the only animals conspicuously absent at the islands. . . . I saw only one wahoo, two yellowfin tuna, and surprisingly small numbers of schooling bigeye jacks. Ten years ago, when I last visited the islands, I saw schools of yellowfin tuna and bigeye jacks *numbering in the thousands, and I saw dozens of wahoo hovering over offshore pinnacles. . . .*

"We witnessed a Mexican commercial long-line fishing boat (The Bluefin) *pulling its 70-mile-long line just two miles offshore from the island. . . . Unless commercial long-line and gill net fishing laws restricting fishing near these islands are more effectively enforced, I fear there will soon be little left to film at the Revillagigedos Islands."*[45]

CHAPTER TEN

Too bad fish can't vote. But then neither can our children or our grandchildren.

— SYLVIA EARLE, *Sea Change*

Taking the Chance

Natural History and No-Take Zones

After my trip to Mexico, I felt interested not so much in accumulating experiences
and knowledge of the creatures of the sea but in finding ways to preserve that richness of life and habitat I had been privileged to get to know.

It was in the home waters of our local Channel Islands that questions and debates about conservation began in earnest for me. It seemed like a harmless enough
thing, a dive trip for a few days off San Miguel Island. But the deeper I dived into
the underwater world there, the more problems and discontent I found.

CHANNEL ISLANDS NATIONAL PARK, CALIFORNIA, 1990s

After a long and rolling night motoring through rough seas, our Ventura,
California–based dive boat, *Chance*, found calm winds and cloudless skies
at dawn. A mountain rose out of the thin mist, its golden flanks covered with
sage and lemonade-berry bush, land unsullied by human construction. This
was California the way Portuguese explorer Juan Cabrillo first set eyes on it
in 1542.[1] A quick look at the rose-colored sunrise and the chart posted in
the galley revealed we were not at our destination, San Miguel Island, but
north of Santa Cruz Island and bearing due east, toward Anacapa Island.

151

Despite the pristine appearance of Santa Cruz, there were grumbles among the passengers, for it was clear that we had abandoned plans to anchor off San Miguel. The most western of the chain, San Miguel is the crown jewel of Channel Islands diving, a place where the California current strikes hardest, bringing cold, nutrient-rich waters down from the north. Here a diver can experience the same marine biota found off northern California and Oregon. Six species of seals and sea lions breed on the island's westernmost point, Point Bennett, and rainbow-hued anemones carpet the underwater canyons. But the skipper of *Chance* turned back during the night from stormy seas and 40-knot winds off San Miguel to take the boat to Santa Cruz and Anacapa, where warm water flowing north from Baja made things balmy. Cap'n Crunch, as our crew called him behind his back, banged the boat's hull on the pier last night and was taking no chances today.

Five of the eight Channel Islands, a chain that rises from the eastern Pacific about 50 miles offshore from Santa Barbara to San Diego, form one of our newest national parks. President Carter signed the bill creating it in 1980, including one nautical mile of ocean surrounding each island, 125,000 acres of submerged land. To divers, of course, the terrain beneath the sea and the living web of invertebrates, fish, and marine mammals that live there are what the park is all about.

The source of the profusion of life in the Channel Islands is a gravy train of nutrients pulled to surface waters by upwelling. Found on midlatitude, western sides of continents, where trade winds pull away surface water to bring up deep, rich water, upwelling regions form only a small percentage of the ocean's area. Yet the food webs they create are disproportionately large and vibrant. John Ryther, of Woods Hole Oceanographic Institution in Massachusetts, wrote that "upwelling regions, totaling no more than about one-tenth of 1 percent of the ocean surface (an area roughly the size of California), produce about half the world's fish supply."[2]

Cold, deep water bears a wealth of nutrients. As freshwater ice forms in the Antarctic, heavy, salt-dense, oxygen-rich water sinks and begins a slow march clockwise along the sea bottom—all the way around the Pacific Rim.[3] A similar phenomenon occurs in the Arctic Ocean off Greenland.[4] Along these ocean-sized circles, the icy, dark, benthic current collects marine snow, the particulate fallout of organic life. Some of the collected decaying material is lysed by marine bacteria into carbon from sugars, nitrogen from proteins, and phosphates from nucleic acids; some of it remains in colloidal or cellular form.[5]

No matter what the form, all of the decaying protoplasm in the water column, once combined with sunlight, bears the potential of becoming potent marine fertilizer. Colder, deeper water also holds more oxygen, essential for respiration. Whether the marine snow drifts in midwater or just above the bottom, it has the propensity to fuel marine food webs; once it reaches the bottom and becomes part of the sediment, it becomes trapped, lost in geological time.[6] Although there is a rich and as yet poorly understood biota (the benthos) that lives on the bottom of the abyss, pressure and lack of heat and light restrain these life forms from using up much of the oxygen and nutrients found in bottom water and sediments.[7]

To bring the fertilizer back up to shallow water requires some planetary help. Warm air, rising from the equator and then sinking at high latitudes, and Earth's rotation, with the resulting Coriolis force, work in concert to power trade winds on the surface in the tropics and subtropics. These steady, unrelenting winds churn circular, hemi-ocean-sized currents, called gyres, that rotate clockwise in the northern hemisphere and counterclockwise in the south.[8] Part of the North Pacific Gyre, the California Current, an immense, cool, south-flowing saltwater river from Alaska, starts to veer west at Point Conception, striking the northern Channel Islands.

Here an oceanic escalator is activated. Wind-driven water, powered by uneven heating (greater at the equator, lesser at higher latitudes) and by the Coriolis force, diverges from the coast. Cold benthic water rises to the surface to replace it, bringing up marine snow nutrients and oxygen to supercharge the photic zone—the upper region of the ocean that supports photosynthesis.

There is some disagreement about the depth from which the trades pull this water. Some recent sources suggest that wind-driven upwelling brings nutrient-rich water from just under the photic zone, or a few hundred meters deep.[9] Other, more traditional viewpoints support the idea that much deeper waters may be brought to the surface.[10] From whatever depth, similar conditions of upwelling—and biotic profusion—can be found in analogous zones off the western coasts of South America, Africa, and Australia.[11]

There is seasonal variation to upwelling, as well. Shallow-water nutrients reach their zenith in the winter months, when there is no warm-water layer on the surface to hold the cold-water nutrients down below. Sunlight, though, peaks in midsummer and powers photosynthesis best then. Primary producers such as phytoplankton reach their highest numbers in early spring, when nutrients and sunlight reach optimal compromise. Zooplankton, their predators, follow with a population surge later in the spring.[12]

As mentioned above, upwelling produces unexploited nutrients in a novel habitat—a sort of oceanic island analogue. But there is an additional factor that makes the Channel Islands marine world so special. Here the Cal-

ifornia Current, carrying those rich nutrients from Point Conception upwelling, meets a warm, north-flowing California countercurrent, the David-
son Current.[13] This aquatic collision creates a multiplicity of oceanic mi-
croenvironments, mixing organisms and nutrients from offshore Baja with
those of Alaska and Canada. The result is a biological dynamo: an incredible
array of wildlife and a vibrant food web. Cyanobacteria, marine protozoa,
diatoms, zooplankton, invertebrates, fish, birds, and marine mammals all
thrive here in bewildering diversity.

Microscopic bacteria, who have their own food web with protozoa,
viruses, and colloids, create perhaps half of the primary photosynthetic production fueled by the upwelling and current mixing.[14] Some of the organic
material created in this microbial loop does not pass on up to phytoplankton, zooplankton, and other larger organisms; some does.

Analogous to this natural complexity, overlapping human bureaucratic
jurisdictions surround the islands of San Miguel, Santa Rosa, Santa Cruz,
Santa Barbara, and Anacapa like layers on an onion. There is the offshore
one-nautical-mile boundary around each island that contains the oceanic
portion of 20-year-old Channel Islands National Park. A second line drawn
at three nautical miles outlines the fishing regulatory jurisdiction of the California Department of Fish and Game. At six miles a third boundary forms
a National Marine Sanctuary, under the federal Department of Commerce,
representing 1,658 square miles of ocean.

The Channel Island land holdings of the National Park Service are some-
what limited; the service owns the small islands of Anacapa and Santa Bar-
bara, the large island of Santa Rosa, and 10% of Santa Cruz, of which the
Nature Conservancy owns the other 90%. San Miguel is owned by the U.S.
Navy, but it is park-managed. Of the remaining three, Santa Catalina, just off
Los Angeles, is private property, and San Clemente and San Nicolas, like San
Miguel, belong to the Navy.

Complex as their human ownership is, the islands also have a diverse geologic history. Around 14 million years ago, volcanic activity in the region
was high, and parts of the islands were formed. Since then, plate tectonics
have buckled the borderland and strained the underlying crust, creating
many faults. As little as 20,000 years ago, scientists believe the northern islands formed a super island called Santarosae; this broke into today's four islands as the final period of glaciation receded and sea levels rose.[15]

Our first dive exploration was at Anacapa, in green water, murky and unsettling. There is a no-take zone here, a 37-acre slice of sea. Here endangered
brown pelicans, now making a comeback with the banning of DDT and the
subsequent thickening of their egg shells, have one of the largest rookeries

in the Western Hemisphere. A crowd of fishing craft (our captain counted 25) hovered in a bay just beyond the rookery, angling for yellowtail.

Off Anacapa we found little wildlife, except for a few hermaphroditic brown sea hares, each possessing a complete set of male and female sexual organs.[16] Mats of blue urchins carpeted the bottom. Perhaps because of the high urchin populations, we saw no kelp. Cruising west to Santa Cruz, the biggest of the chain, we found clear water and a fine kelp forest that was recovering from the effects of the 1997–98 El Niño warming and storms. At 40 feet of depth, I set out through the forest, swimming through giant columns of verdant, swaying branches. Here and there a bright orange garibaldi swam through day-glow-green leaves.

Within the kelp fronds flashed yellow-orange senoritas, their tails marked with black eye spots to confuse predators. Fish that prey on tiny crustaceans, worms, and parasites plucked off other, larger fish that come to be cleaned, these members of the wrasse family bury themselves in the sand at night for safety, with only their heads protruding.[17]

Also on the sandy floor between the holdfasts of the kelp forest skulked bottom dwellers such as the shovelnose guitarfish and the round sting ray, who dine on burrowing worms, crabs, and shrimps. California halibut may be found here as well, although I didn't see any; they are stealthy fish that lie in ambush on the sand, to rise up and snatch perhaps an unwary passing sargo or kelp bass.

Turning back 20 minutes later, a feeling of being watched came over me. Divers have perished in these waters, victims of white shark attack. Most recently, a white attacked and killed an urchin diver, Timothy McFadden, off San Clemente Island. Pete Halmay, also an urchin diver with 30 years of Channel Islands diving under his weight belt, told me how he handles the threat of sharks:

"We keep our heads down, and that way we don't see them," he said, with a macho chuckle. A tall, lean man with graying hair and a humorous twinkle that shines through weather-beaten eyes, he adds, "We hope they keep their heads down, too, so they don't see us." Growing serious, he said, "There's too many sea lions, and it's bringing lots of great whites down from the north."

That spooky feeling persisting, I ignored Halmay's advice and scanned all four quadrants, down, then up. Aha. A harbor seal rested upright near the surface, staring down at me, curious.

Unlike the gregarious and friendly sea lions, harbor seals are more reserved in nature. Five feet long and white spotted, they range from Mexico to Alaska. Sometimes they will approach a diver, but often they steer clear. An exception is found in La Jolla, my home town near the Mexican border, where a pod of 100 or so have taken over a breakwater cove known as the Children's Pool.[18] Their feces caused closing of the beach there, to scuba divers' consternation, but children love watching wild animals up close (my two sons included). In the past I have seen these harbor seals nurse as passersby pet them; nowadays they own a roped-off section of beach and are unmolested. But there in the wilds of the Channel Islands, the seal was looking at me with cautious eyes, ready to vanish in a moment's notice.

Harbor seals rest bolt upright at the surface, with just the nose protruding from the water, a behavior known as bottling. Perhaps my bubbles startled this one from his snooze. Or, perhaps, it was resting from its hunting of sardines and squid. The seal stared down at me as it hung motionless some 10 feet from the surface.

The thrill of a single seal, a garibaldi here, a sheephead there, may not represent the way these national park waters were in 1542, when Cabrillo sailed them. Peter Matthiessen, in his historical chronicle *Wildlife in America*, documented the slaughter of seals along the California coast during the nineteenth century:

> [T]he British whaler *Port-au-Prince* took 8338 Guadalupe fur seals from the San Benito Islands in 1805, and a Yankee crew slew 73,402 on the Farallon Islands, off San Francisco, between 1810 and 1812. The Russians, however, were the most solidly implanted, importing Aleut hunters from their Alaskan posts to handle the labor of carnage. They ranged as far as Guadalupe Island, off Baja. . . .[19]

Added British historian Clive Ponting: "In total, about a quarter of a million elephant seals were killed along the coast of California. . . ."[20]

Huge schools of fish must have swarmed in California waters to sustain such numbers of pinnipeds, although there is no way to prove it. California gray and blue whales were also plentiful; they, too, were hunted to near extinction and only now are making a recovery.

Jeremy Jackson, an ecologist at Scripps Institution of Oceanography, recently collaborated with 18 other marine biologists from across the United States and Australia to try to get a handle on these sorts of historical aspects of predation by humans.[21] They looked at paleoecological records from marine sediments from 125,000 years ago, archeological records from human coastal settlements after about 10,000 years ago, historical records from the fifteenth century onward, and recent ecological records from the past century. The study concentrated on four habitats: the kelp forest, coral reefs, tropical/subtropical seagrass beds, and estuaries. In each case, they found remarkable effects from top-down human predation.

Overfishing had major effects on ecosystems, according to Jackson and colleagues, with most changes in the Americas and the Pacific beginning after European colonization and exploitation. But aboriginal overfishing also played a role, as exemplified by the decline of the sea otter and the sea cow in the northeast Pacific. The researchers concluded that deleterious effects from overfishing, such as bacterial and algal dominance of ecosystems, often did not appear immediately. This was due in part to ecological redundancy. Recall the kelp forests, where sheephead, spiny lobsters, and abalone, predators and competitors of sea urchins, delayed the collapse of California kelp forests to "urchin barrens" following the extirpation of sea otters.

After the fur and whaling industries laid waste to California's coast, other industries took their turn. John Steinbeck's *Cannery Row* is today only a historic relic, victim of the collapse of the Monterey sardine fishery in the mid-1900s. In the 1930s, as many as 550,000 tons[22] were taken annually in California, from what was estimated to be a biomass of three million tons.[23] Although it has been argued that climate changes, specifically the 1958 El Niño, contributed to the demise of the sardine, unsustainable fishing played a role. Today, under tight management, sardines, like gray whales, have recovered, with annual catches around 65,000 to 100,000 tons[24] out of a biomass estimated at around one million tons. Nowhere close to recovering is the California salmon fishery. The latest enterprise to implode is the abalone industry.

Marine biologists Robert Jay Wilder, Mia Tegner, and Paul Dayton wrote this about worldwide fishing:

> A scenario of serial depletion is repeatedly played out, where humans fish down the food chain, depleting one valuable species and then moving on to the next; a result is that the composition of species in ecosystems may be changing. Valuable cod are replaced by "trash fish," and overall catch value falls. . . .[25]

This behavior, "fishing down the food web," has been described by others.[26] Because switching target prey maintains catch sizes by tonnage for the short-term, the practice gives fishermen and accounting departments the false impression that the ocean is full of never-ending bounty, when in reality fish stocks are being depleted.

As for pinnipeds, numbers of sea lions and harbor seals, like the one that returned my curious stare, have come back because of the Marine Mammal Protection Act. Fur and elephant seals, though, have been much slower to recover. The California coast is now graced by 30,000 or so harbor seals; in the past, they were hunted for dog food down to 1,000 animals, their whiskers sold as pipe cleaners. But today they are unharassed, unlike the bolder sea lions, who may end up with an illegal bullet wound after they strip a longline or jump into a seine net to feast.

Leaving the harbor seal to work my way through fishless, tall fronds of kelp, I pondered anew that in a national park, in what many consider de facto wilderness, there is for-profit harvesting of game. An additional region extends six miles offshore from Channel Islands National Park, the marine sanctuary ostensibly protected by the National Oceanic and Atmospheric Administration (NOAA). Commercial and recreational fishing occur in both the marine sanctuary and the aquatic portion of the park. NOAA, a division of the Department of Commerce, prohibits shipping and offshore oil drilling in the six-mile strip but draws the line at preserving fish. Although the concept represents an important first step in preserving living oceans, "marine sanctuary" is somewhat of a linguistic stretch. Similarly, "wilderness" and "national park" are not quite synonyms.

Much has been made of the network of marine sanctuaries placed within the 200-mile border swath of ocean that surrounds every portion of coastal United States and is internationally recognized as an "exclusive economic zone"—the vast region environmental journalist David Helvarg calls the "Blue Frontier" in his book of that name.[27] Created in 1972, the marine sanctuary program grew from public frustration over the 1969 Santa Barbara oil spill and reported military dumping of nerve gas and nuclear waste off the East Coast.[28] But the oil and gas industries and the Departments of Defense and Commerce opposed their creation, although the latter contained NOAA, the organization designated to manage them. During the first seven years of their existence, Congress failed to fund these sanctuaries. Today, 12 sanctuaries protect 18,000 square miles of ocean, a mere one-twentieth of one percent of our economic exclusion zone. All the law creating them really does, though, is outlaw dumping, mining, and oil and gas drilling. To what ultimate purpose the sanctuaries evolve into remains to be defined.

Marine sanctuaries do not preclude previously established commercial fishing activities.[29] This stems from the "multiple use" philosophy inherent to the Department of Commerce. Although there is nothing wrong with the concept of everyone getting a piece of the pie, both in the wild and at the negotiating table, as the multiple use construct allows, there is something inherent to the Department of Commerce oversight that grants trump cards to profit over conservation policies.

How NOAA ended up in this department, rather than, as some would consider more logical, the Department of the Interior, whose job is to manage and protect America's public and wild lands, is an interesting story. It may well have had more to do with personal spite than rationality, according to an account in Helvarg's *Blue Frontier*.[30] Apparently, President Nixon was outraged in 1970 by a public letter from then Secretary of the Interior, Walter Hickel. The letter, advising Nixon to pay attention to students protesting against the Vietnam War, made the president, who had just begun an invasion of Cambodia, "go ballistic."[31] Nixon promptly moved the newly formed NOAA, envisioned as a watery twin to NASA, from the control of his "adversary" Hickel to the Department of Commerce, headed by the loyal Maurice Stans.[32] The effects from this move are yet reverberating 30 years later.

Natives of La Jolla are the beneficiaries of a local marine preserve maintained by the City of San Diego, where the taking of any marine creature, invertebrate, fish, or bird, is prohibited.[33] Small though it is, fishing boats line the borders of the preserve, for large, breeding stocks of protected in-shore fish sometimes stray outside, and smaller fish abound. It is a true marine sanctuary, tiny like the one off Anacapa, and one of only four in California. The preserve offers world-class diving; one can join millions of breeding squid in January or snorkel amid dozens of six-foot mating leopard sharks in August. It works, not only for scuba enthusiasts like me, but for fishermen as well.

Robert Jay Wilder, in his book *Listening to the Sea*, points out that there are 220,000 square miles of state and federal ocean off California, but only 14 square miles, or 0.006%, that are closed to fishing. Of the 156,000 square miles that make up the terra firma portion of the state, in contrast, 6,109 square miles, or 4%, are protected as park land and are off limits to hunters.[34]

I checked my compass and made a 180-degree turn to return myself to the *Chance*. Navigating in a featureless green jungle can be disorienting. Of course, one could always surface and look for the mother boat, but bobbing up and down is a good way to get the bends, and there were thick patches of fog remaining. The best thing to do was to trust compass and watch.

Kicking along through the kelp, it occurred to me that to discover a large marine national park and sanctuary so close to home, and then to find fishing within, was the same as discovering that you could go to Yellowstone and shoot a tame, six-point royal elk without risking jail time. The world's first national park does, in fact, allow fishing, although hunting is anathema to the National Park Service (only sustenance hunting by native American tribes is allowed in certain Alaskan parks).

Even though trout play an important role in the greater Yellowstone ecosystem, a vital link in the food chain for bears, osprey, otters, and white pelicans, they are fair game for humans. Catch and release is the rule for the native cutthroat trout populations of Yellowstone. With three million annual visitors, though, many of them fishermen, there is a high probability that many of the surviving fish sport ragged lips and pierced body parts.

I looked at my air gauge—300 pounds. Time to surface and see how close I was to *Chance*, time to find out if the boat was visible at all. It was a good morning, but my impression of few fish was reinforced throughout the dive. Perhaps the arbitrary decision to protect cuddly mammals and to allow the hooking of scaled, piscine inhabitants underscores a basic conundrum that has bedeviled the National Park Service since its inception. The question is whether a national park's primary purpose is the preservation of true wilderness, or the provision of less than perfect wilderness for the enjoyment of as many people as possible.

To my relief on reaching fresh air, the boat rocked on the swell only 50 yards distant. High above us lay the unsullied, golden flanks of Santa Cruz Island. The Nature Conservancy owned these mountains; I wondered if the private, nonprofit organization, a group that has done an admirable job of preserving land wilderness throughout the world, might find a way to extend its benevolent influence into the surrounding seas. Most probably not, came the thought, because national law prohibits private concerns from owning tidelands and subtidal regions.

Swimming back on the surface, my thoughts returned to national parks. The National Park Service hoped to restore a missing link to the wilderness that is Yellowstone. The return of the wolf, legal challenges notwithstanding, depends on cold cash paid to surrounding ranchers who have lost livestock. I wonder if a similar scheme could work here in these overfished, nutrient-rich waters.

On board the *Chance* after my dive, I got a moment alone with the skipper, who, despite his nickname, struck me as an intelligent sort of guy. Years ago he was a champion free-diver and spearfisherman. Five feet 10 inches tall and burly, in his late 50s, with weathered eyes that peered through many a coastal fog, the man did not like my ideas about the value of no-take zones.

"Frankly," he said, "we can't afford to keep this boat running hauling around underwater photographers. Spearfishing is our bread and butter. We take out 20 boatloads of fishermen for every group of shutterbugs."

I pointed out that diving has brought lucrative windfalls to places like Bonaire in the Caribbean and Hanauma Bay in Oahu, sites that have true marine refugia. The captain was unimpressed.

"These no-take zones people are talking about," he said, "what if the wind comes up and we run for shelter into an anchorage in a no-take zone, and the feds find fish and spears? We'll get arrested but be innocent. They'll probably try to place the most productive areas of these islands off limits, too. . . ."

"What about commercial fishermen?" I asked.

"Now there's your problem," he replied. "Take squid. This year, after El Niño, there has been no squid fishery. Nothing. But the past two years, anybody with $200,000 of boat and expenses made a million a year, minimum. Net, mind you. Profit. They cleaned up on the opal squid.

"Still," he continued, "as far as places like San Miguel go, the weather is bad enough to protect the fisheries. If the fog doesn't get you, the wind and surf will. Most days you can't get near it. I've seen a 60-knot wind kick up in an hour. . . ."

Later, I talked to Doyle Hanan, a California Department of Fish and Game biologist who specializes in squid and pinnipeds. Hanan told me that the market price for squid was $400 per ton, that during the boom years most boats fished 10–20 days a month for four or five months, and that the largest boats could hold 100 tons. A little math told me that in one year you could, with the biggest boat and the best weather, before paying fuel costs, the crew, or boat mortgage and repairs, gross over $3,000,000.

Hanan acknowledged that after two record years of squid landings, coincident with the arrival of the 1997–98 El Niño, the squid fishery dropped dramatically. In answer, the state Department of Fish and Game instituted a permit system and weekend closures. According to Marcy Remco, the squid specialist for the Department of Fish and Game, catches for the next two years rebounded to record range, with 90% of the catch coming from the Channel Islands.

"Squid have life spans less than a year, and their year-to-year abundance is largely determined by environmental conditions," Remco told me. "We're working on modeling for management, but we don't have . . . the same kind of data and models we do for other coastal pelagics like sardine and mackerel, where we've had 60 or 70 years to develop complex population models."

In other words, fishermen are taking wild creatures before scientists have the ecology modeling in hand. Because of their short life spans, for example, squid are known to be associated with rapid turnover and population growth.

"That may itself," biologist David Au at the National Marine Fisheries Service told me, "generate chaotic fluctuations of abundance."

Scientists such as Au recognize that population shifts in biological systems are caused in rough equal measure by feedback mechanisms, or deterministic forces, and by random stochastic events, or noise.[35] Figuring all this out to the point where predictions of sustainable fishing take can be made with assurance will require sophisticated use of chaos theory and other complex, and at present, poorly understood processes.

In *Listening to the Sea*,[36] Robert Jay Wilder suggests that governments enforce the "precautionary principle." This idea advocates that it makes more sense to err on the side of caution when taking wildlife, until research has confirmed that a given amount of game can be captured without overharvesting an ecosystem.

Remco acknowledged to me how important squid were in the food web:

They are a critical forage item for marine mammals, large fish like tuna, many species of whales and dolphins, birds. . . . It's really tough to figure out what the forage needs of the entire ecosystem are; our scientists here at the lab have generated a preliminary estimate of what the consumption needs of squid are for the California sea lion population . . . it's tough to quantify for the entire ecosystem, but we're working on it.

While we can say there's probably not a shortage or overutilization of the squid resource, we're also willing to say . . . that we don't really know. We don't have enough biological information to confirm one way or the other, and we *would* like to be precautionary. . . .

Pete Halmay has spent a lifetime underwater at all the Channel Islands, first as an abalone diver, then as an urchin diver. He is not adverse to no-take zones per se, but cautions, in line with the precautionary principle, that nursery areas for all species must be included:

"If we can find the nursery areas, those source areas of marine organisms, and close them, everybody will buy into it," he told me. "Close the nurseries, and we'll have more fish. But if you close off the wrong area, and push fishing into those small places where animals reproduce, you'll just make things worse."

That night we anchored off Santa Rosa Island, working our way closer and closer to what now seemed a mythical destination—San Miguel Island. There was a damp chill in the air, and stumbling about on deck in the evening fog, I shivered, partly in anticipation of the morning and partly in fear of hypothermia, because an encounter with the reef had ripped my dry suit and forced me to dive with a not-too-thick wet suit.

Sometime during the night the crew raised anchor and diesel engines rumbled. *Chance* was moving again. She tossed, she turned, and we knew, nestled in the warm cocoons of our bunks, that she was headed west. At dawn I crawled topside to a hot cup of coffee and a cold blast of chill fog. A thick kelp forest surrounded us; a distant splash echoed through the curtain of water vapor and hinted of the life that awaited us. We were at Wycoff Ledge, off the legendary isle. There was dense fog, but the sea and air were calm.

Surveying the cold, gray, ominous scene, Greg Ochocki, my dive partner on this trip, smacked his hands together in delight.

"Now this is the San Miguel I know and love!" he shouted, grinning.

After more coffee and a thousand calories of thick French toast lathered with butter and maple syrup, I slipped into my gear and hopped into the waters of the California Current.

Ice-cream headache! The water had turned bitter cold. I worked my way down the anchor line and looked for Ochocki. True to underwater photography form, we were buddy diving—"same day, same ocean." He was nowhere in sight, and that was fine with me.

The walls of the canyon at 70 feet were covered with club-tipped anemones. Shining my light through the gloom, vivid shades of pink, orange, purple, and red leaped out at me. These radially symmetric, aggregating cnidarians are related to jellyfish and corals, possessing tentacles with bulbous tips filled with poisonous nematocysts. Like corals, they reproduce sexually at times but also divide by asexual fission.

A chestnut cowry climbed over the anemones and rocks, its shining shell marked with gold and brown, its orange-brown mantle extended. For the cowry, the kaleidoscopic invertebrates were dinner. It might also take a white-spotted rose anemone, or an orange puffball sponge; both were easy to spot and doing well in this rocky canyon.

Knobby sea stars and orange bat stars, voracious echinoderms, made slow, deliberate moves, perhaps searching for their barnacle and mollusk prey. A shell-less, yellow, snaillike lemon nudibranch, another small carnivore, prowled along the wall as well. As I discovered each new creature, all thoughts of cold disappeared and my sense of wonder expanded.

Switching off the light, I saw that the anemones still looked red. The late Conrad Limbaugh, of Scripps Institution of Oceanography, also noticed this and wondered why, because red light is filtered out by water at this depth. He went on to show that the animals fluoresce: for reasons unknown, they take in blue light and emit red.[37]

A large fish, lying in wait, perhaps, for a wandering crab, nestled within this garden of nematocyst-bearing invertebrates, brilliant dabs of blue along its flanks. Large eyes and an eye stripe identified it as a copper rockfish. Maybe it was too big to be bothered by the anemone toxins, or perhaps a lifetime of exposure had granted it immunity.

Topside, gassing off nitrogen, I thought about a conversation I'd had with Gary Davis, a biologist who studied these waters for the National Park Service. Davis is spearheading the federal proposal to place 20% of Channel Islands National Park ocean off-limits to fishing. The issue is complex, in part because California Fish and Game has ultimate jurisdiction over the disputed waters.

"I understand your proposal got some fishermen pretty stirred up—on several occasions,[38] hundreds of commercial fishermen protested the no-take zone proposal at park headquarters in Ventura," I said to Davis. "What evidence exists about the value of these marine protected areas?"

"More than 30 studies on Philippine coral reef fish, on New Zealand temperate reef fish, on Florida lobsters, and many other species show that no-take zones, even very small ones like you have in La Jolla, produce two or three times as many fish as do fished areas," replied the biologist, who has a deep voice and a calm, relaxed demeanor. "And the fish are a lot bigger. You get more big fish, fish that breed well, and you get export to surrounding areas.

"Understand," continued Davis,

California Fish and Game came to us first. They asked us to report on the state of the wildlife in Channel Islands National Park. We studied the area and realized that things are being depleted. Five species of abalone, rockfish, giant red urchins, kelp bass, sheephead . . . a long list of popular species are in decline in the park, and we were concerned about that. Fish and Game agreed; they were concerned, too, and asked us what to do about it. That's where our suggestion for some no-take zones came from. When populations fall below 40% from their unfished levels, those populations start to get shaky in terms of their sustainability. So we suggested a very modest 20% experimental no-take zone as a beginning, to help gather data. . . .

John J. Reynolds, the Pacific West regional director for the National Park Service, explained in a formal letter to U.S. Senator Dianne Feinstein why no-take zones were needed:

Current sport fishing landings . . . contain fewer and much smaller nearshore rockfishes, California sheephead, white seabass, kelp bass, and other popular fishes than landings of just a few years ago. . . .

Simply refining size and bag limits, or adjusting closed seasons, will not rebuild these depleted populations.[39]

Reynolds pointed out that although scientists have shown the no-take zone strategy worldwide to restore fisheries and biodiversity,[40] there are few studies from the United States, because there are virtually no large unfished areas along our coasts. For example, no-take zones comprise only 0.2% of the ocean contained by the 104 so-called marine protected areas in California.

The 1998 proposal infuriated Channel Island fishermen, and today, although tempers have cooled, many are still opposed to the idea. Zeke Grader of the Pacific Coast Federation of Fishermen's Associations (PCFFA), told me that the evidence just isn't there to support no-take zones:

> Frankly, we're appalled at the lack of science in some of this. I talked with a friend of mine who spent a lot of time in Australia, in their Ocean Watch program, and he says little real research is being done. There are a lot of people quoting other people's papers. If you get right down to it, there's only about two or three studies that have been done.

Added Pietro Parravano, the president of the PCFFA: "The question I have for what I call the rightwing conservation groups, is, what is their goal, do they want fishing at all, or do they want responsible fishing? That's the bottom line."

On the *Chance*, between dives, we saw a pilot whale surfacing some 50 yards beyond the kelp. Two cold-braving souls snorkeled out to join the whale in what appeared to be a feeding frenzy, with brown pelicans plunge-diving, sardines and mackerel painting the water in a mosaic of splashes, and a sea lion darting in and out. For a moment I entertained the idea of joining them, but then recalled the last dive of James Robinson, who perished here off San Miguel four years ago, another white shark victim.

The skipper grimaced at the two snorkelers after reciting to them relevant passages from the Marine Mammal Protection Act. "They stand a good chance of joining the food chain. It hasn't been that long since a shark claimed a diver at this very spot. The big boys are here, make no mistake about it. And that mess in the water over there, that's a free-for-all."

I had asked Gary Davis about pelagic species, fish that live in the water column, such as tuna, mackerel, and schooling sardines. "Pelagics overall are in somewhat better shape than in-shore species," he replied, "although everything in the sea is connected. But we're performing triage, as at an accident scene, and the in-shore species seem to be suffering the worst."

Philip Gallo, a San Diego State professor, wrote a scathing letter[41] to the editor of the *San Diego Union-Tribune* arguing that burgeoning sea lion populations are the reason fish populations are shrinking. He pointed out that a sea lion eats 8% of its body weight every day, and fish depletion comes from the overpopulation of the protected pinnipeds and the lack of apex predators such as white sharks and orcas. Protected by federal law, California sea lion numbers have risen to over 100,000. I asked Davis about this, and he repeated that everything in the ocean is interconnected:

> But if you study what pinnipeds eat, and we have, you'll find they eat squid, octopus, and pelagics. They don't eat the in-shore species we're trying to save. You have to understand how old some of these reef fish are, 20, 30, even 100 years old. And they don't move much, they stick to their portion of reef. And the older they are, the more they breed. These are the fish we're trying to bring back.

There is some disagreement with his assessment of pinniped prey. San Diego marine scientists researched California sea lion and harbor seal diets near San Nicolas Island from 1990 to 1993.[42] Squid did make up 64% of sea lion diets and 24% of seal diets. But rockfish off this Channel Island, one of the kinds of reef fish Davis is talking about, made up 30% of sea lion food and a whopping 69% of the harbor seal menu.

Meanwhile, fishermen have continued their disapproval of the recommendations. "I see the future as being pretty grim," said Bob Fletcher of the Sport Fishing Association, to the Associated Press.[43]

But no-take zones may be here to stay. James Bohnsack, a scientist with the National Marine Fisheries Services, published studies showing that the no-take zone surrounding Cape Canaveral resulted in populations of game fish twice as high as in fishing areas.[44] The Florida Keys National Marine Sanctuary now has 23 no-take zones and record numbers of grouper, spotted sea trout, drum, mullet, and snook. Local fishermen have learned to troll around the boundaries of these zones. Whether the increased fish in the reserve represent a real increase in number or movement of fish away from fishermen is a more difficult question.

Bohnsack thinks there is a true increase in number and size: "An unusually large number of world record fish were landed," he said,[45] "in the immediate surrounding area."

After initial tense confrontations, all parties, including fishermen, scientists, environmentalists, and government agency representatives, agreed to meet as a Marine Reserve Working Group (MRWG). John Ugoretz, from the California Department of Fish and Game, the agency that has ultimate jurisdiction over fishing in the three-mile band of ocean surrounding the islands, is optimistic that the MRWG can reach consensus.

"It's amazing to get a group of people as diverse as that together and actually talking," he said. "They've gotten away from blame, which is a good thing; they understand that there's a variety of causes for fish decline and that in some cases there's certain species that haven't declined."

Tom Raftican, a MRWG member and the president of United Anglers of Southern California, would like to see less emphasis on no-take zones and, instead, better fishery management of recreational fishing: "We've got areas throughout our park system that are catch-and-release," he told me. "Let's learn from that lesson."

Zeke Grader, of PCFFA, represents small-to-medium commercial fishing operations and insists that there is not enough good science to lock up fishing areas yet. "You need to have a combination of fishermen working with scientists," he told me. "The scientists know what to look for, but they don't have as much experience with the ocean—the fishermen are out there all the time. You need the two of them working together . . . that's how you'll get good science and make the right decisions."

In September 2000, the MRWG asked a group of those scientists, including Stanford biologist Joan Roughgarden, to make recommendations to meet consensus goals for restoring Channel Islands fisheries. They summarized over 100 studies and proposed expanding the no-fishing zone to 50% of the Channel Island's National Marine Sanctuary waters. The researchers likened the Channel Islands kelp forest to a ghost town once flush with black bass, cod, and ground fish.[46]

"We have a surprisingly unanimous story to tell. From a purely conservation point of view—the bigger the reserve, the better," Roughgarden said.[47]

I asked biologists Gary Davis and John Ugoretz if, in fact, Channel Islands catches had dropped by tonnage or by fish size. They agreed that on the surface, catches looked decent, but that this was deceptive. Said Davis:

> If you look at the perspective of the fishing community, things appear stable. The fleets work smarter, they have bigger, faster boats, and they have GPS that allows them to find smaller and smaller patches of suitable habitat. By working smarter and learning about their resources, they are able to keep catch rates stable over long periods of time—until things crash. Their solution is to find a similar resource to exploit from the same area using the same gear.

For example, here in Southern California, the abalone fishery moved through five species, one after another, then they moved on to red urchins, and then they moved on to sea cucumbers. And now they're working on the wavy top snail. . . .

Fishing is hard work, and it's a big risk. But as long as there's new territory, or a new species, those in the industry get a return on their investment, and everything looks OK to them.

To fishermen, Davis noted, there is little knowledge of populations of harvested animals, or of ecological and competitive interactions between the animals left behind. Such things, according to the biologist, remain invisible to those fishing topside: "From the perspective of the fishermen, things look pretty good. From the perspective of those of us who study the populations underwater, it's shock and horror. This is the disconnect we're trying to bridge."

The weather improved, and we cruised around to the north side of San Miguel, to where the brunt of the California Current and the northerly swells struck hardest. We slipped into a dive spot called Wilson's Rock, a flat, sloping bottom area, where mats of club-tipped anemones, even more dense than those at Wycoff, met our eyes. Here I found that delight of the underwater photographer, a Spanish shawl nudibranch, *Flabellina iodinea*.

Imagine an ordinary garden slug. Wait! Don't crush it, or cast it into the neighbor's yard. Paint it a bright purple. Paste a long pair of undulating, purple oral tentacles to the head. Behind them glue on two rhinophores—mysterious, sensory tubes—and paint them crimson. Now add 50 or so breathing stalks to the back and color them red at the bases, fading into orange at the tips. Call these cerata. Inject toxins to go along with the coloring, to back up the threat such gaudy displays make to predators—their "aposematic" coloring. Now cast thousands onto the slopes of Wilson's Rock dive site, have them eat sponges, and let them lay eggs in pink and red flowerlike whorls.

There, you have the Spanish shawl.

For all the wonder of the brilliant nudibranchs, I couldn't help but notice—there were no fish to be seen.

"Might be because the reef is so smooth," said the skipper later, in answer to my question.

The weather got still better, and the captain decided to try the most westward chunk of above-water stone, Richardson's Rock. "We're bound to where it ends, boys and girls," he announced. "The last land between California and Japan."

As *Chance* swept along to the west, a cry came out from the bridge: "Dolphins, everywhere!" Common dolphins now surrounded us. I tried to count and gave up after 50. The gray water boiled with dolphins as three, four at a time rode our bow wave and then sped off to the greater pod in the distance. The common dolphin, *Delphinus delphis*, is anything but common in appearance, with its robust, hydrodynamic-shaped teardrop body and beautiful black, ochre, gray, and white markings.

Delphinus feeds on near-shore pelagics, such as squid, herring, and sardines. Obviously, this pod was doing well. We saw a number of mothers with small, close-following young. But as quickly as they appeared, the entire assembly vanished.

"That was a small pod," said the skipper. "I've seen them in the thousands rather than the dozens."

At Richardson's, there were swells coming in from at least three directions. Staring at the water from the boat made me dizzy. Jumping in, I found that at 60 feet deep, there was still a lot of surge. My weight belt buckle came loose in the commotion. I almost dropped it and bobbed to the surface but, instead, caught the thing and wiggled it back on. After settling down to pay attention to my surroundings (rather than worry about underwater life-support systems), I noticed sheets of anemones and invertebrates but, again, no fish. There were, however, clouds of tiny euphaiisid shrimp that would obscure my camera viewfinder and then disappear.

After one dive, we all agreed to move back east, and we next anchored at a secret spot called Skyscrapers. "Even the fishermen don't know about this one," said the skipper.

I slid down the anchor line through green water and clouds of plankton. At 80 feet a complicated series of natural, underwater pillars came into view, each 20 feet or more in height, each carpeted with club-tipped red and pink anemones, each crawling with crabs and cowries. A large red crab, with a five-inch-wide body and legs that made it a good foot or more in diameter, posed patiently for me as I snapped its image—a moss crab, *Loxorhynchus crispatus*, named for the symbiotic algae growing on its back. And there were rockfish everywhere. There were copper rockfish, bocaccio, blue rockfish, and black rockfish. A large school of some unidentifiable species hovered above the boat's anchor line, just at the edge of visibility, maybe 20 feet off.

I was left with unanswered questions. Was it the high relief, the complex reef topography that gave shelter to these fish and crustaceans from marine predators? Or was it that the topography kept away the nets and lines of human predators? Or could the skipper be right, and this place was truly a secret, unfished spot?

Our last dive took us back to Wycoff. Enthused by the bounty at Sky-scrapers, I took along a wide-angle lens, hoping to catch the whole scene, the brilliant anemones, the fish, the kelp towering above. It wasn't easy. Once again at 60 feet there was surge and photo-fouling plankton in the water column. The biggest problem—here, as at Wilson's and Richardson's, there were no fish to speak of, a rare, small rockfish here, a bold garibaldi there.

In the wild off San Miguel, given all the right conditions, the nutrients and plankton that should support a colorful display of marine diversity, there was every reason to have a healthy ecosystem full of wildlife—something analogous to southern New Zealand or the Revillagigedos Islands. To my eye, though, rockfish, schooling coastal pelagic fish, and edible shellfish like abalone seemed few and far between.

As *Chance* powered us back to the mainland, I mused about squid fishermen, our spearfishing captain, voracious pinnipeds, white sharks ambushing urchin divers, and the findings of marine biologists. Juan Cabrillo died here of gangrene from a broken limb, and his men laid his bones to rest on San Miguel. I wondered just how much biological abundance, piscine or otherwise, he and his hardscrabble crew might have witnessed if they'd been able to look underwater. I wondered if it was a much richer ocean in the sixteenth century and, if so, whether or not no-take zones could bring that wealth of life, that biomass, back to its former abundance.

What was the carrying capacity of the region back then, I wondered, compared with now? Perhaps it was the same, with today's biomass just redistributed toward plankton and other microscopic organisms. Most of all, I wondered if paranoid fishermen might be persuaded that no-take zones could benefit them in the long run.

San Miguel Island receded in the late afternoon mist. A small pod of Risso's dolphins, large animals with square, sperm whale–shaped heads, joined us for a minute, leaping, surfing in our wake. Diesels hummed as *Chance* glided downwind with the swell. In the distance, a spout cut through the dense air. There were shouts; everyone ran to the bow. A California gray, perhaps, a straggler from the migration. We saw another spout, then, the protracted arc of a long, sounding body. A blue whale.

This was the largest animal to grace the earth, bigger than the biggest long-necked sauropod dinosaur; it was as large as 100 feet long, weighed as much as 190 tons, and was able to dive for up to 30 minutes. Primarily feeding on krill, that large, polar, shrimplike zooplankton, these cetaceans also eat California plankton, for nearly 1,000 blues live here along the Mexico–California coast. Once the rarest and most prized target of whalers because of its size, the mammal, now protected, maintained an aura of majesty as it made a long and graceful roll.

An enormous set of flukes dangled for a moment in the evening light; runoff trickling from the tail caught the rose-tinted rays like strands of pearls. Then the whale slipped into the ocean. Nothing remained but a bubbling boil of salt water, the footprint of the leviathan.

As those on board *Chance* stared at the last trace of whale, muted by the magnificence of that most charismatic of megafauna, it occurred to me that there was something ancient and forgotten in this strange national park, so close and yet so removed from the crowded cities of southern California. Here, upwelling of benthic bottom water and mixing currents powered an amazing food web. Here white and blue sharks added the same spice grizzly and black bears lend to Yellowstone and Yosemite. Here exploited creatures might yet find a haven to recover and regenerate.

This was a place where biologists, fishermen, environmentalists, and sport divers might not only find common ground but also, better yet, establish the kinds of precedents that could save underwater wildlife and fisheries throughout the world. In the end, the Channel Islands remain a place whose potential depends on the behavior of that ultimate oceanic predator—the human.

In May 2001, two years of MRWG talks came to an end. Although all parties agreed on goals and objectives, consensus regarding no-take fishing zones became impossible to achieve.[48] Commercial fishermen, environmentalists, scientists, and government representatives all reached rough agreement to establish a complex of marine protected areas. Members of the commercial charter boat sportfishing contingent, however, had reservations about no-take zones in the eastern Channel Islands, especially near Anacapa.[49] California Fish and Game, the National Park Service, and members of the marine sanctuary program will therefore establish the system, or not, without full consensus.

Meanwhile, because of the terms of California's Marine Life Protection Act, state and federal officials have until December 31, 2003, to create a no-take fishing zone system throughout California waters. The commercial charter boat industry remains opposed to this proposal as well.[50]

Government agencies have, however, established a large ecological reserve (where fishing is prohibited) in and around Dry Tortugas National Park in the Florida Keys—one of the largest ever.[51] And, in a landmark decision, the California Department of Fish and Game did ultimately vote to ban fishing permanently in a 130-square mile series of reserves surrounding the Channel Islands.[52]

I couldn't possibly write Jaws today . . . not in good conscience anyway . . . back then, it

was OK to demonize an animal, especially a shark, because man had done so since the

beginning of time, and, besides, sharks appeared to be infinite in number.

No longer. — PETER BENCHLEY

Santa Ana Sharks

Blue, White, and Leopard Sharks

After the trip on the Chance, I felt drawn to my local no-take zone. Because of talks with Gary Davis, I knew it was more than a place for test dives, more than a small wave break for teaching kids how to surf. It was brimming with wildlife for a reason, and that was because fishing there was banished. And despite hundreds of city folk like myself snorkeling and kayaking and swimming, the fish were doing well.

Maybe we could be accused of saving the wilderness for our own selfish use. Such an argument is often applied to environmentalists: "They only want to save pristine areas so they can enjoy them." The problem with this argument, for La Jolla as for everywhere else, is that it assumes that there is no intrinsic value in intact ecosystems (in this case, fisheries), whether they are enjoyed by humans or not, or that animals have no selfish needs — like living — themselves.

In *A Sand County Almanac*, Aldo Leopold wrote, "But all conservation of wildness is self-defeating, for to cherish we must see and fondle, and when enough have seen and fondled, there is no wilderness left to cherish."[1] Despite this all-too-true sentiment, I began to think that enjoying wild, marine places and preserving them are not mutually exclusive activities.

The dualistic idea that man and nature are separate lies at the core of the problem. We humans own DNA only a percent or two different from the chimpanzee genome; our brains, though large, are smaller than the brains of many dolphins;

our use of tools and language, while advanced, no longer can be considered unique within the animal kingdom. Although we may not deserve the brutal dictatorship over nature we now impose, we do own the right to a vote within the democracy of wilderness.

John Muir wrote of this unity, as if he anticipated Leopold's thoughts and wished to disagree. Muir used a bear analogy, but he might have written similar words about whales, or tuna, or sharks: "Bears are made of the same dust as we. . . . A bear's days are warmed by the same sun, his dwellings are overdomed by the same blue sky. . . ."[2]

LA JOLLA, CALIFORNIA, LATE 1990s

My brain was buzzing with too much city as I gathered up wet suit and snorkel gear. A fire truck belched diesel smoke in my face as I walked down a sidewalk and turned into the beach access alley. On my right, the restaurant where tuxedoed waiters served *boeuf tornado* in red wine sauce for $50 a plate; on my left, a $5 million ocean-front home. Raymond Chandler, a native of La Jolla (he called it Esmerelda in his books), sent his hard-boiled hero, Marlowe, down here when the gumshoe needed a break from Los Angeles.

The Santa Ana winds blew strong at the beach, where the smell of rotting kelp and salt mixed with sage and ocotillo. A few people wandered about on the sand. No one was in the water, water that was calm and cobalt blue. Air blowing from eastern deserts tingled the back of my head and vaporized all moisture, desiccating urban sweat.

I slipped in, the shock of the 62°F Pacific working its magic, washing clear the freeway, melting away the worries of urban living. In a similar moment, at the age of 26, Jacques Cousteau put on goggles for the first time, slipped into the Mediterranean, and grew ecstatic. "I saw fish," he said. "I raised my head and saw a streetcar, then descended again and saw a jungle of fish."[3]

My mask fogging, I stopped for a moment to spit and rinse. Then I surrendered myself to the sea.

There was a hint of suspense, though, even here in the soothing brine. This was, after all, wilderness, not in the sense that one was physically far from civilization, but in the sense that one had entered a new, watery dimension, a place where wild creatures lived, some of them big enough to eat a human being. In short, at sea, even steps from shore, anything could happen.

Where were the leopard sharks? Every summer they came, but not this year. By now, October, they were usually gone . . . somewhere. But this year they came late, and in huge numbers, enough sharks that even the news people got hold of it, a human interest story: "Seeing Slews of Sharks."[4]

They were old friends. My older son, Erik, and I have seen *Triakis semifasciata* many times. Erik will put on his mask and jump to peer over the front of my tanker, a nine-and-one-half-foot-long surfboard. I paddle him out through the surf, and voilà, there they are: five-foot-long beauties, dressed in black and gray camouflage, classic shark profile, long tail. Erik always squeals in delight, his foot slippery in my hand. Sure, he can swim, but not as well as, say, Johnny Weismuller or Mark Spitz. So dad holds on tight.

My fins powered me for a half-mile north over featureless sand, and there was no sign of leopard sharks. Anxiety tinged my exhilaration. Kick after kick, yard upon hard-earned yard, and no fish, cartilaginous or otherwise. The sea seemed empty to me. Still no sign of leopards. I made a 180-degree turn and worked my way back.

The first time I saw a wild shark was in Maui, where a group of three yard-long whitetip reef sharks patrolled a small cave. We ignored them and swam past their gaze into a cavern. Later, off that same island, I ran into an eight-foot gray reef shark. This one did not like the lone bubble-diver that wandered past his section of coral and so arched its back, held its pectoral fins to a vertical position beneath its body, and waggled from side to side. This behavior is shark-speak for "Beat it, buddy . . . or else."

Since then I've been in the water with silvertips in New Guinea, blacktips and gray reefs in Fiji, and hammerheads, browns, and whale sharks in Mexico. Once I went out in a boat 30 miles from San Diego and watched as Doc Anes chummed fish oil and guts over the side for hours. Doc, a quiet, serious character who has a strange glint in his eyes, has been leading shark trips for years. After stirring a bucket of oil and guts with a soup ladle, he reached into a pocket and withdrew a flask with an ominous, murky, thick, dark, brown liquid inside.

"The secret ingredient," he said. "Care for a smell?"

Abandoning my better instincts, I took a cautious whiff of Doc's clandestine reagent. A nauseating stench of refined, distilled, piscine putrefaction assaulted my nostrils. He poured a capful into the bucket and, muttering an incantation, stirred the ungodly mess. Then, spoonful by spoonful, he ladled it over the side.

My three companions, who had been drinking at a wedding the night before, added their own vomitous elixir to the slick that left our bobbing boat and spread for miles. There was, as I recall, a Santa Ana blowing that day as well.

A quartet of sea lions joined us, to the captain's curses, for sea lions eat the bait and often keep away the blue and mako sharks we sought to lure to our boat. Bored, I jumped in to snorkel with the pinnipeds over bottomless blue water.

Sea lions are playful, and these four adolescents were no exception. I suspected they'd swum out from the Coronados, a pair of small, uninhabited rocks only a dozen miles from shore that lie in Mexican territory. While diving off these islands, I'd been surprised by young sea lions swooping down upon me and sticking their noses inches from my mask, while their watchful mothers and bull father kept a wary eye on my behavior. Once, one grabbed a sea cucumber, a slowly motile invertebrate that looks like the vegetable, and threw it at me, inviting me to play some sort of underwater catch.

Not all members of this species are so playful; the big males can get ornery, and when they approach you, a thousand pounds or so of lightning fast blubber and muscle, their huge canines flashing, there is no question who's boss. There are reliable reports of male sea lions driving white sharks, their chief predators, away from haulout sites, harems, and rookeries with bold, frontal attacks. The sharks are ambush attackers, and once they lose the element of surprise, their big pinniped prey are more than willing to take them on.

The sea lion is bold and fearless in other ways, not at all intimidated by humans, unafraid to strip a commercial long line or raid any net. Some fishermen shoot them on sight, willing to risk a $10,000 fine and jail time. A dead one washed ashore last year on the beach at Horseshoe Reef, a bloated, seven-foot-long carcass with a clean entrance wound and cavitated exit wound, the hallmarks of a high-velocity bullet.

This foursome of youngsters, so many miles offshore, thought it was just great that I chose to get wet and swim with them in the chum line over blue water. They rolled and swerved and charged me, sometimes even mock-threatening me with long spews of bubbles. Once three shot by in a sea lion sandwich, the one in the middle emitting bubbles from the other two squeezing him. I was in photographer hog heaven, snapping away as they swam in their underwater ballet.

Four rolls of film and as many hours later, Doc was getting stewed. He muttered. He grumbled. He poured capful after capful of his precious "secret ingredient" into the gut bucket. At last, an eight-foot blue shark showed. With its long, graceful pectoral fins and beautiful torpedo silhouette, it cruised into the chum line. Feeling a bit silly, I returned to the boat to don a scuba outfit and climb into the aluminum cage we'd brought. Doc, meanwhile, dressed himself as for a joust (with help from the skipper) in chain-mail shark armor.

Not a part of his body was unprotected; the suit included woven metal gloves and hood. He entered the water with a terrific splash, lowering himself outside the cage, chunks of dead mackerel sticking out of his buoyancy compensator vest. In a matter of seconds, the blue came down on him from above, placed its jaws squarely over his metal-covered head, and ground away.

What an image. Here was this underwater Lancelot, his entire head inside the grinding jaws of a shark poised above him. My shutter finger twitching, I clicked pictures madly, sure they would appear on a magazine cover someday, no doubt with *Time* or *National Geographic*. Then Sir Lancelot started tapping on my camera.

"Cut it out," I yelled, angry bubbles coming out of my regulator.

The mad knight, ignoring the perilous situation of his head, kept tapping on my lens.

"Doc," I screamed. Here was this guy, about to be guillotined by a hungry blue shark, and all he could think about was how to mess up my shot. How could I record this amazing event with a chain-mail glove covering my lens?

Then I looked down at my camera. Anes was trying to help me, after all. I was the idiot. The 15-mm lens, ignorant of all these events, remained covered by its black lens cap.

Only days before my snorkel at the reserve, a friend invited me to go cage diving on his dive boat, this time for white sharks. Seems there's a population of great whites off a certain Mexican island that few people know about. Only a month before my friend was there, surrounded by five fish, each well over 10 feet in length. This was his first time using a cage, and he and his crew suspended it with twin inch-thick hawsers. When some blood spilled on one of the ropes, a 15-foot white swam over and gave the line a playful, inquisitive bite, slicing it in an instant. That left the two inhabitants of the cage with one rope holding them over 240 feet of water. If a shark chewed through the second line, they would have had an interesting swim back to the boat.

On board was a researcher who studied the predators at the Farallon Islands off San Francisco, a scientist who had done some radio tagging of the little-understood animals. Results of his study showed that the whites fed on a seal and then swam out several hundred miles into blue-water ocean for three or four days.[5] They then returned to feed again. What they did on these long trips, other than digest, remained a mystery.

Because it takes some time to process hundreds of pounds of food, biologists think most white sharks don't fancy the scrawny, blubberless flesh of most humans. That is why people can survive an attack by a white: The predators shoot up from below, take their initial bite, then back off.[6] While they wait to let you bleed to death, they evaluate the taste of your flesh. If there's not enough fat, you are off the hook. Although surviving that initial bite can be problematic, Peter Klimley, another researcher who studies whites in the Farallon Islands off San Francisco, speculates why most people survive: "If they ingest something that's not energetically profitable, they're stuck with that for a few days," he said.

Commenting on three recent attacks in northern California in which people had been hit and released, he said: "Can you imagine? These sharks are seizing people and holding them very gingerly to make this decision."[7]

What is "gingerly" to a white shark may be a relative term. In 1963, off Aldinga Beach, South Australia, Rodney Fox, a contestant in the state spearfishing contest, was in search of a large dusky morwong, a cartilaginous game fish, some three-quarters of a mile offshore. A second after he noted a strange stillness in the water, a white pointer (Australian for great white shark) hit him on his left side and dragged him through the water. He flailed, attempting to gouge the animal's eyes, and it let him go. The white then attacked a second time and took him down to the bottom, where, distracted by a fish in Fox's tethered game float, the shark again released him, only to tow the bleeding man on an underwater Nantucket sleigh ride. At last the shark's teeth cut the float line, and Fox made it to the surface.

Through a long series of lucky medical events, Fox made it to the hospital and survived, although his lungs and stomach were exposed and only his torn wet suit held his body together.[8] To this day, Fox is still diving. In fact, he specializes in shark dives and has been a leader in the movement to protect Australia's white pointer, the very beast that nearly killed him.

Unlike whites, who specialize in marine mammals, the other three man-eaters, the bull, the oceanic whitetip, and the tiger, are more cosmopolitan in their feeding habits. Once they start feeding, they don't stop.

Like the other lamnid sharks, the salmon shark of Alaska and the mako shark, whites are semi–warm-blooded, keeping their body temperature 5–10°C above the environment by a countercurrent network of blood vessels.[9] Like tuna, billfish, and swordfish, they have the edge on other fish, because their brains and swimming muscles stay warm.

The routine for attracting whiteys is the same as for blues: you dump buckets of slaughterhouse blood and fish guts overboard for hours, and then the big guys and gals come knocking. Into the aluminum you jump for the thrill of a lifetime.

Chumming is unnatural, to say the least. Some have compared it to shooting a zebra in the Serengeti to attract lions. It's artificial. It's disgusting. It's filthy. It can induce seasickness in the hardiest of sailors. I hate it. But it works.

Flip Nicklin, a marine mammal contract photographer for *National Geographic* (and the son of Chuck Nicklin), told me, "I do feel that we should think long and hard about feeding wildlife to get a picture. It would not be tolerated in most terrestrial situations."

The most dangerous thing about chumming is that it teaches sharks to associate humans with food. This might be bad for people, because it could get man-eating fish to seek out small boats, surfers, and swimmers.

But regarding humans as a food source is even worse for sharks, because commercial hunting of the long-lived, slow-reproducing animals for their fins and flesh threatens their survival. Numbers of sharks all over the world have diminished, and as they become more and more rare, in a vicious feedback loop, shark-fin soup's price and glamour in Oriental markets, shark steak's popularity on the menu, and using shark cartilage as an antidote for arthritis and cancer only increase.[10]

Ah, the cancer myth: sharks live forever, they never die unless killed by violence, they never get neoplasms. A pathologist at George Washington University, John Harshbarger, studies malignant tumors in animals. He reported at a recent meeting of the American Association of Cancer Research that sharks, and their cartilaginous relatives, rays and skates, "can and do develop cancer."[11] Yet sales of shark cartilage supplements are rising to multimillion dollar levels each year. The best thing any shark can do, at the first hint of placebo-seeking humanity, is to turn tail and swim away.

The reproductive strategies employed by sharks are complex and, sometimes, bizarre.[12] Primitive sharks (the horned shark, for example) lay eggs (oviparity), the baby sharks relying on yolk reserves for nourishment. More advanced sharks utilize ovoviviparity or aplacental viviparity—the embryos remain in the mother shark's uterus and utilize a yolk sac attached to the maternal digestive tract. Tiger sharks, angel sharks, and some nurse sharks are examples of species that use this strategy. Some sharks carry things even further, exhibiting what scientists call oophagy, or the eating of eggs. White sharks, makos, sand tigers, and threshers gobble up, as embryos, any ovulating eggs appearing during their mother's pregnancy. In a raw display of natural selection, successful sand tigers, in fact, eat all other siblings in utero before turning to their mother's eggs.

Finally, the requiem (gray reef and silvertip sharks belong in this group) and hammerhead sharks utilize placental viviparity, in which the yolk sac evolves into a placenta. This system of supplying embryos with nutrients is very similar to that found in mammals.

No matter what their strategy, rates of maturation and reproductive turnover in sharks are unhurried—many species breed only every other year and have 13-month gestation periods. Sharks have gotten away with this leisurely reproduction for more than a hundred million years because they are efficient predators, but they cannot handle modern fishing methods like drift nets and longlines.

"The oceans of the world are being purged of sharks," writes Sean Van Sommeran, a marine biologist and director of the Pelagic Shark Research Foundation, a nonprofit organization devoted to the research and study of sharks.[13] In the United States, commercial fishing mortality of sharks is around 20,000 metric tons per year; statistical analyses and computer models indicate that catches above 12,000 metric tons are unsustainable. These numbers are dwarfed by longline tuna fishery data dating from the 1950s of Japan, Korea, and Taiwan, where shark by-catch rates have been estimated to be in the millions of fish per year. Sharks are not the targets—they are unwanted "trash fish" destroyed by the indiscriminant mechanism of industrial long-lining. Crews on international fishing vessels do make a routine, though, of slicing fins from sharks caught as by-catch (prices in Hong Kong for shark fins can be more than $250 per pound[14]) and dumping the maimed animals into the sea to die.

Not all species of sharks are endangered, for elasmobranch fishes (sharks and rays) number nearly 800 species, and there is wide variety in fecundity and maturation age. Pierre Kleiber has been studying blue shark populations with the National Marine Fisheries Service (NMFS) out of Honolulu. He took longline catch data of blue sharks from Japan and Hawaii and gill drift net data from Japan, Taiwan, and Korea and crunched the numbers with an analytical computer model that works to explain the production and abundance of populations. Kleiber assured me that steps were taken to ferret out the veracity of the data, to ensure that there was no underreporting. Much of the Japanese "size sample data" (information about the size of the fish in the catch) came from longline training vessels, such as the *Ehime Maru*, the vessel sunk by the surfacing American submarine off Oahu in 2001.

After manipulating the data and trying worst-case scenarios, Kleiber found that blue shark populations were holding out. "You may be surprised that I am getting this optimistic result given that it's a shark we're dealing with, and sharks are known to be very vulnerable to fishing pressure," he wrote me via e-mail from a tiny atoll somewhere in the middle of the Pacific.

He attributes this result to several factors. One is that small-mesh gill drift net fishing was abandoned in the 1980s. More important may be the fact that there is a spectrum of vulnerability among all the species of sharks, and blue sharks appear to be on the low end of it. They have large litters—26, on average, in the Pacific. Shark biologists figure the breeding interval to be one to three years, but at those litter sizes, a shark breeding only once in a lifetime would still be fecund.

"If we were catching one of the shark species at the other end of the vulnerability spectrum at the rate we've been catching blue sharks," Kleiber said, "it would have crashed long ago, which brings up the point that our worries might better be focused on other species that are relatively rare in the catch, such as mako or thresher."

David Au, at the NMFS in La Jolla, told me that there is still concern that fishing will push the blues into danger, because, as discussed in chapter 10, fluctuations in populations may vary in response to both feedback mechanisms (from top-down predation by humans or bottom-up limitation of prey) as well as stochastic reasons (unpredictable events such as climate change or current shifts).[15] For this reason, the NMFS will urge caution in the harvest of the blue shark.

Consider that in the Atlantic, fishermen turned to dusky and sandbar sharks when cod, haddock, and flounder fisheries became depleted in the early 1980s. The NMFS encouraged this switch, and today populations of these sharks have dropped 70–90%.[16] Charles Karnella, administrator of the NMFS Pacific Islands Area Office in Honolulu, admitted that we know very little about the numbers of blue sharks. "All the information we have is fishery-dependent data," he told the Los Angeles Times[17] in 1998, "and what we'd like to do is have fishery-independent data on the size of the population."

The effect of diminishing sharks on the oceanic food web, although not clearly understood, may be to increase midlevel predators and, in turn, possibly, to decrease fish and plankton at the base of the food chain. The diminishment of these ancient, cartilaginous fish may have broad, far-reaching effects on the ocean that humans can only guess at now; it is possible that marine ecosystems might suffer in ways not currently suspected.

As with other large, slow-reproducing denizens of the deep (whales, for example), for shark populations the ocean definitely has limits. There may be enough fishermen with enough high-tech equipment worldwide to endanger populations or even, eventually, to cause extinctions if humans

BLUE SHARK, THIRTY MILE BANK, SAN DIEGO,

CALIFORNIA *". . . there is still concern that fishing will push the blues*

into danger. . . ."

don't change their ways. Fortunately, we have, here and there, offered some assistance.

The white shark, *Cacharodon carcharias*, hunted with impunity even before *Jaws*, now enjoys protected status in California since the passage of Assembly Bill 522.[18] Because of the efforts of such people as Rodney Fox, the white pointer is also protected in Australia. Blues, makos, and tigers are less lucky and can still be fished legally in most places. Fishing in Mexico, unfortunately, is another story. With a valid Mexican license, the legal limit remains a single white shark per day. Of course, what happens at sea is rarely affected by fear of legal retribution. Mexico, for example, has declared waters surrounding the Revillagigedos Islands, south of Cabo San Lucas, to be a marine sanctuary, but there is poor enforcement. The Sea Watch website regularly publishes online photos of such infractions.[19] The United Nations has rendered oversize drift nets illegal, but there is no enforced proscription of the use of nets longer than the maximum 2.5 km or, for that matter, of any other form of high-seas poaching.[20] Abandoned "ghost-nets" continue fishing for many years, their catch unharvested but still dead.

Chumming may be but a distant relative of the overfishing of sharks, but a relative it is, nevertheless. I passed on joining the white shark trip; my consolation prize was to be found here in La Jolla, snorkeling a mile from home.

The odds of seeing a white shark in this corner of ocean were about zero, I thought, scanning the empty, underwater Gobi Desert below, my fins flicking up and down like a pair of wounded fish. True, one may have devoured a young woman in 1994 a few miles to the south, while she was having a solo, nude swim one night off Ocean Beach. Telltale teeth imprints were found on what was left of her body; whether or not she drowned first before the shark came is unknown. A few yards to the north, near Scripps Pier, an oceanography grad student fell victim during a scuba dive in 1959. The attack was witnessed, but no body was found. Just months ago lifeguards at this very beach saw several 12-foot whites patrolling offshore. But on this day? No way. On the other hand, the odds of my seeing leopard sharks should be very good.

I continued to kick to the south. Nothing. The vast plain of sand stretched beneath me, unchanging. Visibility was about 15 feet. No kelp. No fish. *Nada*. Maybe it was the Santa Ana, maybe it was thinking about big fish, but my sense of uneasiness and apprehension grew.

I swung closer to the reef. Emerald-green surf grass appeared, swaying in the undersea wind that is ocean surge and current. Not an alga like kelp, *Phyllospadix* is a true, flowering, vascular plant or angiosperm. It possesses tremendous anchoring power in its roots, allowing it to withstand the pounding and buffeting of winter waves. These roots also help surf grass produce 1,000 grams of carbon/m²/year, a rate four times that of nearshore phytoplankton. Nitrate-binding anaerobic bacteria found within the subtidal mud produce fertilizer that the surf-hardened roots extract.[21]

A school of sargo, marked across the back by a single black slash, small fish the size of my palm, darted around me. A kelp bass poked through the algae, its mouth wide open, gills pumping water slowly. But there was no sign of leopards.

Turning north a second time, I reentered the sandy plains. A bat ray glided by, soaring, its wings, giant pectoral fins, moving with ballet grace. A couple paddled close in a yellow, tandem kayak. Treading water, I spat out my snorkel and asked, "Have you seen any sharks?" They shook their heads. They, too, were looking for leopards.

We moved on in parallel. There was a fluttering movement near shore. I tracked it down, then back to the surface. A western grebe. Strange to see a bird underwater. At home in the air or sea, it moved like a rocket, feet paddling, wings tucked tight and hydrodynamic.

For some minutes I followed the bird, watching it peck the bottom for shellfish. A long shadow darted by—a shark.

Sharks, rather. In twos, in threes, in tens. Leopards. Motionless, I watched from the surface. Were they mating? Hunting? Hunted?

A frond of kelp uprooted from its holdfast and swayed in the surge. The green blades provided the only shade from the Santa Ana sun around for miles. Sharks churned the sand beneath it. I kicked closer. In a flash, they accelerated to warp speed and disappeared. But more took their place. Mesmerized, I glanced beneath me. Only inches from my belly were three, four more. Harmless, but so alive, so alien, so wild.

A round sting ray glided along. The sharks ignored it. They were preoccupied, with what I knew not. There were dozens, hundreds. All swam in the surf line, just above the sand, milling, doing their mysterious shark thing. Lacking a swim bladder, if they stopped moving, they sank to rest on the sand. But few ceased their classic side-to-side body swing. Each had a unique pattern of black spots on a gray background and an asymmetrical tail, the upper lobe elongated.

They feed on fish eggs, sand crabs, and clams. If given the chance, they will take bony fishes, octopi, and lobsters. Bottom dwellers themselves, they enter shallow, muddy bays with the tide, then leave as it ebbs. Their maximum length is seven feet. Their danger to humans, nil. Their flesh is tasty, and they form an important part of the commercial shark fishery.[22]

"They occur seasonally within the sloughs and bays of California," wrote Jon Kao, a scientist focused on studying leopard sharks at Moss Landing Marine Labs, "places that provide birthing and nursery habitat during the spring and summer months."[23]

Kao noted that leopards, like most sharks, have late ages of first reproduction and low fecundity and growth rates—they are as susceptible to overfishing as the white. "The decline of an apex benthic predator such as the leopard shark could have wide-scale community effects," wrote Kao, who is doing research on the animal's food consumption rates.[24]

The buzz in my brain faded, the crackle of shrimp and the roar of surf taking its place. An hour later, I was no closer to understanding what the cartilaginous fish were doing, but I was closer to something else. Far from the city, I rested, nestled at home in the palm of nature.

Why chum whites far away in Mexico, when you could see leopards at arm's length here at home? Relaxed, I bobbed in the swell, the sun warming my black wet suit, my limp body a blade of drifting kelp.

CHAPTER TWELVE

Shuttling as they do like silver threads between upland and ocean, abyss and summit,

salmon tightly stitch the interlock between continent, torrent, and tide, binding together

everything humans do to land or water. And we do much. . . .

—CARL SAFINA, *Song for the Blue Ocean*

Swims with Salmon

Dipping into the Turbulent Waters of the Pacific Salmon

Just after renewing interest in my home waters, I slipped away on another trip. The journey this time, though, kept me within the United States. Alaska—the Serengeti of North America. A place where wild caribou in the hundreds of thousands live in the northern Brooks Range. Here Denali Peak—some in the lower 48 still call it Mt. McKinley, even though the man it is named for never set foot in Alaska—rises more than 20,000 feet. Under its shadow can be found timber wolves, Dall sheep, moose, fox, and wolverine. The oceans off Alaska are also abundant, teeming with fish, crabs, birds, and mammals. Here the same battles occur as all over the globe, between those who would save and those who would exploit wild nature.

ALASKA, 1999

The icy July waters of Kachemak Bay, Alaska, felt shocking only to my face and hands as I slid over the gunwale into sunlit Tutka Lagoon. Chris Banos, the Boston Whaler's owner and our guide, a big, blond man with a hearty grin and a grizzly bear handshake, had been almost giddy as we donned our dry suits and snorkel gear.

"We've had all manner of fishermen, tourists, and photographers on this boat," he said, laughing, "but I can't remember the last time a client jumped over the side."

My friend Greg Ochocki and I had come to the Kenai Peninsula to see salmon in their native habitat. Here in Tutka Lagoon were, according to reports we heard in Homer, Alaska, several hundred thousand pink salmon—also called humpies—returning to their natal home to spawn. To get to the lagoon, Chris had to wait for the slack period of low tide; then, we shot in with the rising tide through a 20-foot-wide channel with one 70-foot salmon purse seiner in front of us and another behind.

On slipping into the water, we saw that the visibility was less than perfect. Dark green water surrounded us, full of phytoplankton taking full photosynthetic advantage of the long sub-Arctic days. Diatoms, tiny creatures wrapped in silica shells, are the most abundant phytoplankton,[1] and they flourish here in the north. Dinoflagellates, also found in polar waters but more common in the tropics, possess attributes of both plants and animals, spinning through the water like microscopic whips as they build sugars from sunlight and carbon dioxide.[2] In the far north, as in the high-latitude south, no thermocline exists, thermocline being that oceanographic term for the abrupt junction of warm surface water and cold, oxygen- and nutrient-rich deep water. Off Alaska, there is no warm water. So there are plentiful phosphates and nitrates mixing near the surface to feed these phytoplankton during the brief summer, when there is at least some sunlight.

The photosynthesizing plankton here in Tutka Lagoon were in turn grazed upon by zooplankton, principally copepods, segmented critters one-half millimeter in length, T-shaped from large antennae, and bearing a single, central eye. Copepods, perhaps the most abundant animals in the oceans, gobble up phytoplankton with an odd, jerky feeding motion at an incredible rate; for this reason, the standing crop of primary producers in the sea is much lower than on land, where trees and plants tie up organic matter in stems and trunks for many years. Total plant marine biomass is estimated at 1–2 billion metric tons, while terrestrial biomass is 600–1,000 billion metric tons. And yet both ecosystems produce around 50 billion metric tons per year.[3] Copepods have a lot to to with this fast and efficient turnover.

Both diatoms and copepods lay enmeshed in a rich food web, a maze of interconnected animals, microbes, and plants nourished by oxygen-rich, glacial meltwater. This web links ocean and land through the miracle of salmon.

But on this day, if there were salmon here, they were not hungry. No. They were here for a different reason.

We snorkeled our way off a shore dense with spruce and hemlock trees, hovering over a shallow bottom thick with submerged logs. If the salmon were present, we didn't see them.

Ochocki went east, I went west. Ten minutes passed, then half an hour. The cold water began slipping in around the seals at my wrists, hands, and feet. Shaded by the trees, the water had an ominous feel to it.

A sunken snag blocked my swimming path. As I grabbed a branch to pass around it, the water beneath me exploded. Hidden under the tree, numbering in the hundreds, humpy salmon shot out in all directions, their cover blown, their fear of my intrusion plain.

Silver bullets with blue-green dorsal skin, each a uniform three feet long, they exuded energy and power. Now, swimming along the coast, I could see them everywhere.

Ochocki was yelling at me from his side of the lagoon; I raised my head out of the water to hear him better. "There's millions of them here. Billions!"

I swam over to Tutka Creek, where freshwater met the brackish lagoon. The surreal mixing of the two types of water made things underwater look like an Impressionist painting, a kind of salmon Seurat. Here the fish would pause, then shoot by me to charge though the blurry junction of liquids.

There was a catch to our wilderness adventure. These weren't really wild fish. They were hatchery fish, spawned in the lagoon in trays, raised in pens, fed food pellets, and released as smolts to fend for themselves in the Gulf of Alaska. The survivors were now returning two years later, their genetic program leading them back by scent and other cues to where they were born, this small estuary and the seiners' nets.

In the center of the lagoon floated the hatchery, a large pontoonlike dock. A pair of seiner boats were moored there, unloading a portion of their catch to provide roe and sperm for future fish. That was the deal—the fishermen got to fish, the hatchery got free breeding stock. And federal and state funds paid for it. On the surface, this was a good investment of the taxpayers' money; as we explored the subject, though, it became clear that there were problems with artificial breeding of salmon.

To understand the nuances of hatchery versus wild requires that one understand the complex life cycle of the Pacific salmon, really a collection of five species, chinook or king, pink or humpy, sockeye (from the Native American word *sukkai*) or red, coho or silver, and dog or chum. In the same genus, *Oncorhynchus*, are the steelhead and coastal cutthroat trout, seagoing races of inland trout species. Like the Atlantic salmon, *Salmo salar*, all these fish are anadromous, wild fish born from eggs in fresh, riverine water that migrate downstream as smolts to mature in the oceans and then migrate back up to their natal spot to spawn. Like the opal squid, once Pacific salmon spawn, they die. Atlantic salmon, steelhead, and coastal cutthroat, however, may live to repeat the process again.

Imagine one gravid female salmon, an intrepid fish hunting herring somewhere far from land. A deep, inner voice calls her to find, using clues that science still has not uncovered, the stream from which she emerged as a smolt years before. How she uses salinity, temperature, magnetism, light, and oceanic geography to find this stream is unknown. How the same voice calls her prospective mates to join her from across the vast reaches of the northern Pacific, how they all reach this freshwater outlet together, is another facet of the mystery. But not only does our fish time things to meet the males, she also times it at the moment in spring, summer, winter, or fall (up and down the Pacific coast, different species and strains procreate in all four seasons) when water flow is best at this stream for her particular dash to procreation.

Each stream in salmon country forges genetic cues in each race of salmon, telling that run where to go and when. Living in fresh water requires a radical shift in metabolic paradigms, and there is only so much time for our fish to mill and stall outside the home river. An enormous sand bar offshore from northern California's Mattole River, for example, is finally breached by great swells in the late fall, beginning that river's run of king salmon.[4] In like fashion, each race of each species of wild salmon has adapted to subtle details of survival for their own particular watershed. They represent, perhaps, intraspecial genetic diversity at its finest.

So imagine our egg-bearing salmon charging upstream, into the freshwater that her now-remodeled kidneys must excrete. Past sea lions and brown bears, over rapids and waterfalls she charges. On reaching her birthplace, our fish is battered and abraded. Pale fungus grows on her sores. She cares not for food; she has but sex, eggs, and sperm on her salmonid mind. The climb back into the mountains has used up most of her bodily reserves, and she begins to metabolize her own flesh. Every organ system is weakened or sacrificed save one: the reproductive system.[5]

She searches for gravel in briskly flowing water a foot deep, gravel big enough to resist the current; on finding the spot, she lays sideways and clears a 15-inch-deep hole, a redd, with forceful tail strokes.[6] At the deepest part of this redd she digs an ovipository, and her excavating may take hours, even days. When it is done the right male, having been busy himself driving off younger "jack" males, is there, arching over her back, trembling with lust and drive. At the moment of truth, they discharge: she, the delicate pink eggs, maybe a thousand; he, the milt, milky and dense with sperm. She covers the eggs from upstream, sweeping them with her tail, burying them in the loose interstices of gravel. Coelomic fluid from the egg switches on the sperm cells; another substance guides these motile packets of energized DNA, leading them to a closing hole called a micropyle. There are but a few brief seconds when fertilization is possible.[7]

Two, three more nests our salmon builds—she is not one to put all her eggs in the same redd—and then she is done, spent, listless, and finally dead. Her corpse, and the corpses of her suitors, drift and rot to feed otter, bear, insect, and the web of life that is the forest. Her body will serve as fertilizer for her hatchlings. So salmon harvest the thin stew of the sea and carry it high into lush alpine forests, where about half of the nutrients feeding that ecosystem are of marine—that is to say, salmonid—origin.

Imagine now one little salmon, born in the gravel cradle its parents fashioned, a redd lying in a clear-running, cold mountain stream. If we could take ourselves back in time, this stream could be as far south as what is now northern San Diego County, as far north as the Alaska Peninsula. Hatching from the small, reddish pink egg is a little fish called an alevin, a hatchling that still has a yolk attached. It remains there in the gravel with its siblings, maybe a thousand of them, growing for two or three months.[8]

When the yolk food is finally absorbed, the alevin plucks a gulp of air from the surface, forms a swim bladder, and becomes a fry. Baby food for the fry includes mayflies, caddisflies, stoneflies, and the like; when fry produce camouflage green and brown spotted markings, they become parr.

For our one little parr to have survived this long, many things must have gone right. As an egg, it needed porous gravel free of clogging algae. As a fry and parr it needs old-growth forest, complete with fallen, submerged snags, dead hemlock, fir, and spruce trees that provide a young fish with nooks, eddies, and crannies, a place for protection from predators: trout, terns, eagles, otters, bigger salmon, gulls, mink, and herons. It needs clean, cold, oxygen-rich water, not water full of sediment-laced runoff from clear-cut mountainsides. It does not do well in water that floods down watersheds unimpeded by snags and other natural barriers.

Having survived so many dangers (for nine in ten hatchlings die by this time), the parr now undergoes a process called smoltification, a metamorphosis into a narrow, seaworthy, fusiform shape, a body that is dark blue-green on the back, silver on the sides, and whitish on the belly—the classic oceanic coloring scheme known as countershading. Physiological changes turn the smolt inside out, as kidneys change from salt-absorbing to salt-excreting, from water-excreting to water-sparing. This kind of internal metamorphosis is the hallmark of all anadromous fish.

Smoltification occurs at the time of year for that watershed when the baby salmon's home river is rushing high, full of foods such as larvae and copepods. As at other stages in a salmon's life, it requires luck to survive predation, but also luck of a different sort. Hydroelectric dams with swirling turbines can impede its path to the sea.[9] Once the changes start, the smolt must reach the ocean in days—its renal physiological clock is ticking, and it cannot survive having saltwater kidneys in freshwater. Over the millennia, each race of salmon is imprinted with the right time to make its dash, when the river is running highest and avails the least amount of swimming. There is nothing worse for our smolt than the miles of slack water lying upstream from a great dam, unless it is the turbines of the dam themselves.

These propellers turn as fast as 75 rotations per minute; too large and slow to puree the fish, turbines subject young salmon to turbulence, hydrostatic pressure changes, and shearing, forces that may explode their swim bladders and kill them, or make them vulnerable to predators. A conservative estimate is that 8–10% of all smolts in a run die at each dam and pool —and many rivers in the Pacific Northwest have multiple dams.[10]

On reaching the ocean, the smolt encounters salt water for the first time, and a new host of hungry hunters. Mortality continues to be high among our young salmon's siblings, as sharks, dolphins, pinnipeds, gulls, and loons feed. But the fish grows rapidly and soon becomes a fleet predator in its own right, traveling some 10 miles per day, ranging wide over a cool ocean.

Years pass, yet another metamorphosis occurs, and the wheel spins once more. It is a convoluted and strange life cycle. And yet, each stream being different, there are countless variations to the theme. Each river and run of fish has its own tight fit, the salmon timing their ascent and descent to perfection. Rainfall, salinity, predators, insects—they all ebb and flow during the year even as tides change through the day and the month.

Pink and chum salmon hatch near the sea, in places like Tutka Lagoon. The big chinooks may find their way hundreds of miles inland, some to elevations a mile above sea level. Cohos spawn in small streams in places like the Tongass rain forest of Southeast Alaska. And sockeyes work their way up winding streams to brook-fed lakes. Chenik Lake, on the Alaska Peninsula, is just such a breeding ground.

We'd flown from Homer across the Cook Inlet in a single-engine, bright red, Otter float plane piloted by a crusty, bearded, 40-ish bush pilot named Ken. In taxiing up to the dock in Homer, Ken barked at me as I reached to help fend the plane from the dock. "Don't touch that!"

"He means you!" said Ochocki, grinning at my uncouthness. It was clear that Ken held disdain for non-sourdoughs from the lower 48—people like myself. That was fine by me, as long as he got us across the 100 miles or so of treacherous water separating the Kenai Peninsula from the Alaska Peninsula. The cloud ceiling on the trip was never more than one hundred feet, and beneath us three cross swells churned the water.

Southern Alaska is a collision zone for the Pacific and North American tectonic plates, as well as high-latitude storms. Contact between these floating layers of planetary crust has created the Himalaya-like, 20,320-foot Denali Peak and the rest of the Alaska Range; at some places where the plates subduct under each other, as in the Aleutian trench, they produce weak points that allow hot gases to boil to the surface. Although the murky atmosphere hid them, I knew active volcanoes surrounded us: Iliamna, Redoubt, Denison, Katmai. And so we were more than happy to spot the odd collection of buildings that forms Chenik Camp. Up the coast, as we circled to make our approach, grizzly bears feeding on salmon dotted a small river at a series of waterfalls.

The Chenik lodge was built on disputed land by one Mike McBride, member of the New York–based Explorer's Club and an Alaskan naturalist and entrepreneur. Although the camp has existed for almost 20 years, McBride has no clear title to the land, and other Alaskans, especially a pro-bear-hunting coalition, want him and his lodge removed.

We hiked the quarter mile from camp twice a day to sit on a grassy cliff some 50 feet above the stepped falls of Chenik Creek. Along the way, sweet odors of fireweed, wild iris, and Burnet rose wafted from our wildflower-strewn path to hang in the sea breeze lifting off Cook Inlet. We were accompanied by a bear mace– and shotgun-toting guide (12-gauge, single-slug, five-shot). At the outlet of the stream, a female brown bear, named Solstice by the camp staff, fished with a two-year-old cub named Sparky. Her prey? Sockeye salmon, each fish a silver bullet weighing three or four pounds, each fish intent on charging up the falls to a clear, cold freshwater lake some five miles inland from the sea.

It was hard to say what was more dramatic, the valiant efforts of the salmon, dodging in terror from the claws and advances of Solstice, or the bear herself, 600 pounds of speed and grace, ravenous in her preparation for winter. The salmon would school at the mouth of the creek, waiting for high water. Here a harbor seal would dine on the unwary, as would a collection of bald eagles and sea gulls. Then high tide—and Solstice—appeared, and the fish charged inland. The bear, her apprentice cub watching, would pounce and, if she missed, chase a salmon for 20 or 30 yards at racehorse speed, water splashing in all directions, her footing somehow secure on the rough and slippery terrain. She was successful on about half of her leaping attempts; far more salmon swam by and escaped than were seized, but the unlucky caught fish were each devoured in a matter of seconds, their remains left for the gulls and eagles.

Solstice made it look easy, but the cub, Sparky, showed how hard catching salmon for a living could be. In five days, we never once saw this 200-pound bear catch one. Try as he would on many attempts, the bear failed, adrenaline-charged fish escaping claws and teeth time and again. Frustrated, the cub followed its mother, seizing half a salmon when it could, enduring a paw slap or bellow when the old gal got tired of a teenager that had hung around, perhaps, a little too long.

For years people like ourselves have sat in silence watching this tragi-comedy, this high-tide duel between salmon and grizzly bear. Similar viewing sites pepper the Alaska Peninsula, most famously at the falls in Katmai National Park and at McNeil River. Over the years the bears have learned to ignore the humans on the cliff sides or wooden platforms. Never has anyone needed to shoot a bear; it hasn't hurt, of course, that the brown giants are stuffed with salmon. Of course, should hunters win the court battles over Chenik Creek, the bears there, conditioned to ignore their traditional human enemies, will make easy targets.

One day Ochocki and I hiked up to the lake. Donning masks and snorkels, we found sockeye schooling in clear, cold water as they rested before their final push to spawning sites in tiny brooks above the shore. It was like swimming in air, frigid, aquatic air; beneath us, every detail of the bottom lay apparent through the crystalline freshwater, the gravel clean and perfect for salmon nurseries. Above us conditions were ideal, too: flies and other insects everywhere, willows and tundra on the surrounding hillsides holding topsoil and preventing runoff. There was no need for a hatchery here; this pool of freshwater with its feeder streams was the perfect place for piscine orgasms of eggs and sperm. A place to die for—Chenik Lake.

So what was wrong with trying to help nature along a bit, with attempting to duplicate Chenik Lake conditions in Tutka Lagoon? Nothing, one might answer, and everything.

In a sense, hatcheries work because hundreds of thousands of fish return from the sea on a regular basis to keep afloat an important industry. But over the long term, major flaws in the system appear. Hatchery fish have limited genetic diversity, and the fish that managers breed for future stocks are picked at random. Over time, salmon like the pinks we swam with in Tutka evolve into a monoculture and, as such, become less able to adapt to changing water temperatures, predators, and infections. Raised in pens until they

GRIZZLY SOW WITH SOCKEYE SALMON, CHENIK CREEK,

ALASKA *"It was hard to say what was more dramatic, the valiant efforts*

of the salmon . . . or the bear herself. . . ."

smolt, they make perfect hosts for viral, fungal, bacterial, and parasitic invaders. Released into the open ocean, they now compete with wild fish and carry those diseases—and their poorly differentiated genes—with them.

As hatcheries pump up salmon numbers, fishing is increased, with resulting increased pressure on wild stocks. The facilities themselves introduce chemical pollution and reduce water quality, diminishing stream flows, destroying habitat, and causing upriver nutrient depletion.

Perhaps the most insidious danger of hatcheries is that they hide the destruction of forest ecosystems. As dams are built for hydroelectric power and flood control, as forests are shaved in clear-cuts, hatcheries are offered as mitigation for the eradication of anadromous fish like salmon.

The U.S. Army Corps of Engineers dammed Oregon's mighty Rogue River in 1977. Even at this late date, the Corps failed to install fish ladders to provide a way for salmon and steelhead to return to natal sites above the dam in the high country surrounding Crater Lake and vicinity. Instead, they built the Cole Rivers Fish Hatchery, a place that cranks out four million salmon and trout per year. I have visited the hatchery with my sons, and we've watched men in boots clearing algae with scrubbers from concrete, fish-filled pens. Since no fish can get past the dam, an enormous rock-filled structure, the construction project signed the death warrant of many races of wild fish over a huge watershed. A writer for the Corps penned the following in an official brochure about the dam and the resulting Lost Creek Lake, using what can only be described as classic Orwellian doublespeak:

> The technologically advanced and unusual intake tower regulates water temperature by combining lake water from different depths in a mixing chamber before releasing it downstream. This cools the normally warm summer water of the Rogue River, improving conditions for fish migration and survival.[11]

As wild stocks are depleted, it is the loss of genetic diversity, that ability to adapt to changing streams and conditions, that may be most important.[12] For only this complexity of DNA will protect these fish, over the endless tide of time, from the global warmings and glacial periods, the El Niños and La Niñas, and the rise and fall of salmonid microbial predators.[13]

Numbers of salmon in upriver habitats are limited by hatcheries, and the loss of dying spawners and fry from the habitat can have far-reaching effects on many species. Bears, otters, and eagles need to eat dead salmon; the bodies of dead adults provide nutrients that bolster streams for wild parr. The trees themselves depend on salmon fertilizer. Research suggests that one salmon per square meter per year is needed to maintain pristine, intact old-growth forest ecosystems.[14]

Then there is the fact that hatcheries are expensive. Data from the Pacific Rivers Council[15] show that out of $1.3 billion spent on salmon by government agencies over the decade from 1981 to 1991, 41%, or $537 million, was spent on hatcheries, money that could have been spent on improving or preserving habitat, on research, or on changing dam systems to help return wild smolt to the sea and wild spawning adults to their natal sites.

Hatcheries like the one we explored in Tutka or south-central Oregon have been touted as a panacea for the practices that have devastated salmon industries in the Pacific Northwest, from northern California on up to Washington State. Clear-cutting of forests and damming of rivers, in conjunction with overfishing, have led to the loss of millions of dollars of jobs and revenue, not to mention fish. Only 16% of salmon runs in the lower 48 states are *not* declining. The rest are dying. More than 300 salmon populations in these states are at moderate to high risk of extinction; 100 have already been destroyed. Reversing this will take money and political will, both of which are diluted by hatchery programs.[16]

Hatcheries have an evil twin as well. Fish farms, prevalent in Norway and elsewhere across the Atlantic, hold Atlantic salmon in pens, where they grow to adulthood before being shipped to market. The ill effects of hatcheries, including the genetic problems, are magnified with this technique. Not the least of the problems is that the fish must be fed. For each pound of salmon raised, some three pounds of ocean-produced fishfood must be provided, thus increasing fishing pressure (freshwater farms grow herbivores like catfish and tilapia and are much easier on the environment).[17]

Salmon aquaculture leaks tons of feces and surplus food, polluting shoreline ecosystems; Norway's farms emit as much nitrogen as does the untreated waste of four million people. A third of "wild" salmon found in Norwegian rivers possess fish-ranch DNA.[18] Worse still, the farms have spread to the Pacific, to North America in the 1980s and to Chile in the 1990s; Pacific fish farmers still use the adaptable, fast-maturing, and long-spawning Atlantic salmon. Hundreds of thousands of escapees[19] from the net pens disrupt wild Pacific salmon populations by introducing disease, interbreeding,[20] and competing for habitat.[21] Because of these problems, the government of Alaska, to its credit, banned salmon aquaculture from state waters in 1990.

Recently, a deadly virus has been found across the Atlantic, infectious salmon anemia virus.[22] This infection causes bleeding, lethargy, and then death; it first appeared in monoculture fish farms in Norway, where seals and storm waves damaged marine net pens and allowed mixing of farmed and wild animals. Now the virus has been found in wild salmon in the Magaguadavic River in New Brunswick, and in Scotland. Arguably in worse shape than their Pacific cousins, wild Atlantic salmon are at their lowest recorded levels, having dropped from 800,000 in 1975 to less than 80,000 in 1998.

In reviewing the environmental wars of the late twentieth century, one might make the case that an error was made in the tactics of preventing the clear-cutting of old-growth forests. A web of life complete with thousand-year-old Douglas firs, cedars, and hemlocks and their dead, hollow snags, the forest contains a mosaic of insects, mammals, birds, and reptiles. As with tropical forests, most of that biomass is held above ground. After the logs are hauled away, the depleted soil cannot regenerate itself to anything approaching the glory of old growth. And the great trees themselves create their own weather, entrapping and condensing moisture. When they are logged, there often is less precipitation, and when the rain does come, it floods, carrying soil and sediment in rapid, uncontrolled runoff.

Ninety percent of ancient forests in the Pacific Northwest have been logged, most of them clear-cut, with 5% preserved in national parks and wilderness areas. That has left the remaining 5% for loggers and environmentalists to fight over. For biologically sound reasons, conservationists fashioned the spotted owl, a creature that depends on ancient snags for nesting, into an icon, an animal that formed the basis of legal battles using the Endangered Species Act to attempt to halt the final destruction of old growth.

But the spotted owl became the butt of jokes, a focal point for local bitterness. People were not willing to give up their short-term livelihood for the sake of an obscure creature, or perhaps they were unable to understand the value of the complex ecosystem the animal represented. Although many legal battles were won because of it, the little bird proved to be a public relations disaster.

In retrospect, the salmon is making a better icon. Salmon need old-growth snags and wooded hillsides as much as the owls—the young salmon need submerged dead logs for protection from predators and heavy spring flows, and they require the clear water healthy, unlogged watersheds give. Instead of owls versus jobs, the debate is now the more utilitarian jobs versus jobs, for the salmon industry, at one time, anyway, had a value comparable to that of the logging industry. It has the additional cachet of being a renewable extractive industry.

Despite the claims of many foresters, it takes 500–1,000 years to create a temperate rain forest; because of the soil nutrient problem, regrowth or secondary growth can only be a sorry attempt at rejuvenation. The enduring salmon, with their life cycles of two to five years, are more forgiving if overharvested, although once a population is destroyed it is difficult, but not impossible, to reestablish. In the battle of clear-cuts versus salmon, fish might have proved to work better than owls. They may still serve to heal watersheds across the region.

The Alaskan salmon story is different from the tales of woe that emanate from the lower 48—not because the runs are bigger (unbelievable numbers of wild, huge salmon once passed under the Golden Gate or up the Columbia River, fish that are long gone),[23] but rather, because of its vastness and relative remoteness, there are still many native races of salmon to be saved. And nowhere in Alaska have the battles been fiercer, or the stakes higher, than in southeastern Alaska's Tongass, the nation's largest national forest, a place where clear-cuts have already replaced much of the wild salmon.

Ronn Patterson stood at the helm of his 50-foot vessel, *Delphinus*. In his 50s, gray haired with a crinkly eyed smile and a gentle and humorous manner that masks iron-hard convictions, Ronn is the owner and skipper of a live-aboard whale-watching boat in southeastern Alaska. He spent 15 years as a biology professor at University of California at Berkeley—he used to teach nature; now he lives it. He pointed to a green swath of the Tongass just east of Frederick Sound on the Alaska mainland, a place that loggers had worked 50 years ago, a clear-cut that soared from the coast up to the snowy, high reaches.

"Look closely," he said. "Do you see any new western hemlock or Sitka spruce there?" It was a rhetorical question. After 50 years, only small pines were scattered amidst a field of alder, the dense shrub that makes the Alaskan bush impenetrable.

"The Forest Service cut much of this timber based on a 100-year rotation—but because of the short summers and dark winters, that, as you can see, is unrealistic."

Ronn explained how in the 1950s the U.S. government felt the need to make an effort to bring year-round jobs to the Alaskan panhandle and maintain a presence in a sparsely populated land not far from the Cold War enemy, the Soviet Union. Our government persuaded two companies, the Alaska Pulp Corporation, a Japanese-owned concern, and the Ketchikan Pulp and Lumber Company, a shell for the timber giant Louisiana-Pacific, to build huge pulp mills in Sitka and Ketchikan, respectively. Each was granted enormous amounts of lumber from the Tongass by the forest service at dirt-cheap prices.

Some years later, Ronn continued, the petroleum industry needed access to Native-claimed lands in the North Slope and across the state from Prudhoe Bay to Valdez, for a proposed oil pipeline. After much backroom brokering, wheeling, and dealing, Congress passed and President Nixon signed the 1971 Alaska Native Claims Settlement Act. This law was designed to put to rest all Native claims to Alaska and to allow the exploitation of the state's vast natural resources. ANCSA, as it came to be called, conveyed 44 million acres and $962.5 million to Alaska's native peoples, in exchange for "the extinguishment of all land claims forever."[24]

There was one catch—the money and land would be held in corporations, in which every Alaskan native would hold stock. These corporations would then be required to pay shareholders cash dividends. The almost predictable result, explained Ronn, was clear-cut logging of nearly every stick of timber on ANCSA land in the Tongass National Forest.

ANCSA was silent on subsistence, on living off the land. It demanded cash. And so the Tlingit of Southeast Alaska, the people most dependent on salmon, on Sitka deer, on all the benefits that old-growth forest granted, were forced by powers beyond their control to cut their home and former livelihood down.

Ronn's take on ANCSA and the Tongass was not unique. Writes Kathie Durban, an investigative reporter for *The Columbian* in Vancouver, Washington, in her book, *Tongass: Pulp Politics and the Fight for the Alaska Rain Forest*:

> The forest had provided sustenance to countless generations of Tlingit and Haida. It had taught them the natural order of things. It had informed their spiritual beliefs and inspired their traditional ceremonies. Now, according to the provisions of ANCSA, it must be leveled and exported to the highest bidder.[25]

The story of the Tongass is not yet over. Whistleblowers like William Shoaf, himself once a "timber beast," forestry slang for an eager lumber cutter, sacrificed their jobs and nearly their sanity to fight the nonsustainable logging that resulted from the two pulp contracts and ANCSA.[26] Environmentalists teamed up with fishermen from towns like Petersburg, where economies were based on salmon and selective logging. After decades of legal wrangling, by the late 1990s the government succeeded in freeing Alaska from the giveaway pulp contracts.

But the legacy of the logging era remains. More than half of the salmon in

CLEAR-CUT MOUNTAIN, TONGASS NATIONAL FOREST,

VIEW FROM FREDERICK SOUND *"The almost predictable result,*

explained Ronn, was clear-cut logging of nearly every stick of timber on ANSCA land

in the Tongass. . . ."

southeastern Alaska are hatchery salmon, because many of the wild runs have been extinguished by clear-cuts. Because chum and pink salmon are two-year species, they are the primary hatchery fish. Fishermen can only get pennies a pound for these low-grade salmon; meanwhile the chinook, coho, and sockeye dwindle.

Ronn summed up the trend toward hatchery fishing in Alaska: "There's good data on the tonnage of salmon caught here, and over the last ten years, that tonnage has remained steady. But the number of fish caught to produce that has doubled: the average fish caught today is half the size of what it was only a decade ago."

But all is not gloom and doom in Alaska's panhandle. One morning I arose just before dawn to find *Delphinus* anchored off Admiralty Island, now a national monument with most of its forests and, by extension, its wildlife, intact. Like the other huge islands that, along with a strip of mainland, make up Southeast Alaska, Admiralty is a terrain (also spelled terrane), a kind of continental fragment, a miniature tectonic plate. Some terrains, such as Prince of Wales Island to the south, originated in tropical climes, their limestone testimony to ancient corals. Many of them, their lime eroded by heavy rain, possess extensive caverns underground, karst formations that hold Pleistocene skeletons and other secrets.

After geological forces ran these plates into the mainland, throwing up magnificent mountains on both islands and mainland, glaciers scoured deep fjords, like the one in which *Delphinus* was now anchored. Plentiful nutrients and long summer days make this a phytoplankton paradise and, by extension of trophic levels, an inland sea rich in herring and halibut. Three species of whales ply the fjords, along with harbor seals, river and sea otters, and a host of other marine mammals. Admiralty, Baranof, and Chichagof islands, the so-called ABCs, also have grizzly bear populations. It was salmon, though, that served the native Tlingit so well, salmon that formed schools so dense that stories were told of walking on fish to cross streams. Salmon anchored the food web of this region, salmon and its essential, symbiotic, botanical counterpart, the ancient forest.

Moving to the stern deck, I stood still to absorb the scene. A jellyfish dilated and contracted in the still, chill waters around the boat. Toward shore, 20-foot tides scoured rocky banks. Here, beyond intertidal anemones, decorator crabs, and bull kelp, lay a forest primeval. Towering hemlocks and spruce were draped in moss and lichens, the verdant understory open and inviting. A zephyr fanned through the ancient trees, bringing subtle scents of the sea, of the forest, of tidewater glaciers. The air was so fresh and clear that I wanted to bottle it and take it home.

As the deck rose and fell from a muted swell, a splash sounded a musical note 20 yards away. Salmon. There was a soft whoosh overhead as a bald eagle, its yellow eyes spying breakfast, lowered razor-sharp talons to take a wild coho in a blinding, splashing instant. The big bird, weighed down, managed to haul its prey to a distant spruce, where it sounded the rise-and-falling melodic, flutelike whistle that is so musical and so antithetical to the animal's fierce visage. The silver salmon was not a hatchery fish. It belonged to a wild strain, its DNA dedicated to an Admiralty stream that did not need man's help.

Far off sounded the bellowing and hooting of a chaos of badly tuned cellos, the distant, echoing roars of a Steller sea lion colony. Distant snow-covered peaks caught each riff and sent it back in a fading echo. Nearer thrummed a tubalike bass note, a slow, rhythmic blast that came in pulses every five minutes or so. For a moment, alone on the deck, bathed in the golden light of an Alaskan dawn, I thought it might be the rumble of distant surf on a far-off beach.

Then the tuba player appeared, cruising near *Delphinus*, only a few feet from shore. As the young humpback sounded to raise a barnacle-encrusted set of flukes, a pair of harlequin ducks winged by, their plumage of maroon and teal set against the blue of morning. Again the eagle whistled, this time answered by another white-headed raptor. Now a lone grizzly wandered onto the beach, scooping and crunching clams, shell and all, ignoring a Sitka deer grazing 100 yards distant. A loon called, a ghostly sound I'd not heard since my boyhood in Minnesota. And behind it all, the Steller sea lions brayed and roared in the distance.

For hours this wild orchestra performed a symphony for a Southeast Alaskan morning, a work of nature that rivaled anything Brahms or Mahler composed. I began to understand why people were so passionate about the Tongass. Here the land, air, and sea, woven together by pine, eagle, and salmon, form a wilderness sublime.

In Tutka Lagoon, having had our fill of snorkeling with salmon, we pulled ourselves back onto Chris Banos's Boston Whaler. Chris, jovial as always, told us he'd been talking by radio with the seiners in the lagoon.

"They all think you two have gone 'round the bend. Joe there, the skipper of that nearest boat, he says, 'Forget Dances with Wolves. We're gonna call these guys Swims with Salmon.' Do you want to get in their net and take some closeup photos?" he said. "I asked 'em, and they said it would be OK."

We agreed, and a moment later, Chris pulled up close to one of the boats that was making a set. The crew waved and smiled. We jumped into the green water and swam over the buoys of the net. The seiner's engines hummed, the sound amplified underwater.

Salmon in the purse seine sped in circles, trying in vain to escape. They ignored us as they wheeled and shot from one side to the other in their shrinking space. After years living in the vast reaches of ocean, after surviving cold storms and fleet predators such as the lamnid salmon shark, cousin of the mako and white, this net was their reward.

It became clear that I'd better get out to avoid being pulled into the air by the hydraulic pulley. I slipped over the buoys and floated there on the surface, staring at the mass of fish, unable to turn away, a rapt bystander. The fact that they were hatchery fish seemed irrelevant. The salmon pressed tightly together against the webbing of the net, their mouths open, gaping, their gills pumping and fanning, their eyes lit wild with fear.

Perhaps, it occurred to me, it was not death that they feared—for they would soon die no matter what. Perhaps it was more a sort of frustration over the inability to spawn, over the cruel net blocking their driving need to consummate the end of a long and perilous oceanic journey. A moment later, the power block lifted them out of their element and converted them into a harvested commodity.

As the fish twisted in their death throes, it gave me solace to know that somewhere across the Cook Inlet, at shining Chenik Lake, high above the sea, other salmon remained wild and free. It was a comfort to realize that, across the Kenai Peninsula and to the south and east, places like Admiralty Island still harbored wilderness symphonies, natural scores that wild salmon conducted.

Here and there across the Northwest lie such unsullied places, intact watersheds where hatcheries are not needed, where the ritual of "spawn and die" can play itself out as it was meant to. Not all of these streams are in Alaska; some course through British Columbia, Washington, Oregon, and California. In places like these, having survived bear claws and orca jaws, dams and hungry fishermen, the "silver threads" that tie fresh and salt water together undergo their final metamorphosis.

As they spiral along their tragic, life-sustaining cycle, the genes of each run are molded into a perfect fit for each unique valley. Perhaps like no other creature, these fish form the keystone of symbiosis between land and sea. From the first swallowed air bubble to spawning and death, these salmon, the fittest, the wildest, the best, embody like no other creature Earth's magical connection between forest and ocean.

Oceanography grows from many disciplines to address questions as to how the ocean works

as a system, as an ecological biogeochemical system. And I believe unless we understand

that, we will simply be making quick fixes. . . . — F A R O O Q   A Z A M

Mystery Marine Microbes

Exploring a Honey-Thick Ocean

As salmon tie together ancient trees and even more ancient ocean, so living cells in the sea connect climate, currents, creatures, and chemicals. Surrounded by a group of loyal explorers and an international web of like-minded scientists, people like Farooq Azam are peering into this microcosmic space, looking into what may prove to be the core reactor of life's machinery on Earth. To understand how oceanic viruses, bacteria, protozoa, and plankton work together, Azam and his colleagues in laboratories and institutes around the globe synthesize microbiology, chemistry, geology, and physics into a new kind of oceanography. The findings of these biogeochemists over the last 30 years are startling.

Because Scripps Institution of Oceanography is but two miles down the road, and because Dr. Azam was gracious to let me join his lab for a day, I was lucky to get a glimpse into a new and magical world. It is important to realize that similar labs exist, also filled with brilliant, inquisitive minds, at the Monterey Bay Aquarium Research Institute, at Woods Hole, at Laboratoire Arago on the Mediterranean, at SUNY, at the University of Hawaii, and at institutions elsewhere on the planet. But even though oceanographic knowledge is making leaps and bounds, marine researchers receive a disproportionately lower fraction of the moneys poured into other realms, especially medicine and space research.

"We're testing a new dark-field microscope," said Farooq Azam on a sun-drenched day at Scripps' Hubbs Hall. Perched on the fourth floor, his office overlooked a Pacific roiling with waves from a passing storm. "Care to see?"

A relaxed, patient man with a bushy mustache and gleaming, intelligent eyes, Dr. Azam led me into a crowded laboratory where a group of postdocs, grad students, and visiting foreign professors chatted in low, intense tones. Azam is from Pakistan, where he received bachelor and master's degrees at the University of Punjab in Lahore. He got his doctorate in microbiology in the Czech Republic but didn't make a real name for himself until, as a visiting microbiologist at the University of California at San Diego, he was invited to help out at Scripps Institution of Oceanography on a problem involving bacteria and diatoms.

Once he realized how little was known about the nanometric world of the oceans, how much potential for discovery existed there, and how important for the planet those discoveries might be, he never left. True scientific acclaim came with his contributions to "microbial loop" theory. Posed first as a collection of questions by Lawrence Pomeroy of the University of Georgia[1] and then refined by Thomas Fenchel of Denmark,[2] this theory, for which Azam has provided key experimental evidence, postulates that much of the fixed photosynthetic energy in the sea does not rise through a food chain to higher life forms, but circles in a tight web entirely at the level of viruses, bacteria, and protozoa.[3]

The historic paradigm of a "grazing food chain," whereby all photosynthetic production, and the fate of carbon, moves from phytoplankton to zooplankton to fish, led to the belief that microbes could be ignored.[4] That view is now replaced with the knowledge that the microbial loop may be responsible for as much as one-half of oceanic primary production.[5]

For this and other achievements, Azam, now full Professor of Biology at Scripps, received the Rosenstiel Award for outstanding distinction in oceanographic science. Only six such awards have ever been made.

But clearly all this has not gone to Azam's head. He maintains an open, humble demeanor. He delights in pointing out various professors emeritus we see wandering the corridors of Hubbs Hall. He discusses their discoveries in reverent tones. And, he welcomes naive visitors like myself who interrupt too often and ask simplistic questions.

In the microscope room we found a cocktail party without the drinks.

MARINE SNOW AT 1,000 METERS DEPTH, MONTEREY

CANYON, CALIFORNIA *"This is a chunk of marine snow,*

part of the ongoing fallout. . . ."

Accents from France, Mexico, and Germany caught my ear. Excited, casually dressed scientists were talking in small groups of twos and threes, exuding intense, barely contained enthusiasm, as if they were riding on the bridge of, perhaps, one of Magellan's vessels, bound on a voyage of discovery. On a bench, the new microscope illuminated slides with side lighting, and, using fluorescent stains and a high-powered lens, researchers were using it to look at marine bacteria. On an attached computer screen, I stared at a large blue blob covered with tiny white dots.

"This is a chunk of marine snow,[6] part of the ongoing fallout of organic matter given off by upper-level marine animals and plants," a graduate student in a T-shirt explained. "Such snow continually drifts to the bottom. Those white specks are bacteria surrounding it."

In a calm monotone, Azam launched into his explanation of biogeochemistry. Listening, I felt like a passenger in an accelerating scientific Ferrari.

> In a cubic centimeter of surface seawater, there are between 500 thousand and one million bacteria. Everywhere. We have looked all over the world, in the Antarctic, in the Bay of Bengal, here in La Jolla. If you plot a log/log plot, you get, of course, some scatter, but roughly, we find the same thing. Always we find this density. We have also found the number of bacterial species . . . to be consistent at around twenty per cc, although the species vary widely.
>
> The ratio of viruses is 10 to 1, so there are about 10 million viruses in every milliliter. Smaller than that are the colloid particles, of which we find 100 million in every cc. [cc (cubic centimeter) is a synonym for milliliter].

As I listened to Azam, it occurred to me how much work went into each fact he tossed off. For example, to say, "We've found one million bacteria in every milliliter of water," had many implications. First, someone had to figure out how to count the bacteria themselves. Because they are smaller than terrestrial bacteria, although possessing the same amount of DNA, finding ways to stain and quantitate marine bacteria was a major challenge in itself. In the 1970s, for example, use of fluorescent staining and microscopy,[7] a major breakthrough at the time, estimated only about 100 bacteria per liter of surface water. Most of the bacteria were missed because of their small size, which permitted them to pass through the plankton filters then in use. Only modern nucleopore filters could snare them.[8] Such filters, in combination with other techniques, such as differential interference microscopy, epifluorescent staining, scanning and transmission electron microscopy, remote sensing, and satellite oceanography, have become keys unlocking a hidden universe for marine microbiologists.

After figuring out how to stain and count, of course, many hundreds of samples needed to be collected from sites all over the globe and properly treated, the bacteria measured, and the data reviewed. Thousands and thousands of hours of data collection, number crunching, false starts, and theorizing from people working worldwide must have gone into making this one simple statement a reality.

"Our focus here in the lab, really, is on adaptations," Azam went on:

> We're trying to find out what it takes to live as a bacterium in the sea, how those adaptations lead to structure in the sea, and how they affect the ocean's carbon cycle. We are looking, for example, at sinking particles. Bacteria on marine snow grow very, very slowly. They aren't just sitting there, though; they have, in their cell surface, high numbers of lytic enzymes: lipases, proteases, phosphatases. As particles fall, they are being solubilized by these enzymes. The bacteria aren't growing larger, perhaps because they are so dense and crowded, but they are leaving behind a plume of organic matter.

For a moment I pictured the oceans of the world, this bizarre snow falling everywhere, bacteria working on it, leaving behind a cloud of nutrients. Azam continued:

> If you think in terms of the carbon cycle of the ocean, carbon dioxide is taken in and fixed within the upper ocean by photosynthesizing bacteria and plankton, and, with other nutrients, turned into sugars, protein, and DNA. If this falls out as marine snow to the bottom, you have a very efficient flux of carbon out of the atmosphere . . . to the bottom, where it can only reappear at the surface after a period of thousands of years. But, if bacteria are using the snow and oxidizing it through the process of respiration, the depth at which the carbon is oxidized becomes very important. Upper ocean: it will equilibrate. Deep ocean: it's not going to come up.

Once again, Azam was pointing out the essential multidimensional nature of the ocean, the same complicated essence of the sea that helped to make dolphin brains, those organs involved in three-dimensional mapping, so big. The sea at the surface is another world from the sea on the bottom.

Azam broke off for a moment to peer at the microscope. Wiggling *Vibrio cholera* now filled the screen. Bacteriophages can infect *Vibrio*, a common marine bacteria, and intercalate (form a chemical bond) into the cholera

DNA, changing it into a pathogen that, if untreated, can kill a human with watery diarrhea. Further complicating things, scientists have linked high organic loads from human runoff with cholera pandemics. They also find the bacteria to be associated with certain small crustaceans.[9] Unlikely linkages and interactions such as these underscore that webs rather than chains dominate interactions in the sea.

Azam jumped back into our conversation:

> The second thing we've found in the sinking particle system: if you look at these hydrolytic enzyme activities, the enzymes that cleave sugars have less activity than the enzymes that cut up proteins and phosphatases. The consequences? Carbon-rich compounds are not being harvested as efficiently as proteins and DNA. This is important to the carbon cycle, for nitrogen and phosphates are left behind in the upper waters, and more carbon is fixed, that is, sinks. So every cycle, more and more carbon is sent down to the bottom, and the efficiency of this carbon pump is increased. Carbon is fixed more efficiently than ammonia and phosphate.
>
> People have observed in the past that as particles sink into the ocean, they become carbon-rich, nitrogen-poor, and phosphate-poor. So . . . bacteria maintain the momentum of the carbon cycle in the upper ocean, and they do it by pumping out these different ratios of enzymes.

If my understanding was correct, then, bacteria helped or hindered carbon fixation depending on both their depth in the water column and the ratio of the various molecular meat cleavers they employed. Clearly, this was a complex and poorly understood system. But the implications for carbon fixation and global warming were just as transparent as the various relationships were murky.

I asked Azam his opinion of a scheme some scientists have proposed to accelerate the fixing of carbon in tropical oceans. The central areas of oceanic gyres, such as the Sargasso Sea, are vast, nutrient-poor regions of the world. The late John Martin, a chemical oceanographer, discovered low levels of iron in such waters and noticed on satellite images that where wind-blown desert dust struck the sea, plankton blooms followed.[10] To test this, oceanographers added iron to waters near the Galapagos Islands, and a large growth of plankton ensued, with resulting decreased nitrate and carbon dioxide levels measured.[11] Some engineering-minded souls would seed the oceans with vast quantities of powdered iron. This would cause massive plankton blooms, increase uptake of carbon dioxide, and ameliorate the greenhouse effect — or so goes the theory. Martin distanced himself from this use of his research: "Such experiments are not intended as preliminary steps to climate manipulation."[12]

Azam laughed and shook his head at my question about eco-engineering.

"What is so amazing to me with every finding we make is our level of ignorance, rather than our level of knowledge," he said. "We have only yesterday discovered the diversity in the sea of life, and surely we don't know how this system works. To perturb it in such a profound way, to change the base of the food web by increasing the productivity would be . . . crazy."

At this point, a bright-eyed young oceanographer, Forest Rohwer, joined the conversation. He sported a single gold earring and a shock of untamed black hair. Trained as a molecular human immunologist, he too (like Azam and myself, at least temporarily) left the medical world for this synergistic study of the sea. A prodigious learner, in only three years in the field he'd become fluent in oceanography. Said Rohwer:

That water from the equatorial tropics is flowing into one of the most productive parts of the ocean, the region around Papua New Guinea, for example. Those reefs, quite possibly, depend on the input of nutrients flowing in from across the ocean.

Azam added:

Normally that phosphate and nitrogen flows out and supports life in other places. If you just harvest carbon, nitrogen, and phosphorus right there, somewhere else you're going to have starvation. So you're not just changing the ecology of that part of the ocean, you're changing the ecology of a significant part of the whole world.

The rationale for the iron proposal is that when you have a bloom of algae, a larger proportion of it will fall down as marine snow. If you let the water go all over the place, you don't have this intense production, and a smaller proportion will flow to the bottom. So the argument is that by creating blooms around the equator, you will have a larger fraction of that productivity fall to the bottom.

But we know so little, so little about sedimentation.

Now Dr. Fereidoun Rassoulzadegan spoke up. The Director of Research at the zoology department of the University of Paris, the kind of august visitor Azam's lab often receives, he pointed out how in the Mediterranean Sea, prevailing winds from North Africa carry Saharan dust high in iron into the water. A quiet-spoken, relaxed man with a beard and rectangular silver glasses, he chewed a long-stemmed pipe and spoke perfect English.

Dr. Rassoulzadegan explained how iron oxides form from this desert dust, compounds that have a tremendous affinity for phosphates. Because, as phosphate or other nutrients become limited, bacteria can accelerate their processing much faster than can phytoplankton, bacteria use up the remaining nutrients. The result is little algae and phytoplankton in the Mediterranean Sea.

"That's why the Med is so blue—low numbers of phytoplankton," said the French oceanographer. "It has lots of productivity at the microbial/bacterial loop level, but nutrients often can't rise up the food web to higher life forms."

Azam went on to explain another cycle, the silicon cycle. Diatoms, the most abundant phytoplankton in the sea, require silicon to grow and reproduce. Beautiful, intricate one-celled organisms that assume a variety of bizarre and whimsical shapes under the microscope, diatoms use what is, essentially, glass for their skeleton.[13] Covering this silicaceous body is an organic matrix. One of Azam's colleagues, Kay Bidle, has shown that marine bacteria can attack dead and living diatoms using hydrolytic enzymes, like the ones they use on marine snow.[14] Once the matrix is gone, the silica dissolves into the water column and can be used by other diatoms.

Diatoms, like computer chips, have an absolute requirement for silicon, and bacteria play a major role in how silica moves through the ocean. Because bacteria use about half of the organic matter derived from oceanic primary production, their role in the cycling and fate of both carbon and silicon, as well as nitrogen and phosphorus, is enormous.

What is most striking, though, is that all this has been elucidated only in the past 20 years.

In 1951 Rachel Carson and Oxford University Press published one of the most remarkable books ever, *The Sea Around Us*, a best-selling, classic work of nature writing about the ocean for the lay audience. Revising it in 1960, Carson brought the book up-to-date for that time. Marine biologist Jeffrey Levinton wrote an afterword to the 1989 edition that added a summary of discoveries from the intervening three decades.

The book remains a wonder, for Carson's lyric imagery makes the sea an unforgettable, living world. Today, however, at the rate that paradigm shifts in how the oceans work are occurring, in part because of discoveries by people like Azam and his peers, a revision could now be written almost every year.

Carson wrote, for example, the following sentence: "The [sardine] fishery could not exist except for upwelling, which sets off the old, familiar biological chain: salts, diatoms, copepods, herring."[15] Her classic food pyramid, from inorganic salts, to phytoplankton, to zooplankton, to fish, we now know to be a bit constrained. Today, we could write, ". . . from salts, to polymerized colloids, to bacteriophages (viruses), to archaea, to bacteria, to protozoa, to diatoms, to copepods, to herring." Then we would need to add that the microscopic side of this complex web often, but not always, runs independently as a parallel system. We might also want to mention the semi-contained jellyfish web. Tomorrow we will, no doubt, need to add more levels and qualifiers.

To understand how tardy some of these critical discoveries are, let us consider, for example, *Synechococcus cyanobacter*. One of the ocean's most abundant bacteria, it was not described until 1979. In the North Atlantic, the North Pacific, and the Sargasso Sea, it is now believed to be the primary producer, the largest fixing agent of carbon into usable organic compounds in the ocean.[16]

Another example, *Prochlorococcus marinus*: In 1988 Sallie W. Chisholm, a professor at MIT who at one time worked with Azam, discovered this creature, now thought to be perhaps the most abundant organism on the planet.[17] Also a photosynthetic cyanobacter, *Prochlorococcus* forms tiny cells smaller than conventional bacteria that number from 70,000 to 200,000 per milliliter of seawater. Preferring low-light ocean for its photosynthetic machinery, this picobacteria, because of its large numbers, churns out a major fraction of oceanic organic production.[18]

But these bacteria are only creatures in the domain of the prokaryotes. Eukaryotes, the largest domain, include the kingdoms of plants, animals, fungi, and protists (single-celled, nucleated organisms that include protozoa, diatoms, and dinoflagellates). A third and new domain, Archaea, has just been recognized. Like the prokaryotes, archaeans do not have membranes around their nuclei, nor do they possess organelles such as chloroplasts and mitochrondria.[19] Yet the creatures in this realm have unique lipids in their cell membranes that resemble neither bacteria nor eukaryotes. At first, archaeans were not thought to be in the ocean, except rarely, at hydrothermal vents, where warm, reducing, sulfide-rich fluid seeps power newly discovered biological communities in the deep ocean. Researchers at the University of Hawaii, for example,[20] found archaea at a depth of 1,000 meters on the summit of Loihi Volcano, the next Hawaiian island. Many of the organisms found in these vents live at high temperatures and use chemosynthesis; they build sugars with reduced sulfur compounds from the vents (H_2S) rather than using water (H_2O) as in solar-powered photosynthesis. The discovery of archaeans, life forms that have a biochemical heritage as related to humans as to the bacteria they resemble, caused a major restructuring of thought and practice in the search for both extraterrestrial life and the origins of life on Earth.[21]

"Now," said Azam, "the work of Fuhrman and Delong[22] shows 20% of what we thought were marine bacteria to be archaea, and they are everywhere. We don't know much about them, nobody has cultured them, and yet, they may be extremely important."

Because of the vast scale of the oceans, and because of the dizzying numbers of microbes found in a single microliter of salt water, any such discovery requires oceanographers to go back to the drawing board. With each new discovery, they must reconsider food webs and atomic ecologic cycles, such as the carbon cycle, the silicon cycle, the nitrogen cycle, and the phosphorus cycle.

Inebriated by these scientific revelations, our party migrated outdoors for lunch at the Scripps cafeteria, where Dr. Azam held forth at a round table. Only yards away, giant surf pummeled the sand just south of Scripps Pier. On his left, Dr. Rohwer; on his right, two professors of oceanography from Europe, one from Paris and one from Germany, and a graduate student from Copenhagen. No one seemed to mind my basic questions, perhaps because so many disciplines were involved and every conversation seemed to bring new perspective to this world of just-elucidated mysteries. Or perhaps the scientists were just being kind.

There was so much to learn. To bacteria, for example, the biogeochemists have found that seawater does not behave like a liquid.[23] In part because of glucosal and proteinaceous colloids, chains of molecules wrapped in three dimensions, seawater at the microliter level is more akin to honey and has a honeylike structure. It is also true that at very small scales, when the velocity of fluid or particles is very slow, viscous forces dominate within fluids.[24] And a soup of polymers behaves differently from simple, unlinked molecules dissolved in water—one mole of dissolved dextran, a chain of sugars, acts much differently from one mole of dissolved glucose, a simple sugar. A monomer of sucrose behaves very differently from a polymer of sucrose. And the sea is chock full of such chains.

Phytoplankton exude these glycopolysaccharides, long sugar polymers that Rohwer and Azam have nicknamed "slime," to attract bacteria, who then graze on the chains and produce ammonia and phosphates as wastes. These act as fertilizer for the plantlike phytoplankton. Corals and kelp also secrete mucuslike slime, perhaps for similar reasons.

Each microliter of salt water, it turns out, has its own complex structure. Writes Azam: "Seawater is an organic matter continuum, a gel of tangled polymers with embedded strings, sheets, and bundles of fibrils and particles, including living organisms . . . [a place where] diverse microniches can support high bacterial diversity."[25]

"Our understanding depends on the terms we create," said Dr. Hans-Peter Grossart, a visiting professor from the University of Oldenburg, Germany. A soft-spoken blond, his words were few but his comments cogent. "We have to overcome the terms fluid or liquid, and particle. We need new terms to characterize the world of the bacteria."

"When you think about bacteria in the ocean," said Azam, "you don't have much sheer force. It's a still scene."

"What about the surf?" I asked, nodding toward the raging waves, breaking in green and foam-drenched salt water so close to us. "Does it affect the bacteria?"

"No. They don't feel it. They don't 'see' the surf," replied Azam. "Since we don't have intuition at that level, we think, oh, they're bouncing around. But they're not. They're still. Although they can move, if they want."

"And very fast," said Grossart. "They can travel at 100 micrometers per second and stop in one nanosecond, within one angstrom. There is no momentum in their world. None."

"They can move incredibly fast for their size," said Rohwer.

"Up to 1,100 micrometers per second," said Azam.

"Five hundred body lengths per second," said Rassoulzadegan.

"Tuna can't swim that fast," said Azam.

"It all comes back to how we should be looking at the world," said Rohwer. "Rather than from the top down, we might want to learn how it works from the bottom up."

"The bottom line," concluded Azam,

is that much of carbon fixation and decomposition, and nutrient cycling, is due to microbes of one sort or another. And they live in worlds that are unexplored. We're just beginning to understand how those worlds are structured, how those interactions occur, and how the food web is organized at that level by organisms of that size. Much of the biomass in the world ocean is at that scale. Much of the activity, much of the biogeochemistry occurs there. It's a realm that is unexplored in the ocean.

The excitement and anticipation each scientist radiated was infectious. Here at the edge of the Pacific, these people were staring into the heart of the equipment that ran the planet. Tiny microbes, in all their complexity, in all their vast numbers, formed the base of Earth's ecology.

When one shifts the scale of thinking about the ocean to this microscopic world, the ocean becomes immense, a veritable universe. Yet nutrients such as iron or silicon can become bottom-up barriers to growth. If Azam's work holds over time, and the numbers of bacteria and viruses that can live in a given patch of water hold constant, then there exist other limits, including the top-down limit of predation by protozoa and other grazers. And yet, within the vastness of the abyss, the bottom water, and the vent communities of the chemosynthetic zone, it is possible that a multitude of undiscovered microbial niches and habitats exist.

For example, many of the larger planktonic protozoa that graze on bacteria, especially Foraminifera and Radiolaria, contain symbiotic photosynthetic bacteria.[26] Other bacterial grazers, planktonic ciliates, retain functioning chloroplasts from their food.[27]

No doubt there are limiting growth factors for the microbial loop as there are for the classical food chain: sunlight, predation, temperature, and nutrients. But mutualistic symbioses like these expand such boundaries.

The combined budget for biogeochemical oceanography, it must be noted, is minuscule compared to the billions spent on space research or human medicine. The U.S. government spends about $14 billion each year studying outer space, but only $160 million each year studying marine biology.[28] Is the work important? Considering that the most abundant organism on Earth was only discovered in 1988, one could say, no, the work is more than important. It is, in a world threatened by the rising seas and increased storms of global warming, essential. And urgent.

Here is this strange, alien microcosmic ocean of gel and honey, an ocean we thought, in our ignorance, to be liquid and flowing. Here are uncounted trillions of strange life forms new to science and fundamental in shaping our planet. Yet an unknowing human world doesn't seem to care, and the researchers work on a relative shoestring.

All I could do, after Azam and the others ran back to their laboratory and life's work, was stare at the pounding surf and try to fathom the world of those bacteria. As each wave rose up and broke, *Synechococcus cyanobacter* were spinning about, starting and stopping, working their way through an intricate and diverse gel of colloid and marine snow, looking for something to lyse and eat, avoiding strange predators and infectious viruses. The base of a giant ecosystem, one that spans the seas, present all through the water column, they controlled the history and biochemistry of the living oceans and, by extension, Earth.

Yet, these microbes were oblivious to a surfer on a wave gliding overhead. Like some distant nebula, he was too big and too far off to really matter.

Amid nameless sparks, unexplained luminous explosions, abortive glimpses of strange

organisms . . . a definite new fish or other creature.— WILLIAM BEEBE

The Deep

A Lecture by Sylvia Earle and a 1,000-Meter Dive with Jim Barry

After meeting with Farooq Azam, I realized there was a lot to learn from ocean-*ographers. So, upon finding out from Chuck Nicklin that his old diving buddy,*
Sylvia Earle, was giving a talk at the Newport Beach Library, in Orange County,
I made sure to get an early seat. My high expectations were not disappointed. But
first, a small, protected, orange fish would provide living testimony to the heart of
her lecture. And later, her own attraction to the unexplored abyss would lead me to
greater depths as well.

SOUTHERN CALIFORNIA, 2001

One afternoon I found myself donning mask, fins, and snorkel for a visit to Horseshoe Reef, on a mission. Over a month earlier, a powerful spasm of in-the-water surf-photography mania had seized me. After shooting most of a roll of what my deluded mind thought to be award-winning action snaps of Brian the Scotsman ripping giant winter surf, I'd paddled into the heart of the impact zone. After some hours of swimming like a madman under monstrous waves, ducking surfers that shot by at 20 miles an hour or more, my hands were numb, my body exhausted, and only one unexposed image remained in my Nikonos V camera.

The wave of the day darkened the horizon, and I treaded water inside as Brian took off on a wicked, hollow left tube. A tiny speck on a pitching wall, he grew closer in the viewfinder until I snapped a picture just as he tucked under the lip into a perfect, deep barrel.

"Oh, boy," I thought, "Cover shot for sure. Maybe *Sports Illustrated*." By then I should have known that such thinking almost guarantees disaster. Sure enough, I then realized that both the lip above me and Brian tucked under it were on a collision course for my head.

A mighty roaring filled my ears. I dived for the safety of the bottom and, a minute or so later, bobbed back up to the air after getting the full Maytag thrashing. My camera did not bob back up with me. Frantic grabbing motions in the foot of surface foam yielded nothing. The Nikonos, and the pictures trapped inside, had found a new home.

Now at last, after five weeks of nonstop big surf, an opportune day of calm, clear water, a full-moon low tide, and sunlit skies appeared. It was a heaven-sent gift to help me find that bright orange rangefinder and its precious roll of exposed film.

A not-so-gentle rip carried me, kicking hard with surf fins, over a sharply etched bottom. Never had the topography of the surf break seemed so complex. There were terraces, gullies, and mounds. At several places the reef rose to a point just beneath the surface, and once again the idiocy of surfing here in big waves seemed clear. Green surf grass waved in the sea-current breeze. Braided hair algae covered miniature canyon walls with dark red shades, and a school of silver, shimmering walleye surfperch surrounded me and then left.

Every 20 feet or so flashed orange, camera-sized blazes of garibaldi damselfish. Soon it would be mating time, and the males were getting their nests and territories ready. Each would try his best to lure a succession of females to lay eggs in his nest. A female might, after mating, try to eat the older, ragged eggs of the female that preceded her, but the male would not allow a single nibble and would scold her on her way.[1]

Making a long series of breath-holding dives, looking for the camera, I noticed that some of the garibaldi darted away from my presence. Others held their ground and even charged, sticking their noses in my mask. After a while I forgot about the lost camera—finding it was a hopeless cause—and I fell into the spell of the garibaldis' world. This one had a square face, that one a thinner sort of look. This one was clearly a coward, that one a hero. Here was one with a missing pectoral fin. As I looked closer, it became obvious that each fish was remarkable, unique, an individual.

Little did I know that watching those damselfish would prime me for

AGGREGATING GARIBALDI, CORONADO ISLANDS, MEXICO

"This one had a square face, that one a thinner sort of look. . . ."

Sylvia Earle's take-home point. In telling us about a two-week dive where she lived in a Caribbean aquatic habitat, fully nitrogen-saturated, she marveled at how when you dived the same reef over and over again, day and night, you began to get to know each fish on that reef.

"Imagine living underwater for a couple of weeks. It's wonderful just getting to know the fish, one on one, the way you get to know cats, or dogs, or horses. We got to know the fish as individuals, not just as j. random halibut, or mister-grouper-over-there-like-all-the-other-groupers. We got to know them as That Grouper That Lives Right There, he's always there, or That Group of Five Angel Fish, the same ones that you recognize as individuals. And fish are just as individual as cats . . . or dogs.

"If there's one thing I want you to remember, one message from today, it is this: All fish are different."

She cleared her throat, paused, and repeated:

"All fish are different."

My trip to meet the famous Dr. Earle was, like that snorkel with the garibaldi, memorable. I drove to the lecture on a busy Saturday, out of San Diego north up the freeway, past city after coastal city, past row after row of condominiums and houses, rolling my small station wagon along the heavy metal river of SUVs and oversize pickups that is Interstate 5 south of Los Angeles. Michael Feldman's comedy show *Whad 'Ya Know* was playing on National Public Radio, broadcast that day from Erie, Pennsylvania. Michael was interviewing an elderly Erie city council member who described in detail how, as a child, he used to catch blue pike:

"Why, you'd throw out a line, and haul in a fish, just as fast as that. And those blue pike, why there was no better fish on the planet to eat. Such a firm, tasty fish . . ."

Feldman went on, in his half-joking way, to point out that the only blue pike left were, maybe, forgotten and frozen in somebody's freezer, awaiting DNA analysis. The blue pike is, and will be forever, extinct.

Earle's message about the sea resonated with the radio talk about the loss of this freshwater fish. Her charisma and speaking prowess were matched only by her resume. A National Geographic Explorer-in-Residence, she founded an Oakland-based engineering firm, Deep Ocean Exploration and Research, a company specializing in repairing, upgrading, and providing expert consulting in the use of small submarines. She has logged more than 6,000 hours underwater over many decades, written a number of books (including the masterful *Sea Change*[2]), and served as both chief scientist of the National Oceanic and Atmospheric Administration and marine botanist-in-residence at the Smithsonian. Perhaps most important, Earle gives lectures around the country in support of the oceans, alerting the world in her own genuine, imploring, and humble way to the problems facing Earth's living sea. There may be other advocates for marine conservation in the world, but there are none better.

She sat next to me during the introduction to her talk, and we shared smiles, a few words, and business cards. Sylvia Earle, grandmother of four, a good-looking woman, a radiant woman. She wore an elegant, tailored black pantsuit, a gold dolphin necklace, and an opal ring and exuded a faint hint of French perfume. Petite and thin, her athleticism was clear as she bounded to the podium and delivered her talk, each word measured, articulate, and patient. She'd give a little-girl excited smile, then assume that firm-jawed explorer's steely stare, then launch a winking, lusty joke—beneath it all, unyielding, clear-eyed, environmentalist determination and a love of life. An unusual person, a real treasure . . . and some grandmother.

Her message was clear and simple. Earth is a water planet: 97% of that water is salt water, and 97% of the remaining 3% is locked up in polar ice. The rest lies in freshwater lakes, groundwater, and rivers. All life, terrestrial or marine, depends on the sea. Without the sea, there would be no rain, no freshwater. And yet, for all the importance of the sea, a place chock full of life, a world where every teaspoon of seawater is crammed with critters from the surface down to the bottom of the Mariana Trench, only 5% has been explored. And only a fraction of what is spent on space exploration is allocated by the government toward probing the oceans.

"Forty-one years ago," she began,

Don Walsh and Jacques Piccard went seven miles down in the Mariana Trench, not far from the Philippines, and looked out their little port hole. They saw eyes looking back at them, a little flounderlike fish. . . .

Today, we fly along at seven miles high, eating lunch, watching movies, I mean, little kids do this, thousands, millions do this every day, yet, in all history, only two people have been down to the deepest part of the sea.

We've got a lot of territory out there yet to explore. I've had great fun in the last few years, getting a taste not only of what we know, but also, most significantly, of what we don't know.[3]

She flashed a slide of the Woods Hole submarine *Alvin*.

This is the ultimate workhorse of little subs; it's been around since 1964, revised many times and updated. It's a truly modern submarine even though it's had a long life, because they keep replacing little bits and pieces; even the main pressure hull has been replaced more than once. It's a wonderful system, but what's not so wonderful is that we have so few such systems. It's as if we only had one Jeep to explore all of North America, well, throw in South America too, or maybe all the continents, because the ocean is such a large part of the biosphere.

She showed us a video of a solo submarine dive off Hawaii in the spring of 2000, where, at about 1,300 feet, she encountered what she thought at first to be a giant squid, but what turned out to be a strange octopus. A beautiful animal, all six feet of it flashed red, silver, and gold. For long minutes the octopus did a kind of marine ballet with Earle and her sub—she would move away, it would follow; it would move away, she would follow. We stared in awe at the smooth, metallic body, the large eyes, the pulsating siphon, the eight graceful tentacles.

Strange wonders await beneath the surface, and compared to, say, the exploration of outer space, investigations of those wonders are neglected. That was the first part of the message. The second was that all that mysterious, unexplored, life-supporting ocean was in deep trouble. An ocean without life is not an ocean, Earle made clear, because it was water-based life that so defined our blue planet. And we humans were doing some serious damage.

Flashing a slide of a living, big-eyed, red shrimp, she said, "To many of us, this means cocktail time. But the shrimp trawlers that bring you this are like bulldozers scraping the forest for acorns and seeds; instead, we ought to learn how to selectively harvest from that forest like squirrels or cardinals."

Earle pointed out that in the 1950s, worldwide fishing totaled some 20 million tons. Today we catch nearly 100 million tons of wildlife every year—we have maintained this rate for some years, but, as discussed in chapter 10, the targeted species have been changing, the size and number of boats have increased, and the technology needed to keep catches high has also expanded. Whether this is sustainable for many more years is debatable; when the crash comes it may well be a hard fall.

Earle discussed how marine animals had millions of years to learn to deal with the eat-or-be-eaten world of the sea, and then along come humans, land-based primates, and the heavy-duty predation we have maintained is too rapid and unprecedented for the marine world to keep up. She used what by now should be familiar examples: bluefin tuna populations, down 90% in 20 years; white abalone, near extinct in California; market squid, little regulation, little scientific knowledge of their ecology, and unstable harvests. Humans kill fish today, according to Earle, with the same reckless abandon we used in killing such birds as the passenger pigeon 100 years ago.

She clearly believed that there were limits to the ocean world, at least regarding the human relationship with the sea through fishing and extracting resources.

On wrapping up the lecture, the biologist fielded an aggressive, truculent questioner:

"Dr. Earle, why don't we, instead of wasting all that money on exploring and finding pretty fish like your octopus, spend it on new ways and techniques to fish without increasing by-catch, like new shrimp devices, new types of nets, and so on?"

Earle paused for a long moment. Her answer was gentle, if firm:

> The problem is that even if we could use only the prey we wanted, like those squirrels and cardinals taking acorns and nuts selectively, there are too many of us to keep the sea out of trouble. I've stopped eating fish, although it is very hard, for I once loved to eat fish.
>
> Think of the health problem—we are using the ocean as the world's ultimate sewer. Scientists now find polychloral biphenyl concentrations in orcas in Puget Sound to be extremely high.[4] These toxins are closely linked to problems with the immune system.[5] Orcas are apex predators. We are apex predators. Think about it.
>
> When you eat fish like tuna or swordfish, it's like eating an eagle, an owl, a lion, or a tiger . . . yet $54 billion is spent every year in fishing subsidies, to help people catch even more fish. . . .

Earle was referring to a study showing that the fishing industry spent $124 billion in 1995 to catch $70 billion worth of fish and other marine life. Government subsidies such as price controls, fuel-tax exemptions, low interest loans, and grants of equipment made up most of the $54 billion deficit.[6]

She paused for a long moment before resuming, slowly, thoughtfully:

> These days, my grandchildren are what matter most to me. I'm not Dr. Earle, or aquanaut, or explorer-in-residence to them. I'm G-mom. Being the best G-mom I can is the important thing in the world to me right now, and that means showing the kids the sea, in all its wonder, in all its diverse glory. I want those little boys, when they grow up, to be able to show a living ocean to their grandchildren, too.

Even though Earle was a staunch conservationist and stalwart defender of sustainable human activities, I wondered if, in her heart, there wasn't another driving force.

After attending her talk and reading *Sea Change*, I decided the woman's true marine love, as founder of the submersible consulting company Deep

Ocean Exploration and Research, Inc., and as Explorer-in-Residence for National Geographic, lay in finding out about what is truly an unknown world: the abyss. Earle likes to get down where few humans have ever been. I saw the glint in her eye whenever she showed a submarine slide. There was a quiver in her voice when she described her ballet with that strange, giant octopus.

It is a strange and mysterious world, this place where the pressure is 100 times atmospheric pressure at the depth of a kilometer. It is a world where squeeze, cold, and darkness limit life, but where bizarre and wondrous animals have evolved—creatures that possess oversize jaws and teeth and strange dangling lures. It is a world where most animals are small, no more than 20 centimeters long. But there are exceptions—Earle's octopus, for example, or the giant squid, which may reach more than 20 meters.

Then there is the strange, hypoxic midwater zone, beneath the top hundred meters where photosynthesis and life abound, and above the bottom water where there is oxygen from polar surface waters and marine snow nutrients. Here in the midwaters large comb jellies and siphonophores, relatives of the Portuguese man-of-war, find still waters unstirred by strong currents and surf. Here they can attain enormous size. In fact, by growing to over 40 meters in length, the siphonophore *Praya* may well be the longest animal on Earth.[7]

Many trophic levels can be found in the water column from the surface to the ocean floor. Surface phytoplankton, gorging on nutrients caused by spring upwellings, provide primary production of glucose. Zooplankton grazers such as copepods, those teardrop-shaped animals with large antennae and a single, central eye, or euphausiid shrimp, also known as krill, rise at night to feed on the phytoplankton. The grazers descend during the daytime to deep, dark waters.

Feeding on these small animals are such carnivores as the hatchet fish, a silver metallic creature with oversize jaws that directs its large, telescopic eyes upward. The retina of the hatchetfish, sitting at the base of a tubelike silver structure topped by a spherical lens, captures available light from above.[8] As the zooplankton migrate to the safety of the deep each day, the hatchetfish awaits them. To protect itself from predators, the animal has evolved a series of bioluminescent photophores along its belly. When the two compounds luciferin and luciferase combine in these organs, light is produced, erasing the hachetfish shadow.[9]

At the fourth trophic level are wide-ranging predators that move through the upper kilometer of ocean at will. These include barracudinas (not barricudas!), sleek, silvery hunters that hang vertically, deep in the water column, ready to explode upward at the sign of prey. Other hunters, such as the dragonfish and the *Chiroteuthis* squid, use lures to draw their prey through subterfuge.

Parallel to this traditional food web lies another web, that of the jellyfish. A dominant midwater group, jellies feed on each other in a complex semi-closed system.

In deep water live strange creatures that are just being categorized and discovered. They include the vampire squid, a living fossil with two large light organs on a body that has eight arms, each equipped with suckers, fingerlike cirri, and light organ tips. Half squid, half octopus, *Vampyroteuthis infernalis*, it turns out, rarely if ever comes to the surface (as I once thought it might in Fiji) and has been seen by deep submersibles in Monterey Bay to have an undulating, dark-brown body with translucent, opalescent blue eyes.[8]

Farther down on the deep seafloor lie stranger creatures still. Here can be found predatory tunicates, bizarre mushroom soft corals, and weird fish such as tripod fish and catsharks. Here are hydrothermal vents with one-meter-long, red tipped tube worms that depend on chemosynthesis rather than photosynthesis for carbon fixation and formation of sugars. These tube worms define the word bizarre—they have no mouth, no stomach, and no digestive track, these having been lost through evolutionary adaptation to exploitation of vents. They instead have a plume to exchanges gases (CO_2, O_2, H_2S), a circulatory system that transports these gases, a gonad, and a trunk, which, by weight, can be nearly 50% chemosynthesizing symbiotic bacteria.[10]

The abyss, I decided, was Earle's dream world, a place where an explorer could bump into a new discovery at every turn. Her idea of fun, I could tell, was to go for a deep spin in a submarine. There must be a reason people feel such a powerful draw down there, I thought, and so began looking to hitch a ride to the deep. Dr. Jim Barry, a marine biologist at the Monterey Bay Aquarium Research Institute (MBARI), invited me, after a few phone calls and some good fortune, to join him for a "little dive to a thousand meters or so."

Barry, a blue-eyed, bearded man with a surfer's physique, trained at Scripps Institution of Oceanography but is now well entrenched at MBARI, the new juggernaut of research oceanography. Blessed with a healthy, no-strings-attached, $40 million annual endowment[11] by the late David Packard (of Hewlett-Packard), MBARI, unlike Scripps, Woods Hole, and other marine science centers, receives little funding from government or industrial sources. Hence, scientists have, arguably, more freedom to study things that the Navy or the oil industry may not be interested in. Barry, for example, studies the ecology of deep-sea cold seeps.

Along continental margins, where tectonic plates meet and compress, water laden with hydrogen sulfide seeps from the seafloor. Like the black smokers and giant tube worms of the more famous hydrothermal vents found elsewhere, these areas are rich in unique biota that have been known only since the 1980s. There are clams, *Cryptogena* sp., filled with symbiotic bacteria that chemosynthesize sugars from hydrogen sulfide. There are giant bacteria visible to the naked eye, *Beggiotoa*, that also chemosynthesize using the energy found in sulfides. There are large, multicolored mats formed by as yet unknown bacteria near the clams. There are galatheid crabs, vestimentiferan worms, and other creatures.[12] For my dive with Barry, it was the clams that received our attention.

Now, you might wonder at Barry's wisdom in taking an often clumsy guy, a chap who drops expensive cameras into the surf, a bull-in-a-china-shop sort who is six feet four inches tall and weighs over 200 pounds, down in a tiny submarine filled with delicate instruments. But Barry knew what he was doing. Unlike Sylvia Earle, he works with a much cheaper, safer type of submarine—the remote-operated vehicle (ROV) *Ventana*. Consider that the manned *Alvin*, the workhorse of manned subs, has logged around 600 dives since the 1960s. Then consider that *Ventana* hit the water in 1988 and has logged more that 2,000 dives. If you want to go deep and do it often, the best way is by robot.

At 7:00 A.M. we left Moss Landing and the aroma of baking sourdough bread and simmering ciappino that wafted from the adjacent Phil's Fish Market. Salt sea-smell enveloped us as *Ventana*'s mother ship, a remodeled oil tender from the Gulf, the research vessel *Point Lobos*, took us over Monterey Canyon, the biggest submarine canyon on the U.S. West Coast. Erosion during glacial times, when seas were much lower, combined with huge landslide events, chronic tidal motion, and what Barry called "episodic storm-caused turbidity flow," to carve out the great rift. It runs up to the Moss Landing harbor and plunges to Grand Canyon-like depths only a short distance offshore.

As we steamed over calm seas to our dive site, a place with the romantic name of Invertebrate Cliff, a team of researchers swarmed over the submersible, an orange-red and black ROV bristling with wires, gauges, robot arms, cameras, specimen containers, and other spaceshiplike gizzyhodges and thingamajigs. A long, yellow cable was coiled up on a giant drum nearby —the power and communications lifeline for the sub.

A quick glance at the high-tech sub reminded me that although she was

ROV VENTANA, MONTEREY BAY, CALIFORNIA *"... an orange-red
and black ROV bristling with wires, gauges, robot arms...."*

cheaper than a manned submersible, it still cost $8,000 a day to operate her. With her many motors, large size, and bright lights, *Ventana* was far from a subtle device. Bruce Robison, a MBARI marine biologist and deep-sea and midwater fish expert, remarked that many creatures are probably scared off by its approach.

"It's like driving a tractor trailer through the trees to study forest ecology," he said.[13]

I asked one of the sub pilots how deep she could go.

"Oh, we're rated to 1,850 meters," he said, "but things work best above 1,100. Below that, the equipment can start to misbehave."

For deeper dives, MBARI scientists use the new 4,000-meter ROV *Tiburon*. On occasion, they develop National Science Foundation grants to work with Woods Hole Oceanographic Institution's manned *Alvin*.

But on this day, for dive number 2,059, Barry wanted to collect some clams from a seep site that lay at 1,000 meters. When we arrived over the spot, some 15 miles offshore, the crew went into a practiced launch routine. A solid crane lifted up the ROV, which was about six feet long and four feet tall and weighed a mere four thousand pounds. As she slipped into the sea, I made a dash for the control room in the bow of *Point Lobos*.

Here, four comfortable swivel chairs sat in front of more than a dozen video screens. There was the main camera, mounted on the lower bow of the ROV. There was an upper camera, an arm camera, a lateral sonar screen, and a camera topside keeping an eye on the crane, as well as slave screens duplicating key scenes. As *Point Lobos* bobbed along, *Ventana* dove into a blizzard of marine snow. I watched, entranced, as we passed 100 meters. The specks of snow shot by the screen like stars bleeding past the view port of a sci-fi spacecraft. There was a difference, though. Instead of a planet or comet every parsec or so, there was a marine creature in the snow every 10 feet or so: a moon jelly, a comb jelly sparkling bioluminescent lights, a familiar *Loligo* market squid, a bright red shrimp, hanging motionless, vertical in the water column, and then darting away. Some kind of strange, white fish, also hanging vertically, also darted away with a serpentine motion.

Sitting entranced, forgetting we were topside, I surrendered to the world of the deep and became one with the sub. I was not alone. Despite the rock music and sports banter of the pilot and researchers, there was a high spirit of diving together in the dark, video control room.

One hour later we reached the bottom and began a two-hour exploration. Cold seeps, clumps of biota one to three yards in diameter, appear here and there, patchy in their distribution. The original Invertebrate Cliff seep had been disturbed by researchers, and Barry wanted a pristine collection of clams for his work. So, to some jocular grumbling from the pilots, we began to explore a vast bottom covered with fine, dark sediment—what was really, I thought, collected, fallen marine snow. Benthic biota appeared every 10 feet or so.

Rattail fish of the Macrouridae family, perhaps the dominant fish of Earth's continental shelves, hovered over the bottom, then scurried away from our lights with rodentlike tails. A rattail maintains a foraging area on the bottom; should a whale carcass or other windfall appear, an animal follows scent trails, abandoning its normal hunting ground to feed. Adjacent fish move in to exploit these undefended forage sites and follow rattails to the source in what marine biologist Bruce Robison calls a "collapsing territories process."[14] Soon the dead carrion is covered with scavengers. Fishermen, using drag nets, market *Nezumia* rattails as "grenadiers." Consumers like their low-oil-content flesh and mild flavor but have no clue as to their lifestyle.

Mushroom soft corals the size of basketballs extended nematocyst-bearing tentacles, pink stalks with red fernlike structures growing from their bulbed tops. Sea cucumbers made their way through the muck. A strange fish called a California slickhead appeared in our headlights, then disappeared. Gorgonians and sponges dotted vertical walls.

I saw what appeared to be halibut lying still on the sea floor, trusting their camouflage, but Barry corrected me.

"Those are deep-sea flatfishes: deep-sea sole, *Embassichthys bathybius*, and dover sole, *Microstomus pacificus*," he said.

Deep-water collection studies done during the 1970s surprised researchers—there was tremendous biodiversity in what appeared at first glance to be a stable, uniform environment.[15] In the 1980s, for example, researchers investigating the ocean bottom found an average of 4,500 organisms per square meter. The scientists found 798 species in 21 samples of one square meter; 46 of the species represented new discoveries.[16] Along with this diversity can be found common traits—bioluminescence, used in mating and predation; slow metabolism, due to the cold; and long-livedness, also temperature related. Other traits seen in the benthic community are gigantism and fragility; pressure is not a major problem because internalized forces balance the external squeeze.

At last we found what Barry was looking for—a pristine, meter-wide, dense, doughnut-shaped collection of clams. Dead surf grass, *Phyllospadix* sp., too deep to find light for photosynthesis, had drifted downslope and become entangled with the clams. Mats of interspersed yellow bacteria hinted that this aggregation of life survived, not on marine snow or dead fallout from above, but on chemosynthesis.

Now began the tedious, delicate work that is marine biology. With two pilots running the remote, the marine biologist directed clam collection and core sampling from three sites. In the center of the seep, at the doughnut hole, sulfide concentrations were high and no clams survived. We collected cores of sediment and clams at the inner edge of the doughnut, the middle of the collection, and the outer edge. It was Barry's hypothesis that the clams at that edge, with lower concentrations of sulfide, would be less robust than those closer to the seep.

For hours we worked the robot as curious fish and invertebrates, taking advantage of the silt, darted in and fed. Sometimes marine snow would envelop the cameras, and then a gentle current would sweep things clean. At last, enough specimen clams were sucked up with our giant vacuum cleaner and enough cores collected in stoppered salami-sized test tubes. We began the long ascent back through the blizzard of marine snow.

"*Cryptogena* clams were first discovered by dredges from HMS *Albatross* in the 1890s," said Barry. "But how they survived at such depths, in such numbers, remained a great mystery until cold seeps were described."

An hour later, the submersible broke the surface, seawater running off her in sparkling rivulets, an octopus hanging on to a specimen container. As we removed the corked core samples, a stopper gave way and a small pile of sulfurous mud landed on the deck. I reached down and stuck my finger into the sediment. It was fine, the smallest grain imaginable, and reeked of sulfur. It reminded me of Paint Pot geyser mud from Yellowstone.

Meanwhile Barry was hard at work shucking clams, measuring blood pH, and examining gills.

"Look at the flecks on these gills," he said. Sure enough, the clam gills were dotted with yellow.

"To *Cryptogena*, sulfur is like gas in the tank," he said. "Should the seeps slow, and we think they do from time to time, the bacteria on board will still have fuel for carbon fixation."

We opened one of the clams from the middle region of the doughnut ring. As expected, the gills of this clam, a bigger, older animal, were bright yellow—really loaded with sulfur. Then we checked a clam from the inner edge of the ring—bright yellow gills, but smaller. Perhaps the growth of these animals was limited by too much sulfide.

Barry's work would take him and his team late into the night. He hoped to get enough data to add a bit more hard knowledge about the world of the deep. As I jumped off *Point Lobos* onto the solid ground of Moss Landing, two things struck me.

Once again, symbiosis lay at the core of marine ecology, in this case cold seep clam/bacteria chemosynthesis. And, once again, every clam turned out to be different.[17] Just as with the garibaldi on Horseshoe Reef, just as with Sylvia Earle's Caribbean reef fish, every one of Jim Barry's clams was different.

Every animal, in its own strange invertebrate way, was a unique, distinct individual.

It is not enough to understand the natural world. The point is to defend and preserve it. . . .

—EDWARD ABBEY

Blue-Water Cop

Interview with Paul Watson

Sylvia Earle is not the only marine biologist who no longer eats seafood. To radical environmentalists the question of whether to eat fish or not is a no-brainer. Eating flesh, for them, is a mistake—immoral, bad for the environment, and disgusting to boot. After the following interviews, I began to see why they feel that way. Of course, eco-activists carry their convictions much farther. No one, though, carries things farther than Paul Watson.

CALIFORNIA, 1999

Water poured off glistening gunmetal in white rivulets as a slow-moving mass rose up out of the water. My first startled thought: submarine. The blowing spout, foghorn loud, convinced me otherwise. This was a California gray whale, heading south from rich, Alaskan feeding grounds to warm, Mexican breeding bays.

Even while sitting alone on a surfboard far from shore, I felt no fear at being within spitting distance of an animal 40 feet long, a beast that could

send me to Davy Jones with a single tail swipe. No, because of peace between humans and whales, the International Whaling Commission (IWC)
moratorium of 1986, neither of us had anything to fear from each other. Or
did we? On the high seas, in the realm of the gray whale, the albacore tuna,
and the spinner dolphin, there is only one real law, and it is a simple one.
Might makes right.

Beyond each nation's 200-mile exclusive economic zone, there is no
game warden. Even within the zones, it is easy to take illegal fish and cetaceans, because most countries lack the ability to patrol their vast aquatic
holdings. DNA sequencing[1] of whale meat sold in Japan, for example, has
been reported in both scientific and popular literature to show that only
one-half[2] to three-quarters[3] is from legal minke whaling; the rest comes from
dolphin, porpoise, and illegally killed baleen whales.

U.N. Resolution 46/215 bans the use of drift nets longer than 2.5 km.
Outlawed gill nets, many 40 km or more in length, kill large numbers of
nonmarketable fish, marine mammals, and birds ("by-catch" is the fishing
industry euphemism) along with their intended victims. If lost by the mother
ship, "ghost" nets float for years, sweeping sea life from huge swaths of
ocean. No one, however, puts any muscle behind the U.N. regulation, and
violations occur. How often is impossible to know, because there is no one
to patrol the salty reaches of a water planet. No one, that is, except for a man
some would call an extremist pirate, his small group of volunteers, two
ships, and a submarine.

I caught up with Paul Watson in his cozy, book-lined office in Los Angeles (since this interview, he has relocated to the Pacific Northwest and then
moved south again to Malibu), where various mementos of past battles dec-
orate the shelves: a brass door knob, battered and sliced with a hatchet by
a murderous mob of drunken Canadian sealers, a razor-sharp Taiwanese
flensing knife, thrown in frustration at his ship, *Sea Shepherd*, after it rammed
and destroyed a million-dollar drift net. From this room, Watson ran the Sea
Shepherd Conservation Society, a small, radical, grassroots environmental
organization, and based his teaching of ecology at UCLA and the Arts Center in Pasadena. He did not meet my expectations of a man who is responsible for, among other deeds, the sinking of eight illegal whaling ships and
one sealing ship, the ramming of two Japanese drift-net vessels, the ramming of a Mexican tuna seiner, the destruction of a whale processing plant,
and the ramming of a Taiwanese drift netter.

I anticipated a thin, wild-eyed fanatic with Charles Manson eyes, a little
twitchy, maybe, someone who deserves a spot in psychiatry's *Manual of Mental Disorders*. Instead, to my surprise, Watson turned out to be a congenial,

somewhat roly-poly, relaxed man who listens as well as he talks. He sports a head full of untrimmed silver locks and wears sandals and a black sweatshirt with the word "CREW" stenciled across the back. He is married, has a college-aged daughter, and spends his free time translating ancient religious texts. Articulate, scholarly, at times impish and refreshingly politically incorrect, he is betrayed only by a certain, subtle glint that appears in his eyes whenever he gets passionate about the ocean. And that is often.

Born in Canada, Watson ran off to sea at an early age and traveled to exotic ports in Africa, Asia, the Middle East, and Europe, working for the Scandinavian merchant marine and the Canadian Coast Guard.[4] In 1970, at the age of 20, he sailed with a group called the Don't Make a Wave Committee to protest nuclear testing by the United States Atomic Energy Commission on the island of Amchitka in the Aleutians. Two years later, with a handful of companions, he turned that committee into the Greenpeace Foundation. He left Greenpeace in 1977 when it became too bureaucratic and cumbersome for his taste. At that time he formed Sea Shepherd, the society he still leads more than two decades later.

Searching for a suitable goal for his new organization, Watson learned of a pirate whaling vessel through painstaking research by a British conservationist, Nick Carter, who spent years studying unregulated whaling. Carter discovered a fast whale catcher, formerly of the Dutch Antarctic whaling fleet, now rebuilt with a stern slipway and an onboard freezer—a self-sufficient, whale-killing factory.

Since 1968 she had operated under differing names, flags, and owners, working her way all over the Atlantic, in both north and south latitudes, killing every whale she came across, from every species and of every age. Her harpooners cared little about international bans on killing humpback and blue whales.

Carter's research showed this ship, the *Sierra* (her third name), to have violated the whale conservation and fishing regulations of many nations; she was forbidden to enter British ports, and her owners had been brought to court in the Bahamas and in South Africa. A motley international crew manned her, along with four employees of a Japanese fishing company, her meat buyer. According to Watson, they directed the crew to keep prime cuts of whale tail and to jettison the rest of the whale carcass.[5] This rogue whaler even had a mutiny: her skipper, a Norwegian, was allegedly shot and left for dead on a dock in Angola in 1974 by the first mate, another Norwegian.[6]

Although she violated numerous laws and treaties, the international community was powerless to do anything about the *Sierra*. With financial help from Cleveland Amory's Fund for Animals, Watson bought a 200-foot British trawler, named her *Sea Shepherd*, and set out to find the pirate ship. By 1979, when he discovered the whaler two days east of the Azores, she was estimated to have killed 25,000 whales.

The *Sea Shepherd* chased the Sierra into Leixões harbor in Portugal, where Watson let ashore all of his crew but two, Jerry Doran and Peter Woof. With a firm hand at the helm, Watson ran the ice-strengthened, concrete-reinforced bow of the 779-ton *Sea Shepherd* three times into the whaler. Her captain screamed at him in Norwegian and a crewman shot at him with a rifle. Watson bellowed in return, "This is for the whales, asshole!"[7]

The Portuguese government, knowing Watson's expertise in using news services and publicity, let him go. Indeed, none of the many campaigns he has since mounted against fishing and whaling pirates has resulted in a single criminal or civil conviction. More important, he is adamant that no human has ever been hurt by either his acts or those of the Sea Shepherd Conservation Society.

Behind the man's deeds stands an unusual philosophy, a concoction of Sun Tzu's *Art of War*, Miyamoto Musashi's *Book of Five Rings*, and Marshall McLuhan's perceptions of media ("the medium is the message"). At the core of his thinking lies what he feels is the great dichotomy in how humans view the world.

Watson believes the root of today's environmental catastrophes (human-caused mass extinctions, deforestation, overfishing, overpopulation) is anthropocentrism, the human-centered point of view that prevails today. Most of us, according to Watson, are separated from nature. We pay little attention to the natural world, other than for purposes of exploitation, and are primarily concerned with things human.

On the other side of a great divide are those who view the world with biocentrism as their guiding philosophy. Such people, Watson included, believe that all forms of life are sacred and important, plant and animal as well as human, and that humanity must take its place, with some humility, as a part of a greater, intertwined whole.

It occurred to me that lots of environmentalists might embrace a biocentric philosophy—but they don't go out and sink illegal whaling vessels. I asked Watson how he gained the brazen strength of his convictions.

"I was raised in a fishing village in New Brunswick, Canada," he answered:

I grew up with fishing all around me. But it all started, really, the one summer I spent near a beaver pond. Every day I went swimming with this beaver pup, and it became my best friend. But the next year, when I went back, I couldn't find the beaver anywhere.

We started asking questions about trapping there, and we began to destroy trap lines and to free animals in the traps . . . my brothers helped me, and my sisters. We used to throw the traps in the St. Croix River. We also disrupted duck and deer hunts.

I think that any time people find they have a connection to something they will protect it. If you love something, you might even kill for it.

Watson knows how to play the media-centered anthropocentric game. He has taken movie actresses to the icebound Magdalen Islands to photograph them with cuddly harp seals. He rams ships, cuts loose and sinks their drift nets, and films everything, photographers and reporters forming key members of his crews. He gets into the news as much as he can, aiming not for environmental magazines that preach to the converted, but for general newspapers and TV. A German and Canadian production consortium is in the process of producing a multimillion-dollar motion picture (starring James Marsden, directed by John Badham) based on Watson's autobiographical book, *Ocean Warrior*.[8]

Explains Watson:

The media thrive on blood, sex, scandal, and celebrity and are a barren desert for facts, reality, and solutions. If it bleeds, it leads. If it's important, it's ignored, leaving us with little choice but to communicate through the media with dramatic actions and one-liners. The media make the rules and force us to play the game, and if we play the game too well, they accuse us of manipulating them. It's a very fragile line.

At the time of my interview (1999), Watson had just returned from a trip to the Pacific Northwest, where Makah tribesmen want to return to traditional whale hunting. Earlier Sea Shepherd ships, including a small submarine, prevented the Makah from killing any gray whales.

(In July 2000, the U.S. 9th Circuit Court of Appeals prohibited continued "indigenous" hunting of gray whales by the Makah native group, stating that they did not meet requirements of the Environmental Protection Act. Before that, in May 1999, just after my interview with Watson, the hunters did succeed in killing a lone baby gray whale. Possibly, the whale killed was the famous JJ, a stranded baby gray that was nursed to health after much effort—some would call it misguided effort—and a million dollars by Sea World of San Diego. JJ, released into California waters early in 1999 with a radio transmitter, promptly scraped the device off on the bottom and became, as we doctors say, "lost to follow-up.")

A medic for the Lakota at Wounded Knee and an honorary member of the Oglala Lakota, Watson is usually an active supporter of Native Americans. Not this time.

We jaywalked across a busy boulevard for lunch at a Thai restaurant. Watson feels the Makah are being used as pawns by the Japanese and Norwegian whaling industries, who claim that they, too, have a need for reviving traditional, subsistence whaling. The Makah, he said, sold most of their harvested whale oil, only to abandon whaling by 1920 as kerosene became common and whale oil prices collapsed. The tribe, said Watson, applied to the IWC for permission to whale for cultural subsistence, not for food subsistence. He feels sure that if the door is opened for the Makah, Japan and Norway will resume whaling under the same "cultural" pretext.

I asked him about a report that he painted the sub black and white to simulate an orca.

"It worked," he said, through a mouthful of steaming, yellow curry tofu. Watson is a vegetarian, although he doesn't make a big deal about it.

> I don't know if it kept the grays away, but the killer whale paint job worked to intimidate the Makah. The U.S. government, though, was going to arrest me if I played whale sounds in the water. They said if I played orca singing in the water, I would be charged with harassing the whales, under the Marine Mammal Protection Act, and given a $10,000 fine.
>
> I told them I didn't understand. How come you can shoot one with a five-and-a-half-inch long shell from a fifty-caliber rifle, but you can't play music to them?

Later I found myself wondering if there really was a problem on the high seas, or if Watson was overreacting. To get an academic perspective, I talked to Harold Mooney, a biologist at Stanford University and chair of a 25-member, blue-ribbon national panel. Mooney's committee, a branch of the National Research Council, published a recent report on the state of the world's fishes, *Sustaining Marine Fisheries*.[9] The news is grim.

"Basically," Mooney told me, "fishing is overcapitalized worldwide. There are too many heavily mortgaged boats with high-tech items like sonar and global positioning systems, and they are fishing for too few fish."

According to the report, 30% of the world's fish stocks are overfished and 44% are fished at or near the point where they cannot keep producing current yields. For corporate fishing ventures, unlike traditional family fishers, reasons for holding back and saving brood stocks of fish for the future are less than cogent. Powerful incentives for catching as many fish as quickly as possible include beating competitors to a diminishing and finite resource. If you don't catch all the fish today, somebody else will catch them tomorrow.

The scientists call for radical changes, including making 20% of inland waters off-limits to fishing, as an aid to spawning, and assigning exclusive fishing rights to replace open competition and overall limits. They fall short, however, of endorsing the kind of aggressive policing Watson practices.

To get an alternative view on overfishing, I went to At Sea Processing, a Seattle trade association representing eight large pollock fishing companies. Pollock, used in processed fishsticks and fish patties, represents by weight the biggest fish resource for the United States. I asked Barbara Nombalais, the spokesperson for the organization, whether overfishing was a problem.

"No," was her emphatic answer:

> The people out there studying the fish, the National Marine Fisheries Service, tell us our catch is sustainable. We're in it for the long haul. Our companies have huge investments in ships and other facilities. We want to protect those investment. That's why we support fishing allocations, or privileges, as we like to call them. We want to avoid the 'race to fish,' unfettered competition that wipes out fish populations.

I asked her if she'd heard of Paul Watson.

"Yes, of course, we know Watson up here—he's involved in antiwhaling. But we don't whale."

I spoke with a pinniped expert (who shall remain unnamed) at the same National Marine Fisheries Service that Nombalais mentioned. This biologist admitted that some of his study subjects were doing poorly, and that, although an ecosystem shift might be responsible, it could also be related to pollock fishing.

"Steller sea lions, large, yellow-maned marine mammals, are declining," he told me. "It's probably food-related. They feed on hake and pollock. There's no evidence, but it's thought that they are food limited, and the harvest of the fish may have an effect on the survivorship."

Alaska's sole member in the House of Representatives, Republican Don Young, has an anthropocentric take on the pinniped: "My concern's for the fishermen facing those high seas. I haven't seen a Steller sea lion that's voted for me yet."[10]

Jerry Lieb is the legislative director of Greenpeace's ocean campaign. Greenpeace, founded by Watson and several others, sends out ships to monitor the high seas, like the Sea Shepherd Conservation Society, although they stop short of sinking illegal vessels. Recently, for example, a Greenpeace ship chased a vessel catching the newly fished, almost extinct, and now protected

Patagonian toothfish (sold as Chilean sea bass) halfway around the Pacific. I learned from Lieb that Greenpeace is suing the National Marine Fisheries Service for setting excessive quotas for factory trawlers—like those At Sea Processing represents. According to Lieb, the Steller sea lion is threatened with extinction. On the World Conservation Union's red list of species, it is endangered and has suffered a 50% decline or greater over the last 10 years.[11]

The ecosystem in the Aleutians has undergone a phase shift from a vibrant kelp forest to a desolate urchin barren (see chapter 12). Unlike the California kelp forest, there were not many other predators of the kelp-devouring urchins besides the sea otter. Recently, sea otter populations have plummeted, and that has caused the phase shift. According to J.A. Estes, of the University of California, and associates,[12] this is probably due to killer whale predation. And orcas, who have co-inhabited the Aleutians with sea otters for many years, have only recently started eating the small, furry mammals.

The reason, according to Estes, is the collapse of Steller sea lion populations, the usual killer whale prey, across the northwestern Pacific. Pinniped forage fish, especially pollock stocks, have decreased in abundance, due most probably to higher ocean temperatures and heavy fishing pressure.[13]

Greenpeace's Lieb laughed when I asked him about Watson, who has never been reticent about castigating the bureaucracy of Greenpeace.

"I know Paul Watson very, very well," said Lieb, diplomatic after his chuckling:

> While he doesn't practice the same philosophy himself, Greenpeace has a practice of not denigrating the efforts of other environmental organizations. Everyone's shooting for the same goal. We may have differences on how to get there, but it's more productive to focus our attentions and our energies on the folks who are conducting the illegal activities.

There is some evidence of those illegal activities, although discovering just what goes on over a vast, watery world can be elusive. *Sustaining Marine Fisheries* discusses DNA studies of retail fish markets in Japan.[14] Here, vendors offer—at prices as high as $70 a pound—dried jerky, belly bacon, and canned meat, all from cetaceans and some from illegally killed baleen whales, including fins and humpbacks.[15]

The large marine mammals have made some gains since the moratorium of 1986. There are some 23,000 gray whales worldwide, for example, their numbers growing at 3% per year. Humpbacks are increasing at 10% per year and number more than 30,000. But blues, the largest animals to live on Earth, remain rare and number only about 10,000 individuals.[16]

Roger Payne, a biologist who has spent his life studying whales, lists some of the ongoing threats to their existence: illegal whaling, drift nets, propeller injury, overfishing, and food-chain concentration of organohalogen pollutants. In short, their future is not assured. He writes, in the book *Among Whales* on illegal Soviet whaling:

"Recent revelations by high-ranking officials of the Russian Federation indicate that throughout the modern whaling era the Soviets . . . systematically cheated, and on a massive scale. . . ."[17]

Payne is a staunch advocate of protecting marine life, but he feels that radical actions such as those of Paul Watson are not the best way to go:

"If one lives by the sword," he writes of eco-saboteurs, "one dies by the sword."[18]

In an article in *The Atlantic Monthly*, William Aron, William Burke, and Milton Freeman offer what Watson would term an anthropocentric argument in favor of hunting the great marine mammals. They maintain that because many species, such as minkes, small baleen whales that now number one million animals, are not endangered, Japan, Norway, Russia, and Iceland should be allowed to resume whaling. They dismiss outright any biocentric thoughts that individual animals might be worth sparing just for being whales: "Whales have been studied intensively for decades, and there is still no strong evidence that they are uniquely intelligent. Many species throughout the animal kingdom demonstrate behaviors and abilities just as complex as those demonstrated by whales."[19]

Paul Watson, of course, thinks this argument is specious. Unlike Aron, Burke, and Freeman, he has driven a Zodiac between a pod of sperm whales and a Russian whaling ship. Trying to block the line of fire, he and his partner, Robert Hunter, thought their 1975 Greenpeace stand would prevent whales from being harpooned. They were wrong. The whalers fired an explosive harpoon, barely missing Watson's head as, "with a dull thud followed by a muffled explosion," they slaughtered a cow sperm.[20]

Sperm whales like the pod Watson encountered off northern California are, evolutionarily, one of the oldest of whales. They are also the kings and queens of deep diving, making long two-hour dives to a mile of depth in search of their favorite prey, squid. Not above eating fish or small cephalopods, sucker marks on their skin prove that they also tangle with one of the oceans's most unknowable and feared creatures: the giant squid.

Sperms have a unique organ in their massive foreheads, a melon filled with that finest of rare oils, spermaceti. Scientists theorize that the sperma-

SPOUTING HUMPBACKS, FREDERICK SOUND, ALASKA

"   *canned meat. . . . some from illegally killed baleen whales, including fins and*

humpbacks."

ceti helps whales focus their echolocation sounds—sperms click and locate prey like dolphins, only their "click" is more like a sledge hammer blow. Some researchers believe that they may use the sounds, focused into a powerful aquatic sonic ray, to stun and immobilize prey and to communicate with each other over thousands of miles of ocean. Another theory is that the oil, by changing under pressure to a solid state, aids a whale in maintaining neutral buoyancy at great depths.

Sperms are mighty, mythical animals. Herman Melville, in fact, based his epic novel on a real whale, a 70-foot leviathan named Mocha Dick, a bull sperm that inhabited the southeastern Pacific off Chile and turned a pale white with age. Until its death in 1859 at the hand of Swedish whalers, Mocha Dick sank seven wooden whaling ships and 20 boats during his hundred years of life.[21]

As Watson watched the cow sperm bleed to death, a similar whale now surfaced from the depths. The large bull sperm, "60 tons of irate muscle and bone,"[22] rose and sounded next to the small Zodiac. Told by whale researchers that this was an attack situation, Watson and Hunter thought they were finished. Instead, the ocean erupted as the bull launched himself headlong at the Russian kill boat. The harpooner was ready. He fired again. And again.[23]

In an open letter to the people of Scandinavia, published in 1988 in a major Norwegian newspaper, Watson explained what led the Sea Shepherd Conservation Society to sink half of Iceland's whaling ships and destroy a Reykjavik whale processing station:

> Slowly, very slowly, a gargantuan head emerged from the water and the whale rose at an angle over and above our tiny craft. Blood and brine cascaded from the gaping head wound and fell upon us in torrents.
>
> We were helpless, we knew that we would be crushed within seconds as the whale fell upon us. There was little time for fear, only awe. We could not move.
>
> The whale did not fall upon us. He wavered and towered motionless above us. I looked up past the daggered six-inch teeth and into an eye the size of my fist, an eye that reflected back intelligence and spoke wordlessly of compassion and communicated to me the understanding that this was a being that could discriminate and understood what we had tried to do. . . . I realized then and there that my allegiance lay with this dying child of the sea and his kind. . . ."[24]

Watson uses the U.N. Charter for Nature to justify his actions on the high seas. Arrested in 1993 by the Canadian government for harassing—with butyric acid stink bombs—Cuban fishing vessels on the Grand Banks, where a cod industry 400 years old is now moribund, his charges could have resulted in a sentence of three life terms plus 10 years. A Canadian jury found him innocent based on the charter, setting strong legal international precedent.

"The Charter for Nature was proposed by Zambia and voted into law by the General Assembly in 1982," said Watson, as we talked at the Thai restaurant. "One country voted against it. The United States. The United States votes against all those types of things."

"It's a sovereignty issue?" I asked.

"Yes," he replied. "But the charter laid out that there is an obligation to protect and conserve the environment. There's a section that states that nongovernmental individuals and organizations have a right to intervene to uphold the laws. Specifically, section 21E says this right exists especially in areas beyond national jurisdictions."

"Beyond the 200-mile limit?" I questioned.

"Exactly," he said.

I found it hard to believe that one man, his followers, and a few ships could be more than insignificant blips on the high-seas radar screen, if a nation like the United States could be reticent about being the world's land policeman. How could a small organization like his, I wondered, succeed at being the cop of the oceans?

"Well, we hope the effort will snowball," said Watson.

But I don't see any government, including the U.S., taking a stand to protect the ocean. . . .

Jacques Cousteau once said that if the navies of the world had any sense of responsibility, they would be out there protecting the world's oceans and stop playing war games with each other. The navies could do a lot; they see a lot, they just ignore it.

But one area where governments *do* intervene on the high seas, and one thing the U.S. government specifically does, is drug interception. Now if you have the power to intercept drugs on the high seas, then you sure as hell have the power to intervene against illegal fishing, whaling, and exploitation activities. But they don't see it that way.

As if to prove Watson's point, the U.S. destroyer *John Young* seized the Belizean 78-foot fishing boat *Forever My Friend* in March 2001. Military agents found eight tons of cocaine hidden behind steel bulkheads, arrested her 10 crewmen, and towed her all the way to San Diego. The location of the interception—250 nautical miles southwest of Acapulco, 50 miles beyond Mexico's economic exclusion zone.[25]

Several months later, the Coast Guard cutter *Active* boarded and seized the 151-foot *Svesda Maru*, also registered in Belize. The 13 tons of cocaine on board may result in potential life terms in U.S. prisons for the 10 Russian and Ukrainian crewmen aboard. The location of the interception? 1,500 miles due south of San Diego, putting it over 500 miles from Clipperton Island, a French protectorate and the nearest land.[26]

Maverick enforcement of vague international law out on blue water can be more than lonely—it can be brutally dangerous. Taking a sip of Thai iced tea, Watson stabbed sea-roughened fingers onto our restaurant's starched white tablecloth, counting a long list of murdered environmental activists: Chico Mendez, Dian Fossey, Fernando Pereira, Karen Silkwood. After the episode with the Taiwanese drift netter, Kaohsiung fishermen placed a $25,000 reward on Watson's head—assuming it was separated from his body. I asked him if the ransom is still being offered.

"Oh, I don't know, I never really gave it much thought," he answered.

I questioned whether he was planning any trips to Taiwan soon.

"Oh, if I had to go, I'd go there," he said, laughing.

A lot of the drift netting, although that boat was Taiwanese, is controlled by the yakuza, the Japanese mafia. We're dealing with three different mafioso groups, including the Russian mafia on the sturgeon/caviar issue and the Colombian mafia over the tuna/dolphin issue.

The slang for cocaine in Colombian is *atun blanco*, the white tuna, because they use the tuna boats to smuggle the cocaine. The Cali cartel owns 48 of those tuna seiners. And then we find that we're always up at odds with the yakuza. If you're a modern-day gangster, the oceans are where you want to go, if you don't want to get caught and you want to make lots and lots of money.

The miracle is that we've managed to survive at all. . . .

As I left Paul Watson, a man unafraid to live or die by the sword, he was busy plotting his next move on the endless fencing arena that is the ocean. One activist and a small group of volunteers, living on donations, gamble their lives to take on drift netters, whalers, and the crushing momentum of centuries of anthropocentrism.

Before submerging myself in the ocean of cars that is Los Angeles, I asked Watson how he sustained himself over the years, how he managed to keep balanced, how he kept his love of nature.

"Just get me out to sea," he said. "That's all I need. I know where I belong. And it ain't in the rain forest. It ain't in the mountains, and it ain't in the desert (he laughs). Just get me out to sea."

I wondered how this sort of extreme radicalism, this special brand of newsworthy violence against property, compared in environmental efficacy to the demonstrations and corporate courtroom tactics of Greenpeace, to academic dissertations like *Sustaining Marine Fisheries*, or even to benign articles about depleted fish and whales that millions read in *National Geographic*. Could Watson be alienating as many people as he convinces? Does he care?

Certainly some would plant him square in the middle of the animal rights movement, in the thick of the free-the-fur-factory-mink and release-the-lab-chimp crowd. Yet Watson, whale-sized ego and all, stands alone as a unique environmental icon. Not for him the furtive, violent act with the anonymous phone call: he leaps to the pulpit and brandishes his bold deeds, daring the world to take notice. No other conservationist combines his media savvy, his long list of achievements (or crimes, depending on your point of view), and his dedication of body, brain, and soul to the sea.

Others would call Watson an anarchist, someone who takes the law into his own hands; they'd brand him a shameless publicity seeker, an eco-profiteer who gets his meal ticket from gullible liberals and their donations, suckers who have bought into his overblown view of eco-paranoia. Still others, who shall go unnamed, find the man to be "but one step from the Unabomber."

The spectrum of man's relationship to nature runs the gamut from extreme anthropocentrism, as represented by abortion clinic bombers and doctor shooters, to radical biocentrism, as represented by those who torched the ski development in the Colorado mountains. The news treats the edges of that spectrum in different ways, and Watson is not alone in trying to manipulate that process. For example, the media watch group, Fairness and Accuracy in Reporting, or FAIR, compared reportage of the October 1998 arson of several unoccupied buildings at the Vail ski resort with the slaying, also in that month, of Dr. Barnett Slepian, an obstetrician who performed abortions. In 500 newspaper and broadcast stories on the killing of Slepian, reporters used the term "terrorist" or "terrorism" six times. In contrast, the terms appeared 55 times in the 300 media reports on the Vail arson. FAIR attributes this ten-fold difference to a concerted PR campaign promoting the idea of "ecoterrorism" by an anti-environmental NGO funded by several multinational lumber, chemical, and petrochemical corporations.[27]

Watson is clearly in the monkey-wrenching biocentrist camp, but unlike the Vail arsonists, his style, rather than repelling an apathetic majority, attracts a certain amount of sympathy. Why? He chooses his targets carefully, picking bona fide bad guys; he strikes with finesse, keeping people from get-

Blue-Water Cop

243

ting injured or killed; and then, after the fact, he accepts full responsibility for his deeds, handling the media like a savvy politician.

Ramming the *Sierra* became a defining moment in Watson's life, the first of many victories, a crowning achievement that saved thousands of whales. It made a difference to other lives as well. Shortly afterward, Knut Hustvedt, the Norwegian harpooner on the ship, appeared on NBC's *Amazing Animals*. Asked (as reported in Watson's book, *Ocean Warrior*) if the violent act made him angry, he replied:

> At first it did, but it also made me think about what I was doing. To me, whales were just big fish. We killed them and made money. I never thought about them as intelligent creatures. When I saw people willing to take such risks to protect them, I began to think about what I was doing. I will never kill a whale again.[28]

Others, of course, such as Roger Payne, do not believe that violence, even if used only against property, can ever be condoned. They feel that the turn-around in whaling laws and treaties came about not because of radicals like Watson but from the public's immense love of whales, fueled in part by books such as George Small's 1971 *The Blue Whale* and from years of effort by patient scientists.[29] These centrists hung in there with facts and little hyperbole, taking unfair, humiliating hits both from politicians representing the whaling nations and from many environmentalists.

My own thoughts on Paul Watson are ambivalent. I have misgivings about vigilante-style behavior and maintain respect for the law. Yet Watson and a few others like him (e.g., Greenpeace) are pretty much alone in making a physical presence in blue water and attempting to enforce international laws of the sea. Immediate human needs and desires seem to me overly emphasized today, with nature—and, by extension, future human generations—all too often getting short shrift. Anthropocentrism dominates popular thought and culture. I'd rather the U.S. Navy and Coast Guard worry as much about illegal drift nets and whaling as they do about controlling the drug trade. Because, at present, they don't, that leaves only people like Watson . . . and those patient scientists.

Then there are the gray whales and the Makah. Threatened species versus indigenous people: Perhaps only Solomon could find a solution to balance the rights of these two embattled groups. There can be no arguing that the history of Euro-American conquest of Native Americans over the past five centuries has been catastrophic to the latter group's culture, health, and existence. Anthropologist Henry F. Dobyns, for example, estimated that 95% of Native Americans (whose pre-Columbian population is believed by many anthropologists to have been much larger than ever suspected) died from smallpox, measles, and other Euro-Asian diseases that swept the American continents during the first century of contact.[30]

But there is also evidence that many different waves of peoples have swept the Americas in the past 14,000 years, and there may have been multiple cycles of conquerors and vanquished.[31] The current controversy over the so-called Kennewick Man bones might, in fact, be fueled by the possibility that the 9,300 year-old skeleton could be one of those vanquished.[32]

Can the rights of animals and indigenous peoples both be preserved? Perhaps. Some would even say such humans are, in fact, the best candidates for showing the rest of us how to coexist in a sustainable state with wild nature. Ethnobotanists, for example, have learned much about the use of rain forest pharmaceuticals from jungle shamans.[33] Some anthropologists have gone further, suggesting that precolonial natives modified much of the "pristine" landscape to serve their purposes. C. Charles Mann, writing in *The Atlantic Monthly*,[34] summarizes this notion, a view that includes the idea that the Amazon rain forest might be, in essence, a garden of nut and fruit trees tended over the millenia by Native Americans whose botanical skills far outstripped those of European invaders. In a similar way, the grassland prairies of North America may have been fire-created buffalo and elk farms.

Others, though, would say that this sort of Rouseau-like concept of the "noble savage" is nonsense. They would point, for example, to recent evidence that early hunters caused mass extinctions in both North America and Australia, killing off animals such as the saber-toothed tiger, the wooly mammoth, and the 100-kilogram *Genyornis*, the heaviest bird ever known.[35]

Writes ecologist Michael Soulé:

Some of the wounds on nature's body are old and scarcely detectable without paleo-forensic research. The most profound of these is the absence of the megafauna—dozens of species of large animals, including mammoths, mastodons, giant ground sloths, native horses, camels, American lions, and cheetahs. They disappeared about eleven thousand years ago, soon after the arrival to North America of sophisticated hunters from Asia.[36]

There is good evidence, nevertheless, that in the ensuing 10,000 years between the North American megafauna extinctions and the coming of the Europeans, many native tribal groups evolved ways to live in a sustainable manner with the wilderness. Perhaps this was related to their biocentric philosophy and religion. In the Pacific Northwest, for example, the taking of salmon was controlled by strict conventions and taboos.[37] The health of the

Northwest salmon populations when the Europeans arrived, compared with the many destroyed runs of today, speaks to the efficacy of native management.

In another example, inland tribes recognized the importance of beavers as keystone species (although that term, of course, is a modern one). Writes Vine Deloria, Jr., of the University of Colorado, a Lakota Sioux himself:

> Beavers were understood as the critical animals in many areas because they built dams that retained water and made surrounding areas very fertile. Until the fur trade, when the beaver were virtually exterminated, the species was generally left alone except when the need for food became critical.[38]

Salmon runs and beavers were, of course, not the only wild populations that, until the last 500 years, were healthy. Native Americans, whether they were linked to the megafauna extinctions or not, proved to be much better stewards of wildlife than did their European conquerors. Whales, pinnipeds, old-growth forests, prairies, buffalo, passenger pigeons, great auks—the list of wild creatures and habitats that were in decent shape before Columbus, but today are diminished or extinct, is extensive.

However, Jackson et al.,[39] in their historical study of overfishing that ranged from 125,000 years ago to the present, suggest that, at least for the ocean, ancestral humans were not necessarily being kind to the marine environment, but were limited by primitive technology.

"Contrary to romantic notions of the oceans as the "last frontier" and of the supposedly superior ecological wisdom of non-Western and precolonial societies," writes Jackson and his 18 co-authors (including the late Mia Tegner), "our analysis demonstrates that overfishing fundamentally altered coastal marine ecosystems during each of the cultural periods we examined."[40]

Even if one were to buy that indigenous peoples are our best chance to learn how to live with nature, and there is much evidence to support this idea, there are those who believe that problems exist with that argument as it pertains to some members of the Makah. The Sea Shepherd organization, for example, holds the opinion that the Japanese fishing industry has a close relationship with individuals within the tribe.[41] If so, Watson could be justified in worrying about such pro-whaling industrial nations using the Makah's "cultural subsistence" argument as an excuse to resume large-scale whaling.

Then there is the opinion of others that, even given their community's social problems, problems that many Native American tribes face today, the

Makah can still stand up and defend themselves, get legal help, and vote. Unlike the whales, according to this point of view, they can shoot back, in a figurative as well as a literal sense.

Take the case of one tribal member, Alberta Thompson, age 77, who worked as a program clerk at a senior center on the reservation for 15 years. According to Thompson, when claims surfaced that she used office time to make a telephone call to a whale protection group, her employers let her go.[42]

"They fired me for being against the hunt," she said to me in an interview in June 2001, giving me her take on the real reason she lost the job. A sweet woman with a kind face and oversized glasses that accentuate beaming eyes, Thompson has a calm demeanor that masks a stubborn will to do what she thinks is right.

I asked her if she had ever seen gray whales as a child in northwestern Washington.

"There never were any here. If you had a chance to interview Isabel, who is 101, she was just a girl when they brought the last whale ashore. That had to have been at least 80 years ago. So, I would have never seen them."

Mrs. Thompson worked with elderly Makah since she was a young married woman. Unlike many young people in the tribe today, she understands the Makah language and spent long hours listening to the old people talk.

"We had forefathers that . . . knew what to do, and they saw the depleting of the whales and so they decided not to go whaling."

Considering herself a patriot to two nations, American and Makah, she also worked as a welder in Seattle during World War II. It was logging, though, that first made her stand up and speak in public.

This company lived here on the reserve, and took us for five cents a stump . . . my husband was a logger; if I knew then what I know now, he would not have been a logger. I don't like this clear-cutting. We were fighting the clear-cutting here, my friend and I, then this whiting fishery came on; we went against that. Then this whaling thing came and we went full force on that. My friend stepped down, but I stayed with standing up for the whales.

I asked her what motivated the whalers. (Makah whalers and the Makah Tribal Council were, unfortunately, unavailable for interviews for this chapter, despite a number of attempts on my part.)

In 1995, they made a deal with Japan and Norway to build a plant here to process the whale meat and sell it to Japan and Norway. But they didn't do their homework, because our treaty says, in Article 13, that we Makah have agreed not to sell whatever we caught in the ocean to the Indians of Vancouver or to any other citizen.

So then they found out what was in there, and they started hollering "tradition."

Jean-Michel Cousteau, son of Jacques Cousteau, arrived in Neah Bay with "a plateful of money," relates Thompson, and he offered to help set up and finance a whale-watching business to take the place of whale hunting. "They laughed at him," she said, a rare hint of bitterness in her voice.

But Cousteau also took Thompson to San Ignacio Lagoon in Baja California, where, for the first time in her life, she saw a gray whale. Retelling the story, Thompson became animated, her voice excited:

I've never been the same. The baby came up first, and I was way back by the motor, and he came past all these people, looked me right in the face, and stayed there until I touched him and talked to him. Then his mother came up on the other side, and she sprayed me with water, and she stayed there until I touched her and talked to her. And that's all she did, she brought her baby there, and then they stayed there for a while, and then they went under the boat we were in. It was just awesome. I've never been the same.

Whales, or any marine animal for that matter, are arguably even more disenfranchised than Native Americans. To a biocentrist, it is only logical that they need help to a greater degree than do Natives, and from anywhere they can get it, be it radical or mainstream environmentalism. To an anthropocentrist, on the other hand, such a notion is nonsense.

That, then, gets us to the key question about a certain radical environmentalist. Is Paul Watson a hero, or an egotist interested only in publicity? Some might opine that only when one knows how much money is flowing in and out of an ecoactivist's checkbook can one make a balanced judgment on such matters.[43]

Nevertheless, after meeting Watson and talking to him, I found myself both sympathetic to his genuine love of animals and nature and understanding of his need to use the media to galvanize an apathetic public. Perhaps I am naive and susceptible to the influence of the man's considerable charisma. Alberta Thompson, though, who knew Watson well, agreed with my read of the man:

When people heard he was coming here, I heard all kinds of stories, "He's going to bomb the parade, he's going to kill [tribal fisheries minister] Dan Green," on and on they went. Where they got those ideas, I don't know, because that was the farthest thing from Paul's mind, to bomb, or to kill someone.

"Some people don't like him," she continued, with her soft-spoken, characteristic bluntness, "because he does things. He doesn't hold back any punches. Did you hear about what he did to those boats with the 35-mile-long drift nets?"

Offshore in the fog, the California gray slid by my surfboard in the slow, powerful ballet of a weightless giant. I glimpsed a fathomless, black eye, rimmed with white barnacles. A wild, unknowable intelligence stared at me for a moment, then, with a flick of mammoth flukes, the whale left me unharmed and awash in wonder. I recalled what Alberta Thompson said of grays: "The thing I felt as the whales and I talked . . . was a spirit of trust. . . ."

She was right, I thought. These mammals at the apex of oceanic evolution, along with fish, turtles, and the rest of Neptune's creatures, deserved better from us humans. But altering the ancient habits (or the continued growth) of six billion people would not be easy—so many of us think of the ocean as a limitless food bank and nothing more. And time was not on the side of the wilderness.

Preserving blue-water wildlife might indeed require a fundamental, biocentric shift in culture and thought. Perhaps a radical like Paul Watson, a man who believes there are limits to the ocean, might catalyze that kind of sea change. He is a man who sees humanity as a cruel and foolish soon-to-be winner in a violent, out-of-control, zero-sum sea game. He has chosen for himself the role of blue-water cop, and he selectively enforces laws that favor whales, seals, turtles, and fish.

But, just maybe, a gentle soul who refuses to back down and speaks her mind might, in the end, prove to be an equally powerful force.

Someone, say, like Alberta Thompson.

The National Marine Fisheries Service filed a brief on March 18, 2002 to federal courts estimating a population of 26,000 gray whales. New NMFS regulations will allow renewed hunting of the cetaceans. Makah whalers duly prepared to resume their hunt of five animals per year—but, this time, using harpoons and cedar canoes.

"We are stewards of our resources," said Keith Johnson, president of the Makah Whaling Commission, to the Associated Press. "We are not hunting the last whale."[44]

Meanwhile, there are new hazards facing whales on the high seas. Low Frequency Active (LFA) sonar, a development of the United States Navy, emits low-frequency pulses of sound ranging up to 240 decibels that bounce back to a listener. While this may make detection of high-tech, ultra-quiet enemy submarines more feasible, it may also cause deafness, disorientation, and a host of other problems in whales and dolphins.[45] In 1996, shortly after the testing of up to 230 decibels of LFA systems in the Mediterranean, 13 Cuvier's beaked whales stranded alive and died along a nearby coast. Usually whales beach together, but these whales were scattered—an atypical event leading Greek marine biologist A. Frantzis to believe their deaths were LFA-related.[46]

The environmental impact report the Navy prepared for the public on LFA sonar did admit to potential risk to 43 species of whales.[47] But, at present, the U.S. Justice Department claims that the National Environmental Policy Act, the "Magna Carta of environmental law,"[48] a law that forces review of government actions for their environmental effects, does not apply beyond the three-mile maritime territorial limit. Thus, naval activities in the nation's 200-mile oceanic exclusive economic zone—and beyond—would not require any environmental oversight.[49] This would allow the Navy to use LFA sonar offshore unimpeded by any qualms regarding health effects on whales.

CHAPTER SIXTEEN

A Palau Journal

A Visit to the Ultimate Underwater Paradise

OCTOBER 31, 2001, WESTERN PACIFIC

An hour east of Guam, at an altitude of 35,000 feet, a massive tropical depression appeared in sunset colors outside our starboard window. The pilot made a wise, wide detour, but the circular, churning, moisture-laden thunderstorm, dressed in lightning-sparkled reds, oranges, grays, and blacks, towered above the plane. The spellbinding sight served as a reminder of the power of nature. Whether or not it would be an omen of what lay ahead was unclear.

It had been five years since I'd visited the western Pacific. My hopes were high, my cameras, strobes, and regulator overhauled and ready. Equipment preparation, air travel, and research in textbooks, guidebooks, and oceanography literature left me itchy, excited, and exhausted—all at once.

Palau: the ultimate underwater destination, a scuba wonder of the world. To a diver, the reefs and marine wildlife of this small archipelago, 500 miles east of the Philippines and 500 miles north of New Guinea, form the standard against which all other tropical destinations must be measured. David Doubilet, the *National Geographic* marine photographer, called the region "one of the great coral reef systems in the world."[1]

Home to more than 50 inland marine lakes, Palau also has a coralline corner where two saltwater rivers converge, drawing mind-numbing multitudes of pelagic fish. It is home to unique and bizarre mushroom-shaped limestone islands; undercut by waves and topped with dense jungle, these Rock Islands sprinkle a lagoon protected by a large, barrier reef. To someone interested in marine island biogeography and coral reef biology, it was a logical destination.

NOVEMBER 1, 2001

My time sense off kilter, I arose from my hotel bed at 5 A.M. and took an early morning stroll. The city of Koror, home to 12,000 of the nation's 18,000 people, was quiet. I wandered to the end of a paved road on what is called T-Dock and looked out to sea.

There were butterflyfish in the clear water. Three women, middle-aged and smiling, were having a dawn constitutional swim in the harbor. We started to chat, and I asked them about an old friend, a nurse from Palau I'd known in Hawaii over 20 years ago.

"Oh sure, I know her," said one of the women. "She started a nursing school here, but now she lives on Guam."

Small place, Palau. Not all was perfect, though, in this petite paradise.

An island dive master gave me a lift through the bustling streets of Koror. A California expatriate, he was tan, relaxed, and calm, not the sort given to rash opinions or exclamations. He confided in a quiet, almost apologetic voice,

"The coral got hit bad in the '97–'98 El Niño."

"How bad?" I asked.

"Well, let's just say that before 1998, we had more dive sites than we knew what to do with. We'd spend a trip on a liveaboard exploring here, there, everywhere, and then finish off with the grand finale, Blue Corner. The whole week or 10 days would blow everyone's mind. Now," he said, "we start at Blue Corner, and hope to dive there as much as we can."

An hour later, I met Tova Bornovski, who, with her husband, Navot, owned the Fish 'N Fins dive shop and the liveaboard dive boat *Ocean Hunter*. Tova and Navot, both Israeli citizens, sailed the 60-foot boat across the Pacific with two small children, stopping for months at a time to explore and dive such places as the Galapagos and Tahiti. They have led a life that many would envy but few are crazy enough to attempt.

Tova, a vivacious, curvy brunette, had a warm, welcome smile. Knowing my time was short, she made a few phone calls from the dive shop, and in an hour, after running through a tropical, torrential downpour, I sat down at a workshop on Marine Protective Areas (MPAs) at the Palau International Coral Reef Center.

The Honorable Noah Idechong, a representative of the Palauan congress, made the opening remarks. *Time Magazine* has awarded Idechong a Hero for the Planet Award for his work on MPAs; he is also a Goldman environmental prize winner and the executive director of the Palau Conservation Society. Now he urged the various scientists at the workshop to give him support for expanding the current MPA system, now managed by the states, to the federal level.

"Give me a working plan for national control of MPAs, and I promise to do everything I can to push it through the legislature," said Idechong.

Palau is an independent nation with a Compact of Free Association with the United States. After much dickering and argument about nuclear weapons, the citizens of the country in 1994 voted to give the United States future options to build bases on the island for $450 million in aid. This money has fueled the islands' bureaucracy and economy but will stop in 2008.

With 16 states, governors, assorted chiefs, a national government, a national legislature, and state legislatures, Palau is, perhaps, the most overgoverned place on the planet. "Never have so few been governed by so many,"[2] is an old joke on Palau. If they were all like Idechong, I thought, it might not be a bad thing.

At the workshop, I met Ann Kitalong, from the Office of Environmental Response and Coordination. "Somewhere around 30% of our corals died," she said, answering my inquiries about the health of the reefs. "We're trying to brainstorm here and find ways to help the coral recover."

The trouble began in the summer and fall of 1997, when the usual trade winds bringing warm—but not too warm—water from the eastern Pacific died. Seawater in Micronesia and other parts of the western Pacific turned cool, dipping below 70°F. A warm tongue of water grew to prodigious size from the flank of equatorial South America and stretched across the eastern Pacific. This was the infamous El Niño of 1997.

A year later, trade winds returned with a vengeance as La Niña, El Niño's contrary sister, arrived. These winds pushed the massive tongue of warm water westward. On the islands of Palau, as elsewhere in Indonesia, the Philippines, and throughout Oceania, water temperatures rose to record levels. Scientists have dubbed this entire cycle of events an ENSO, or El Niño southern oscillation.

The result? Over three months, from September to November of 1998, many *Acropora, Porites*, and other corals that covered reefs in Micronesia and elsewhere in the Indo-Pacific turned white. This bleaching occurred as zooxanthellic algae, the essential symbiotic partners of each coral polyp animal, died en masse from overheating and the effect of the sun's radiation. Sometimes such bleaching, if followed by optimal conditions, may prove only temporary. Unfortunately, the reefs of Palau proved vulnerable. Much of the coral cover failed to recover in the months that followed.

Especially hard hit were the peaks of dropoffs, places like the reef flats of famous Ngemelis Wall. Other well-known dive sites such as Coral Gardens were also hammered. The walls themselves, bathed in cool currents, and shallow areas, where warm water was common before El Niño, fared better.

Palau was hardly alone as a victim of the 1997–98 ENSO. In the Indian Ocean, the Maldives, Kenya, and the Seychelles suffered massive bleaching. Throughout Indonesia, Thailand, and New Guinea there were similar dieoffs of hard corals.

Bleaching episodes on tropical reefs continue to proliferate worldwide. Peter Glynn, a coral researcher at the University of Miami, was one of the first scientists to begin studying bleaching after the 1982–83 ENSO caused catastrophic coral mortality in the eastern Pacific.

"All major coral reef regions have been affected," he writes, "including areas in the eastern, central, and western Pacific, Indian Ocean, and western Atlantic."[3]

One might wonder how local efforts like MPAs can affect recovery from worldwide problems such as global warming. Yet, if areas resistant to bleaching are protected from siltation, pollution, overfishing, and other stresses, they can provide larvae to speed recovery throughout affected areas. These relationships were documented in a Nature Conservancy report from a similar workshop held in Hawaii.[4]

Palau already had a good MPA program. Palauan fish populations, some of the most biodiverse in the world, remained healthy throughout the ENSO disturbance. Many fish, especially angelfish, butterflyfish, triggerfish, and surgeonfish, eat filamentous algae, which otherwise can take over and smother baby corals in places where coral cover is depleted. There is good agreement among marine ecologists that overfishing, in combination with hurricane waves and sea urchin mortality, caused the current lack of coral cover in the country that has become a classic case of reef mismanagement, Jamaica (see chapter 5).[5]

There are several reasons why Palau, over the centuries, developed a marine conservation ethic, called *bul* in Palauan. Frequent interisland warfare kept the population down and made it dangerous for fishermen to venture far from home reefs. During times of peace, bad weather also kept small craft close to local coasts. From these historic constraints grew today's lagoon and reef tenure system. Islanders control the right to fish and allow outsiders to take fish only with permission.[6]

During the twentieth century, German, Japanese, and American cultural influence replaced the barter economy of traditional Palau with a cash economy. Although fish populations suffered as a result,[7] attempts to institute sustainable use of resources, in combination with the tenure tradition, have made the *bul*, or conservation ethic, much stronger in recent days in Palau. The meeting I attended was an example of this.

As I absorbed lectures at the workshop, I noticed the weather clearing. An hour later, a bush pilot named Gary strapped me into the rear of a Piper fixed-wing aircraft, unscrewed the adjacent door, and took off.

A collection of jewels appeared, densely vegetated limestone islands scattered like emeralds over clear waters of blue. Where the reefs were visible, brown, green, and white appeared. I leaned out of the door into the slipstream and wrenched back inside as the 100-knot wind tugged at my camera.

Gary took the plane over Seventy Islands, a collection of uninhabited rock islets that are off-limits to boaters, divers, fishermen—taboo to everyone. If anyone ever wanted to make an experiment examining the effects of diving, fishing, and boating on coral reefs, Seventy Islands would make a perfect control.

On the way back, we flew over a new dolphin exhibit. Like the Roatan, Honduras tourist pens (see chapter 8), this for-profit oceanarium had large, outdoor enclosures for bottlenose dolphins. Tourist in-the-water encounters took place here, the typical snorkels, swims, and dives. The dolphins were imported from Japan, because spinners were the usual local cetaceans. At the airport, we refueled the Piper, and I had to take responsibility for burning, in one-half hour, six gallons of aviation fuel. Not good for my global warming conscience.

After a brief nap, it was back to the dive shop. Tova told me that the muck diving off the pier was splendid, and I spent a long hour searching for mandarin fish, green and red finger-sized gobies that were to mate that night when the moon would be full. What with my hyperactive energy, though, I found it hard to sit in one spot and wait for the little guys to come out and play.

I zipped all over the harbor at a depth of about seven feet, checking out a brilliant blue *Tridacna* giant clam, wide open, its algae busy photosynthesizing. There was a cuttlefish hanging still nearby, its camouflage a dappled red. Then a juvenile sweetlips appeared, an orange and white character that fluttered all over the reef. This odd creature cast a spell on me, and I spent the rest of the dive following its circuitous movements. It seemed that its coloration and nervous swimming would be sure to attract predators. Perhaps this was an example of aposematic color, that common warning of poison to potential attackers seen in nudibranchs, poison dart frogs, and snakes, but the adults were a favored Palauan game fish. It couldn't be for mating, or to assist parents that were long gone.

So then, why? Many other types of juvenile fish also carry gaudy pigmentation. Here was a mystery of piscine natural history.

NOVEMBER 2, 2001

This morning Troy Ngiralkelau, a Fish 'N Fins dive master, took me out in the skiff to photograph mangroves. Troy was way cool; nothing got him rattled. A slim, quiet man, he was a betel nut *afficionado*; he kept his bag of nuts, clam-shell lime, and tobacco handy for those quiet moments when Westerners might, say, enjoy a glass of beer or wine.

We motored a few hundred yards from the dive shop and mangroves surrounded us. I slipped into the tepid water; although it was far cooler than the 95°F of the fall of 1998, it was 85°F and made the use of a wet suit superfluous.

Snorkeling half in the bathtub-warm water, half out, watching schools of juvenile fish work their way through the mazelike mangrove roots, I felt a deep sense of calm. This was a nursery, after all. Baby fish felt safe here, and so did I.

Later that day, after the usual chaotic loading of gear and the standard safety lectures, six of us dive tourists and three crew took off for a week at sea on *Ocean Hunter*. This was what my tired brain and body craved. This was why I spent 24 hours traveling to get here.

Our first dive site was a Japanese wreck from World War II, the *Iro Maru*. A victim of a submarine attack in 1944, the *Iro* was a big oiler, some 500 feet long, lying in 50–120 feet. Just a short distance from Koror, she was covered with razor clams, small clams living on the big ones; black corals also grew throughout the superstructure. Large, unafraid batfish hovered over her, and orange anthias fish were everywhere. The wreck was a beauty. After rumors of gloom and doom, I was expecting death and desolation, but the *Iro* was encrusted with life.

For our second dive we motored down to the Southern Rock Islands. Kenneth Johnny, the Palauan skipper of *Ocean Hunter*, hoped to see mantas in the channel dredged there by the Germans in the early 1900s. Kenneth had been skipper for years; he was the nephew of Francis Toribiong, the Palauan who explored and discovered many of today's dive sites. Kenneth was on the macho side, an amateur wrestler and reader of combat novels; not for him the betel nut. Like Troy, though, he made over 500 dives a year.

We hit the water, shot to the bottom, and fought a powerful current. Kenneth took us to a popular manta cleaning station, where we hooked on to the bottom with four-inch, nonbarbed reef hooks tied to our buoyancy compensators. There was a full moon tonight, and, because the moon and the sun's gravity combined, there were high high tides and low low tides, with strong currents at midtide. Floating there a few feet above the reef, we found the roaring current gave the impression of flying. Looking around, for the first time I saw the effects of the ENSO.

My guidebook, written by Francis Toribiong and Tim Rock, a Guam nature journalist, said, "The channel itself is quite shallow, but the coral gardens around it are deeper and beautifully manicured by nature . . . forests of staghorn coral provide protection for clouds of damselfish."[8]

We found the expected sand in the channel. But the "manicured gardens" were nonexistent. Instead, there were acres of dead coral, broken staghorn *Acropora* for the most part, with bits of green algae growing on them. There were, though, large numbers of varied fish everywhere we looked. Two big gray reef sharks patrolled the current just in front of us. There were schools of fusiliers, male–female pairs of butterflyfish of many different species, and whitetip reef sharks. One of the gray reefs, hanging lazily in front of us, darted to the surface, grabbed something, and sped back down, resuming its lazy serpentine swim. The speed of the attack was daunting. Just this past month Kenneth and Troy saw a tiger shark take a manta ray here.

My air almost gone, I signaled to Kenneth my intention to ascend and slowly rose to a 15-foot safety stop. My anxious searching for the buoy where we were supposed to end our dive was a failure. At the surface, I inflated a large, orange safety sausage, a six-foot long, tubular sack. In the distance, to my relief, was *Ocean Hunter* and an alert Troy.

Palau has six-foot tides rushing in and out of the lagoon formed by its barrier reef. In addition, the equatorial countercurrent and the equatorial current meet in the Philippine Sea to the west. There is a lot of moving water, and that, along with the close proximity to the Fertile Triangle, is why so much sea life is found here. Palau diving is high current diving.

There have been incidents.

Stories circulate about how, some years ago, the skipper of a small dive boat off Peleliu, the southernmost island in the archipelago, developed engine trouble, motored to port for a new part, and abandoned six Japanese divers. On his return some hours later, they were nowhere to be seen. A search with every available boat on the island was mounted. One diver, a young woman, was found drifting 10 days later, a diary she kept on her dive slate revealing that she survived for six days before exposure and dehydration killed her.

Just this year, or so the tale from Kenneth and Troy went, a cook on an Australian liveaboard went for an unannounced swim. Not knowing his chef was in the water, the skipper pulled anchor and moved to a new spot. After some hours, when lunch failed to appear, everyone put two and two together and went back to look for him. But he was never found.

Knowing these stories, I bought an emergency position indicator radio beacon (EPIRB) before leaving San Diego, and a dive box to hold it that was rated down to 40 meters. When I gave the frequencies to Kenneth, he chuckled, as if it was unnecessary, and in truth, it proved to be so. But later we found out that, a year ago or so, yet another group of divers got swept off and lost at Peleliu. An aerial search found them all two-and-a-half hours later.

We all carried safety sausages. Of course, there was much ribald humor about how to inflate one's sausage, whether it was "flaccid" or "erect," how long it took to "get it up," and so on. But behind the jokes there was a touch of anxiety, anxiety that faded with Troy and Kenneth's proven competence.

NOVEMBER 3, 2001

It poured throughout the night, and all on *Ocean Hunter* slept like zombies. It takes rain to make paradise. Still on California time, I rose at 5 A.M. and watched the sun come up, its beams sneaking between thunderheads, subtle pastels of the tropics painting the sky, fish splashing in the ocean.

We dived at Turtle Cove, again in full current, again hooking on to the reef. True to the name, we saw green sea turtles. Gray reef sharks circled in front of us, as at German Channel.

Then we tried New Drop-off, or West Ngemelis Wall. Again, we hooked on in current and saw green sea turtles and gray reef sharks. During a second dive at West Ngemelis we found a prime section. Here I discovered invertebrate life that equaled or surpassed anything in New Guinea or Fiji. Soft corals, sea whips, and gorgonians lined a vertical wall. The obligatory turtles and gray reef sharks made their usual showing. Clouds of plankton-eating rainbow runners flashed by in schools. Stopping to photograph a choice section of reef, I could not find a place to set my fingertip to brace myself—there was no spot bare enough to avoid damage, either to my finger or to the reef.

While the others ate lunch, I snorkeled over to a place Kenneth called Coral Gardens, hoping to find shallow coral heads in three feet or so of water. I was on a mission for that perfect over–under image, where half the image is above the sea and half below. Coral Gardens, unfortunately, was a disappointment. Dead and broken staghorn coral was everywhere. The bottom had some fish, but by and large, much of the sea life was gone.

Compare my experience with that of James D. Watt. A professional underwater photographer, Watt wrote this for a 1997 piece in *Discover Diving*:

> Coral Gardens is a picture perfect coral setting. . . . It is another wonderful spot for split image photographs and photos with a lush coral background. The coral grows to within two feet of the surface from depths of up to 90 feet. Be careful! The coral in this area is very thick and very delicate. Once can spend literally days in this pristine setting.[9]

We made an afternoon dive here at a deeper area of Coral Gardens. There was no improvement. Most of the coral was dead. There were still active cleaning stations, angelfish, and *Tridacna* giant clams amidst the carnage, though, so all was not lost.

Kenneth wanted to make a night dive here, because we knew the spot. We found lionfish, a scared clownfish in an anemone, and scattered shrimp with eyes glowing, reflecting our flashlights. Here and there could be found baby staghorn corals, their bright blue tips waving tentacles in the current. Topside, Troy told me that a gray reef shark nibbled on my fins while I was photographing the lionfish.

"Coral Gardens?" one of my boatmates said. "Coral Cemetery is more like it."

The main course at dinner was a grouper caught by Arly, our cook, while we were out diving. I had to pass. Grouper, to me, were naive fish that were easy to spear; eating them was something like eating golden retriever. Plus, I was well fed with other courses.

Exhausted after five dives, my head found the pillow early. Tomorrow, with the full moon two days gone, we would chance Blue Corner.

Up again at 5 A.M., high with anticipation, I greeted a cloudless sunrise. The winds were calm, and Kenneth took the boat to Blue Corner, a pass in the barrier reef where a strong tidal current ran over a corner of reef about 45 feet deep that jutted into the open sea and dropped to the depths.

Carl Safina called his first dive there "the fastest, most slow-motion forty-two minutes in my life."[10] Rock and Toribiong's guidebook says:

> Blue Corner off Ngemelis Islands consistently sizzles with electric fish action. Large sharks are common, as are small sharks, sea turtles, groupers, schools of barracuda, snappers, small tropicals, Napoleon wrasse, bumphead parrotfish and even an occasional moray eel or sea snake. . . .[11]

They also warn, "The currents can be powerful and tricky at times, sweeping ascending divers right off the point. Be sure to watch for down and up currents running along the walls. . . ."

We hit the cobalt clear water charged with excitement; a cloud of silver fish with bold blue stripes on their sides promptly engulfed us. Kenneth advised us at the briefing to get down to 90 feet or so, to avoid the current. At that depth, the wall leading to the corner was packed with gorgonians, soft corals, hard corals, sponges, ascidians, and tunicates. This was the kind of multiple-phyla-impregnated reef that a place only 500 miles from Indonesia and the Philippines ought to be.

The others passed overhead, and I paused to photograph a beautiful gorgonian jutting six feet out from the wall, its base jammed with *Dendronephthya*. To nail the perfect photo, with fan, soft corals, sunburst, and solar rays, required shooting straight up into the sun. My bubbles, as always, intruded upon the image, so I was forced to hold my breath—something only an underwater photographer would understand, certainly not a recommended policy for general scuba diving.

Just as my last, languid bubble cleared the picture frame, out of the corner of my eye came a dozen big, dark shadows.

Sharks. Gray reefs, in a school, and heading right overhead. Gasping, both from trying to hold my breath at four atmospheres of pressure, and from the perfection of the moment, I fired away with my Nikonos, giddy with adrenalin.

In outdoor photography, it must be understood, there is no end of anticipation and disappointment. If you put yourself out there in the wilderness enough, nature will grant you the odd golden opportunity. Sometimes. And usually only for a moment. If I had a dollar for every blown photo, for every critter that popped up only to disappear, for every overexposed, out-of-focus, underexposed, blurred, or otherwise screwed-up image my camera delivered, my doctoring night job would be history. My office has a large wastebasket that is invariably filled with cast-off slides after a wilderness expedition.

So, along with using 35-mm film and cameras, I also shoot what Tom Johnson, the first mate of the Alaska diveboat *Delphinus*, calls "neurochromes." These most reliable of exposures are preserved in the cerebrum by neural circuitry. They are perfectly exposed, although they can fade with time. My neurochromes of that moment at Blue Corner were awesome.

Gray reef sharks in a school. Hello? Swimming in perfect position under a sunburst? Soft corals *and* a big sea fan? All in one place? Jazzed over my luck and realizing that one-third of my air (one thousand of three thousand pounds) was gone, I left the sea fan and the relative calm water at 90 feet to look for the others.

There was no one in sight. The current pulled me harder and harder during the ascent. Now it rushed me along, the wall sliding by faster, the sea fans and corals barely registering. There was a cloud of fish and bubbles ahead. I hooked myself to the top of the wall as my mask flooded. The current was howling. After fixing my mask, no small task holding a camera with twin strobes in a five-knot oceanic river, I looked around. Next to me flew Wayne, a Southern Baptist minister from Louisiana, a heavenly grin on his face.

To our left was a school of barracuda, maybe 100 fish. To the right, an even bigger school of jacks. They hung overhead, facing into the current, keeping their places with only cursory flicks of their tails. A pack of gray reef sharks, the ones I'd been photographing, hung motionless in the current dead ahead, waiting, perhaps, for a lapse in attention from the smaller fish, or for current-borne food from the open sea.

The top of the reef was rubble. Whether it was the current, the El Niño, or heavy diving pressure, little live coral survived here. Martin, my on board roommate, a Dane who now worked in Seattle, dived here six years ago and reported that it was the same then. On average, 100 divers per day explore Blue Corner. Today, however, there were only the six of us plus Troy hooked in a cluster on the reef flat, just above a wall that dropped deep into blue water.

An immense blue-green fish with thick lips, an animal that must have weighed over 200 pounds, lumbered up to nuzzle Troy. Obliging, the divemaster slipped a scrap of food out from the pocket of his trunks and fed the big guy. This was the Blue Corner resident Napoleon wrasse. Able to live to 100 years and grow to more than seven feet long and 400 pounds, these fish and their gibbous lips are one of the few predators of crown-of-thorns sea stars.[12] They are also prized fare for the live restaurant fish trade. This one was more than friendly. Troy gave him a hug. The fish seemed to like it, moving between us, engaging our attention. As with the other fish, the current seemed inconsequential to Napoleon's movements.

I shifted position and was all but swept away. The beauty and efficacy of fish hydrodynamics was apparent.

Then the current delivered a tight school of 30 Japanese divers from the liveaboard *Palau Sport*. Blue Corner became, over about five seconds, Grand Central Station. It was time to go. We released our hooks, drifted over the reef flat, safety-stopped together at 15 feet, and hopped aboard the waiting *Ocean Hunter*.

Blue Corner was everything it was supposed to be.

NOVEMBER 5, 2001

We chugged south to Peleliu, the site of an intense World War II battle during September, October, and November of 1944. Today it was home to 800 Palauans, an elementary school, and some of the highest voltage dive sites in the islands. Here were the most powerful currents, here the best chance to see tiger sharks, pilot whales, and whatever else the sea dished up. This was also a place where current-related dive accidents could occur.

Kenneth told us about a diver visiting *Ocean Hunter*, a confident fellow who insisted on taking two bulky camera/strobe systems underwater at Peleliu Express, the site with the strongest currents. Kenneth advised the gentleman not to overburden himself, but the man said, "How long have you been diving? I've been diving for 20 years. I know what I'm doing."

Kenneth replied, "How long have you been diving Palau?"

The guy took both systems underwater. The dive lasted about five minutes. Kenneth found him pinned to the wall by the current, a camera in each hand, both his mask and his wits lost. After the rescue, there were no more discussions about diving experience.

We slipped in at a spot called White Beach Wall, where kind conditions prevailed, soft corals were abundant, and hard corals were all dead above 30 feet. Next, we visited Peleliu Coral Gardens. There were plentiful nudibranchs here, gaudy giant clams, and varied and numerous reef fish.

Again, above 30 feet, there was not much but broken and deceased stag-horn coral.

We pulled into a channel still lined with rusting steel breakwater beams built by the U.S. Navy's Seabees in 1944. Kenneth arranged for a guide to take us around the battlefields, and Willy, a native of Peleliu, greeted us.

"As you can see," said Willy, "Peleliu today is very beautiful. But in 1944 it was different. There was not a living plant after the shelling. There was terrible heat and the smell of corpses. But, as you can see, the mother nature has come back; all is green and growing."

Willy took us to a monument at Orange Beach, the D-Day invasion site. He pronounced Orange "o-ran-gee." On a simple cross made of steel rebar was propped a G.I.'s helmet, rusted with age, a shrapnel hole clearly visible. Willy supplied us with the staggering numbers: 8,000 dead American soldiers, 10,000 dead Japanese, most young men in their late teens or early twenties.

It was an eery moment, standing there with the cross, staring at the idyllic beach. Coconut palms, betel nut trees, and ironwood trees, lianas winding around their trunks, waved in the southwest wind. On the sand a baby coconut plant was growing out of the remnants of shell rind—the mother nature.

Willy had copies of citations for six Medals of Honor given for soldiers at Peleliu. Five were for men who threw themselves, knowing it meant certain death, onto live grenades to save their buddies. The sixth was given to one Captain Pope, who led a charge to take a small hill and held it through a night of countercharges and hand-to-hand combat. In the morning, wounded but still alive with a handful of men down to their last dozen bullets, he was relieved by fresh troops. The hill, now called Pope's Hill, was abandoned to be recaptured later in the battle.

Walking around Peleliu was a moving experience. Perhaps it was the droning of Willy, our guide, rattling off stories and statistics. Perhaps it was my own mind set, the warlike events of September 11, 2001 still front and center in my consciousness. Perhaps it was the rusted tanks with ferns growing in them, the howitzers buried in the Japanese tunnel system, or the wreck of a Zero fighter plane in the dense jungle. Perhaps there remained ghosts in that jungle: the spirits of men who died from flame-thrower scaldings, mortar shell explosions, and bayonet wounds.

Today the local men fished, the women gardened taro. Some sold marijuana, a major, if clandestine, cash crop. There was a ferry to Koror, a four-hour trip for two dollars. Fresh water came from filtered, collected rainwater.

We returned to *Ocean Hunter* and prepared for a night dive at, once again, Peleliu Coral Gardens. The tide was changing, and I resolved, if a current was running, to abort the dive.

We jumped off the skiff into a two-knot rip. 'Plan your dive and dive your plan,' goes the dive mantra. I aborted, and Kenneth picked me up and dropped me off to dive the channel muck near the Seabee beams, where I found a hermet crab wearing a cone shell and a cowrie climbing on the corroded steel. There were a few saltwater crocodiles here, it was said, and the thought kept me moving as I explored the mud alone in the dark. At least there was no current.

The others returned, safe but muttering. The current had worsened, and there was more apprehension than photography on the dive. It is a good general rule not to dive at night if there is a current.

NOVEMBER 6, 2001

We returned to the Southern Rock Islands and dived at Big Drop-off or Ngemelis Wall, Turtle Wall, and a place called Barnum Wall. Without exception, the walls were crammed with invertebrates: soft corals, gorgonians, and healthy hard corals. Gray reef sharks and green sea turtles appeared on each dive. At Barnum Wall, as I kicked over from the boat, a curious turtle swam straight at me on a near collision course. At the last moment it slowed and peered deep into my flat-port camera lens. Was it observing its reflection? Or was it drawn to me because of my handsome, reptilian features?

On the same wall, I found a number of cleaning stations manned by *Labroides dimidiatus* wrasse, colorful characters three inches long with yellow dorsal stripes, a bold black lateral stripe, and bright blue bellies. Like their counterparts in the Caribbean, with a cautious, nonthreatening approach from an observer, they continued to service a multitude of customers.

As I'd noted before with the Roatan wrasse (see chapter 8), the busiest cleaners seemed to pick an underwater landmark, a large brain coral, a jutting sea fan, something that stood out to both fish and divers. I found a trio of the most popular cleaners at a peninsula of reef that stuck out into the current. First they tended to a mature sweetlips, a grouperlike, somber adult that had the opposite nature of the juvenile that fluttered over the Fish 'N Fins harbor muck. Next, a reticulated butterflyfish showed up, an animal with a pointillist pattern painted on its sides. The *Labroides*, making deft sure movements, nipped at gills, mouth, fins, and tails of both fish; then their customers moved on.

Business for my three wrasse then slowed. They swirled around their corner of reef, flashing their colors. It pays to advertise.

A school of yellow-tailed fusiliers swarmed in, maybe two dozen fish. The cleaners went crazy. Fusiliers do not sit still well, and it was obvious that these clients were impatient. The wrasse went into hyperdrive, darting from one fish to the next, nibbling, pecking, blurs of blue, black, and yellow. They looked like a pit crew changing tires at the Indy 500.

I clicked off a last photo, laughing into my regulator, and left to give the cleaners some peace and quiet. On my swim back to the boat, a jellyfish pulsed in the blue water. A collection of juvenile fish darted within the deadly tentacles.

We made a late afternoon dive at German Channel, looking for mantas once again. The routine was familiar: find the cleaning station, hook on to the reef, float in the current. I looked up and saw hundreds of jacks at about 50 feet of depth. Closer to the surface were thousands of baitfish, too distant to guess at species. The two shoals hovered at their respective depths, facing the current.

Just as I was about to turn and look elsewhere, the jacks broke the facade of tranquility. As one they darted, a mass of muscle and teeth, up into the heart of the school of bait. Ready for the threat, the shoal darted toward us in a kind of underwater Immelman turn, a giant S-curve. So many fish moved so fast over such a great distance that they produced a loud, roaring sound, something akin to a 30-foot wave breaking. A moment later, the bait vanished, and only the jacks remained, some, perhaps, having scored dinner.

That afternoon we explored a sandy slope off Ngerchong Island, a place lined with dead staghorn coral, where Kenneth showed us a pair of cuttlefish. They were guarding their nest site, a thorny (and very much alive) golden brown invertebrate that I'd not seen before. Dozens of white eggs were hidden deep within the thorns. As we watched one of the parents, it changed from a complex crimson pattern to a plain brown with black checkerboard stripes. We backed off, and it flicked back to the old pattern.

Wayne drew us into a circle. An underwater seascape painter friend of his, an avid diver, had died of cancer. Wayne held a small vial of the man's cremated remains. In his best preacher fashion, he opened the vial, waved his hands in a solemn gesture, and scattered the ashes near the cuttlefish.

The wind picked up, and we took the skiff on a bone-jarring 20-minute ride to the drop-offs. We hit Ngemelis Wall again, Blue Corner, and Blue Hole. The skiff rides and the multiple high voltage dives began to tire us. At the last site, a big underwater cave with cathedral-like light streaming down, Kenneth took a plastic bottle half-full of water and twisted it in his hands, making a strange, squeaking sound. A moment later two gray reef sharks appeared, interested, very close.

NOVEMBER 8, 2001

The southwest wind was still howling, and we moved into the shelter of the Central Rock Islands. The Rock Islands are the ancient tips of reefs, pushed upward and covered with jungle. Their bases are undercut by waves, mussels, and sponges eating into the old coral. We passed over calm waters through these scattered uplifts of limestone. Dense tropical foliage covered each one.

The forest growing atop each limestone cap was impenetrable. As underwater, a close look showed exceptional variation, wide varieties of green hues and leaf types. Palau is also home to a wide variety of birds—a casual glance from the boat revealed white swallows, white-tailed tropics, and a common white-headed pigeon.

We motored down a long channel dotted with small islands and found a small pier made of pressure-treated wood. This was Mecherchar Island, the gateway to one of Palau's crown jewels.

Within the uplifted limestone of the archipelago, limestone built by corals long ago, lie over 50 marine lakes. Filled with filtered salt water that rises and falls with the tides, they represent isolated, insular ecosystems. We were to visit the best known, Jellyfish Lake.

Leaping ahead of the others, carrying three cameras and snorkel gear, I trotted up a steep 100-foot hillside dotted with limestone steps. Halfway up was a strange tree that leaked black sap. Resisting an impulse to touch it, I remembered a quote from David Doubilet, who spent a month photographing here for *National Geographic* in 1981: "Poisonwood trees drip a black, molasses-like sap that causes human skin to erupt like plastic bubble packaging."[13]

Rounding the top, short of breath, I saw a lake below through the foliage.

STINGERLESS JELLYFISH, MERCHERCHAR LAKE, PALAU,

MICRONESIA *"In the center of the lake, maybe 50 yards out, were some dimples*

in an otherwise smooth surface."

At the base of the hill lay a small dock, surrounded by mangrove trees. By now I was dripping in sweat from heat, humidity, and exertion. The water felt cool and refreshing; tannins leached from vegetation gave it a brownish tinge.

On the eastern shore, small white anemones undulated tentacles, waiting for prey that might venture too close. In Jellyfish Lake, the ecosystem is simplified and isolated. Of the two species of jellyfish found in the midwater lake ecosystem, the pale, white *Mastigias* are the most fascinating. With no prey or enemies demanding the need for nematocyst-bearing tentacles, evolution has led them to a different lifestyle. The *Mastigias* have lost their stingers and taken on symbiotic zooxanthellic algae, as *Tridacna* clams and hard corals have done. Living in this island of salt water, they are no longer hunters. They have become farmers; their only predators are the white anemones.

In the center of the lake, maybe 50 yards out, were some dimples in an otherwise smooth surface. The morning sun was already above the jungle, and I kicked toward the disturbance—a jelly, maybe five inches across, its bell contracting, moving toward the surface, bringing its algae to the photosynthesis source. There was another, another, and soon, dozens.

For a long time I swam with the jellies, diving down and looking up at them, floating in the clear lake under cumulus clouds and blue sky. When one swam against my hand, it felt like a bag of living water.

The *Mastigias* jellies took a hit in 1998, as did the hard corals. In 1999 diveboats stopped bringing in tourists, for there was nothing to see and it was felt best to limit any intrusion into what had proved to be a delicate ecosystem. But the creatures had made a comeback.

I swam back, traded cameras, and snorkeled along the west shore. Here were ancient mangroves with three-inch-long black-belted cardinalfish flitting through the root systems, their big eyes checking me out. I wondered how the fry of these fish made it into the lake, filtered through the lime along with the tides.

Should any animal venture to the depths of the lake, death awaits. Below 50 feet lies a dense layer of deoxygenated water contaminated with natural hydrogen sulfide. Exposure for more than five minutes can be fatal.

The last to leave the lake, I raced back to the skiff and, on return to *Ocean Hunter*, noticed shallow water and corals next to the Rock Islands. While the others ate breakfast, I snorkeled around several of the islets. Some were only 30 feet in diameter. In the shallows were cauliflower coral and circular, blue-colored, close-growing *Fungia* coral; there were more and healthier stony corals here than on the outer reefs.

We visited a place called Clam City, where Palauans raised *Tridacna*, or giant clams. Mature clams, 50–100 years old, can grow to four feet in length and weigh over 500 pounds. The clam farmers have placed the mollusks here in about 30 feet of shallow water on a sandy bottom, where currents carry larvae to the east and west.

The clams, now spread open to the sun, their mantles shimmering with unique patterns of blue, tan, green, and brown, sheltered tiny orange gobies and a variety of damselfish. One can swim over an open clam, but maintaining perfect buoyancy control is important. Should you get too close, the big adductor muscles contract in an instant, each animal having rows of light-sensitive black eyes on the edges of its mantle. I was careful not to cast my shadow on them, to protect both the animals and myself.

Poachers are wiping out the big mollusks on coral reefs all over the western Pacific. Often they take only the adductor muscles and leave the rest of the animal to rot; numbers of giant clams have dropped catastrophically. Places like Clam City may prove essential to *Tridacna* survival.

Still exploring the Central Rock Islands, we stopped at a site called Soft Coral Arch. It was a shallow dive with a brisk current and cloudy, silty water. But on either side of a narrow channel were *Dendronephthya*, yellow, red, pink, brown, blue, purple. Hundreds of colonies, living on top of one another, inhabit this small passageway. As in Fiji, there was little other life living on or with them.

My last dive was on a wreck near Koror, where Kenneth showed me a stunning nudibranch, jet black with a single blue, decorative band. He showed me another species, a white one with a complex brown pattern. My dive computer pulled me to the surface as he tried to show me a third

---

NOVEMBER 9, 2001

Today was my nitrogen washout day. With time to burn after packing and rinsing out camera systems in fresh water, I took a cab through Koror's sweltering streets, roads crammed with trucks and people chatting on cell phones, to another clam facility, the Palau Mariculture Demonstration Center. Here long concrete pools sheltered *Tridacna* of all ages, from little guys an inch in diameter and a six months old, to six-inch clams that were maybe five years old, to big two-footers that were decades old.

Some of the clams are planted around the islands, some are sold to restaurants, and others are sold to aquarists. Shipping and keeping the mollusks alive, one of the operators told me, was not an easy matter—often the containers bound for the United States, where the bulk of the tropical aquarium trade goes, got hung up in the Philippines in transit and the clams died.

I rang up Patrick Colin, the president of the Coral Reef Research Foundation, and dropped by to pick up a scientific paper he offered to give me. Colin is a gray-bearded fellow with a gruff manner, a manner belied by his generosity. His lab was a working institution not intended for tourists. There were microscopes, tanks, refrigerators, and underwater camera gear scattered on crowded benches. Colin's wife and fellow researcher, a tan brunette, was busy examining some samples. I told him how much I liked his guidebook, *Tropical Pacific Invertebrates*,[14] and asked him about the hard coral mortality that we'd seen firsthand.

"Unfortunately, the worst hit places in Palau are some of the spots sport divers visit most often," he said. "Many of the shallow areas in the northern and central Rock Islands were spared, perhaps because the corals were more adapted to warm water. But divers commonly don't explore them."

Estimates of the exact amount of coral that died because of the 1998 warming vary, but in his published report of the event, Colin and colleagues[15] from Brown University looked at nine sites using what marine biologists call a point-intercept technique. They placed three 20-meter transect lines in each of the sites and characterized coral every 10 cm along those lines as healthy, bleached, recently dead, or "other" ("bare substrate, dead coral skeletons, or space occupied by other organisms"[16]).

Their findings? 54% of living hard corals (also called scleractinian corals) became bleached at depths of three to five meters, and 69% of hard corals bleached at 10–12 meter depths.[17] Although some of these study corals eventually recovered, others did not. But larvae were appearing and settling down to renew the reefs.

"Herbivore fish populations in Palau remain healthy," said Colin that afternoon, "and that is aiding coral recovery."

ENSO-induced bleaching events, it occurred to me, may be a standard part of evolving life on coral reefs. Just as the recent fires in Yellowstone National Park rejuvenated that ecosystem even as they destroyed vast acres of forest, the reefs in Palau, after their brush with El Niño, might well return more robust and diverse than ever.

"We may see some different species of corals and zooxanthellic algae replacing those that died," said Colin. "There probably is selective pressure now for organisms that are both less sensitive to heat and less prone to damage from typhoon wave action."

I asked the researcher about his position on the continuum of opinion among marine scientists regarding the survivability of coral reefs, a spectrum represented on one side by cautious optimists, such as Richard Grigg of the University of Hawaii, and, on the other, by the alarmists, such as Phillip Dustan of the Cousteau Society and the College of Charleston.

"I'm in the middle," Colin said. Coral reef resilience is a matter of perspective and time frames, he pointed out. Grigg, for example, is a geology-oriented oceanographer, whereas Dustan is a marine biologist. The former thinks in terms of millions of years; the latter, in decades.

"One thing for me has definitely changed, though," Colin said, referring to his experience with El Niño's effect on Palau's coral reefs. "I had my doubts in the past, but now, I am a believer in global warming."

I knew from talking to Colin that my own brief trip to Palau was barely enough to scratch the surface of the complexities of coral reef biology, El Niño–induced die-offs, and fish populations. How much better to stay for a month, a year, or a lifetime—yet a week of diving, 30 varied mini-explorations, still spoke volumes. There is nothing subtle about an acre of dead staghorn coral, nor can one ignore vivid red sea fans and squadrons of gray reef sharks on a healthy tropical wall.

That evening, Tova and Navot invited me over with some other lucky guests for a feast. We tore into a delicious meal of yams, roast lamb, and papaya fruit salad, and washed it all down with some good California merlot. There was an assorted, international company of Israelis, Spaniards, Palauans, and Americans, and the conversation flowed with the wine. We spoke of the 20 divers killed in Belize by a recent hurricane when their diveboat capsized. We talked about Yap, Truk, the Solomons, and New Guinea. We talked about currents, and Navot admitted that whenever *Ocean Hunter* went to Peleliu he was kept awake at night by worry. An athletic, vital fellow who studied marine architecture and is a licensed shipwright, Navot told me of two long trips the Bornovskis had made to the Galapagos Islands. It was a familiar story.

"The first time we were there, unbelievable. Massive schools of hammerheads, silky sharks, dolphins. . . . The second time, 10 years later, still unbelievable . . . but less."

Gail, their five-year-old, delighted me after dessert by showing off her addition skills. According to Tova, she was a skilled swimmer and snorkeler. Her blue eyes sparkling, her face full of mischief, she made it hard for me not to think of my four-year-old son, Nicholas.

It was time to venture back among the thunderstorms. It was time to fly home.

Whenever I find myself growing grim about the mouth; whenever it is a damp drizzly

November in my soul . . . then, I account it high time to get to sea as soon as I can. . . .

—HERMAN MELVILLE, *Moby Dick*

Damp Novembers of the Soul

A Swim in Gaia's Blood

CALIFORNIA, 2001

Today was a hard, November day for me; instead of surfing or diving, I worked a long shift in the hospital, taking care of a man with a bad heart and then a woman with grievous injuries from a motor vehicle accident. But the medical world with its sealed, windowless operating rooms spat me out with enough time before dark to slip away for a swim. That mile-long bicycle ride from my house down to the beach took only seconds. There was the usual struggle to slip on the wet suit, the crunchy feel of the sand, the dive into the cool, refreshing waters, the shore break rocking my body in a rhythmic cadence, the cormorant floating nearby, watching me with curiosity. Everything became better.

I began to stroke through the water, stretching forward with my hands, giving gravity a rest. A strand of loose kelp caught me around the neck, and it took a moment to disentangle myself from the familiar algae. My glasses off and the light fading, I opened my eyes underwater and saw beneath the orange shimmer of a garibaldi. Whether it was a male guarding a nest of eggs or a wandering female was not clear. But it didn't matter. Everything that was wrong with the world had been made right.

I stroked harder now, pulling with all my might, feeling the chill of California's water, hoping to warm up by exercise. The tide was high, but waves were feathering out on the reef and drew me farther out. At last, I wheeled toward shore and stroked with everything in me. A wave picked my body up and cast it forward. The surf took me for a dozen rides—my torso arched for the butterfly stroke, my legs moving, cetaceanlike, in the dolphin kick. After a while my mind settled and drifted to the philosophical.

Melville's Ishmael and I are not the only ones who go to sea, to the wild, for solace. Roger Payne, a whale researcher born and raised in New York City, has spent many years in such wild places as Patagonia researching the lives and habits of the aquatic mammals. This is what he writes of the effects of the wilderness tonic:

> It is a sort of celestial phlogiston, which comes from flowers and vast beaches and deserts and oceans populated by species other than our own. This substance restores souls, and sets minds straight, and rebuilds moralities, and cleans up the wreck and wrack and rust that we generate by endlessly rubbing against our fellow humans. . . ."[1]

Wilderness, and especially saltwater wilderness, is a vital thing. Yet, if one believes the sometimes strident rhetoric of nature and environmental organizations, much of this wild nature is threatened. Some people, of course, dismiss these doomsday predictions as self-serving propaganda. The problem environmentalists face is that the degradation of nature is real, but slow enough that it must be measured over decades and centuries, species by extinct species, wilderness by lost wilderness. And most of us don't respond to such time frames. We think in minutes and hours, days and months. We worry more about today, less about tomorrow, and not at all about 100 years hence.

In 1978, an eccentric British atmospheric chemist and inventor named James Lovelock published a book entitled *Gaia: A New Look at Life on Earth*. In this work, he proposed the poetic notion that humans ought to consider Earth to be a single living organism. According to Lovelock, our planet, which he personified by calling Gaia, the Greek name for the Earth Goddess (a term William Golding suggested), is not only a living organism[2] but also adapts in mysterious, almost intuitive ways to changes on a planetary level to maintain chemical and meteorologic conditions at a steady state.

This theory took a broadside of withering criticism from scientists such as British geneticist Richard Dawkins, Colorado climatologist Stephen Schneider, and Harvard geochemist H.D. Holland. Foremost among their objections was the hint of teleology that infused Lovelock's writings, the idea that Gaia was somehow a conscious being. Lovelock took these complaints to heart and modified his theory in the 1988 book *The Ages of Gaia*.[2] He deleted any hints of new-age consciousness and showed by computer modeling how life, through natural selection and response to climate changes, could regulate planetary conditions.

Although Lovelock's ideas of a sort of ideal Gaian steady state may be attractive to some, to others he missed the boat—there have been, through geological time, wild swings in Earth's climate. This dynamic, caused by positive feedback loops of ice, solar rays, orbital planetary wobbling, and the shifting of oceanic currents and tectonic plates, has led to abrupt and, for biological systems, deadly changes.

For example, Joseph Kirschvink of Caltech believes that the cause of the biological outpouring of phyla of animals that occurred 540 million years ago, the "Cambrian explosion," may have been caused by extraordinary geological upheaval. Life on Earth turned upside down, because Earth itself turned upside down. One giant continental landmass, called Rodinia, disintegrated into pieces that regathered into another supercontinent, Gondwanaland. Kirschvink showed how sedimentary rocks record abrupt shifts in ocean chemistry, and uranium–lead isotope dating techniques prove that these changes occurred rapidly. The entire surface of Earth may have even rotated 90° over the geologically brief 15 million years, in a phenomenon called "inertial interchange true polar wander," a sort of reconciling of unsettled planetary moment of inertia.[3]

As the continents shifted, marine currents also reorganized, causing dramatic shifts in the global oceans. This, writes Kirschvink, "should have fragmented any large-scale eco-systems that were established, generating smaller, more isolated populations and leading to a higher evolutionary branching rate. . . ."[4] The result? Quite possibly, the Cambrian explosion.

Even though Earth seems to be a stable place, it isn't. Thirty years ago, for example, no one believed that anthropogenic (human-caused) change on a global scale was possible. Today we have learned from the 1978 Coastal Zone Color Scanner satellite (now defunct) how phytoplankton blooms change in the sea.[5] We know that hatchery salmon alter phytoplankton numbers in the subarctic North Pacific[6]—something that would never have been believed in 1970. Because of the decline of Steller sea lions and harbor seals in coasts of the same region, in part from overfishing of pollock and related fish, killer whales have switched from pinnipeds to sea otters (see chapters 6, 15), whose population has plummeted by 90%; meanwhile urchin populations, their preferred food, have soared, and kelp forests, on which urchins graze, have declined 90%.[7]

These sorts of anthropogenic abuses become even more obvious in contained bodies of water, regions that act like islands in reverse. The Black Sea, for example, communicates with the Mediterranean only through the Straits of Bosporus. In 1982, an invasion occurred of stowaways lurking in the ballast water of a ship traveling from the Americas. The invaders, jellyfishlike ctenophores, then devastated local fishing. *Mnemiopis leidyi*, for two decades, made up about 95% of the Black Sea's wet-weight biomass—a huge domination. Not only did the ctenophore, which had no natural enemies in the insular Black Sea, kill fish directly, but it killed their food as well—zooplankton, larvae, crustaceans all fell prey to the stinging *Mnemiopis* tentacles.[8]

Another hitchhiking comb jelly, *Beroe cucumis*, found its way into the Black Sea, probably also by ships' ballast water. This time the invader proved to be beneficial, for *Beroe*, a smaller, three-inch-long organism, dines on the five-inch-long *Mnemiopis*. The result has been an unexpected, dramatic recovery of a moribund fishing industry.[9]

On an even larger scale, of course, there is the issue of anthropogenic increases in carbon dioxide in the atmosphere—the greenhouse effect first proposed by Swedish chemist Svante Arrhenius in 1896 and brought to attention in the twentieth century by Roger Revelle and Hans Suess in 1957.[10] By 1990, there was general consensus among 200 climatologists worldwide that greenhouse warming was real and the consequences would be serious.[11] By 2001, two independent studies, one from Scripps Institution of Oceanography and the other from the NOAA funded Princeton, N.J., Ocean Climate Laboratory, linked human activity with at least a 95% certainty to global warming.[12] Few scientists, some perhaps funded by oil company money, argue against the possibility that humans are accelerating global warming.[13] Even President George W. Bush, not the staunchest of environmentalists, lacked the chutzpah to deny that carbon dioxide emissions from burning fossil fuels are warming the world. He cited economics, not scientific uncertainty, as the chief reason the United States would not abide by the Kyoto protocol to reduce emissions.[14]

There are a few "clean" contrarians who appear not to be tainted by oil money, for example, meteorologist Richard Lindzen of Massachusetts Institute. He maintains that global warming is not affected by human carbon emissions, believing that negative feedback from ongoing increased cloud cover and water vapor will actually cool Earth. But Lindzen does acknowledge[15] that Earth in the past century has warmed about 0.5°C, and that during this time period humans have increased atmospheric carbon dioxide by around 30%.

It would a fine thing if Lindzen is correct and Earth, Lovelock-like, will be able to self-correct the ongoing warming. Many scientists doubt this is happening. No one, though, pretends to have rock-solid certainty about anything involving ongoing climatic processes.

"Climate is an angry beast," summarized climatologist Wallace Broecker, "and we are poking it with sticks."[16]

Scientists have learned that ratios of oxygen isotopes in water and ice correlate with global temperatures. Using this tool, international teams have been pouring over ice cores from Greenland, and the results are unsettling. Richard Alley, a National Academy of Science geophysicist, likened the wild climate and temperature fluctuations to a lamp switch getting flipped off and on by a rascally three-year-old.

"Dozens of rapid changes litter the record of the last hundred thousand years," he told *New Yorker* staff writer Elizabeth Kolbert.[17] "If you can possibly imagine the spectacle of some really stupid person bungee jumping off the side of a moving roller-coaster car, you can begin to picture the climate."

One steady-state factor that does seem to support Lovelock's theory is the percentage of oxygen in the atmosphere. For several hundreds of millions of years, at least, it seems to have remained, as best as we can tell, around 21%. Even at this level, rain forests and grasslands become flammable during today's droughts. According to Lynn Margulis and Dorion Sagan, if oxygen concentrations were a few percent higher, living organisms such as plants would spontaneously combust and fires would consume the planet; a few percentage points lower, and aerobic organisms would succumb from lack of oxygen, or asphyxiate.[18]

But there is little question that we humans are making our presence known to the planet, or that there have been many alterations in the past. For example, fossil studies of polar ice show that a rapid rise in carbon dioxide (and, presumably, temperatures) up to preindustrial levels, occurred 12,000 years ago, a rise that Lovelock attributed to the sudden death of a large percentage of marine algae.[19] And 18,000 years ago, during the last ice age, massive ice caps sucked water from the oceans and lowered sea level 410 feet from where it is today.[20] The consensus of most scientists, based on a view of Earth as a dynamic, changing place, is that the idea of a steady-state planet is erroneous.

Nevertheless, the broad concept of Earth as the living Gaia tempted me, out there day-dreaming in the sea, to look at the planet from a health perspective. To be more accurate, an analogy comparing the biosphere of Earth to a living creature intrigued this physician and self-taught naturalist, a person with one foot square in the world of medicine and the other mired in the wilderness. Other celestial objects, such as Mars or the Moon, did not stand much chance in being considered alive. Yet Earth as an organism could fit into the organ-system paradigm we doctors use to understand health and disease.

Comparison of the human body with our home planet is not a new exercise. Leonardo da Vinci, for example, saw the four Greek elements of fire, air, water, and earth in both our bodies and Earth. Our own human heat was similar, he reasoned, to volcanic lava, our breath to air released during earthquakes, our blood to underground springs, our bones to the rocks. Stephen Jay Gould wrote that such analogies "represent a mirror of human centrality in the scheme of universal things . . . yet another manifestation of the ancient sin of pride."[21] But I wondered whether one could find traces of the macrocosm within the microcosm and vice versa, and if insight might not result from the use of such a tool.

The human body, a collection of cells that is mostly water by weight, possesses a circulatory system, a conduit powered by a heart pump that carries saline blood, oxygen, carbon dioxide, nutrients, and wastes throughout the body. The biosphere of Earth also possesses a circulatory system, the water cycle, evaporation, clouds, rain and snow, freshwater rivers, and, of course, that great venous repository of saline water, the ocean. Within the ocean there is further circulation, as immense cold-water currents circulate over the deep abyssal plains, carrying nutrients far and wide on the floor of a watery globe. Instead of using a heart powered by biochemical energy, this circulatory system is powered by the sun. But on a macrocosmic, planetary level, it serves much the same role as blood, carrying food and wastes to all corners of the living planet, providing, like blood, the essence of life.

Another example of the body/planet comparison might be seen in the respiratory system, the nose, trachea, bronchi, and, most important, the millions and millions of alveoli, where a network of capillaries greets each breath of air, dumps waste carbon dioxide, and gathers in oxygen. On a planetary scale, Earth's atmosphere flows in and out of billions upon billions of collective organisms, some, like humans, producing carbon dioxide, and others, like plants, cyanobacteria, and phytoplankton, also producing oxygen and using up carbon dioxide. Air flows in and out of the ocean, as oxygen is absorbed into water and respired by zooplankton and fish, as plankton, bacteria, and marine algae suck up carbon dioxide and release oxygen.

Just as in the human alveoli the respiratory and circulatory system are intertwined, so air and water intertwine on Earth.

There are other analogies we could make between the planet, on a macro scale, and the body, on an organism level. Both have a daily cycle of wakefulness and sleep, or day and night. Both have a life cycle, for just as surely as each human is born, grows from babyhood, lives, and dies, so a planet, even our Earth, is born from cosmic dust, coalesces, rotates, solidifies, perhaps flourishes with life, and then becomes lifeless rock as the sun turns into a terminal nova.

There is also a dark side of the body/planet analogy we might consider—disease. A human can receive multiple traumatic injuries from a car accident; so can the planet get smacked by a large meteorite and suffer, on a grand scale, a similar sort of indignity. A human can smoke cigarettes for a lifetime and develop a host of cardiopulmonary problems; so can the biosphere become inundated with pollutants from industrial processes. Endocrine disorders, changes in tiny amounts of messenger molecules, lead to a host of human diseases, from growth hormone problems to immune problems to thyroid illness. On Earth, hormone-mimicking pollutants such as polychloral biphenyls, atrazine, endosulfan, alkylphenols, and others have led to weakened immune systems, diminished sperm counts, and subtle, but increasing, feminization and loss of fertility in a wide range of species.[22]

Perhaps the most obvious, if painful, analogy between human medicine and planet medicine involves cancer. For a host of reasons, some genetic, some environmental, cells in the human body periodically undergo transformation to begin producing in a wild and uncontrolled fashion. Sometimes the body can spot these renegades and destroy them, but other times malignant cells gain the upper hand, stealing nutrients, invading healthy tissue, and forever growing until death of the host results. So too, on Earth, species can run amok.

It is no secret that *Homo sapiens* has caused an accelerated number of extinctions. In fact, some scientists have likened the current wave of human-caused extinctions to the five previous mass extinctions found in the fossil record, including the one caused by that Caribbean meteorite 65 million years ago.[23] Getting a handle on rates of species loss is fraught with difficulty, one problem being that science has yet to make a full inventory of the planet's biota. New species are still being discovered, although most biologists nevertheless believe extinction rates from anthropogenic habitat destruction to be high. Some scientists, however, such as David Woodruff at the University of California at San Diego, think modern emphasis on species conservation, in part engendered by the political and legal utility of the Endangered Species Act, remains misdirected: "Some of us advocate a shift from saving things, the products of evolution, to saving the underlying process, evolution itself," he said.[24]

Kirk Winemiller, a fish biologist at Texas A&M University, agrees: "Why not save functioning ecosystems that haven't been despoiled yet?"[25]

Using this kind of philosophy, such organizations as the Nature Conservancy are enlisting wealthy donors and buying up huge tracts of land—to just let them be. Unfortunately, this cannot be done with the commons that is the sea.

But even if our current preoccupation with endangered species may be overly narrow, it is a fundamental of Wilson and MacArthur's theory of island biogeography that, as the area of habitat falls, the number of species living in it drops in proportion to the third to sixth root. Using a middle value, the fourth root, if 90% of a habitat is eliminated, one-half the species disappear[26]—presumably to become extinct. And there is little doubt that humanity is doing much to eliminate wild habitat, whether by chopping down trees on land or bottom trawling at sea.

Because species in this planetwide scenario become extinct faster than new ones appear, the result is a net decline in biodiversity. This, of course, is the exact opposite of what happened to create the species-rich coral reefs of New Guinea. It is also distinct from the idealized steady-state island equilibrium between immigration and extinction.

Six billion human omnivores, without a doubt, are taking from many other species their carrying capacity, the air, freshwater, land, prey, and nutrients that groups of organisms need to survive.[27] If one is a fervent anthropocentrist, the ascendance of mankind at the expense of other species is only right and just. If one were to hold a biocentrist point of view, one might consider the explosive growth of humans on the biosphere, a growth that, ironically, has been aided by physicians such as myself, to act as a cancer.

During another November, this one in 1982, I lived on the island of Oahu. Perhaps because of the strongest El Niño event since 1969, the ocean was warm, well into the 80°F range. The normal trade winds were absent. We surfed perfect, glassy eight-foot waves off the Hyatt Kuilima Hotel (now the Turtle Bay Hilton) near Kahuku Point at Turtle Bay, a protected spot that usually gets only three-foot surf. Then one of the many hurricanes that spawn off Acapulco in southern Mexico started careening toward Hawaii.

Hurricanes feed and grow on water warmer than 80°F. This one, dubbed "Iwa," was no exception. This was the hurricane that Rick Grigg mentioned in his paper on corals, the one that reduced coral coverage near Honolulu from 60–75% to 5–15%.[28] The storm, once again, was a magnitude 5 cyclone and packed winds greater than 150 mph.

The missile destroyer *Goldsborough* left Pearl Harbor during the blow, seeking the safety of blue water. The ship reported 30-foot waves near the harbor, and it was not a safe passage, for five crewmen were injured, one fatally.[29] Iwa slammed into Kauai the hardest, but it hit the North Shore of Oahu hard as well.

I remember taping the windows of my apartment to keep the broken glass under control. The air grew increasingly humid and gray, until around 4 P.M. the winds started shrieking. I ventured out the door only once, staggering through a wall of moving air, to see a coconut palm bend to the horizontal. Hanging on to the outdoor stairway for dear life, I watched as a powerful gust tore off the crown of the tree; it disappeared to the east, a huge, wind-blown projectile. Then sheets of rain began to pour from the west, jetting sideways, stinging, painful to the skin. That was enough for me. I dragged a couple of mattresses into a windowless hallway and, unable to do anything more, went to sleep.

The next morning, all was still. In the distance, 25-foot waves thundered, a sound we were to hear for days. There was no power, no telephone, no water. I worked my way to the hospital, winding around trees and trash on the road, just slipping under a downed power line.

The hospital emergency room was chaotic, of course. Most of the injuries were minor. I'll never forget one patient, though. He lived in a pole house that took heavy flooding from the big waves and rain.

"Doctor," he said, his face contorted in agony. "There's something in my ear."

I took a quick peek with an otoscope. Apparently not only humans looked for safe, quiet places to ride out the storm. Inside the man's ear was a flurry of chitinous legs. I poured some warm mineral oil inside, for a clean, quick kill. It didn't work fast enough. My patient screamed. Then he smiled as I pulled out the mother of all insects.

How a two-inch-long Hawaiian-sized cockroach could fit into a human external ear canal, I'll never know. All day long a constant parade of nurses and lab technicians paraded in to look at the giant, dead bug. They couldn't believe it, either.

If planetary temperatures continue to increase due to the greenhouse effect, coastal areas, where about half the world's population lives, may well see more and more such hurricanes. To repeat, cyclones "feed" on water warmer than 80°F.

As more and more people appear on the planet, they seem drawn to live on coastlines, where they build concrete sea walls and rock jetties and lay down rip-rap boulders to armor these coasts. This hardening (or "newjerseyization"[30]) of the coast, combined with upstream dams blocking sand flow, depletes naturally protective beaches.[31] Similarly, in a slow and relentless way, more and more wetlands, protective areas for storm surges (and nurseries for juvenile fish), are drained and diked for development. Mangrove forests, sea grass beds, and salt marshes protect coast-dwelling humans and marine creatures alike; all are being destroyed worldwide. When the "gales of November come early" and the power of nature unfolds, such cities as New Orleans, Miami, Tampa, lower Manhattan, and San Juan will get hammered, no matter how much concrete is poured. If sea levels rise, lowland states such as Florida and countries such as Holland, Bangladesh, and the Maldives will become inundated with salt water.

United States weather-related claims totaled $17 billion during the 1980s. During the 1990s, this figure jumped to more than $60 billion. As a result, members of the insurance industry, convinced of the connection between more powerful storms and global warming, have begun to differ with "big oil" over the rate at which humanity ought to switch from fossil fuels to a new energy regimen. David Helvarg, in his book *Blue Frontier*, reports how a coalition of the insurance industry, certain environmental groups, and low-lying island nations has begun "to counter the go-slow approach of fossil-fuel lobbyists and the OPEC nations."[32]

Perhaps more than anything, rising seas and temperatures might be thought to manifest the carcinogenic effect of humans on an ocean planet. However, because of the complexity of climate research and scientists' inability to provide experimental controls, some uncertainty as to cause and effect will pervade any future global warming periods or ice ages. But even if we exclude climate, many anthropogenic mishaps remain: clear-cutting of temperate and tropical rain forests; destruction of coral reefs, mangroves, and wetlands; overfishing; human-caused extinctions; pollution with such long-lived compounds as PCBs—the list is extensive.

Easter Island, one of the most isolated spots on Earth, holds what oceanographer Tom Garrison at the University of Southern California calls a "cautionary tale."[33] Archeological research has shown that the southeastern Pacific island, colonized by human voyagers around 350 A.D., went from a lush land with dense forests, seabirds, and fisheries to a treeless wreck of "withered grasses and scorched vegetation"[34] by the eighteenth century. The settlement on Easter Island peaked at 7,000–10,000 people by the year 1400 or so, but that population was well above the island's carrying capacity. Overuse of agriculture and overfishing led to crop failures (from worn-out soil) and loss of forests (from building canoes to fish ever farther afield), and the hard times led to increased religiosity.

In a kind of god-worship gone dysfunctional and extreme, the warring and stressed islanders transported a multitude of giant stone statues to special religious sites, requiring the use of even more lumber for transport. By the year 1550, no one could build boats, because all the trees were gone; there were no more nesting seabirds to exploit, and anarchy and cannibalism prevailed.[35] Captain James Cook estimated the human population to be only 200 when he arrived at the island in 1774.

Once again, we need to consider whether lessons from island biogeography, in this case human island biogeography, might be extrapolated to larger ecosystems. One could analogize that our own modern worship of materialism and unfettered anthropocentrism is leading us down an Easter Island-like, dysfunctional path on a global scale. If our degradation of the environment on a planetary level continues, one could have legitimate concerns about whether our civilization on Earth—what might be thought of, perhaps, as the ultimate island—might not, on a different, drawn-out time scale, come to a similar end.

David Quammen, the author of *The Song of the Dodo*, that elegant work that makes island biogeography so fascinating, wrote in *Harper's Magazine* about a possible future ecosystem, a world dominated by weedlike generalists, a planet with land masses crowded by roaches, rats, starlings, crows, and kudzu—and little else.[36] Even skeptics might acknowledge that such an alarmist vision does, at least, have a small-scale precedent in Easter Island.

Marine ecologist Ivan Valiela agrees with the general concept of humans causing weeds. In a discussion of succession in newly appearing patches of nutrients or newly disturbed marine regions, he notes that, in empirical studies, human exploitation with intense pollution holds back succession: "At severe levels of contamination or exploitation," Valiela said, "only a few of the more weedy species survive."[37]

It might be argued that what is most important for us humans to consider is the question of what the future holds for our oceans. For me, at least, it took a hurricane to make it clear that even though we live on land, the sea may well hold our destiny.

Does human life in the oceans, then, play nothing more than a nasty, zero-sum game? Or can we find a way to learn from humble creatures like corals, zooxanthellae, goby-shrimp symbionts, and cleaner fish?

There are six billion of us humans, I thought, who harvest 100 million metric tons of seafood each year. To amuse myself, I performed some rough mental calculations; 100 metric tons equals 1.0×10^8 tons, which equals 1.0

$\times 10^{11}$ kilograms. Because each kilogram of seafood is mostly protein and represents about 4.0 kilocalories, humans harvest about 4.0×10^{11} kilocalories of protein from wild animals in the sea. Let's say each of 6.0×10^9 humans consumes their fair share of this protein. Each human, then, would get to eat 66 kilocalories per year from this harvest. Because we require, as adults, about 2 kilocalories per day, this seafood, if all of it went down our gullets, and not into catfood or fertilizer, would give each of us, at the most, about one month per year of our food, or 12%.

Using U.N. data, James Nybakken, a marine biologist at Moss Landing Marine Laboratories and author of the textbook *Marine Biology: An Ecological Approach*, argues that the total catch of fishes for human consumption represents an even smaller amount, "perhaps 1% of all human food, but a significant 10% of the protein intake."[38]

However we calculate our consumption, it is plain that the ocean produces only a small percentage of what we humans need to feed ourselves. This is so, in part, because of the fewer trophic levels occurring in terrestrial ecosystems; there are only two levels from feed corn to livestock (and one if we eat the corn only) as opposed to the five or more levels (including microscopic trophic levels) often found at sea. There is a roughly 90% loss in energy from one trophic level to the next and, as a corollary, a 10 fold increase in organic pollutants (see chapter 7). An example of this sort of bioconcentration may be found in the studies Sylvia Earle mentioned that showed PCB levels in Puget Sound orcas to be the highest ever measured in any animal.[39]

In addition to this difference in number of trophic levels, vast regions of the oceans have relatively low primary productivity. In the central gyres carbon is fixed by photosynthesis at a low rate (see chapter 13).

Ecologists D. Pauly and V. Christensen of the Fisheries Center in Vancouver have studied the amount of primary production required to support the fish that humans skim out of the sea; they estimate people use 24–35% of global marine productivity in upwelling and shelf systems, where the majority of the fish are to be found.[40] If the world's oceans are considered globally, the primary production required to sustain today's average reported yearly catches of 94 million tons, plus the estimated 27 million tons of bycatch (discarded, undesirable biomass), is about 8%. Although this number may seem modest compared with the amount of primary production required for human use from the land (35–40%), Pauly and Christensen believe prospects for increases are dim.

The bulk of oceanic carbon fixation occurs in the open sea or gyre systems, with much of that in the microbial loop. Most fishing in gyres is for top predators, such as yellowfin and skipjack tuna, that "roam desert-like expanses to find scattered food patches."[41] To move down trophic levels here is not feasible.

I've described several times how fishermen around the world in up-welling and shelf regions are fishing down the food chain, going after less and less attractive prey, moving toward the primary consumer trophic level. We have a definite impact on the higher trophic levels by our heavy preda-tion. We may sustain our one month or one week of seafood per person per year for a while, but eventually, unless we start eating phytoplankton and bacteria, we will continue to reduce standing crops of commercial fish species. We will hit a wall.

We humans represent a whole lot of biomass—if each of us weighed about 70 kilograms (what in medicine we call "the ideal 70-kg man"), we would represent 4.2×10^{11} kilograms, about four times the weight of our annual and, most probably, unsustainable fishing harvest.

As oceanographer Richard Grigg told me,[42] "100 million metric tons (100 billion kg) of seafood, divided by 6 billion people, is 17 kg per capita per year. About one medium-sized tuna. Slim pickings for sure."

The bottom, inescapable line—there are too many of us. Although we certainly need to work on related evils such as overfishing, eutrophication, and global warming, human biomass—human standing crop—is the key problem.

Paul Ehrlich figured this out long ago. He began his science career as a tropical butterfly ecologist. In 1965–1966 Ehrlich and his wife, Anne, also a scientist, spent a sabbatical year traveling around the world to gain a per-spective on the taxonomy, evolution, and ecology of these colorful, flying in-sects.[43] Everywhere they went, though, to their surprise, was barren, over-grazed, and deforested—even places they imagined to be "unspoiled tropical paradise," such as New Guinea and the Solomons.

The result was a book for the public entitled *The Population Bomb*, pub-lished in 1968.[44] Although since then many persons on both the right and the left have criticized the Ehrlichs for alarmism and premature warnings (they failed to predict the now-weakening "green revolution" in agriculture), ecologists today from both political sides still respect them. When the book was published, there were 3.5 billion people on Earth. Today there are 6.0 billion. And yet only 1.5 billion even approach a standard of living we in the West would call acceptable.[45] Rain forests are disappearing, salts infest irri-gated lands, ozone holes are growing, aquifer tables are dropping, CO_2 and temperatures are going up, species are going extinct, hypoxic dead zones are appearing in places like the Gulf of Mexico,[46] and it is all because there are too many of us and we consume too much.

According to the Ehrlichs, we are living on Earth's capital, not her income.[47] Through our numbers and our high rates of consumption, we are blowing our inheritance. That is Paul and Anne Ehrlich's analogy.

After studying the sea and thinking about all that biomass getting hauled out of the ocean, it is hard to doubt the reality of their message. An island biogeographer might analogize that, as a K-selected (slow-growing, large-sized) species, we have exceeded our carrying capacity. My own physician analogy was that humanity had become, pure and simple, a planetary cancer.

The only acceptable cure, it seemed to me, the one that was relatively painless, was birth control. To a doctor, the idea of death control, of letting the Four Horsemen of the Apocalypse (War, Pestilence, Famine, Death) run free in response to eventual Malthusian certainty, seemed unacceptable. To an anesthesiologist with training and experience in surgery, operations like vasectomies and tubal ligations seemed effective and simple.

Prevention is always better than treatment in the medical world, if you can do it. We physicians can keep people alive a long time—given our knowledge and technology, there is no reason for a couple to have more than two kids to replace themselves. But achieving successful birth control, or zero population growth, seems at times a political nightmare, if a scientific necessity.

Lately, worldwide population growth rates have diminished, leading some to claim that the problem is over. They are wrong, for even if we level our numbers off at nine or ten billion late in the twenty-first century, as is probable,[48] we are still far too numerous. Today at six billion, for many if not most humans, there is insufficient freshwater, soil, food, and waste disposal. At six billion we are not sustainable; the Club of Rome, an international group of distinguished scientists, has estimated that carrying capacity for humans on Earth is around three billion.[49]

Partha Dasgupta, a Cambridge economist, has made attempts to factor in the natural environment in calculations of wealth, well-being and optimum population size (unlike many economists and econometricians). His book, *Human Well-Being and the Natural Environment*, concludes with an elegant mathematical proof showing the optimum population to be a quarter of carrying capacity. Write Dasgupta, "If carrying capacity is 10 billion people, optimum population is 2.5 billion."[50]

Because of the bio-energy flows discussed in chapter 7, our position in the planet's food web, how high or low we eat on the food chain, is key in determining how heavily or lightly each of us tramps on Earth. The carrying capacity for sustainable human life is dependent on where we position our-selves on the food web; the number of us that can live here depends on our ratio of vegetarianism to carnivory.

Likewise, the number of species—and their respective carrying capacities—with whom we choose to share our planet is an optional item.

Meanwhile, humanity grows. And the fish go.

Garrett Hardin, a biology professor at the University of California, gave a remarkable address to a meeting of the American Association for the Advancement of Science in Logan, Utah, in June 1968. "The Tragedy of the Commons"[51] has become a classic, but the concept of the title has stuck better than the more radical conclusion of the lecture.

Hardin uses for his title analogy a common pasture shared by villagers. The grassland is open to all. For centuries, such an arrangement works well, until population reaches the carrying capacity of the land. At that point, "commons" generates "tragedy," or what the philosopher A.N. Whitehead called the "solemnity of the remorseless working of things."[52]

Each herdsman desires to prosper and so maximize his gain, and thus adds to his flock. The upside is immediate gain for the individual; the down-side, the additional overgrazing, is shared by the entire village. For each ra-tional tribesman, the gain outweighs the loss, and each reaches the same conclusion: own more livestock. Inevitably, the commons is ruined. The world is limited, Hardin is telling us, and therein lies the rub.

He takes this analogy to the sea:

> The oceans of the world continue to suffer from the survival of the phi-losophy of the commons. Maritime nations still respond automatically to the shibboleth of the "freedom of the seas." Professing to believe in the "inexhaustible resource of the oceans," they bring species after species of fish and whales closer to extinction.[53]

Forget conscience regarding population control, argues Hardin, for those who lack it and have more children will produce a larger fraction of the next generation than those with more susceptible consciences. Eventually, those with conscience will be eliminated.

Hardin's solution, one that no doubt will trouble the left, the right, and the middle, yet one that may be eventually inevitable: mutually agreed-upon coercion by society to limit childbirth. How and when that may be achieved will be debatable, difficult, but ultimately doable. No doubt it will generate some injustice.

"Injustice," he notes, "is preferable to total ruin."[54]

Adrift in the vast ocean, finished with my goring of various oxen, tired of poking a needle in the collective eye of humanity, I continued swimming and bodysurfing, bodysurfing and swimming. As always when in the sea, nagging thoughts about some toothed predator engulfing me with a single swallow gave me pause. Perhaps one of the planet's infection-fighting, giant-celled, macrophagelike sharks would sense my flailing on the surface and re-cycle my protein, fat, and DNA. Such thoughts gave me a thrill, for big, in-tact predators meant big, intact wilderness. Or, perhaps, I might survive and continue cogitating over the world's problems, railing against forces far stronger than myself.

Again and again I let the waves take me for short, sweet dolphinesque rides. Finally, after a long hour, deep, free-associating thoughts of Lovelock and Leonardo dissipated and relaxed their hold. I swam far outside, to a point well beyond the breaking waves, and taking a deep breath, dove down 20 feet or more. My body went limp, every spasm of thought and anxiety left me. The cool, decisive pressure of the ocean surrounded me, a fetus in the womb of Nature.

On the surface, after a whalelike exhalation of air, I swam to the reef, re-juvenated. Turning around for a pace-changing backstroke, I saw a familiar dark line looming on the western horizon. It was a wave bigger than the oth-ers. Excited, I stroked hard to get my water speed up, felt the rise as the wave lifted, and pushed my arm forward to mold my body into a surfboard. Now the wave was my master, carrying me on its smooth shoulder, a passive projectile of flesh and bone, a dark speck in the deepening dusk.

The wave reached a transition. A burst of white water and foam hurled my body across Horseshoe Reef, shaking me with a familiar violence In that galloping white horse, in that tipping point from smooth laminarity to chaotic turbulence, could, perhaps, be found the ultimate analogy for hu-manity and Earth.

Or maybe not.

As the swell relaxed its grip and white water again became calm and blue, city lights sparkled through the saltwater mist, calling me back to land. Ready to carry on, my mind was washed clean, the damp, drizzly November of my soul transformed into the warmth and sunlit optimism of May.

When god-like Odysseus returned from the wars in Troy, he hanged all on one rope a dozen

slave-girls of his house-hold whom he suspected of misbehavior during his absence.

This hanging involved no question of propriety. The girls were property. The disposal of

property was then, as now, a matter of expediency, not of right and wrong.

—A L D O L E O P O L D , *"The Land Ethic," from A Sand County Almanac*

The Sea Ethic

Teach the Children Well

Thus began the final chapter of Leopold's famous book, as he penned ideas for a new kind of land ethic, for treating the soil and ecosystem in a manner driven by more than just monetary interest. His opening point was that over thousands of years ethics change and grow. People today would be aghast at treating women in such a way and would no doubt arrest Odysseus on the spot as a mass murderer. In "The Land Ethic," Leopold made the case for growth in our current ethics, for extending ethical treatment from other humans to the land, the water, the wildlife, and the plants.

The forestry biologist went on to define ethics in ecology as a giving up of certain freedoms for the sake of community and symbiosis.[1] He described the biotic community as a food pyramid, with a flow of energy through all members of that community, and he suggested that ethics for modern society must transcend economics. Like Paul Watson, he divided the world into two types of persons, his type A persons resembling Watson's anthropocentrists; his type B persons, biocentrists. Only through seeing mankind as a member and responsible subject of the larger biota, according to Leopold, can ethical treatment of land and soil be promulgated successfully.

One May afternoon on Maui's west side, my son Erik and I have stolen away, leaving a tired four-year-old, Nicholas, to nap with Diane, my wife. We're staying at a condominium on family holiday. This morning, the four of us went for a voyage in one of Lahaina's glass-bottom boats, where the little guy and his big brother each received a card with pictures and names of common Hawaiian fish. They picked out yellow tangs, raccoon butterflyfish, cornetfish, and moorish idols. But look and look though they might, they missed spotting any of Maui's green sea turtles.

Nick is just learning to swim and has fallen fast asleep, his cherubic face content, his little body exhausted from holding his breath and diving down after his toy white shark in the swimming pool. A few months ago he couldn't even put his head underwater; now he's learning fast. He tells me he's going to be a diver when he grows up.

Erik, age seven, has been practicing with swim fins, mask, and snorkel. At last, his blond hair turning green, his swim muscles firming up, he lets me know he is ready by churning four lengths of the pool at top speed.

We drive north past hotels, condos, and golf courses until vegetation takes over and civilization recedes. We follow a footpath under a dense, junglelike canopy, complete with giant banyans and hanging lianas. Lava banks and the profuse vegetation still the trade winds, but the air remains sugarcane sweet. On the banks of a stream that winds through the forest, a local Hawaiian, a thin man with a long ponytail crouching on the back of a battered pickup, is chopping a coconut with a machete. He smiles as we walk by. At last we arrive at Honolua Bay, now a Marine Life Conservation District—that is to say, a no-take fishing zone.

Erik and I slip on our gear and slide into the warm, clear water. It feels good to have his solid, 70-pound muscle mass next to me. He has mastered the art of powering through the water, kicking with fins, and doing the Australian crawl without rolling his snorkel underwater. Suddenly he screams into his mouthpiece and points.

"A reef triggerfish!" he exclaims, coughing, nearly inhaling a mouthful of water. I'm grateful he didn't try to pronounce the Hawaiian name, meaning "grunts like a pig," *Humuhumunukunuku-a-pua'a*, or he might have drowned. We have found Hawaii's state fish, endemic and thriving. Shaped like an egg, with bizarre green, black, blue, and yellow markings, the fish, also called a Picasso triggerfish, picks at algae on the bottom, pausing to expel a cloud of silt from its gills.

Erik is snorkeling in the ocean for the first time. I, too, am seeing the ocean for the first time, through his eyes.

In this urbanized world, many children today have never experienced wilderness, as I was so lucky to do in my own youth. Many have no idea what beautiful landscapes and seascapes Earth can create without the hand of man to mar and alter. Many have never set foot within what John Muir termed "cathedrals of nature"—wild places like Yosemite Valley or Honolua Bay.

One hundred years ago and more, such encounters were common, even for urban youth. Wetlands, called swamps then and mostly now drained, enabled children to discover amphibians, reptiles, and birds. There were few sea walls and dams, and beaches had more sand and were much healthier than they are today.

Nowadays it may require work to give children a chance to know nature. On the other hand, because of Jacques Cousteau, Émile Gagnan, and their marvelous invention, scuba, marine wilderness exploration opportunities that were unknown before now abound.

E.O. Wilson, in his book *Biophilia*, proposed the thesis that humans possess an instinctive attraction to living things, what he defines as "the innate tendency to focus on life and lifelike processes."[2] My experience as a child in Minnesota and as a father in California corroborates Wilson's theory, for children seem to need little encouragement, only the opportunity, to study wildlife.

As described at the beginning of this book, my Wyoming summer as a teenager with Paul Petzoldt, who instilled the idea that wilderness was sacred and that marring it in any way was a sin, left a deep mark. As the years have wound their way, I've become a strong believer in the need for using Petzoldt's ethic and expanding it to the sea.

Some of my best adventures have occurred taking small boys on long explorations at low-tide beaches and reefs near our home in La Jolla. My family and I have enjoyed soaring brown pelicans, aggregating anemones covered with armor made from bits of shells, and hermit crabs hiding in tiny borrowed homes. We've spent hours combing the sand for worms, sand fleas, and other hidden treasures. As the kids explore tide pools and beaches, we adults have done our best to inspire them to respect other living things. We try to teach unobtrusive observation, for as Wilson wrote: "As we come to understand other organisms, we place a greater value on them, and on ourselves."[3]

It has not been easy getting across to the two young imps this gospel of sharing the world with other species. Sharing does not always come naturally. But that is the heart and soul of Leopold's land ethic and, by extension, the sea ethic. One must give up a little selfish something to let the mystery of marine symbiosis reveal itself.

We are blessed to have a wild shore close to our home. The opportunity to encounter the many creatures and situations written about in this book has also been a wonderful gift.

We are well aware of our good fortune on being alive while there is still much living marine wilderness. In thanks, we do our best to lead our lives in as pure a manner as we are able. We "recycle, reuse, and reduce" as much as possible. We try to eat low on the food pyramid for health reasons, because of biomagnification of toxins, and for environmental ones, because of the 90% loss of energy at each trophic level. "Eating low" limits our impact. And we've taken permanent steps to restrict our family size.

We aspire to lead a life that does not damage the environment, but our failings are great, and the road to eco-perfection, especially within our consumer-oriented society, is uphill and rocky. There is much to be said, though, for striving to live without harming nature, even if one does not always succeed. But that may not be enough.

Concrete things need to be done to conserve our living oceans, and they need to be done soon. Changing our philosophical approach is the beginning. But eventually, action at national and international levels must evolve from ethics. Appeals to conscience, such as "think globally, act locally," make a good beginning, but as Garrett Hardin wrote,[4] they may prove to fail in the long run. Here is an arbitrary short list of concrete steps we can take that may prove more effective:

1. In the United States, as elsewhere in the world, we can integrate state, federal, and local jurisdictions of coastal areas. At present, too many interests collide on the coasts, and because of the resulting chaos, all too often those with the cash, not the accurate science, get their way. Often when this happens, the marine environment suffers.

2. We can pull the National Oceanic and Atmospheric Administration from the Department of Commerce and place it in the Department of the Interior.

3. The U.S. Navy and Coast Guard, and all the world's navies for that matter, can work at enforcing violations of international fishing and whaling laws on the high seas with the same zeal that they enforce drug laws. Or, perhaps, some kind of multinational marine policing group could be formed, a sort of U.N. Ocean Patrol.

4. Consumers, restaurant owners, and chefs can become informed as to which fish come from sustainable fisheries and which do not—and make

their menu choices accordingly. The Monterey Bay Aquarium, for example, posts just such a list on the Internet.[5]

Better yet, the U.S. Food and Drug Administration could ban the sale of fish from unsustainable fisheries, such as orange roughy or Chilean sea bass (Patagonian toothfish).

5. No-take fishing zones can be greatly expanded in all waters worldwide. Such zones must be enforced (see item 3 above). If and when the current massive depletion of the world's fish populations is corrected, the size of the zones can be decreased. The practice of shark-finning needs to be banned worldwide, as well, and the ban enforced. Bottom trawling needs strict controls, too.

In essence, marine-protected-areas will become control experiments, preserves of marine biodiversity, bona fide regions of true wilderness. They will be "a portion of a garden set apart for things to grow wild,"[6] places where "Earth and its community of life are untrammeled by man."[7] They will provide a benchmark for the measuring of other, less wild marine regions — a benchmark that has been lacking and is sorely needed.

6. An immediate and sustained effort can be made to preserve and encourage populations of wild salmon. Preservation of ancient forests and wild rivers (in themselves admirable goals), and modifying or eradicating certain dams will all be required to achieve this goal. Money now spent on hatcheries could be transferred to this end.

7. Protection of cetaceans, our intelligent cousins of the sea, is ethical and essential. We need to continue to maintain the hard work done by so many to ensure the survival of these creatures.

8. An immediate and sustained effort to understand, conserve, and protect coral reefs needs to be integrated worldwide. All the problems facing these treasures of the sea — local, regional, and global — need to be addressed. That includes global warming.

9. Funding for research of the sea, from physical oceanography to the study of marine animal, plant, microbial, and protist ecology, should be increased by a factor of 10. The precautionary principle makes too much sense to ignore, and good, hard science must lead us, not short-term economic concerns. As Richard Rosenblatt, a marine biologist from Scripps once said, "Everyone is entitled to their own opinion, but they aren't entitled to their own facts."[8]

As a corollary of this, we ought to map, explore, and study the depths of the sea with the same level of finance and abandon with which we have approached outer space. Recall that the United States spends about $1 every year on marine biology research for every $88 it spends per year studying outer space.[9] The big question facing NASA these days seems to be, "Is there life out there?" We know there are strange and mysterious life forms in the abyss, but we know so little about them, they might as well be on Mars.

10. Last, but most important and most difficult, we need to control ourselves. We need to achieve a stable human population, and if our current population is not sustainable, as shown by the best and most rigorous ecological studies available, we should aim over time, through attrition and birth control, to reach a level that is.

Garrett Hardin may indeed have had it right. Mutually agreed-upon coercion might well be the only way this will ever happen. As a corollary, and just as important as controlling our numbers, we shall most probably need to use similar methods to curb our consumption of nonsustainable resources.

A weaker, but more realistic, alternative to such draconian measures would be for governments in the developed world and the international community to embark on an ambitious population control campaign in developing countries. This would need to include both radical expansion of voluntary family planning programs and pressing for the education of women—a development that in and of itself leads to decreased birth rates. To give poor people confidence in having smaller families, the first world also needs to mount sustained public health efforts in the third world, where nearly all future global human growth will be concentrated.[10] Many of the poorest nations, those in Latin America, Asia, and Africa, harbor the lion's share of Earth's biodiversity, both terrestrial and marine.[11] To give the above effective aid to these countries is to give aid to the environment.

Of course, as long as developed countries continue with their profligate consumption of natural resources, their moral authority in the third world regarding population control will continue to be undermined. The United States, with some 5% of the world's people, consumes 25% of its petroleum,[12] for example, and lends itself to oftentimes bitter criticism from poor countries with population problems.[13]

"Even though debates between [North] and [South] often become shrill, each vision is partially correct," writes the Cambridge economist Partha Dasgupta about this argument of population versus consumption. "There is no single environmental problem."[14]

After reading the above list, one might accuse me of pie-in-the-sky idealism. There is no denying that none of these action items will be easy to implement or maintain. The most important, the last, will surely be the most difficult. Yet today, Odysseus would never dare own slave girls (in most parts of today's world), much less slay them. Tomorrow, we may yet become responsible caretakers of the oceans. We ignore such progress in ethics and action at our peril. And, if each person does but one little deed to turn things around, the cumulative effect will be overwhelming.

So. Remember the two-part question I proposed in the preface? *Are there biological limits, over time, to the ocean? Or is life a non-zero-sum game?*

I guess it should be clear by now that there are limits to the vast and endless ocean. To the blue whale, the whale shark, and the white abalone, the ocean has walls. Extinction is the ultimate limit that they and all rare creatures face. Even to the blindingly numerous prochlorococcus and synechococcus bacteria, there are barriers, for growth of marine bacteria can be rate-limited by iron and other nutrients. Phytoplankton are limited by lack of sunlight, by cold temperatures, by lack of availability of phosphates, silica, oxygen, carbon, and nitrogen, and by grazing from zooplankton.

"Islands" of water occur throughout the ocean, regions of upwelling, enclosed areas such as the Black Sea and Jellyfish Lake, and oceanic rings that spin off from such currrents as the Gulf Stream. "Island" ecosystems such as coral reefs or kelp forests, with their high productivity, act as marine oases. Whether immigration to these islands equilibrates with extinction, as MacArthur and Wilson felt happens on terrestrial islands (see the preface), remains an unknown. Yet there seems to be evidence that, because of islandlike limits, some of the theory of island biogeography may indeed apply to marine systems.

Over time, though, to microbes that form symbiotic relationships, self-organizing with other life forms to create entirely new types of creatures, these limits, these walls start to crumble. To cnidarians that follow reticulate evolutionary patterns, species may well come and go based on the whim of the currents. As life in the ocean evolves, then, there may be changes in what the limits are.

As far as our knowledge of the sea goes, new discoveries, relationships, and species are found daily. In the realm of human science, there are no limits to the sea. We can always learn more.

What about game theory and reality? To predator and prey, to tuna and sardine, to herring and copepod, life is a zero-sum game. To human fishermen who want to catch "all the fish," this is doubly true. The relationship between hunters and hunted may well be thought of as the dominating interaction at sea.

But to corals and zooxanthellae building new reefs in tropical waters, to humans sinking decontaminated ships as artificial reefs, to salmon that bind grizzly bears and forests with sardines and open oceans, life may not be a complete win/lose proposition. From algae within giant clams to chemosynthetic bacteria in cold-seep clams, from cleaner fish and their customers to anemonefish and their anemones, reciprocity and mutualism appear everywhere in the ocean. So, while the sea has limits, both zero-sum and non-zero-sum games are played there, often in parallel.

Our questions are most important regarding the human relationship to the sea. Our predatory actions provide powerful downward trophic pressure on life in the sea. And yet, we possess the ability to change our ways, for we have free choice and conscious brains. We can choose between predation and cooperation, unlike the white shark. We also hold the ability to control our own numbers and the degree of our predation.

The ocean is a complex, open system, where life self-organizes in an unstable, nonequilibrium state. We can never be sure about knowing it all; we will never find ourselves in total command of every detail of every feedback loop, aware of every keystone species, knowing exactly how every human-caused perturbation will affect the grand system.

Given the best data we have, however, we can make intelligent projections and guesses. We understand from chaos/complexity theory[15] that the ocean, like all complex systems, may be highly sensitive to initial conditions. If we take now as the initial condition (although, given our history, that is a stretch), there is still reason to be optimistic. We may see the value in being precautionary, in establishing plentiful no-take zones, preserving rare species from extinction, limiting trawling and fishing, and in general doing everything we can to support diversity and biomass in the sea.

By making the initial conditions of today as beneficent as we can to marine biota, we should reap great rewards in the future. We might well be able to expand the limits of the ocean, create more opportunities for life, more high-relief reefs, more kelp forests. Conversely, even if the ocean seems limitless and vast, humanity's current abuse of the complex marine system, if not altered, may provide conditions that lead to disaster.

Because there is evidence that some if not most life can play a non zero-sum game, we can learn from theoretical models like the Prisoner's Dilemma. We can learn from field observations of cleaner fish and symbiotic corals and algae. We can be "nice." We can avoid being "envious." We can strive for mutualism instead of competition for competition's sake.

Certainly the real engines of life and evolution on the planet, the bacteria, play both non-zero-sum and zero-sum games. They lead their tiny, immense-in-the-aggregate lives both as supreme competitors and as essential symbionts.

The bacteria don't care what we humans might decide to do with our relationship with the ocean and, by extension, with Earth. They will most probably triumph over any pollutant, climate change, or overpredation of fish we throw at them. They evolved during the unstable and savage Archaean Aeon, and they will continue to prosper in their mindless, efficient way. What we primate-mammalian-vertebrate-eukaryotes do with our small slice of time here on the planet is up to us. We can vote for diversity, or we can vote for overpopulation and a "planet of weeds."

We can only look to the future. When we work to keep the surf clean and the water unpolluted, when we leave fish for a wild dolphin, when we protect a kelp forest, we do it for our children, and their children, and so on forever.

But, again, we do such things for more than just our corner of sprawling humanity. We do them to make ourselves less a cancer and more a cure. To help conserve a coral reef, a wild sea mount, or a whale breeding ground is to become a steward for the inhabitants of the sea themselves. Only in this way can we redeem our good citizenship in the saltwater wilderness.

Erik and I continue swimming out toward the point between the two bays. We remain in marine-protected waters. Dense clouds of fish cascade by us, waterfalls of living organisms. Purple coralline algae cover the bottom, as do healthy hard corals, colored rich browns and greens by their zooxanthellae. Here and there lies the brilliant crimson of a slate pencil sea urchin. A school of big gray chubs, *nenue* in Hawaiian, slide by just beneath us, pecking at the coral. We float for a minute, watching, entranced. Years ago, one autumn as a bachelor surfer, I rode perfect, grinding 10-foot tubes over this very spot. But today there is no surf. Today is much better.

There is another chortle from my son. Only seven, he can spot wildlife with the best of naturalists. He shows me a snowflake moray, a white snake-like creature with black spots undulating over the bottom. Then he spots a second, bigger one. Now he's quivering with excitement.

"Cool," he says. On and on we swim. The chubs, seeming to follow us, are now nibbling algae near the point. We stop to watch them some more, relax, and catch our breath. Each *nenue* is a foot or more in length; there are 20 or so working their way along the rocks, like deer grazing on a meadow.

The tropical sun warms us and dapples the reef in a mosaic of light. Erik is moving again. The bottom falls off, 10, 20 feet deep; we can see wave-induced dunes on the sand, parallel to the shore. Here and there oases of coral punctuate the Sahara-like seafloor.

For a moment I recall a boogie-boarder who died off Kauai, his leg taken by a tiger shark. The big carnivores are rare, but around—protected though

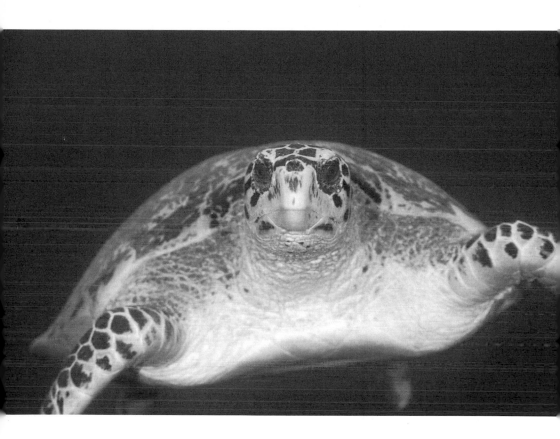

GREEN SEA TURTLE, PALAU, MICRONESIA *"What hurricanes,*

what predators, what oceans have these big reptiles experienced?"

it may seem, Honolua Bay retains its wild integrity. I put one arm around Erik and hold him close. The chill of my parental paranoia lessens with our shared warmth.

"It'll have to take us both," I say to myself, holding him even tighter.

Now my son almost swallows his snorkel. "Turtle!" he says. And sure enough. A green sea turtle, *Chelonia midas*, is resting on a coral head, a crimson-and-blue saddle wrasse nibbling algae off the turtle's back. There is a geometric, abstract pattern on the shell. We spot another turtle, and then another.

Every detail of the turtles, lying still in 20 feet of crystalline water, is there beneath us to observe. A small cloud of damselfish, some black, some yellow, disturbed by our arrival on the surface, have returned to join the wrasse in cleaning the reptiles. They work their way over the shells, the heads; they even pick clean turtle eyelids.

Each turtle is well over three feet in diameter. I wonder how old they are—some can live well over 100 years. I wonder what hurricanes, what predators, what oceans these big reptiles have experienced.

For long minutes Erik and I hover over the aquamarine seascape, the turtles ignoring us, the cleaners absorbed in their industrious pecking. Then we swim on, alert, wide-eyed, ready to discover more.

Notes

Preface

1. M. Bramwell, ed. *Atlas of the Oceans* (Chicago: Rand McNally, 1977), p. 26.

2. Committee on the Ocean's Role in Human Health, *From Monsoons to Microbes: Understanding the Ocean's Role in Human Health* (Washington, D.C.: National Academy Press, 1999), p. 90.

3. *Webster's New Twentieth Century Dictionary*, 2nd ed. (New York: Prentice Hall Press, 1983).

4. Ted Kerasote, ed., *Return of the Wild: The Future of Our National Lands* (Washington, D.C.: Island Press, 2001), p. 19.

5. J. Conrad. "Initiation," in *The Oxford Book of Sea Stories*, T. Tanner, comp. (New York: Oxford University Press, 1994), pp. 5–6.

6. Richard Grigg, Professor of Oceanography, University of Hawaii, unpublished written communication.

7. D.E. McAllister. "The Crisis in Marine Biodiversity and Key Knowledge," *Canadian Club of Rome Proceedings*, Autumn 1999.

8. Associated Press, "Wide Expansion of No-Fishing Zone Urged; Santa Barbara Boats See Ruin of Industry," *San Diego Union-Tribune*, 28 September 2000.

9. H. Mooney [Chairman, National Academy of Sciences Committee on Ecosystem Management], *Sustaining Marine Fisheries* (Washington, D.C.: National Academy Press, 1999).

10. R.H. MacArthur and E.O. Wilson. *The Theory of Island Biogeography* (Princeton, N.J.: Princeton University Press, 1967).

11. David Quammen. *The Song of the Dodo: Island Biogeography in an Age of Extinction* (New York: Simon and Schuster, 1996).

12. Ibid.

13. G.P. Jones and U.L. Kaly. "Conservation of Rare, Threatened and Endemic Marine Species in Australia." In: L.P. Zann and P.K. Kailola, eds., *State of the Marine Environment Report for Australia*, Technical Annex: 1, The Marine Environment (Canberra, Australia: Ocean Rescue 2000, Department of the Environment, Sport and Territories, 1995), pp. 183–191.

14. J.E.N. Veron. *Corals in Space and Time* (Sydney: University of New South Wales Press, 1995), p. 51.

Chapter 1

1. S.H. Ridgway, "The Central Nervous System of the Bottlenose Dolphin," in *The Bottlenose Dolphin*, S. Leatherwood and R.R. Reeves, eds. (San Diego: Academic Press, 1990), pp. 69–97; L.G. Barnes, "The Fossil Record and Evolutionary Relationships of the Genus *Tursiops*," in *The Bottlenose Dolphin*, S. Leatherwood and R.R. Reeves, eds. (San Diego: Academic Press, 1990), pp. 3–19; J.F. Eisenberg, "Dolphin Behavior and Cognition: Evolutionary and Ecological Aspects," in *Dolphin Cognition and Behavior: A Comparative Approach,* R.J. Schusterman, et. al., eds. (London: L. Erlbaum Associates, 1986), pp. 261–270.

2. J.S. Lilly, "Animals in Aquatic Environments: Adaptation of Mammals to the Oceans," in *Handbook of Physiology—Environment*, D. B. Dill, ed. (Washington, D.C.: American Physiological Society, 1964), pp. 741–747.

3. L.M. Muhkametov, "Sleep in Marine Mammals," *Experimental Brain Research* suppl. 8, (1984): 227–238.

4. D. Reiss and L Marino. "Mirror Self-recognition in the Bottlenose Dolphin: A Case of Cognitive Convergence," *Proceedings of the National Academy of Sciences* (2001)98: 5937–5942.

5. M.C. Caldwell et al. "Review of the Signature-Whistle Hypothesis for the Atlantic Bottlenose Dolphin," in *The Bottlenose Dolphin* S. Leatherwood and R.R. Reeves, eds. (San Diego: Academic Press, 1990), pp. 199–234; V.M. Janik and P.J.B. Slater, "Whistle Usage in Bottlenose Dolphins: Signature Whistles as Contact Calls," in *Abstracts of the World Marine Mammal Science Conference*, Monaco, 20–24 January 1998, p. 68.

Chapter 2

1. David Quammen, *The Song of the Dodo* (New York: Simon and Schuster, 1996), pp. 230–231.

2. A. Fielding and E. Robinson, *An Underwater Guide to Hawaii* (Honolulu: University of Hawaii Press, 1993), p. 18.

3. D. Kampion, "The Lifecycle of Ocean Waves," in *The Book of Waves: Form and Beauty on the Ocean* (Niwot, Colo.: Robert Rinehart International, 1989), pp. 38–49; W. Bascom, *Waves and Beaches: The Dynamics of the Ocean Surface* (Garden City, N.Y.: Anchor Books, 1980).

4. R. Grigg, *Big Surf, Deep Dives and the Islands* (Honolulu: Editions Limited, 1998).

5. Ibid.; Bascom, *Waves and Beaches*. W. Bascom, *The Crest of the Wave* (New York: Harper and Row, 1988), p. 6.

6. Grigg, *Big Surf*.

7. N. Young, *The History of Surfing* (Palm Beach, N.S.W.: Palm Beach Press, 1983), p. 60.

8. David Quammen, *The Song of the Dodo* (New York: Simon and Schuster, 1996), pp. 316–317, 320–321.

9. Ibid.

10. R.W. Grigg, "Effects of Sewage Discharge, Fishing Pressure, and Habitat Complexity on Coral Ecosystems and Reef Fishes in Hawaii," *Marine Ecology Progress Series* 103(1994): 25–34.

11. I. Valiela, *Marine Ecological Processes*, 2nd ed. (New York: Springer-Verlag, 1995), pp. 121, 294–296.

12. Ibid.

13. R.W. Grigg, "Coral Reefs in an Urban Embayment in Hawaii: A Complex Case History Controlled By Natural and Anthropogenic Stress," *Coral Reefs* 14(1995): 253–266.

Chapter 3

1. M. Bramwell, ed., *Atlas of the Oceans*, (Chicago: Rand McNally, 1977), pp. 18–19.

2. E. F. Ricketts, et al., *Between Pacific Tides*, 5th ed. (Stanford, Calif.: Stanford University Press, 1985), pp. 434–437.

3. J.L. Garfield, *The San Diego-La Jolla Underwater Park Ecological Reserve* (San Diego: Picaro Publishing, 1994), p. 56.

4. J.W. Nybakken, *Marine Biology: An Ecological Approach* (San Francisco: Benjamin Cummings [Addison Welsley Longman, Inc.], 2001), pp. 118–119, 123, 445, 481–482.

5. E.D. Goldberg, *The Health of the Oceans* (Paris: UNESCO, 1976).

6. Nybakken, *Marine Biology*.

7. Ibid.

8. Ibid.

9. Roger Payne, *Among Whales* (New York: Delta Books, 1995), pp. 42–44, 269–270.

10. Ibid. E. Palmer, et al., "The Relationship Between Structure, Function and Innervation in the Skin of the Bottlenosed Dolphin," *Proceedings of the Zoological Society of London* 143(1964): 553–568.

11. Payne, *Among Whales*.; R. Harrison and M.M. Bryden, eds., *Whales, Dolphins, and Porpoises* (Oxford, England: Facts on File Publications, 1988), pp. 50–51.

12. M. Snyderman, "Eyeball to Eyeball with a 40 Tonne Whale," in *Whales, Dolphins, and Porpoises*. R. Harrison and M.M. Bryden, eds. (Oxford, England: Facts on File Publications, 1988), pp. 214–215.

13. M.M. Walker, et al., "A Candidate Magnetic Sense Organ in the Yellowfin Tuna," *Science* 224(1984): 751–753.

14. Nybakken, *Marine Biology*.

15. S. Ridgeway, "Physiological Observations on Dolphin Brain," in *Dolphin Cognition and Behavior: A Comparative Approach*. R.J. Schusterman, et al., eds. (London: L. Erlbaum Associates, 1986), pp. 31–59.

Chapter 4

1. E. Hanauer, "The Perils of Diving for Even the Experienced," *San Diego Union-Tribune*, 10 January 2001. Letters to the Editor.

2. Ibid.

3. J.L. Garfield, *The San Diego-La Jolla Underwater Park Ecological Reserve* (San Diego: Picaro Publishing, 1994).

4. Ibid.; M. Snyderman, *California Marine Life* (Niwot, Colo.: Roberts Rinehart International, 1998), pp. 56–57, 123–125.

5. Tom Garrison, *Oceanography: An Invitation to Marine Science* (Pacific Grove, Calif.: Brooks/Cole Biology, Thomson Learning, 2001).

6. J.W. Nybakken, *Marine Biology: An Ecological Approach* (San Francisco: Benjamin Cummings [Addison Welsley Longman, Inc.], 2001), pp. 55, 204, 385.

7. Ibid.; J.H. Ryther, "Photosynthesis and Fish Production in the Sea," *Science* 166(1969): 72–76.

8. M. Tegner and P. Dayton, "El Niño Effects on Southern California Kelp Forest Communities, *Advances in Ecological Research* 17(1987): 243–279.

9. Paul Dayton, personal written communication, 23 March 2002.

10. Quoted in J. Williams, "Ebb and Flow—Kelp Beds Stand up to Nature's Changing Plans," *San Diego Union-Tribune*, 17 February 1993.

11. T. Rodgers, "Sewage Hearing Draws Predictable Testimony," *San Diego Union-Tribune*, 14 March 2002.

12. Quoted in S. La Rue, "Death Beds: San Diego's Once-Rich Kelp Habitat Is in Serious Decline," *San Diego Union-Tribune*, 23 April 1997.

13. J.B.C. Jackson, et al., "Historical Overfishing and the Recent Collapse of Coastal Ecosystems," *Science* 293(2001): 629–638.

14. Ibid.

15. Endangered and Threatened Species; Proposed Endangered Status for White Abalone. NOAA/NMFS Docket No. 990910253-0118002; ID No. 041300C, RIN 0648AM90. *Federal Register* 65(5 May 2000).

16. I. Franklin, "Evolutionary Change in Small Populations," in M.E. Soulé and B.A.Wilcox, *Conservation Biology: An Evolutionary-Ecological Perspective* (Sunderland, Mass.: Sinauer Associates, 1980), pp. 135–149; Michael Soulé, "Thresholds for Survival: Maintaining Fitness and Evolutionary Potential," in *Conservation Biology: An Evolutionary-Ecological Perspective*, M.E. Soulé and B.A. Wilcox (Sunderland, Mass.: Sinauer Associates, 1980), pp. 111–124.

17. G.P. Jones and U.L. Kaly, "Conservation of Rare, Threatened and Endemic Marine Species in Australia," in L.P. Zann and P.K. Kailola, eds., *State of the Marine Environment Report for Australia*, Technical Annex: 1, The Marine Environment (Canberra, Australia: Ocean Rescue 2000, Department of the Environment, Sport and Territories, 1995), pp. 183–191.

18. Ibid.

19. C.M. Roberts and J.P. Hawkins, "Extinction Risk in the Sea," *Trends in Ecology and Evolution* 14(1999): 241–246. J. Lamarck's quote also appeared in this paper.

20. Ibid.; Jones and Kaly, "Conservation"; J.T. Carlton, et al., "The First Historical Extinction of a Marine Invertebrate in an Ocean Basin: The Demise of the Eelgrass Limpet *Lottia alveus*," *Biological Bulletin* 180(1991): 72–80.

21. Jones and Kaly, "Conservation."

22. M.E. Gilpin and M.E. Soulé, "Minimum Viable Populations: Processes of Species Extinction," in *Conservation Biology: The Science of Scarcity and Diversity*, M.E. Soulé, ed. (Sunderland, Mass.: Sinauer Associates, 1986), pp. 19–34.

23. David Quammen, *The Song of the Dodo* (New York: Simon and Schuster, 1996), pp. 269–270, 572.

24. Jones and Kaly, "Conservation."

25. Quammen, *Song of the Dodo*.

26. Endangered and Threatened Species, *Fed Reg* 65.

27. Roberts andHawkins, "Extinction Risk."

28. Ibid.

29. E. Culotta, "Is Marine Biodiversity at Risk?" *Science* 263(1994): 918–920.

30. Committee on the Ocean's Role in Human Health, *From Monsoons to Microbes: Understanding the Ocean's Role in Human Health* (Washington, D.C.: National Academy Press, 1999), pp. 93–94.

31. Quoted in *Discover Magazine*, "Location Plays a Key Role in Squid Lovemaking," reprinted in the *San Diego Union-Tribune*, 28 January 1998.

32. Snyderman, *California Marine Life*.

33. Ibid.

34. William Beebe, "A Half-Mile Down: Strange Creatures, Beautiful and Grotesque as Figments of Fancy, Reveal Themselves at Window of Bathysphere," *National Geographic*, December 1934, p. 702.

35. R.T. Paine, "A Note on Trophic Complexity and Community Stability," *American Naturalist* 103(1969): 91–93.

36. J. Levinton, Dept. of Ecology and Evolution, SUNY Stony Brook, unpublished written communication, 8 May 2001.

37. T. Rodgers and E. Jahn, "Autopsy of Diving Instructor Is Inconclusive," *San Diego Union-Tribune*, 17 February 1996.

38. Union-Tribune News Service, "White Abalone Put on Endangered Species List," *San Diego Union-Tribune*, 30 May 2001.

Chapter 5

1. Tom Garrison, *Oceanography: An Invitation to Marine Science* (Pacific Grove, Calif.: Brooks/Cole Biology, Thomson Learning 2001), pp. 191–192.

2. Ibid.

3. P. Dustan, Dept. of Biology, College of Charleston, and Science Advisor, Cousteau Society, www.cofc.edu/~coral/corallab.htm (cited July 2002).

4. A. Fielding and E. Robinson, *An Underwater Guide to Hawaii* (Honolulu: University of Hawaii Press, 1993).

5. G.R. Allen and R. Steene, *Indo-Pacific Coral Reef Field Guide* (Singapore: Tropical Reef Research, 1994), pp. 1–3, 45, 65, 101–102; P.L. Colin and A.C. Arneson, *Tropical Pacific Invertebrates* (Beverly Hills, Calif.: Coral Reef Press, 1995), pp. 1–2, 7, 12.

6. Richard Grigg, Professor of Oceanography, University of Hawaii, unpublished written communication; D. Doubilet, "Coral Eden," *National Geographic*, January 1999, pp. 7–29.

7. J.W. Nybakken, "Tropical Communities," in *Marine Biology: An Ecological Ap-*

proach (San Francisco: Benjamin Cummings [Addison Welsley Longman, Inc.], 2001), p. 370–433.

8. R. Sullivan, "Fiji Rebels Release 4 Hostages In Standoff," *San Diego Union-Tribune*, 23 May 2000.

9. Colin and Arneson, *Tropical Pacific Invertebrates*; E.H. Kaplan, "Origin of the Coral Reef," in *Coral Reefs* (Boston: Houghton Mifflin Co., 1982), pp. 96–99.

10. Allen and Steene, *Field Guide*. H.S. Ladd, et al., "Drilling on Eniwetok Atoll, Marshall Islands," *Bulletin of the American Association of Petroleum Geology* 37(1953): 2257–2280.

11. Allen and Steene, *Field Guide*.

12. Ibid.

13. Y. Tomono, H. Hirota, N. Fusetani, "Isogosterones A-D, Antifouling 13, 17-Secosteroids From an Octocoral Dendronephthya sp," *The Journal of Organic Chemistry* 64(7)(1999): 2272–2275.

14. W. Fenical, "Marine Biodiversity and the Medicine Cabinet: The Status of New Drugs From Marine Organisms," *Oceanography* 9(1)(1996): 23–24.

15. Penni Crabtree, "Drugs of the Deep," *San Diego Union-Tribune*, 6 September 2001.

16. J. Levinton, Dept. of Ecology and Evolution, SUNY Stony Brook, unpublished written communication. [Donald Gerhart was a graduate student with Dr. Levinton.]

17. Earthwatch Radio, Script Template, "Pharmacy in the Sea," University of Wisconsin, 4 June 1997. (http://seagrant.wisc.edu/communications/earthwatch/archive/1997/earthwatch051611.html, June, 2001.

18. R.J. Wilder, *Listening to the Sea: The Politics of Improving Environmental Protection* (Pittsburgh: University of Pittsburgh Press, 1998), p. 204.

19. E.O. Wilson, *The Future of Life* (New York: Alfred A. Knopf, 2002), p. 15.

20. Colin and Arneson, *Tropical Pacific Invertebrates*.

21. Levinton, unpublished.

22. J.E.N. Veron, *Corals in Space and Time: The Biogeography and Evolution of the Scleractinia* (Ithaca, N.Y.: Cornell University Press, 1995).

23. R.W. Grigg, "Evolution by Reticulation," *Science* 269(1995): 1893.

24. J.E.N. Veron, "The Search for Truth," *Ocean Realm*, Autumn 1997, pp. 82–92.

25. Grigg, "Evolution."

26. Veron, *Corals*.

27. Veron, "Search for Truth."

28. Veron, *Corals*.

29. Grigg, "Evolution."

30. P. Dustan, "Testimony Presentation on Coral Reef Conservation Issues," Subcommittee on Oceans and Fisheries. Chair: U.S. Sen. Olympia J. Snowe, Senate Committee on Commerce, Science, and Transportation, 30 June 1999 Hearing. www.cofc.edu/~coral/cousteau/Senate/PDSenate699.html.

31. Nybakken, "Tropical Communities."

32. Ibid.

33. J.W. Nybakken and S.K. Webster, "Life in the Ocean," *Scientific American Presents*, Fall 1998, pp. 74–86.

34. S. Earle, *Sea Change: A Message of the Oceans* (New York: Fawcett Columbine, 1995), pp. 199–200.

35. Garrison, *Oceanography*; Nybakken, "Tropical Communities."

36. Nybakken, "Tropical Communities."

37. Veron, *Corals*.

38. Ibid.

39. R.C. Babcock, et al., "Synchronous Spawnings of 105 Scleractinian Coral Species on the Great Barrier Reef," *Marine Biology* 90(1986): 379–394.

40. G.A. Wray, "A World Apart: The Larval Lifestyle," *Natural History*, March 2001, pp. 52–63.

41. Grigg, unpublished.

42. Wray, "A World Apart."

43. Levinton, unpublished.

44. S. Simpson, "Aquatic Homebodies," *Scientific American*, January 2001, pp. 22–23.

45. P.W. Sammarco and M.L. Heron, eds., "Bio-Physics of Marine Larval Dispersal," *Coastal and Estuarine Studies* 45(1994): 1–352.

46. Doubilet, "Coral Eden."

47. J.B.C. Jackson, et al., "Historical Overfishing and the Recent Collapse of Coastal Ecosystems," *Science* 293(2001): 629–638.

48. Nybakken, "Tropical Communities."

49. T.P. Hughe, "Catastrophes, Phase Shifts, and Large-Scale Degradation of a Caribbean Coral Reef," *Science* 265(1994): 1547–1551.

50. J.S. Levinton, "Afterword," in *The Sea Around Us*, R. Carson (New York: Oxford University Press, 1989), p. 237.

51. D. Quammen, "Agony in the Garden," in *The Flight of the Iguana* (New York: Simon and Schuster, 1988), pp. 132–139.

52. R. Grigg, "Coral Reef Environmental Science: Truth vs. the Cassandra Syndrome," *Coral Reefs* 11(1992): 183–186; P.D. Walbran, et al., "Evidence from Sediments of Long-term *Acanthaster Planci* Predation on Corals of the Great Barrier Reef," *Science* 245(1989): 847–850.

53. D. Chadwick, "Coral in Peril," *National Geographic*, January 1999, pp. 31–37.

54. S. Simpson, "Fishy Business," *Scientific American*, July 2001, pp. 83–89.

55. C. Zimmer, "The Partitioning of the Red Sea," *Science* 293(2001): 627–628.

56. P. Glynn, "History of Significant Coral Bleaching Events and Insights Regarding Amelioration," in R.V. Salm and S.L. Coles, eds. *Coral Bleaching and Marine Protected Areas,* Report 0102 (Honolulu: The Nature Conservancy, 2001), pp. 36–39.

57. P. Glynn and W.H. de Weerdt, "Elimination of Two Reef-Building Hydrocorals Following the 1982–83 El Niño Event," *Science* 253(1991): 69–71.

58. Jim Barry, Monterey Bay Aquarium Research Institute, personal communication.

59. R.W. Grigg and S.J. Dollar, "Natural and Anthropogenic Disturbance on Coral Reefs," in *Coral Reefs, 7,* Dubinsky, ed. (Amsterdam: Elsevier, 1990), pp. 439–452.

60. J.F. Grassle, "Variety in Coral Reef Communities," in *Biology and Geology of Coral Reefs*, vol. 2, *Biology 1*, O.A. Jones and R. Endean, eds. (New York: Academic Press, 1973), pp. 247–270.

61. Grigg and Dollar, "Natural and Anthropogenic."

62. Grigg, unpublished.

63. Grigg, "Coral Reef."

64. R. Bailey, *Eco-Scam: The False Profits of Ecological Apocalypse* (New York: St. Martin's Press, 1993).

65. T. Goreau, "Post Pleistocene Urban Renewal in Coral Reefs," *Micronesica* 5(1969): 323–326.

66. "Global Coral Reef Alliance, Home Page" Tom Goreau, president. www.globalcoral.org, July 2002.

67. Environmental News Network, "Ask a Naturalist," 25 October 2000. Available: June 2001, www.enn.com/feature/2000/10/10252000/aan.

68. Quoted by S. Kriner and D. Rekenthaler, "Sentinels of the Deep: Dying Coral Reefs Warn of Dangers Ahead." www.diasterrelief.org/Diasters/990127coralreefs/, cited July 2002.

69. (No byline, no story title), www.abc.net.au/science/coral/story.html, cited June 2001.

70. Dustan, Dept. of Biology.

71. (No byline) "Your Guide to the Money in U.S. Elections," Center for Responsive Politics, www.opensecrets.org, July 2002.

72. J.E. Maragos and C. Payri, "The Status of Coral Reef Habitats in the Insular South and East Pacific," in *Proceedings of the 8th International Coral Reef Symposium* (Balboa, Panama: Smithsonian Tropical Research Institute, 1997), p. 311.

73. World Resources Institute, "Reefs at Risk," www.wri.org/wri/reefsatrisk/, cited July 2002.

74. G. Hardin, "The Tragedy of the Commons," *Science* 162(1968): 1243–1248.

75. J.E.N. Veron, "Coral Reefs: An Overview," *State of the Marine Environment Report for Australia*, Department of the Environment, Sport and Territories, Ocean Rescue 2000 (Canberra, Australia: 1995).

76. Levinton, unpublished.

77. Grigg, unpublished.

78. F. Bavendam, "Crinoids," *National Geographic*, December 1996, pp. 118–131.

79. Richard Ellis, *Aquagenesis* (New York: Viking Penguin, 2001), pp. 104–105.

80. Howard Hall, "Current Film Production," www.howardhall.com/currentpro.html. (cited July, 2002).

Chapter 6

1. W.N. Eschmeyer and E.S. Herald, *Pacific Coast Fishes* (Boston: Houghton Mifflin, 1983), pp. 36–39.

2. Stonefish envenomation, apart from rapid ascent after the injury, can, notwithstanding Alan Raabe's treatments and comments, be fatal. *Diver's Alert Network and Alert Diver Magazine* (April 2002, p. 3) recommends
   a) removing any remaining spines or stingers with a tweezers,
   b) placing the injured area in water that is around 113°F/45°C maximum (to denature the toxic protein in the venom) for 30–90 minutes,
   c) washing and irrigating the area with soap and lots of fresh water, and
   d) using stonefish antivenom, if available and appropriate.

3. Associated Press, "Skipper Acquitted in Deaths of 2 Divers," *San Diego Union-Tribune,* 25 November 1999.

4. R. Ellis, *Dolphins and Porpoises* (New York: Knopf, 1989), pp. 68–73.

5. Tom Garrison, *Oceanography: An Invitation to Marine Science* (Pacific Grove, Calif.: Brooks/Cole Biology, Thomson Learning), 2001.

6. J.W. Nybakken, "Tropical Communities," in *Marine Biology: An Ecological Approach* (San Francisco: Benjamin Cummings [Addison Welsley Longman, Inc.], 2001), pp. 370–433.

7. C. M. Yonge, "Giant Clams," *Scientific American* 232(1975): 96–105.

8. M. Holloway, "Cuttlefish Say It with Skin," *Natural History*, April 2000, pp. 70–76.

9. Ibid.

10. E.J. Prager, "Endpoints," *Scientific American*, May 2001, p. 100.

11. P. L. Colin and A.C. Arneson, *Tropical Pacific Invertebrates* (Beverly Hills, Calif.: Coral Reef Press, 1995), pp. 2, 215.

12. Ibid.

13. Quoted in D. Doubilet, "Coral Eden," *National Geographic*, January 1999, p. 7.

14. I. Valiela, *Marine Ecological Processes,* 2nd ed. (New York: Springer-Verlag, 1995), pp. 311–324.

15. Ibid.

16. Ibid.

17. Quoted in Doubilet, "Coral Eden."

18. C.M. Roberts and J.P. Hawkins, "Extinction Risk in the Sea," *Trends in Ecology and Evolution* 14(1999): 241–246.

19. R.H. MacArthur, "Fluctuations of Animal Populations and a Measure of Community Stability," *Ecology* 36(1955): 533–536.

20. Valiela, *Marine Processes*; S. Pimm, "The Complexity and Stability of Ecosystems," *Nature* 307(1984): 321–326; D. Goodman, "The Theory of Diversity-Stability Relationships in Ecology," *The Quarterly Review of Biology*, September 1975, pp. 237–266.

21. W.D. Gardner and W.R. Ashby, "Connectance of Large Dynamic (Cybernetic) Systems: Critical Values for Stability," *Nature* 228(1970): 784; S.P. Hubbell, "Population and Simple Food Webs as Energy Filters. II. Two-Species Systems," *American Naturalist* 107(1973): 122–151; R.M. May, *Stability and Complexity in Model Ecosystems* (Princeton, N.J.: Princeton University Press, 1973).

22. C. Jeffries, "Qualitative Stability and Digraphs in Model Ecosystems," *Ecology* 56(1974): 238–243; D.L. De Angelis, "Stability and Connectance in Food Web Models," *Ecology* 56(1975): 238–243; M.E. Gilpin, "Stability of Feasible Predator-Prey Systems," *Nature* 254(1975): 137–139.

23. Valiela, *Marine Processes*.

24. S. J. McNaughton, "Diversity and Stability of Ecological Communities: A Comment on the Role of Empiricism in Ecology," *American Naturalist* 111(1977): 515–525.

25. J.B.C. Jackson, et al., "Historical Overfishing and the Recent Collapse of Coastal Ecosystems," *Science* 293(2001): 629–638.

26. J.A. Estes, et al., "Killer Whale Predation on Sea Otters Linking Oceanic and Nearshore Ecosystems," *Science* 282(1998):473–476.

27. J. Kaiser, "An Experiment for All Seasons," *Science* 293(2001): 624–627; D. Tilman, et al., "The Influence of Functional Diversity and Compostition on Ecosystem Processes," *Science* 277(1997): 1300–1302.

28. K.S. McCann, "The Diversity-Stability Debate," *Nature* 405(2000): 228–233; D. Tilman, "Causes, Consequences, and Ethics of Biodiversity," *Nature*

405(2000):208–211; F.S. Chapin, et al., "Consequences of Changing Biodiversity," *Nature* 405(2000): 234–242.

29. J. Kaiser, "Rift over Biodiversity Divides Ecologists," *Science* 289(2000): 1282–1283.

30. Ibid.

31. Michael Huston, "Hidden Treatments in Ecological Experiments," *Oecologia* 110(1997): 449–460.

32. Kaiser, "Rift."

33. M. Westenhofer, *Der Eigenweg des Menschen* (Berlin: Mannstaedt and Co., 1942).

34. A. Hardy, "Was Man More Aquatic in the Past?" *New Scientist* 7(174)(1960): 642–645.

35. E. Morgan, *The Aquatic Ape Hypothesis* (London: Souvenir Press, 1999).

36. R. Dawkins, *Unweaving the Rainbow: Science, Delusion, and the Appetite for Wonder* (Boston: Houghton Mifflin, 1998).

37. Garrison, *Oceanography*.

38. Richard Ellis, *Aquagenesis* (New York: Viking Penguin, 2001).

39. P.V. Tobias, "Water and Human Evolution," *Out There* 35(1998): 38–44.

40. Yohannes Haile-Selassie, "Late Miocene Hominids from the Middle Awash, Ethiopia," *Nature* 412(2001): 178–181; M. Evans, "Ethiopian Fossils Could Rewrite the Story of Early Human Evolution," *San Diego Union-Tribune*, 12 July 2001.

41. Jerold M. Lowenstein, "The Paleoolympics: Hominids Race Against the Clock," *California Wild*, Summer 2002, pp. 46–48.

Chapter 7

1. U. Aiavao, ed., "Lions and Emperors," *Lulutai Magazine* (4, 2)(1997): 12–13.

2. R. Harrison and M.M. Bryden, eds., *Whales, Dolphins and Porpoises* (New York: Facts on File Publications, 1989), p. 194; D. Chadwick, "Listening to Humpbacks," *National Geographic*, July 1999, pp. 110–129; Roger Payne, *Among Whales* (New York: Delta Books, 1995), pp. 144–167, 269.

3. R.M. Nowak, ed., *Walker's Mammals of the World,* 5th ed. (Baltimore: Johns Hopkins University Press, 1991), p. 1035.

4. S. Nicol and W. de la Mare, "Ecosystem Management and Antarctic Krill," *American Scientist* 81(1993): 36–47.

5. V. Loeb, et al., "Effects of Sea-Ice Extent and Krill or Salp Dominance on the Antarctic Food Web," *Nature* 387(1997): 897–900.

6. I. Valiela, *Marine Ecological Processes*, 2nd ed. (New York: Springer-Verlag, 1995), pp. 243, 296–304.

7. Payne, *Among Whales*.

8. Ibid.

9. "Tonga Considers Proposal to Resume Whaling," Agence France-Presse: Auckland, 20 May 1995.

10. Valiela, *Marine Processes*.

11. R.M. Laws, "Seals and Whales of the Southern Ocean," *Philosophical Transactions of the Royal Society of London* B270(1997): 81–96.

12. R.M. Laws, "The Ecology of the Southern Ocean," *American Scientist* 73(1985): 26–40.

13. Valiela, *Marine Processes*.

14. Valiela, *Marine Processes*; R.A. Wallace, *Biology: The World of Life*, 5th ed. (New York: Harper Collins, 1990), p. 643; J.W. Nybakken, *Marine Biology: An Ecological Approach* (San Francisco: Benjamin Cummings [Addison Welsley Longman, Inc.], 2001), p. 18.

15. J. Diamond, "'Normal' Extinctions of Isolated Populations," in *Extinctions*, M. H. Nitecki, ed. (Chicago: University of Chicago Press, 1984), pp. 191–246; David Quammen, *The Song of the Dodo* (New York: Simon and Schuster, 1996), pp. 292–293.

16. G.A. J. Worthy, "Physiological Time vs. Real Time: Ramifications for How Large Marine Mammals View the World," in Abstracts of the World Marine Mammal Science Conference, Monaco, 20–24 January 1998, p. 151.

Chapter 8

1. C.R. Robins and G.C. Ray, *Atlantic Coast Fishes* (Boston: Houghton Mifflin, 1986), p. 214.

2. R. Granade, "Dangerous Marine Animals," in *Coral Reefs*, E.H. Kaplan, ed. (Boston: Houghton Mifflin Co., 1982), pp. 258–259.

3. P. Billeter, "Intimate Relationships on the Reef," in *Coral Reefs*, E.H. Kaplan, ed. (Boston: Houghton Mifflin Co., 1982), pp. 246–247.

4. A.S. Grutter, "Cleaner Fish Really Do Clean," *Nature* 398(1999): 672–673.

5. L.B. Slobodkin and L. Fishelson, "The Effect of the Cleaner Fish *Labroides Dimidiatus* on the Point Diversity of Fishes on the Reef Front at Eilat," *American Naturalist* 108(1974): 369–376.

6. R. Axelrod and R.D. Hamilton, "The Evolution of Cooperation," *Science* 211(1981): 1390–1396.

7. Ibid.

8. Ibid.

9. Ibid.

10. Ibid.

11. R. Dawkins, "Nice Guys Finish First," in *The Selfish Gene* (London: Oxford University Press, 1989), pp. 202–233.

12. Ibid.

13. Ibid.

14. S. Earle, *Sea Change: A Message of the Oceans* (New York: Fawcett Columbine, 1995), pp. 199–200.

15. Michael Alvard, "Mutualistic Hunting," in C.B. Stanford and H.T. Bunn, eds., *Meat-Eating and Human Evolution* (New York: Oxford University Press, 2001), pp. 261–278.

16. Ibid.

17. Bruce Winterhalder, "Intragroup Resource Transfers: Comparative Evidence, Models, and Implications for Human Evolution," in C.B. Stanford and H.T. Bunn, eds., *Meat-Eating and Human Evolution* (New York: Oxford University Press, 2001), pp. 279–301; A.R. Hoelzel, "Killer Whale Predation on Marine Mammals at Punta Norte, Argentina: Food-sharing, Provisioning and Foraging Strategy," *Behavioral Ecology and Sociobiology* 29(1991): 197–204.

18. L.A. Dugatkin, "Cooperation in Fishes," in *Cooperation Among Animals: An Evolutionary Perspective* (New York: Oxford University Press, 1997), pp. 45–70.

19. Alvard, "Mutualistic Hunting."

20. L.A. Dugatkin, et al., "Beyond the Prisoner's Dilemma: Towards Models to Discriminate Among Mechanisms of Cooperation in Nature," *Trends in Ecology and Evolution* 7(1992): 202–205.

21. I. Valiela, *Marine Ecological Processes*, 2nd ed. (New York: Springer-Verlag, 1995), p. 108.

22. L. Margulis and D. Sagan, "The Beast with Five Genomes," *Natural History*, June 2001, pp. 38–41.

23. Ibid.; L. Margulis, *Symbiosis in Cell Evolution* (New York: W.H. Freeman, 1981).

24. L. Margulis and D. Sagan, *Microcosmos: Four Billion Years of Microbial Evolution* (New York: Simon and Schuster, 1986), pp. 19, 124–144.

25. Ibid.

26. Margulis and Sagan, "The Beast."

27. Dawkins, "Nice Guys."

28. R. Dawkins, *Unweaving the Rainbow: Science, Delusion, and the Appetite for Wonder* (Boston: Houghton Mifflin, 1998).

29. Ibid.

30. E.S. Hobson, "Feeding Patterns among Tropical Reef Fishes," *American Scientist* 63(1975): 382–392.

31. M. Hall and H. Hall, *Secrets of the Ocean Realm* (New York: Carroll and Graf, 1997), p. 43.

32. Margulis and Sagan, *Microcosmos*.

33. Tom Garrison, *Oceanography: An Invitation to Marine Science* (Pacific Grove, Calif.: Brooks/Cole Biology, Thomson Learning, 2001).

34. Encyclopedia Britannica, "Teleost Fishes," www.britannica.com/eb/article?eu=120758&tocid=0, cited June, 2001.

35. J.B.C. Jackson, et al., "Historical Overfishing and the Recent Collapse of Coastal Ecosystems," *Science* 293(2001): 629–638.

Chapter 9

1. S.J. Joung, et al., "The Whale Shark Is a Live Bearer: 300 Embryos Found in One Mega-Momma Supreme," *Environmental Biology of Fishes* 46(1996): 219–223.

2. S.A. Eckert and B.S. Stewart, "Telemetry and Satellite Tracking of Whale Sharks, *Rhincodon Typus*, in the Sea of Cortez, Mexico, and the North Pacific Ocean," *Environmental Biology of Fishes* 60(February 2001): 299–308.

3. S. Earle, *Sea Change: A Message of the Oceans* (New York: Fawcett Columbine, 1995), p. 180.

4. S. Junger, *The Perfect Storm* (New York: W.W. Norton, 1997).

5. R. Murphy, "Threatened Species, Threatened Livelihood," *New York Times*, 19 July 1998.

6. Ibid.

7. C. Safina, *Song for the Blue Ocean* (New York: Henry Holt, 1997).

8. Ibid.; Earle, *Sea Change*.

9. Safina, *Song for the Blue Ocean*.

10. J.W. Nybakken, *Marine Biology: An Ecological Approach* (San Francisco: Benjamin Cummings [Addison Welsley Longman, Inc.], 2001), pp. 370, 473.

11. D.S. Linthicum and F.G. Carey, "Regulation of Brain and Eye Temperatures by the Bluefin Tuna," *Comparative Biochemistry and Physiology* 43A(1972): 425–433.

12. B.A. Block, "Structure of the Brain and Eye Heater Tissue in Marlins, Sailfish, and Spearfishes," *Journal of Morphology* 190(1986): 169–189.

13. B.A. Block and F.G. Carey, "Warm Brain and Eye Temperatures in Sharks," *Journal of Comparative Psychology* 156B(1985): 229–236.

14. Safina, *Song for the Blue Ocean.*

15. R.L. Roberts, "Ram Gill Ventilation in Fish," in G.D. Sharp and A.E. Dizon, eds., *The Physiological Ecology of Tunas* (San Francisco: Academic Press, 1978), pp. 83–88.

16. I. Valiela, *Marine Ecological Processes*, 2nd ed. (New York: Springer-Verlag, 1995), pp. 339–360.

17. Tom Garrison, *Oceanography: An Invitation to Marine Science* (Pacific Grove, Calif.: Brooks/Cole Biology, Thomson Learning, 2001).

18. J.B.C. Jackson, et al., "Historical Overfishing and the Recent Collapse of Coastal Ecosystems," *Science* 293(2001): 629–638.

19. L. Seachrist, "Sea Turtles Master Migration with Magnetic Memories," *Science* 264(1994): 661–662.

20. D.D. Seifert, "Loggerhead Sea Turtles: The Solitary Life of the Great Ocean Traveler," *Ocean Realm*, Summer 1997, pp. 44–49.

21. D. Reiss and L. Marino, "Mirror Self-recognition in the Bottlenose Dolphin: A Case of Cognitive Convergence," *Proceedings of the National Academy of Sciences (USA)*, 98(2001): 5937–5942.

22. D. Griffin, *Animal Minds* (Chicago: University of Chicago Press, 1992).

23. Sea Watch, "An Overview of the Destruction of the Sea of Cortez," www. seawatch.org, cited April, 2000.

24. H. Hall, Sea Watch website, "Letter from Howard Hall," www.seawatch.org, cited April, 2000.

25. D. Pauly, "Anecdotes and the Shifting Baseline Syndrome of Fisheries," *Trends in Ecology and Evolution* 10(10)(1995): 430.

26. Tim D. Smith, Quoted in Teri Frady, "NOAA Scientist Will Lead Project to Reconstruct the History of Fishing" from NMFS Northeast Fisheries Science Center News, www.nefsc.nmfs.gov/press_release/news01.06.html, accessed July, 2002.

27. D.E. McAllister, "The Crisis in Marine Biodiversity and Key Knowledge," *CACOR Proceedings*, Autumn 1999.

28. M.V. Erdmann, et al., "Indonesian 'King of the Sea' Discovered," *Nature* 395(1998): 335.

29. McAllister, "The Crisis"; World Conservation Union, *"Red List of Endangered and Vulnerable Species,"* www.redlist.org., cited August, 2002.

30. McAllister, "The Crisis."

31. C.M. Roberts and J.P. Hawkins, "Extinction Risk in the Sea," *Trends in Ecology and Evolution* 14(1999): 241–246.

32. McAllister, "The Crisis."

33. D.E. McAllister, "Status of the World Ocean and Its Biodiversity," *Sea Wind, Bulletin of Ocean Voice International* 9(4)(1995): 1–72.

34. Valiela, *Marine Processes.*

35. D. Bryant, et al., *Reefs at Risk: A Map-Based Indicator of Threats to the World's Coral Reefs* (Washington, D.C.: World Resources Institute, 1998).

36. McAllister, "The Crisis."

37. C. Safina, "Scorched-Earth Fishing," *Issues in Science and Technology* 14(1998): 33–36.

38. Roberts and Hawkins, "Extinction Risk."

39. G.P. Jones and U.L. Kaly, "Conservation of Rare, Threatened and Endemic Marine Species in Australia," in *State of the Marine Environment Report for Australia*, Technical Annex: 1, The Marine Environment (Canberra, Australia: Ocean Rescue 2000, Department of the Environment, Sport and Territories, 1995), pp. 183–191.

40. Safina, "Scorched-Earth Fishing."

41. McAllister, "The Crisis"; E. Culotta, "Is Marine Biodiversity at Risk?" *Science*, 263(1994): 918–920.

42. Culotta, "Is Marine Biodiversity at Risk?"

43. Roger Payne, *Among Whales* (New York: Delta Books, 1995).

44. Hall, "Letter from Howard Hall."

45. Howard Hall, "An Eyewitness Account of the SeaWatch visit to Los Revillagigado Islands—March 2002," www.seawatch.org, cited July 2002.

Chapter 10

1. P.C. Howorth, *Channel Islands: The Story Behind the Scenery* (Las Vegas, Nev.: KC Publications, 1986), pp. 10, 26, 37.

2. J.H. Ryther, "Photosynthesis and Fish Production in the Sea," *Science* 166(1969): 72–76.

3. A. Couper, ed., *The Times Atlas and Encyclopaedia of the Sea* (New York: Harper and Row, 1983), pp. 51–53.

4. B. Robison and J. Connor, *The Deep Sea* (Monterey, Calif.: Monterey Bay Aquarium Press, 1999).

5. F. Azam, "Microbial Control of Oceanic Carbon Flux: The Plot Thickens," *Science* 280(1998): 694–696.

6. Tom Garrison, *Oceanography: An Invitation to Marine Science* (Pacific Grove, Calif.: Brooks/Cole Biology, Thomson Learning, 2001).

7. J.W. Nybakken and S.K.Webster, "Life in the Ocean," *Scientific American Presents*, Fall 1998, pp. 74–86.

8. M. Bramwell, ed., *Atlas of the Oceans* (Chicago, Rand McNally, 1977), p. 32.

9. J.W. Nybakken, *Marine Biology: An Ecological Approach* (San Francisco: Benjamin Cummings [Addison Welsley Longman, Inc.], 2001), p. 65; Jim Barry, Monterey Bay Aquarium Research Institute, personal communication.

10. R. Carson, *The Sea Around Us*, spec. ed. (New York: Oxford University Press, 1989), pp. 144–145 (originally published in 1950).

11. Couper, *The Times Atlas.*

12. G. Waller, ed., *SeaLife: A Complete Guide to the Marine Environment* (Washington, D.C.: Smithsonian Institution Press, 1996), p. 55.

13. Howorth, *Channel Islands.*

14. Azam, "Microbial Control."

15. Howorth, *Channel Islands.*

16. S. Hinton, *Seashore Life of Southern California* (Berkeley: University of California Press, 1987), pp. 60, 111–112.

17. M. Snyderman, *California Marine Life* (Niwot, Colo.: Roberts Rinehart, 1998).

18. T. Perry, "La Jolla Aims to Retake Beach," *Los Angeles Times,* 27 November 1998.

19. P. Matthiessen, *Wildlife in America* (New York: Penguin, 1987), pp. 102–103.

20. C. Ponting, *A Green History of the World: The Environment and the Collapse of Great Civilizations* (New York: Penguin, 1991).

21. J.B.C. Jackson, et al., "Historical Overfishing and the Recent Collapse of Coastal Ecosystems," *Science* 293(2001): 629–638.

22. S. Earle, *Sea Change: A Message of the Oceans* (New York: Fawcett Columbine, 1995), p. 186.

23. M. Remco, California Dept. of Fish and Game, personal communication, April 2001.

24. J. Ugoretz, California Dept. of Fish and Game, personal communication, April 2001.

25. R.J. Wilder, et al., "Saving Marine Biodiversity," *Issues in Science and Technology*, Spring 1999, p. 59.

26. Garrison, *Oceanography*; D. Pauly, et al., "Fishing Down Marine Food Webs," *Science* 279(1998): 860–863.

27. D. Helvarg, *Blue Frontier* (New York: W. H. Freeman, 2001), pp. 187–219.

28. Ibid.

29. Garrison, *Oceanography*.

30. Helvarg, *Blue Frontier*.

31. W.J. Hickel, *Who Owns America?* (Englewood Cliffs, N.J.: Prentice Hall, 1971), pp. 247–249.

32. Helvarg, *Blue Frontier*.

33. J.L. Garfield, *The San Diego-La Jolla Underwater Park Ecological Reserve* (San Diego: Picaro Publishing, 1994).

34. R.J. Wilder, *Listening to the Sea: the Politics of Improving Environmental Protection* (Pittsburgh: University of Pittsburgh Press, 1998), pp. 146–147, 161.

35. O.N. Bjornstad and B.T. Grenfell, "Noisy Clockwork: Time Series Analysis of Population Fluctuations in Animals," *Science* 293(2001): 638–643.

36. Wilder, *Listening to the Sea*.

37. Hinton, *Seashore Life*.

38. L. Fernandez, "Fishermen Protest Proposed Channel Islands Restrictions," *Los Angeles Times,* 3 April 1998; L. Fernandez, "300 Denounce Plan to Limit Fishing Area," *Los Angeles Times*, 12 March 1998.

39. J.J. Reynolds, Regional Director, Pacific West, National Park Service. Letter to Hon. Dianne Feinstein, U.S. Senate, 29 May 1998, United States Department of the Interior A3615(PWR-RD).

40. G.E. Davis, "Designated Harvest Refugia: The Next Stage of Marine Fishery Management in California," *CalCOFI Report* 30(1989); J.E. Dugan and G.E. Davis, "Applications of Marine Refugia to Coastal Fisheries Management," *Canadian Journal of Fisheries and Aquatic Science* 50(1993): 2029–2042.

41. Philip Gallo, *San Diego Union Tribune*, letters to the editor, circa 1999, clipping, date not available. Because of new judicial copyright rulings, all archival data from before 2000 are no longer available to the public. I spoke to Dr. Gallo, who also does not have the date of the letter but confirmed its contents.

42. A.E. Henry, et al., "Common Exploitation of Living Marine Resources by Pinnipeds and Humans Near San Nicolas Island, California," in Abstracts of the World Marine Mammal Science Conference, Monaco, 20–24 January 1998, p. 63.

43. Quoted in Associated Press, "Wide Expansion of No-Fishing Zone Urged; Santa Barbara Boats See Ruin of Industry," *San Diego Union-Tribune*, 28 September 2000.

44. J.A. Bohnsack, "Application of Marine Reserves to Reef Fisheries Management," *Australian Journal of Ecology* 23(1998): 298–304; J.A. Bohnsack, "Maintenance and Recovery of Reef Fishery Productivity," in *Management of Reef Fisheries*, N.V. Polunin and C.M. Roberts, eds. (London: Chapman and Hall, 1995), pp. 283–313.

45. Quoted in R. R. Britt, "Something's Fishy at Cape Canaveral," www.space. com/scienceastronomy/planetearth/canaveral_fish_000111.html, cited July 2002.

46. Quoted in Associated Press, "Wide Expansion."

47. Ibid.

48. (No Byline) *San Diego Union-Tribune*, "Effort for Marine Preserve Fails," 17 May 2001.

49. Gary Davis, personal communication.

50. E. Zieralski, "It Takes Citizen Participation For Public Hearings to Work," *San Diego Union-Tribune*, 7 October 2001; T. Rodgers, "Offshore Protection Proposal Stirs Opposition from Fishing Industry," *San Diego Union-Tribune*, 11 July 2001.

51. Davis, personal communication.

52. Laura Wides, "State Panel Bans Fishing In Areas Around Channel Islands," *San Diego Union-Tribune*, October 24, 2002; Kenneth Weiss, "Fishing Permanently Banned Around the Channel Islands," *Los Angeles Times*, October 24, 2002.

Chapter 11

1. A. Leopold, *A Sand County Almanac,* commem. ed. (New York: Oxford University Press, 1987), p. 101.

2. J. Muir, *John Muir, Man of the Mountains*, L.M. Wolfe, ed., 1938, in *Dictionary of Environmental Quotations*, B.K. Rodes and R.A. Odell, eds. (Baltimore: Johns Hopkins University Press, 1992), p. 300.

3. Quoted in R.K. Sobel, "Jacques Cousteau: He Inspired Our Passion for the Oceans," *National Wildlife*, April/May 2001, p. 19.

4. T. Rodgers, "Seeing Slews of Sharks," *San Diego Union-Tribune*, 27 October 1999.

5. P.O. Daily, personal communication.

6. A. Peter Klimley, et al., "The Hunting Strategy of White Sharks (Carcharodon Carcharias) Near a Seal Colony," *Marine Biology* 138(3)(2001): 617–636; A. Peter Klimley and D.G. Ainley, eds., *Great White Shark: The Biology of Carcharodon Carcharias* (San Diego: Academic Press, 1996).

7. Quoted in W.J. Broad, "Great White Sharks," *National Wildlife*, December/January 1999, pp. 50–51.

8. P. Matthiessen, *Blue Meridian: The Search for the Great White Shark* (New York: Random House, 1971), pp. 174–179.

9. C. Safina, *Song for the Blue Ocean* (New York: Henry Holt, 1997), p. 57.

10. M. Tighe, "Asia's Passion for Shark Fins Powers a Cruel Ocean Industry," *Los*

Angeles Times, 20 September 1998; E. Niller, "Sharks: Several Species Are Declining," *San Diego Union-Tribune*, 14 October 1998.

11. S. Nemecek, "Yes, Sharks Get Cancer," *Scientific American*, June 2000, p. 34.

12. H.L. Pratt, Jr. and J.I. Castro, "Shark Reproduction: Parental Investment and Limited Fisheries, An Overview" in S.H. Gruber, ed., *Discovering Sharks* (Highlands, N.J.: American Littoral Society, 1990), pp. 55–60.

13. S. Van Sommeran, "The Pelagic Shark Research Foundation," (Santa Cruz, Calif.:) Pelagic Shark Research Foundation), Available: www.pelagic.org/conservation/, cited July 2002.

14. Tighe, "Asia's Passion"; Niller, "Sharks."

15. O.N. Bjornstad and B.T. Grenfell, "Noisy Clockwork: Time Series Analysis of Population Fluctuations in Animals," *Science* 293(2001): 638–643.

16. Niller, "Sharks."

17. Tighe, "Asia's Passion."

18. Van Sommeran, "The Pelagic Shark Research Foundation."

19. Sea Watch, "Revillagigados Islands Under Continued Attack by Illegal Commercial Fishing," www.seawatch.org., cited July, 2002.

20. Van Sommeran, "The Pelagic Shark Research Foundation"; Tom Garrison, *Oceanography: An Invitation to Marine Science* (Pacific Grove, California: Brooks/Cole Biology, Thomson Learning, 2001).

21. Garrison, *Oceanography*.

22. W.N. Eschmeyer and E.S. Herald, *Pacific Coast Fishes* (Boston. Houghton Mifflin, 1983), pp. 35–36.

23. John S. Kao, "Diet, Daily Ration and Gastric Evacuation of the Leopard Shark (*Triakis Semifasciata*)," Masters Thesis, Moss Landing Marine Labs, California State University, 2000.

24. Ibid.

Chapter 12

1. D. A. Murawski, "Diatoms: Plants with a Touch of Glass," *National Geographic*, February 1999, pp. 114–121.

2. G. Waller, ed., *SeaLife: A Complete Guide to the Marine Environment* (Washington, D.C.: Smithsonian Institution Press, 1996), p. 54.

3. Tom Garrison, *Oceanography: An Invitation to Marine Science* (Pacific Grove, Calif.: Brooks/Cole Biology, Thomson Learning, 2001), pp. 352–353.

4. F. House, *Totem Salmon* (Boston: Beacon Press, 1999), pp. 29–30, 87–89.

5. C. Safina, *Song for the Blue Ocean* (New York: Henry Holt, 1997), pp. 153–156, 219–220.

6. F. Montaigne, "A River Dammed," *National Geographic*, April 2001, pp. 24–25.

7. House, *Totem Salmon*.

8. Safina, *Song for the Blue Ocean*.

9. D.J. Duncan, "Salmon's Second Coming," *Sierra*, April 2000.

10. Ibid.; Montaigne, "A River Dammed."

11. U.S. Army Corps of Engineers, *Lost Creek Lake Oregon* (brochure, n.d.).

12. F. Utter, "Genetic Problems of Hatchery-Reared Progeny Released Into the Wild," *Bulletin of Marine Scientists* 62 (1998): 623–640.

13. House, *Totem Salmon*.

14. Ronn Patterson, personal communication.

15. Pacific Rivers Council, "Coastal Salmon and Communities at Risk: The Principles of Coastal Salmon Recovery" (Eugene, Ore.: Pacific Rivers Council, July 1995).

16. Safina, *Song for the Blue Ocean*.

17. D. Dobbs, "Old MacDonald Had a Fish," *Sierra*, January/February 2000, p. 24.

18. J. Levinton, Dept. of Ecology and Evolution, SUNY Stony Brook, unpublished written communication, 8 May 2001.

19. Dobbs, "Old MacDonald."

20. R.H. Devlin, "Growth of Domesticated Transgenic Fish," *Nature* 409(2001): 781–782; P.W. Hedrick, "Invasion of Transgenes From Salmon or Other Genetically Modified Organisms Into Natural Populations," *Canadian Journal of Fish Aquatic Sciences* 589(2001):841–844; W.M. Muir and R.D. Howard, "Possible Ecological Risks of Transgenic Organism Release When Transgenes Affect Mating Success: Sexual Selection and the Trojan Gene Hypothesis," *Proceedings of the National Academy of Sciences* 96(1999): 13853–13856; I.A. Fleming and S. Einum, "Experimental Tests of Genetic Divergence of Farmed from Wild Atlantic Salmon Due to Domestication," *ICES Journal of Marine Science* 54(1997): 1051–1063; P. McGinnity, et al., "Genetic Impact of Escaped Farmed Atlantic Salmon on Native Populations," *ICES Journal of Marine Science* 54(1997): 998–1008.

21. J.P. Volpe, et al., "Evidence of Natural Reproduction of Aquaculture-Escaped Atlantic Salmon in a Coastal British Columbia River," *Conservation Biology* 14(2000): 899–903.

22. D. Bouchard, et al., "Isolation of Infectious Salmon Anemia Virus from Atlantic Salmon in New Brunswick, Canada," *Diseases of Aquatic Organisms* 35(1999): 131–137.

23. Montaigne, "A River Dammed."

24. K. Durbin, *Tongass: Pulp Politics and the Fight for the Alaska Rain Forest* (Corvallis, Ore.: Oregon State University Press, 1999), pp. 52, 136.

25. Ibid.

26. Bill Shoaf, *The Taking of the Tongass: Alaska's Rainforest* (Sequim, Wash.: Running Wolf Press, 2000).

Chapter 13

1. L. Pomeroy, "The Ocean's Food Web: A Changing Paradigm," *Bioscience* 24(1974): 499–504.

2. T.M. Fenchel, "Suspended Bacteria as a Food Source," in *Flows of Energy and Materials in Marine Ecosystems*, M.J.R. Fasham, ed. (New York: Plenum Press, 1984), pp. 301–315.

3. F. Azam, "Microbial Control of Oceanic Carbon Flux: The Plot Thickens," *Science* 280(1998): 694–696.

4. J.H. Steele, *The Structure of Marine Ecosystems* (Cambridge, Mass.: Harvard University Press, 1974).

5. Azam, "Microbial Control."

6. A. M. Alldredge and M.W. Silver, "Characteristics, Dynamics, and Significance of Marine Snow," *Progress in Oceanography* 20(1998): 41–82.

7. J.E. Hobbie, et al., "Use of Nuclear Stains for Counting Bacteria by Fluorescence Microscopy," *Applied and Environmental Microbiology* 33(1977): 1225–1228.

8. J.W. Nybakken, *Marine Biology: An Ecological Approach* (San Francisco: Benjamin Cummings [Addison Welsley Longman], 2001), p. 84.

9. R.R. Colwell, "Global Climate and Infectious Disease: The Cholera Paradigm," *Science* 274(1996): 2025–2031.

10. J.H. Martin, "Testing the Iron Hypothesis in Ecosystems of the Equatorial Pacific Ocean," *Nature* 371(1994): 123–129.

11. Ibid.; K.H. Coale, et al., "A Massive Phytoplankton Bloom Induced by an Ecosystem-Scale Iron Fertilization Experiment in the Equatorial Pacific Ocean," *Nature* 383(1996): 495–501.

12. Martin, "Testing the Iron Hypothesis."

13. D.A. Murawski, "Diatoms: Plants with a Touch of Glass," *National Geographic*, February 1999, pp. 114–121.

14. K.D. Bidle and F. Azam, "Accelerated Dissolution of Diatom Silica by Marine Bacterial Assemblages," *Nature* 397(1999): 508–512.

15. R. Carson, *The Sea Around Us* (New York: Oxford University Press, 1989), p. 144.

16. F. Azam and F. Rohwer, personal communication.

17. S.W. Chisholm, et al., "A Novel Free-Living Prochlorophyte Abundant in the Oceanic Euphotic Zone," *Nature* 334(1988): 340–343.

18. E.O. Wilson, *The Future of Life* (New York: Alfred A Knopf, 2002), pp. 5–14.

19. Ibid.

20. Richard Grigg, Professor of Oceanography, University of Hawaii, unpublished written communication, 2001

21. Joint Office for Science Support, "Ocean Ecology: Understanding and Vision for Research (OEUVRE)," www.ofps.ucar.edu/joss_psg/project/oce_workshop/oeuvre/report/Entire.pdf, cited July, 2002.

This report, written in 12/9/98, is a summary of ocean ecologic knowledge from the past 30 years as summarized from a National Science Foundation–sponsored workshop of 40 ocean ecologists, held in Keystone, Colorado, 1 6 March, 1998. More than an excellent summary of past discoveries, it provides a road map for the most productive research questions and challenges for the next twenty years.

22. J.A. Fuhrman, et al., "Novel Major Archaebacterial Group From Marine Plankton," *Nature* 356(1992): 148–149; E.F. DeLong, "Archaea in Coastal Marine Environments," *Proceedings of the National Academy of Sciences (USA)* 89(1992): 5685–5689; "Archael Means and Extremes," *Science* 280(1998): 542–543.

23. S. LaFee, "The Jell-Ocean," *San Diego Union-Tribune*, 4 October 2000.

24. J. Levinton, Dept. of Ecology and Evolution, SUNY Stony Brook, unpublished written communication, 8 May 2001.

25. Azam, "Microbial Control."

26. T. Fenchel, "Marine Planktonic Food Chains," *Annual Review of Ecological Systems*, 19(1988): 19–38.

27. D.K. Stoecker, et al., "Large Proportion of Marine Planktonic Ciliates Found to Contain Functional Chloroplasts," *Nature* 326(1987): 790–792.

28. Richard Conniff, "Jelly Bellies," *National Geographic,* June 2000, p. 98.

Chapter 14

1. M. Hall and H. Hall, *Secrets of the Ocean Realm* (New York: Carroll and Graf, 1997), pp. 1–17.

2. S. Earle, *Sea Change: A Message of the Oceans* (New York: Fawcett Columbine, 1995).

3. Sylvia Earle, 4th Annual Martin Witte Distinguished Speakers Lecture Series, Newport Beach Public Library, Newport Beach, California, 17 February 2001.

4. M. Cone, "A Disturbing Whale Watch in Northwest: Washington-Area Orcas Riddled With Toxic PCB's," *Los Angeles Times*, 16 February 2001.

5. For further reading, see: D.H. Chadwick, "Pursuing the Minke," *National Geographic*, April 2001, p. 70.

6. For further reading, see: Carl Safina, "The World's Imperiled Fish," *Scientific American*, November 1995.

7. J.W. Nybakken and S.K. Webster, "Life in the Ocean," *Scientific American*, Fall 1998.

8. B. Robison and J. Connor, *The Deep Sea* (Monterey, Calif.: Monterey Bay Aquarium Press, 1999).

9. Ibid.

10. Jim Barry, Monterey Bay Aquarium Research Institute, personal communication, 2001.

11. J. Adam, "Piloting Through Uncharted Seas" [profile of Marica McNutt, director of MBARI], *Scientific American*, June 2001, pp. 38–39.

12. J.P. Barry, et al., "Biologic and Geologic Characteristics of Cold Seeps in Monterey Bay, California," *Deep Sea Research I*, 43(1996): 1739–1762.

13. Quoted in L. Tangley, "Mysteries of the Twilight Zone," *National Wildlife*, October/November 2001, pp. 52–57.

14. Robison and Connor, *The Deep Sea*.

15. I. Valiela, *Marine Ecological Processes*, 2nd ed. (New York: Springer-Verlag, 1995), p. 316.

16. Tom Garrison, *Oceanography: An Invitation to Marine Science* (Pacific Grove, Calif.: Brooks/Cole Biology, Thomson Learning, 2001), p. 429.

17. J.P. Barry, "The Influence of Pore-Water Chemistry and Physiology on the Distribution of Vesicomyid Clams at Cold Seeps in Monterey Bay: Implications for Patterns of Chemosynthetic Community Organization," *Limnology and Oceanography* 42(2)(1997): 318–328.

Chapter 15

1. C.S. Baker and S.R. Palumbi, "Which Whales Are Hunted? A Molecular Genetic Approach to Monitoring Whaling," *Science* 265(1994): 1538–1539.

2. C.S. Baker, et al., "Molecular Identification of Whale and Dolphin Products from Commercial Markets in Korea and Japan," *Marine Ecology* 5(1996): 671–685.

3. D.H. Chadwick, "Pursuing the Minke," *National Geographic*, April 2001, p. 70.

4. P.W. Watson, *Ocean Warrior* (Toronto: Key Porter Books, 1994).

5. Ibid.

6. Ibid.

7. Ibid.

8. Ibid.

9. H. Mooney, [Chairman, Committee on Ecosystem Management, National Research Council], *Sustaining Marine Fisheries* (Washington, D.C.: National Academy Press, 1999).

10. Quoted in D. Helvarg, *Blue Frontier* (New York: W.H. Freeman, 2001), p. 165.

11. International Union for Conservation of Nature and Natural Resources (IUCN), World Conservation Union, "2000 IUCN Red List of Threatened Species," www.redlist.org, cited July, 2002.

12. J.A. Estes, et al., "Killer Whale Predation on Sea Otters Linking Oceanic and Nearshore Ecosystems," *Science* 282(1998): 473–476.

13. National Research Council, *The Bering Sea Ecosystem* (Washington, D.C.: National Academy Press, 1996).

14. Mooney, *Sustaining Marine Fisheries*.

15. Baker and Palumbi, "Which Whales Are Hunted?"

16. R. Payne, *Among Whales* (New York: Delta Books, 1995).

17. Ibid.

18. Ibid.

19. W. Aron, et al., "Flouting the Convention," *Atlantic Monthly*, May 1999. pp. 22–29.

20. Watson, *Ocean Warrior*.

21. R. Hendrickson, *The Ocean Almanac* (New York: Doubleday, 1984), pp. 83–85.

22. Watson, *Ocean Warrior*.

23. Ibid.

24. Ibid.

25. J.W. Crawley, "Catch of the Day—Drugs: 8 Tons of Cocaine, Fishing Boat Seized by Coast Guard, Navy," *San Diego Union-Tribune*, 4 March 2001.

26. J. Hughes, "Cocaine Seizure at Sea a Record," *San Diego Union-Tribune*, 15 May 2001

27. (No author cited), " 'Terrorists' Attack Ski Lodges, Not Doctors," Fairness and Accuracy in Reporting (FAIR), www.fair.org/extra/9812/buffalo-vail.html, cited August, 2002.

28. Watson, *Ocean Warrior*.

29. J. Levinton, Dept. of Ecology and Evolution, SUNY Stony Brook, unpublished written communication, 8 May 2001.

30. H.F. Dobyns, "Estimating Aboriginal American Population: An Appraisal of Techniques with a New Hemispheric Estimate," *Current Anthropology* 7(4)(1966): 395–416.

31. L.H. Keeley, *War before Civilization: The Myth of the Peaceful Savage* (New York: Oxford University Press, 1996).

32. J. Barnard, (Associated Press), "Bones of Kennewick Man Are in the Court's Hands," *San Diego Union–Tribune*, 21 June 2001.

33. M.J. Plotkin, *Tales of a Shaman's Apprentice: An Ethnobotanist Searches for New Medicines in the Amazon Rain Forest* (New York: Penguin, 1994).

34. C. C. Mann, "1491," *Atlantic Monthly*, March 2002, pp. 41–53.

35. L. Dayton, "Mass Extinctions Pinned on Ice Age Hunters," *Science* 292(2001): 1819.

36. M.E. Soulé, "Should Wilderness Be Managed?" in *Return of the Wild: The*

Future of Our Natural Lands, T. Karasote, ed. (Washington, D.C.: Island Press, 2001), p. 137.

37. V. Deloria, Jr., "American Indians and the Wilderness," in *Return of the Wild: The Future of Our Natural Lands,* T. Karasote, ed. (Washington, D.C.: Island Press, 2001), pp. 25–35.

38. Ibid.

39. J.B.C. Jackson, et al., "Historical Overfishing and the Recent Collapse of Coastal Ecosystems," *Science* 293(2001): 629–638.

40. Ibid.

41. P. Watson and A. Christie, "Proposal for a Resolution of the Makah Whale Hunt Issue, http://www.seashepherd.org/issues/whales/makahhunt20701.html, cited July 2002.

42. Alberta Thompson, "Letter to the International Whale Commission," www.stopwhalekill.org/alberta.html, cited June, 2001.

43. R. Bailey, *Eco-Scam: The False Profits of Ecological Apocalypse* (New York: St. Martin's Press, 1993).

44. E. Murtaugh, Associated Press, "Tribe Families Prepare to Harpoon Whales," *San Diego Union-Tribune,* 29 March 2002.

45. Leigh Calvez, "Deafness in the Depths," *The Ecologist* 30(4)(2000): 48–49; "By the Time We Have Proof," *Ocean Realm,* Spring 2000, pp. 41–47.

46. A. Frantzis, "Does Acoustic Testing Strand Whales?" *Nature* 392(1998): 29.

47. Calvez, "Deafness in the Depths."

48. Katharine Seelye, "Environmental Law Doesn't Cover Ocean Tract, Feds Say," *San Diego Union-Tribune,* 10 August 2002.

49. Ibid.

Chapter 16

1. D. Doubilet, "Inside Palau," *Ocean Realm,* January 1996, pp. 56–70.

2. K. Galbraith, et al., *Micronesia* (Victoria, Australia: Lonely Planet, 2000).

3. R.V. Salm and S.L. Coles, eds. *Coral Bleaching and Marine Protected Areas,* rep. 0102 (Honolulu: The Nature Conservancy), pp. 36–39.

4. Ibid.

5. J.W. Nybakken, "Tropical Communities," in *Marine Biology: An Ecological Approach* (San Francisco: Benjamin Cummings [Addison Welsley Longman, Inc.], 2001), pp. 370–433.

6. R.E. Johannes, "The Traditional Conservation Ethic and Its Decline," in *Words of the Lagoon* (Berkeley: University of California Press, 1981).

7. Carl Safina, *Song for the Blue Ocean* (New York: Henry Holt, 1997).

8. T. Rock and F. Toribiong, *Diving and Snorkeling Palau* (Victoria, Australia: Lonely Planet Publications, 2000).

9. J.D. Watt, "Palau's Special Places," *Discover Diving* 15(July–August 1997): 43–47.

10. Safina, *Song for the Blue Ocean.*

11. Rock and Toribiong, *Diving and Snorkeling Palau.*

12. Safina, *Song for the Blue Ocean.*

13. Doubilet, "Inside Palau."

14. P.L. Colin and A.C. Arneson, *Tropical Pacific Invertebrates* (Beverly Hills, Calif.: Coral Reef Press, 1995).

15. J.F. Bruno, et al., "El Niño Related Coral Bleaching in Palau, Western Caroline Islands," *Coral Reefs* 20(2001): 127–136.

16. Ibid.

17. Ibid.

Chapter 17

1. R. Payne, *Among Whales* (New York: Delta Books, 1995), pp. 310–348.

2. J. Lovelock, *The Ages of Gaia: A Biography of Our Living Earth* (New York: W.W. Norton, 1988).

3. J.L. Kirschvink, et al., "Evidence for a Large-Scale Reorganization of Early Cambrian Continental Masses by Inertial Interchange True Polar Wander." *Science* 277(1997): 541–545.

4. Ibid.

5. Joint Office for Science Support, "Ocean Ecology: Understanding the Vision for Research (OEUVRE)," www.ofps.ucar.edu/joss_psg/project/oce_workshop/oeuvre/report/Entire.pdf, cited July, 2002.

6. A.K. Shiomoto, et al., "Trophic Relations in the Subarctic North Pacific Ecosystem: Possible Feeding Effect from Pink Salmon," *Marine Ecology Progress Series* 150(1997): 75–85.

7. J.A. Estes, et al., "Killer Whale Predation on Sea Otters Linking Oceanic and Nearshore Ecosystems," *Science* 282(1998): 473–476.

8. J. Travis, "Invader Threatens Black, Azov Seas," *Science* 262(1993): 1366–1367.

9. Ben Holland, "Humans Are the Winners in Jellyfish Fight," *San Diego Union-Tribune*, 6 February 2002.

10. R. Revelle and H. Suess, "Carbon Dioxide Exchange between Atmosphere and Ocean and the Question of an Increase in Atmospheric CO_2 during the Past Decades," *Tellus* 9(1957): 18–27.

11. R.A. Kerr, "New Greenhouse Report Puts Down Dissenters," *Science* 249(1990): 481–482.

12. T.P. Barnett, et al., "Detection of Anthropogenic Climate Change in the World's Oceans," *Science* 292(2001): 270–274; S. Levitus, et al., "Anthropogenic Warming of the Earth's Climate System," *Science* 292(2001): 267–270.

13. Kerr, "New Greenhouse Report"; P. Ehrlich and A. Ehrlich, *Betrayal of Science and Reason: How Antienvironmental Rhetoric Threatens Our Future* (Washington, D.C.: Island Press, 1996).

14. R. Gelbspan, "A Modest Proposal to Stop Global Warming," *Sierra*, May–June 2001, pp. 62–67.

15. Quoted in D. Grossman, "Dissent in the Maelstrom," *Scientific American*, November 2001, pp. 38–39.

16. W. Broecher, Lamont-Doherty Earth Observatory, Columbia University, New York. Quoted in B. McKibben, "A Special Moment in History," *The Atlantic Monthly*, May 1998, pp. 55–78.

17. E. Kolbert, "Ice Memory," *The New Yorker*, 7 January 2002, pp. 30–37.

18. L. Margulis and D. Sagan, *Microcosmos: Four Billion Years of Microbial Evolution* (New York: Simon and Schuster, 1986), pp. 111, 271–272.

19. Ibid.

20. Tom Garrison, *Oceanography: An Invitation to Marine Science* (Pacific Grove, Calif.: Brooks/Cole Biology, Thomson Learning, 2001), pp. 103, 380.

21. S.J. Gould, "This View of Life," *Natural History*, April 2000, pp. 32–38, 82–86.

22. Payne, *Among Whales*; T. Colburn, et al., *Our Stolen Future: Are We Threatening Our Fertility, Intelligence, and Survival?* (New York: Plume Paperbacks [Signet] 1997).

23. R. Leakey and R. Lewin, *The Sixth Extinction* (New York: Anchor Books/Doubleday, 1995); J. McClintock, "As We Learn about Biological Diversity, Earth Is Losing It," *San Diego Union-Tribune*, 23 November 2000; F.S. Chapin, et al., "Consequences of Changing Biodiversity," *Nature* 405(2000): 234–242.

24. Quoted in W.W. Gibbs, "On the Termination of Species," *Scientific American*, November 2001, pp. 40–49.

25. Ibid.

26. R.H. MacArthur and E.O. Wilson, *The Theory of Island Biogeography* (Princeton, N.J.: Princeton University Press, 1967).

27. Chapin et al., "Consequences."

28. R.W. Grigg, "Coral Reefs in an Urban Embayment in Hawaii: A Complex Case History Controlled by Natural and Anthropogenic Stress," *Coral Reefs* 14(1995): 253–266.

29. A.N.L. Chiu, et al., *Hurricane Iwa, Hawaii, November 23, 1982*, National Academy Research Council Report CETS-CND-021 (Washington, D.C.: National Academy Press, 1983).

30. O.H. Pilkey and K.L. Dixon, *The Corps and the Shore* (Washington, D.C.: Island Press, 1996), p. 42.

31. Tom Garrison, *Oceanography: An Invitation to Marine Science* (Pacific Grove, Calif.: Brooks/Cole Biology, Thomson Learning, 2001), pp. 314, 380.

32. D. Helvarg, *Blue Frontier* (New York: W. H. Freeman, 2001), p. 116.

33. Garrison, *Oceanography*.

34. Ibid.

35. Ibid.; C. Ponting, *A Green History of the World: The Environment and the Collapse of Great Civilizations* (New York: Penguin, 1991).

36. David Quammen, "Planet of Weeds: Tallying the Losses of Earth's Animals and Plants," *Harpers* (October 1998), pp. 57–69.

37. I. Valiela, *Marine Ecological Processes*, 2nd ed. (New York: Springer-Verlag, 1995), pp. 107–108, 380.

38. J.W. Nybakken, *Marine Biology: An Ecological Approach* (San Francisco: Benjamin Cummings [Addison Welsley Longman], 2001), pp. 461–485.

39. M. Cone, "A Disturbing Whale Watch in Northwest: Washington-Area Orcas Riddled with Toxic PCB's," *Los Angeles Times*, 16 February 2001.

40. D. Pauly and V. Christensen, "Primary Production Required to Sustain Global Fisheries," *Science* 374(1995): 255–257.

41. Ibid.

42. Richard Grigg, Professor of Oceanography, University of Hawaii, unpublished written communication.

43. Ehrlich and Ehrlich, *Betrayal*.

44. P.R. Ehrlich, *The Population Bomb* (New York: Ballantine Books, 1968).

45. Ehrlich and Ehrlich, *Betrayal*.

46. Nybakken, *Marine Biology*.

47. Ehrlich and Ehrlich, *Betrayal*.

48. E.O. Wilson, *The Future of Life* (New York: Alfred A. Knopf, 2002), pp. 29–31; J. Bongaarts, "Population: Ignoring Its Impact," *Scientific American*, January 2002, pp. 67–69.

49. Grigg, unpublished.

50. Partha Dasgupta, *Human Well-Being and the Natural Environment* (New York: Oxford University Press, 2001), pp. 117–118.

51. G. Hardin, "The Tragedy of the Commons," *Science* 162(1968): 1243–1248.

52. A. N. Whitehead, *Science and the Modern World* (New York: Mentor, 1948).

53. G. Hardin, "The Tragedy of the Commons."

54. Ibid.

Chapter 18

1. A. Leopold, *A Sand County Almanac* (New York: Oxford University Press, 1987), pp. 201–226, (originally published in 1949).

2. E.O. Wilson, *Biophilia* (Cambridge, Mass.: Harvard University Press, 1984), pp. 1–2.

3. Ibid.

4. Garrett Hardin, "The Tragedy of the Commons," *Science* 162(1968): 1243–1248.

5. "Seafood Watch: Choices for Healthy Oceans," www.montereybayaquarium.com/cr/seafoodwatch.asp, cited July, 2002.

6. *Webster's New Twentieth Century Dictionary*, 2nd ed. (New York: Prentice Hall, 1983).

7. Ted Kerasote, ed., *Return of the Wild: The Future of Our National Lands* (Washington, D.C.: Island Press, 2001), p. 19.

8. Richard Rosenblatt, professor emeritus of marine biology at UCSD's Scripps Institution of Oceanography. Quoted in Terry Rodgers, "City Wants Grunion-Friendly Beaches," *San Diego Union-Tribune*, 12 July 2001.

9. R. Coniff, "Jelly Bellies," *National Geographic*, June 2000, p. 98.

10. J. Bongaarts, "Population: Ignoring Its Impact," *Scientific American*, January 2002, pp. 67–69.

11. E.O. Wilson, *The Future of Life* (New York: Alfred A. Knopf, 2002).

12. Ged Davis, "Energy for Planet Earth," *Scientific American*, September 1991, pp. 55–62.

13. Partha Dasgupta, *Human Well-Being and the Natural Environment* (New York: Oxford University Press, 2001), pp. 117–118.

14. Ibid.

15. R. May, "Simple Mathematical Models with Very Complicated Dynamics," *Nature* 261(1976): 459–467; J. Gleick, *Chaos. Making a New Science* (New York: Viking, 1987); Z. Sardar and I. Abrams, *Introducing Chaos* (Cambridge, Mass.: Icon Books Ltd., 1999).

A Short List of Related Readings

Carson, Rachel. *The Sea Around Us*. New York: Oxford University Press, 1989.

Brought up to date by Jeffrey Levinton's afterword, this book remains the single best layman's introduction to the ocean and the world of the sea.

Earle, Sylvia. *Sea Change: A Message of the Oceans*. New York: Fawcett Columbine, 1995.

A major work by the Queen of the Sea—a lifetime adventure as related by an oceanwise scientist who cares.

Garrison, Tom. *Oceanography: An Invitation to Marine Science*. Pacific Grove, California: Brooks/Cole Biology, Thomson Learning, 2001.

This classic oceanographic text covers physical oceanography, biologic oceanography, and chemical oceanography, all in a most readable manner. In its fourth edition, this work has been reviewed by some 80 scientists.

Hall, Michele and Hall, Howard. *Secrets of the Ocean Realm*. New York: Carroll and Graf, 1997.

An account of movie-making underwater, a moving first-hand oceanic adventure story packed with natural history and world-class photography.

Helvarg, David. *Blue Frontier*. New York: W.H. Freeman, 2001.

A hard-hitting, thoroughly researched compilation of environmental and political reportage on the state of the seas in the United States.

House, Freeman. *Totem Salmon*. Boston: Beacon Press, 1999.

> *A lyric and well-researched book on the animal that ties sea and forest together—deep ecology at its finest.*

Kampion, Drew. *The Book of Waves: Form and Beauty on the Ocean*. Niwot, Colorado: Robert Rinehart International, 1989.

> *With fabulous photographs and succinct, lyric prose, Kampion makes the ocean come alive for the non-surfer as well as the "major surf dude."*

Nybakken, James W. *Marine Biology: An Ecological Approach*. San Francisco: Benjamin Cummings [Addison Welsley Longman], 2001.

> *Never before has a textbook been so readable, so chock full of pertinent facts, or so filled with classic references.*

Payne, Roger. *Among Whales*. New York: Delta Books, 1995.

> *Payne's love and respect for the biggest animals of all time, as well as a lifetime of science studying them, make this a classic.*

Safina, Carl. *Song for the Blue Ocean*. New York: Henry Holt, 1997.

> *A gem of prose, research, and interviews: from the Atlantic bluefin tuna, to salmon, to coral reefs, Safina paints a striking picture of the beauty and disasters found in today's seas.*

Quammen, David. *The Song of the Dodo: Island Biogeography in an Age of Extinction*. New York: Simon and Schuster, 1996.

> *Although this book is not about the sea per se, it covers the topic of island biogeography in depth. It is a wonderful piece of scientific journalism and nature writing.*

Valiela, Ivan. *Marine Ecological Processes*, 2nd edition. New York: Springer-Verlag, 1995.

> *Not for those who are shy about mathematics or academics, this book is packed with information for anyone who wishes to know more about the mysteries of how life in the sea interacts with itself and the marine environment.*

Index

swimming, capabilities of humans,
94–95
swordfish, Atlantic, 132
symbioses, 64, 229, 294
  clam-bacteria, 224
  coral-algae, 66
  productivity and, 67
  shrimp-goby, 87
  tube worm-bacteria, 223
  whale-barnacle, 33
  zooxanthellae-clam, 88
  zooxanthellae-jellyfish, 268
Synechococcus cyanobacter, 211
syngameon theory, 65, 146

Taiyo Fishing Corporation, 74
Taufa'ahau Tupou IV, King, 102
taxonomy, of corals, 63, 64
Tegner, Mia, 37, 42, 157
teleosts, evolution of, 117
terrains, 200
Texas pipefish, 47
Thailand, bleaching of corals in, 254
Theory of Island Biogeography, 64
thermoclines, 57
Thetis Bank, 136
Thompson, Alberta, 247, 248
tiger sharks, 177
Tilman, David, 92
time hypothesis, 90
Tit-for-Tat strategy, 113, 114
Tobias, Phillip, 95
Tonga, 99
Tongass National Forest, 197
  clear-cutting in, *199*
totoaba, 47
tourism, sustainable, 105
trade winds, 14, 59, 253
  currents and, 153
tragedy of the commons, 75, 286
trawling, 146, 220, 292
triggerfish, 289
trophic levels, 222, 283
tropical storms, effect on corals, 69
tube worms, 223
tuna
  bluefin, 132, 145
  illegal fishing of, 242
tuna nets, 122
turtlegrass, 138
turtles. *See* sea turtles
Tutka Lagoon, Alaska, 186

Ugoretz, John, 166
unicornfish, 110
United Nations
  Charter for Nature, 240–241
  regulation of drift nets, 182
  Resolution 46/215, 231
United Sates, consumption in, 293
upwelling, 128, 152, 284
  seasonal variation in, 153
U.S. Army Corps of Engineers, 194
U.S. Coast Guard
  interception of drugs, 242
  policing, 291
U.S. Navy
  interception of drugs, 241
  ownership of national park-managed
    lands, 154
  policing, 291
  research on underwater breathing sys-
    tems, 121
  use of sonar, 250

Valiela, Ivan, 90, 92
vampire squids (*Vampyroteuthis infernalis*),
  80, 223
Van Sommeran, Sean, 179
Vava'u, Tonga, 99
vegetarianism, 230, 286
Ventana, 224, *225*
Vernon, J. E. N., 64, 67
Vibrio cholera, 207
violence, environmentalism and, 244
viruses, 204
visibility, underwater, 57, 100
viviparity, extinction and, 146–147

wahoo (*Acanthocybium solandri*), 133
Wakaya Island, Fiji, 60
Wallin, Ivan, 115
water pollution, 9, 12, 30
  effect on biodiversity, 90
  from fish hatcheries, 194
  from the Mississippi River, 73
  threat to whales, 238
water temperature
  corals and, 67
  diving and, 57
  effect of El Niño on, 253
  fish abundance and, 237
Watson, Paul, 231–235, 238, 240, 242,
  243, 248, 249
Watt, James D., 259